Muslims at the Margins of Europe

Muslim Minorities

Editorial Board

Jørgen S. Nielsen (*University of Copenhagen*)
Aminah McCloud (*DePaul University, Chicago*)
Jörn Thielmann (*Erlangen University*)

VOLUME 32

The titles published in this series are listed at *brill.com/mumi*

Muslims at the Margins of Europe

Finland, Greece, Ireland and Portugal

Edited by

Tuomas Martikainen
José Mapril
Adil Hussain Khan

BRILL

LEIDEN | BOSTON

Library of Congress Cataloging-in-Publication Data

Names: Martikainen, Tuomas, editor. | Mapril, José, editor. | Khan, Adil Hussain, editor.
Title: Muslims at the margins of Europe : Finland, Greece, Ireland and
  Portugal / edited by Tuomas Martikainen, José Mapril, Adil Hussain Khan.
Description: Leiden ; Boston : Brill, [2019] | Series: Muslim minorities,
  1570-7571 ; volume 32 | Includes bibliographical references and index. |
  Summary: "This volume focuses on Muslims in Finland, Greece, Ireland and
  Portugal, representing the four corners of the European Union today. It
  highlights how Muslim experiences can be understood in relation to a
  country's particular historical routes, political economies, colonial
  and post-colonial legacies, as well as other factors, such as
  church-state relations, the role of secularism(s), and urbanisation.
  This volume also reveals the incongruous nature of the fact that
  national particularities shaping European Muslim experiences cannot be
  understood independently of European and indeed global dynamics. This
  makes it even more important to consider every national context when
  analysing patterns in European Islam, especially those that have yet to
  be fully elaborated. The chapters in this volume demonstrate the
  contradictory dynamics of European Muslim contexts that are
  simultaneously distinct yet similar to the now familiar ones of Western
  Europe's most populous countries"-- Provided by publisher.
Identifiers: LCCN 2019023090 (print) | LCCN 2019023091 (ebook) | ISBN
  9789004404557 (hardback) | ISBN 9789004404564 (ebook)
Subjects: LCSH: Muslims--Non-Islamic countries. | Muslims--Non-Islamic countries. |
  Muslims--Finland. | Muslims--Greece. | Muslims--Ireland. | Muslims--Portugal.
Classification: LCC D1056.2.M87 M873 2019 (print) | LCC D1056.2.M87
  (ebook) | DDC 323.3/8297094--dc23
LC record available at https://lccn.loc.gov/2019023090
LC ebook record available at https://lccn.loc.gov/2019023091

Typeface for the Latin, Greek, and Cyrillic scripts: "Brill." See and download: brill.com/brill-typeface.

ISSN 1570-7571
ISBN 978-90-04-40455-7 (hardback)
ISBN 978-90-04-40456-4 (e-book)

Copyright 2019 by Koninklijke Brill NV, Leiden, The Netherlands.
Koninklijke Brill NV incorporates the imprints Brill, Brill Hes & De Graaf, Brill Nijhoff, Brill Rodopi,
Brill Sense, Hotei Publishing, mentis Verlag, Verlag Ferdinand Schöningh and Wilhelm Fink Verlag.
All rights reserved. No part of this publication may be reproduced, translated, stored in a retrieval system,
or transmitted in any form or by any means, electronic, mechanical, photocopying, recording or otherwise,
without prior written permission from the publisher.
Authorization to photocopy items for internal or personal use is granted by Koninklijke Brill NV provided
that the appropriate fees are paid directly to The Copyright Clearance Center, 222 Rosewood Drive, Suite
910, Danvers, MA 01923, USA. Fees are subject to change.

This book is printed on acid-free paper and produced in a sustainable manner.

Printed by Printforce, the Netherlands

Contents

Preface   VII
List of Illustrations   VIII
List of Tables   IX
Notes on Contributors   X

Introduction   1
José Mapril, Tuomas Martikainen and Adil Hussain Khan

PART 1
Governing Islam and Muslims

1   The Founding of the Islamic Council of Finland   27
   Tuomas Martikainen

2   State and Religion in Peripheral Europe: State-Religion Relations,
   Corporatism and Islam in Portugal and Ireland (1970–2010)   45
   Luís Pais Bernardo

3   The Governance of Islamic Religious Education in Finland: Promoting
   "General Islam" and the Unity of All Muslims   67
   Tuula Sakaranaho

PART 2
Politics of Recognition

4   Concepts of Authority in Irish Islam   91
   Adil Hussain Khan

5   Nation-state, Citizenship and Belonging: A Socio-historical Exploration
   of the Role of Indigenous Islam in Greece   112
   Venetia Evergeti

6   Perceptions of Mis/Recognition: The Experiences of Sunni Muslim
   Individuals in Dublin, Ireland   137
   Des Delaney

PART 3
Public Debates and (In)Visibility

7 Explaining the Absence of a Veil Debate: The Mediating Role of
   Ethno-nationalism and Public Religion in the Irish Context   161
   Stacey Scriver

8 Muslim Migration Intelligence and Individual Attitudes toward Muslims
   in Present-day Portugal   180
   Nina Clara Tiesler and Susana Lavado

9 From the Margins to the Fore: Muslim Immigrants in Contemporary
   Greece   198
   Panos Hatziprokopiou

PART 4
Mobilities and Belonging

10 Iraqi Diaspora and Public Space in a Multicultural Suburb
   in Finland   225
   Marko Juntunen

11 Sudanese and Somali Women in Ireland and in Finland: Material
   Religion and Culture in the Formation of Migrant Women's Identities in
   the Diaspora   245
   Yafa Shanneik and Marja Tiilikainen

12 The Socio-spatial Configuration of Muslims in Lisbon   269
   Jennifer McGarrigle

   References   293
   Index   325

Preface

The initiative for this book originates from the Academy of Finland funded The Governance of Islam in Finland, Ireland and Canada Project. In our efforts to discuss Islam in the contemporary world, we noticed a lack of scholarly interest in the more peripheral countries on today's Europe. Based on this insight we organised an international conference at the Institute of Social Sciences in the University of Lisbon in March 2011. At the conference – *At the Margins of Europe? Muslims in Finland, Ireland and Portugal* – we discussed the pressing issue of the dominance of Germany, France and the UK in setting the agenda for the study of Islam in Europe. As the histories and experiences of these countries cannot reveal the diversity and multiplicity of Muslim lives and institutions on the continent, we felt that it should be high time to focus on lesser-known cases.

We started working on collecting suitable authors, many of whom were already present in the conference, and later expanded the scope to include also Greece. Thereby the four corners of Europe were covered and we would be able to point out the complex historical trajectories through which contemporary Islamic presence in Europe has developed. We hope that our book will also encourage others to bring forth lesser-known European Muslim experiences. The aim of this book, as suggested by the title, is to bring the margins into the wider debate of an increasingly religious diverse Europe.

Finally, we would like to thank the University of Lisbon, for making the first meeting possible, and the University of Cork, who generously hosted us the following year (for the preparation of a project proposal during which we had the opportunity to continue our discussions). We also express our gratitude for the generous financial support of Professor Tuula Sakaranaho (University of Helsinki, Finland) in having the language proofing costs covered. Karoliina Dahl helped us with the bibliography, thank you.

Tuomas Martikainen, José Mapril and Adil Khan

Illustrations

Figures

2.1   Crude rate of net migration in Finland, Greece, Ireland, Italy, Portugal and Spain, per 1,000 habitants   50

2.2   Religiosity in Ireland and Portugal 1981–2008, per cent   51

2.3   Religious service attendance in Ireland and Portugal 1981–2008, per cent   52

9.1   Apprehensions of undocumented aliens in Greece 2006–2014   208

9.2   Extreme right anti-muslim poster   213

11.1   Mebkhara, Dublin, 2010   250

11.2   Hoq, Cork, 2011   250

11.3   Bambar, Cork, 2011   252

11.4   Gabanat al-qahwa, Cork, 2010   254

11.5   Mawlid doll, Cork, 2010   256

11.6   Scarificated faces, Cork, 2011   257

11.7A–B Traditional aqal, Somaliland, 2006   261

11.8   Xeedho, Finland, 2019   263

Maps

12.1   Muslims (over 15 years old) per 1000 inhabitants, by parish, Lisbon Metropolitan Area, 2001   277

12.2   Muslims (over 15 years old) per 1000 inhabitants, by parish, Lisbon Metropolitan Area, 2011   278

12.3   Municipalities and other places, Lisbon Metropolitan Area   279

12.4   Islamic places of worship, Lisbon Metropolitan Area, 2001   280

12.5   Islamic places of worship, Lisbon Metropolitan Area, 2014   281

Tables

0.1   Total population and estimates of Muslim population in Finland, Greece, Ireland and Portugal in 2011/2012   5

2.1   Denominational belonging in Ireland 1981–2008   52

2.2   Denominational belonging in Portugal 1981–2008   53

6.1   Honneth's struggle for recognition typology   140

6.2   Interviewees' perceptions per sphere of everyday life   142

8.1   Means and standard deviation for attitudes toward Muslims, perception of Muslims as terrorists and perceptions of Muslims as a threat to country's culture, by country   191

8.2   Correlations between attitudes toward Muslims, perception of Muslims as terrorism supporters and perceptions of Muslims as a threat to country's culture, by country   194

9.1   Foreign nationals in Greece originating from Muslim countries, 2001–2011   206

12.1   Religious affiliation in Portugal and the Lisbon Metropolitan Area, population aged 15 and over, 1981–2011   273

12.2   Muslim population aged 15 or over in Lisbon Metropolitan Area, by main nationalities and country of birth, 2011   274

Notes on Contributors

Luís Pais Bernardo
is a research officer at the Center for Africa, Asia and Latin-America Studies of the Lisbon School of Economics and Management. He holds a Ph.D. in Sociology from Humboldt-Universität zu Berlin. His research interests include the comparative-historical study of State-religion relations, the politics of secularity and the organizational management of religious diversity.

Des Delaney
holds a Ph.D. from the School of Law and Government, Dublin City University (DCU). His research interests are in the synthesis of philosophy and empirical sociology, particularly in relation to recognition, power, social struggle, and integration issues.

Venetia Evergeti
is a Lecturer at the University of Surrey. Her research interests are situated within ethnic and migration studies and include religious identity and practice of migrant and indigenous Islam in Europe, ethnicity and identity, transnational family responsibilities, and prejudice and social exclusion. She has carried out comparative and multi-sited ethnographic studies on Muslim communities in Greece and the UK and has published journal articles and book chapters on representations of Muslim identities in Britain (*Ethnic and Racial Studies*, 2010), notions of home and belonging in Greek migrant communities in London (2006, 2008), negotiating transnational caring responsibilities (2011), and spatial expressions of Muslim identity in Greece (*Social and Cultural Geography*, 2014). She has also edited a Special Issue on Social Capital, Migration and Transnational Families for *Ethnic and Racial Studies* (2006).

Panos Hatziprokopiou
is Assistant Professor at the Department of Spatial Planning & Development, Aristotle University of Thessaloniki, Greece. His areas of interest are migration; immigrants' settlement and incorporation; diversity, difference, space and place in the metropolis. He has studied religious identity and practice among indigenous and immigrant Muslims in Athens, Greece. His has written extensively on aspects of the above, and his publications include *Globalisation, Migration and Socio-Economic Change in Contemporary Greece: Processes of Social Incorporation of Balkan Immigrants in Thessaloniki* (University of Amsterdam Press, 2006).

Marko Juntunen

is University Lecturer in Arabic and Islamic Studies, Department of World Cultures, University of Helsinki, Finland. His research interests include social, political and cultural aspects of mobility, gender relations and Muslim diasporas in Europe, Iraq and Morocco. His recent publications include 'Constructing Mobile Lifestyles Between Europe and Africa' (*Migration in the Western Mediterranean: Space, Mobility and Borders*, eds. Bernes, Bousetta and Zikgraf, Routledge, 2017).

Adil Hussain Khan

is Associate Professor of Islamic Studies at Loyola University New Orleans. He holds a Ph.D. from the School of Oriental and African Studies (SOAS), University of London. He has conducted postdoctoral research on aspects of Islam in Europe at University College Cork, Ireland. He is the author of *From Sufism to Ahmadiyya: A Muslim Minority Movement in South Asia* (Indiana University Press, 2015). His research interests include sectarianism, orthodoxy, and Muslim identity. He is also interested in questions of authority and aspects of Islam's intellectual tradition.

Susana Lavado

holds a Ph.D. in social psychology from the Institute of Social Sciences of the University of Lisbon, with a thesis focused on how prejudice and discrimination are perpetuated by the majority groups. Her research interests mainly focus on justifications that perpetuate bias and inequality. Currently, she is a post-doctoral researcher at the Nova School of Business and Economics, where she investigates the application of artificial intelligence tools in public administration. Before, she worked as a researcher in international comparative surveys such as the European Social Survey.

José Mapril

holds a Ph.D. in Anthropology from the Institute of Social Sciences, University of Lisbon, with a thesis on Transnationalism and Islam among the Bangladeshis in Lisbon. Currently, he is an assistant professor in the Department of Anthropology at the Universidade Nova de Lisboa and a senior researcher at CRIA, FCSH-UNL, where he is developing a project on re-migration, life course and future among Bangladeshis in Europe. He is also part of the HERA project 'The Heritagization of Religion and Heritage of Contemporary Europe', developing research on heritage-making and the place of Islam in Lisbon. He is a member of the editorial committee of the *South Asia Multidisciplinary Academic Journal* (SAMAJ) and of the advisory council of the European Association of South Asia Studies (EASAS). Since the end of 2018, José is the coordinator of the executive committee of CRIA. Some of his latest publications include *Secularisms in a Post Secular Age: Religiosities and Subjectivities in a Comparative Perspective* (with Erin Wilson, Ruy Blanes and Emerson Giumbelli, Oxford: Palgrave, 2017) and *Death on the Move: Managing Narratives, Silences and Constraints in a Transnational Perspective* (with Philip Havick and Clara Saraiva, Newcastle: Cambridge Scholars Press, 2018).

Tuomas Martikainen
is director of the Migration Institute of Finland. His areas of interest include religion, migration and consumer society. His publications include *Immigrant Religions in Local Society* (Åbo Akademi University Press, 2004) and *Religion, Migration, Settlement* (Brill, 2013).

Jennifer McGarrigle
hold a Ph.D. from the Department of Urban Studies, University of Glasgow and is a researcher at the Centre for Geographical Studies (IGOT) at the University of Lisbon. Her research interests include religion and space, migration, immigrant integration and urban transformations. McGarrigle is currently leading a project on the socio-spatial integration of Lisbon's religious minorities: residential patterns, choice and neighbourhood dynamics. Her publications include *Understanding Processes of Ethnic Concentration and Dispersal: South Asian Residential Preferences in Glasgow* (University of Amsterdam Press, 2010).

Tuula Sakaranaho
is Professor of the Study of Religion and Vice-Dean at the Faculty of Theology, University of Helsinki. She has published extensively on methodological issues in the study of religions and on Muslims in contemporary society. She is the author of *Religious Freedom, Multiculturalism, Islam: Cross-reading Finland and Ireland* (Brill, 2006), co-author of *Islam in Ireland: Past and Present* (Edinburgh University Press, 2015), and guest editor of the *Journal of Religion in Europe* (8/2015) on the governance of transnational Islam.

Stacey Scriver
is a Lecturer in Global Women's Studies, School of Political Science and Sociology at NUI Galway, and Director of the MA Gender, Globalisation and Rights. Her research interests are in the intersections of gender and political and national identity. She has published in numerous journals, including

NOTES ON CONTRIBUTORS

Psychoanalysis, Culture and Society, Journal of Power, Organization, and *Journal of Business Ethics.* She is the editor (with Niamh Reilly) of *Religion, Gender and the Public Sphere* (Routledge, 2013).

Yafa Shanneik

is Lecturer in Islamic Studies at the University of Birmingham. She researches the dynamics and trajectories of gender in Islam within the context of contemporary diasporic and transnational Muslim women's spaces. She works on Sunni and Shia women communities in Europe and their transnational links to the Middle East. She also has a particular research interest in the authority and leadership of Muslim women and the changing nature of women's participation in religious practices in Europe and the Middle East. She has published several articles on gender and Islam and migrant identities in Europe, such as: 'Remembering Karbala in the Diaspora: Religious Rituals among Iraqi Shii Women in Ireland' (*Religion,* 2015) and 'Religion and Diasporic Dwelling: Algerian Muslim Women in Ireland' (*Religion and Gender,* 2012). She also has a particular research interest on Muslim marriage practices in diasporic spaces: 'Shia Marriage Practices: Karbala as lieux de mémoire in London' *Social Sciences.* Special issue: Understanding Muslim Mobilities and Gender, 6 (3): Accessible via: http://www.mdpi.com/2076-0760/6/3/100.

Nina Clara Tiesler

is a research fellow and senior lecturer at the Institute of Sociology of the Leibniz University of Hannover (Germany), and associated researcher at the Institute of Social Sciences of the University of Lisbon (Portugal). She holds a Ph.D. in Comparative Studies of Religion and a *venia legendi* for Sociology and Cultural Anthropology. Her areas of interest are social theory, sociology and anthropology with special emphasis on migration-related phenomena and the genesis of ethnicities. Her publications include *Muslims in Europe: Religion and Identity Politics in New Societal Settings* (in German, Lit-Verlag, 2006; updated in Portuguese, ICS, 2011) and *Islam in Portuguese Speaking Areas* (edited special issue of *Lusotopie,* 2007).

Marja Tiilikainen

is Senior Researcher at the Migration Institute of Finland. Her research has focused on issues such as everyday lived religion, cultural dimensions of health, illness and healing, experiences of migrant women, and transnational families. In particular, she has studied Somali diasporic communities and conducted ethnographic research in Finland, Canada and Somalia. Her publications include '*Wellbeing of Transnational Muslim Families: Marriage, Law and Gender*' (co-edited by Tiilikainen, Al-Sharmani and Mustasaari, Routledge, 2019) and 'Illness, Healing and Everyday Islam: Transnational Lives of Somali Migrant Women' (*Everyday Lived Islam in Europe*, eds. Dessing et al., Ashgate, 2013).

Introduction

José Mapril, Tuomas Martikainen and Adil Hussain Khan

On March 18th 2018, the Islamic Community of Lisbon, the leading representative association for Islamic issues in Portugal, celebrated its 50th anniversary. The celebrations took place in Lisbon Central mosque and among its guests were the Imam of Al-Azhar Mosque, from Cairo, the secretary general of the United Nations, António Guterres, the prime minister of Portugal, António Costa, the president of the Portuguese Republic, Marcelo Rebelo de Sousa, representatives of the Catholic church and other key figures in interfaith dialogue. The celebration lasted two days and had an extensive coverage in news reports, in mainstream media, reinforcing the visibility and centrality of this institution in all things Islamic.

In November (2018), in Athens, a procession celebrating the *mawlid-un-nabi*, the anniversary of Prophet Muhammad, was organized, departing from Omonoia Square, while the negotiations continue for the construction of a central Mosque in the city to serve its growing Muslim population. This is an old claim that, for one reason or another, was never fulfilled since the 80s, in spite several plans to conclude it.

In Helsinki, on the other hand, the polemics around the construction of a central Mosque continue. In spite of dozens of small mosques, several Muslim associations, including the Finish Muslim Union, have been claiming, for years, the construction of a central Mosque in the city, therefore giving equality of place to Islam in relation to other religions. As soon as the project became public though, it was strongly contested by extreme right-wing movements that mobilized several Islamophobic/racist arguments against it.

On Christmas Day last year (2018), the Muslim Sisters of Eire organized the distribution of survival bags (with food, tents, warm clothes, sanitary products, and others) called "Bags for Life," to homeless women and men in Dublin. The objective was to lighten the load of those in need, in this period of the year, and included Muslim and non-Muslim women, with very diverse backgrounds and histories. With this campaign, the association also wants to increase public awareness about the role of Muslim women as Irish citizens and as key actors in promoting the wellbeing of the wider society.

These four initial vignettes hint at the larger objective of this edited volume: all of them address common issues about the public recognition of Islam, claiming a place for Muslims, making citizenship claims through care,

© KONINKLIJKE BRILL NV, LEIDEN, 2019 | DOI:10.1163/9789004404564_002

and manifestations of Islamophobia and racism, in four different countries, Portugal, Greece, Finland and Ireland. The objective of this edited volume is precisely to address these and other issues about Muslims and Islam focusing this time in the margins of Europe. Discussions and research about Islam and Muslims in Europe have tended to focus on a small number of Western European countries due to their large Muslim populations and their social and political significance. Most notably, much of the research concentrates on the experiences of Muslims in France, Germany, the Netherlands, Belgium and the United Kingdom.[1] The exact size of the European Muslim population remains disputed, but data provided by *The Future of the Global Muslim Population*[2] and the *Yearbook of Muslims in Europe*[3] suggests that between 17.5 and 19.1 million Muslims were living in the European Union around the year 2010, which is 3.5 to 3.8 per cent of the total EU 28 population (500 million people). French, German and British Muslims constitute alone, over 11 million and, thus, two-thirds of all European Muslims.

Whereas there are legitimate and worthwhile reasons for the great interest in Muslim lives in these countries, it is nevertheless important to broaden the study of Islam and Muslims to other European countries. For example, Larsson and Račius argue for the inclusion of Muslim experiences from the Baltic rim to balance the view that Islam is a new religion in Europe by reminding us of the need to bring forth the manifold Muslim experiences from different European societies.[4] Many others have also lamented the lack of information from smaller countries, despite its importance. While some steps in that direction have already been taken, including the *Yearbook of Muslims in Europe*,[5] we feel that the study of the diverse experiences of Muslim(s) Europe(s) require more attention on countries with smaller and comparatively understudied Muslim populations in order to continue broadening the picture of European Muslims and Islam. It is precisely with this objective in mind that this edited volume focusses on Muslims at the four corners of the European Union today, namely, Finland, Greece, Ireland and Portugal.

---

1 Marcel Maussen, *The Governance of Islam in Western Europe. A State of the Art Report*, IMISCOE Working Paper No. 16 (Amsterdam: IMISCOE), 6.

2 Pew Templeton Global Religious Futures Project. *The Future of the Global Muslim Population. Projections for 2010–2030.* (Washington: Pew Research Center, Forum on Religion & Public Life, 2011), 161–162.

3 Jørgen S. Nielsen et al., ed., *Yearbook of Muslims in Europe. Volume 5* (Leiden: Brill, 2013).

4 Göran Larsson and Egdūnas Račius, "A Different Approach to the History of Islam and Muslims in Europe: A North-Eastern Angle, or the Need to Reconsider the Research Field," *Journal of Religion in Europe* 3/3 (2010): 351–352.

5 The first Yearbook was published in 2009; see: "Yearbook of Muslims in Europe," Brill, accessed November 5, 2013, http://www.brill.com/publications/yearbook-muslims-europe.

INTRODUCTION 3

The reader might wonder why we have chosen these countries – after all they are quite distinct. This is certainly true but it also somehow true that they share certain common features: first, all had a link to nineteenth and twentieth century imperial and colonial histories – the Russian, Ottoman, British and Portuguese empires – that in turn led to colonial and postcolonial mobilities and migrations, some of which Muslims (although not exclusively), and, as we will see further ahead, influenced incorporation dynamics. Second, during the great population movements following decolonization and, especially, the Second World War, the four countries were overwhelmingly marked by emigration to Central and Northern Europe, where other migrants, among which of Islamic religion, also found their way. This is distinct from much of the research on Muslims in Europe, which is framed in the context of post-WW2 economic development and labour migration. These four cases only recently – the last four decades – became (also) immigrant destinations and this seems to have an array of consequences for the immigration regimes, the place of non-dominant religions and the creation of minorities. As a consequence, and this is the third common characteristic among them, these countries received increasing numbers of migrants only from the mid-1970s onwards,[6] and especially since the 1990s following the advent of new population movements in the larger contexts of the post-Cold War developments, including new forms of cultural, economic and political globalization, and the globalization of migrations.

Finally, not only have the four countries "lagged behind" for decades in the national immigration experience of growing economies, but they have become part of the same discursive realm, both as receivers of information of "migration issues" via media and later through growing immigration and EU collaboration.[7] Thus, in this edited volume, we aim to expand and contribute to the study of European Islam and Muslims by addressing these cases, which have, for one reason, or another, received less attention.

In the remainder of this introduction, we will discuss how different national histories can broaden our understanding about the complex places, locations, predicaments and lived experiences of European Muslims. Having said this, we want to escape the trap of methodological nationalism[8] and therefore we

---

6 The exact timing varied somewhat between the countries (from the mid-1970s to the late 1980s), but the change from a net emigration to a net immigration country has been a shared experience that accelerated in the 1990s in all countries.

7 Stephen Castles and Mark J. Miller, *The Age of Migration: International Population Movements in the Modern World*, Fourth Edition (New York: The Guilford Press), 108–120.

8 Andreas Wimmer and Nina Glick Schiller, "Methodological Nationalism and Beyond: Nation-state Building, Migration and the Social Sciences," *Global Networks* 2/4 (2002): 301–334.

will draw attention to the articulations between particular national histories and more general European or global developments (see for instance, how the political economy of European development – e.g. the application of austerity measures – the global war on terror and the global expansion of Islamophobia and racism have impacted on our interlocutors' lives). In the first section we will briefly present the Muslim history and populations in Finland, Greece, Ireland and Portugal, including the processes of institutionalization and legal regulation of Islamic organizations. The second section of this introduction will focus on the main debates and research on European Muslim and Islam, explaining how the cases addressed in this volume engage and contribute to such discussions. At the end of the introduction, we will present the organization of the chapters.

1 Histories of Muslims and Islam in European Peripheries

Finland, Greece, Ireland and Portugal do not have much common history, but they somehow have long been considered "peripheral" in Europe, not only in a strictly geographic sense but also because they have been surrounded by greater states and powers and also in terms of European policies and politics. The European Union provides a commonality, which the countries share since joining: Ireland in 1973, Greece in 1981, Portugal in 1986 and Finland in 1995. In religious terms, Finland is dominantly Lutheran, Greece Orthodox, and Ireland and Portugal Catholic and all relate in very diverse ways with ideas about church-state relations, secularism and *laicité*.

The four countries have medium-size populations ranging from 4.6 to 11 million in 2012. Muslims constitute between 0.5 and 3.2 per cent of the countries' populations and the minorities are of similar size (50,000–60,000) with the exception of Greece, which has somewhat more (350,000) (see Table 0.1). Together they represent about 3 per cent of all European Muslims. While many of the Muslims are rather new arrivals, all of the countries do have longer constituencies of Muslim populations that help to identify country-specific patterns of adjustments as well as broader European trends. The following country presentations provide basic historical, demographic, institutional and legal facts about Muslims living in Finland, Greece, Ireland and Portugal.

The first Muslim immigrant came to Finland as soldiers and personnel of the imperial Russian army after Finland was annexed by Russia from Sweden in 1808. Kazakh and Tatar military personnel have been recorded since at least the 1830s onwards and were served by garrison imams. Beginning in the 1870s, Tatar Muslim merchants, later with their families, started to arrive from the

TABLE 0.1   Total population and estimates of Muslim population in Finland, Greece, Ireland and Portugal in 2017 - 2019

	Total population	Estimate of Muslim population	Muslim's share of total population
Finland	5,518,752	70,000	1.1–1.2%
Greece	10,816,286	380,000	3.2%
Ireland	4,857,00	63.443	1.1%
Portugal	10,291,027	48,000–55,000	0.5%

SOURCES: CENTRAL STATISTICS OFFICE (2019), HELLENIC STATISTICS AUTHORITY (2019), MAPRIL ET AL. 2019, PAUHA AND KONTTORI 2019, CARR 2019, TSITSELIKIS (2018), STATISTICS FINLAND (2019), STATISTICS PORTUGAL (2017)

Nizhni Novgorod region and became a permanently settled religious minority in a predominantly Lutheran grand duchy. Islamic religious organizations and activities were not recognized by law but were tolerated during the Russian era. The arrival of Tatars came to a halt in the post-October Revolution Soviet Union by the mid-1920s due to stricter border and migration policies. The number of Tatars has always stayed under 1,000 individuals.[9]

After Finnish independence in 1917, the new constitution of 1919 (revised in 1999) declared freedom of religion, and Muslims were gradually granted citizenship. The Freedom of Religion Act of 1923 (revised in 2003) made it possible for non-Protestant religions to organize officially. The first state-recognized Islamic organization was registered by Tatars in Helsinki in 1925 to be followed by another association in the city of Tampere in 1943. Even though small numbers of other Muslims migrated to Finland over the years, they did not organize themselves until 1987 when immigrants from the Middle East founded the third Sunni Islamic society in Finland. Muslim migration started to grow rapidly at the turn of the 1990s when Muslim background UNHCR quota refugees were accepted and the number of asylum seekers grew. People came from various crisis-ridden areas, including the former Yugoslavia (Bosnia and Kosovo), Iran, Iraq, Somalia and Afghanistan. Even small-scale migration from Turkey, Northern and Sub-Saharan Africa, and South Asia took place simultaneously. In the post-Cold War world, Finland somewhat unexpectedly became a destination country for migrants, including Muslims who constituted up to twenty

---

9 Tuomas Martikainen, "Finland," in *Yearbook of Muslims in Europe. Volume 5*, ed. Jørgen S. Nielsen et al. (Leiden: Brill, 2013), 237–246; Tuula Sakaranaho, *Religious Freedom, Multiculturalism, Islam: Cross-reading Finland and Ireland* (Leiden: Brill, 2006), Chapter 6.

per cent of all immigrants.[10] Whereas in 1990 there were an estimated 4,000 Muslims, the number had grown to some 25,000 in 2000.[11]

In 2019, the Muslim population of Finland was an estimated 70,000, mainly recent migrants and their children. The largest national groups were Iraqis, Somalis, Kurds, Turks, Kosovo Albanians, Persians and Bosnians. Converts to Islam are estimated at 1,500 individuals and membership in the Tatar congregations was 610 persons[12] in 2018. The majority of Muslims in Finland are Sunni and about a tenth are Shi'i. There are over 50 functioning prayer rooms, mosques, and many other Muslim organizations. The Muslim population is concentrated in the Helsinki greater area with smaller numbers in other cities. Due to difficulties in entering the labour market for individuals with a refugee background, including discrimination, Muslims are over-represented among the working classes and the less well-off in socio-economic terms in Finland.[13]

In legal terms, Muslims enjoy the same civil rights as any person residing in Finland and their right to religious activities and institutions is undisputed. There is also the possibility of religious education of Islam in public schools.[14] However, Islam is viewed with great suspicion according to figures that show about half of Finns view it unfavourably while only a few per cent view it positively. The figures have stayed about the same since the late 1980s when it was first measured. The attitudes are similar to those of some other religious minorities, such as the Jehovah's Witnesses.[15] Many Muslim majority groups are also among the lowest in the national ethnic hierarchy, and there are studies that indicate that many Muslims experience more than average discrimination in Finland, whether due to nationality, racism, religion, or other reasons.[16]

---

10   Martikainen, "Finland"; Tuula Sakaranaho, *Religious Freedom, Multiculturalism, Islam*, Chapter 6.

11   Abdi-Hakim Yasin Ararse, "Suomalaiset muslimit ja syyskuun 11. päivä," in *Mitä muslimit tarkoittavat? Keskustelua islamilaisista virtauksista Suomessa ja Euroopassa*, ed. Tuomas Martikainen and Tuula Sakaranaho (Turku: Savukeidas, 2011), 145, 147.

12   "Suomen Islam-seurakunta," accessed November 5, 2013, http://www.uskonnot.fi/yhteisot/view/?orgId=85; "Tampereen islamilainen seurakunta," accessed November 5, 2013, http://www.uskonnot.fi/yhteisot/view.php?orgId=441.

13   Martikainen, "Finland," 237–240.

14   Martikainen, "Finland," 240–241; see also Sakaranaho's chapter in this book.

15   Kimmo Ketola, "Uskontotilanteen muutos ja suomalaisten suhtautuminen eri uskontoihin," in *Uskonnon ylösnousemus: Kirkon, uskonnon ja kulttuurin murros*, ed. Tuomas Martikainen and Ville Jalovaara (Helsinki: Magma, 2010), 44–51.

16   Magdalena Jaakkola, *Maahanmuuttajat suomalaisten näkökulmasta: Asennemuutokset 1987–2007* (Helsinki: City of Helsinki Urban Facts, 2009), 52–66.

Islam's presence in Greece is connected with both the historical "Old Islam," which relates to the indigenous Muslim communities that were recognized and legalized as minorities after the construction of the Greek nation-state, as well as the migrant "New Islam," which is a result of the migratory waves towards Greece from predominantly Muslim countries during the last decades.

Most of the territory of contemporary Greece was under Ottoman rule from the fifteenth century until the year 1830 when the country gained its independence and modern Greece was founded. Thereby Greece has a long common history with Islam. Only a small number of Muslims remained in Greece after independence, but due to annexations the number has risen. Historically, the area of Thrace is home to a large community of Greek Muslims of Turkish, Pomak and Roma ethnicity. The position of the Muslim minorities has been recognized in several documents, including the Treaty of Lausanne (1923). The Muslim community was divided into three provinces, each having its own Mufti with a number of administrative, educational and legal tasks. Due to the sometime problematic relations between Greece and Turkey, the treatment of the Muslim minority in Greece has also shifted over the years.

The Greek national identity was originally constructed against the Ottoman Empire, which resulted in the formation of hegemonic perceptions of Islam as a religious and national other. Furthermore, Orthodox Christianity played a key role in the way Greek nationalism developed and even today continues to be one of its pillars. Since the 1990s, and as Greece became also an immigration country, migrants of Islamic religion moved and settled in its main cities, the majority in Athens. These newcomers came from the Balkans, North Africa, the Middle East, Central Asia and South Asia, albeit in small numbers. In 2012, an estimated 350,000 Muslims lived in Greece, of whom over half were new migrants. The figure does not include Albanians who are nominally Muslims. With the economic hardships associated with the application of austerity policies within neoliberal readjustment plans in Southern Europe, anti-Muslim sentiments have also grown.[17]

Currently the institutional and legal position of Islam in Greece is connected mainly with the presence of the indigenous Muslims in Thrace. The Treaty of Lausanne not only recognized them as a minority but further safeguarded their religious and civic rights as Greek citizens. As such, the Muslims in Thrace have full civil rights, including the freedom to establish political parties, vote and run for office and are well represented at the local and municipal level. Furthermore, Islam is legally recognized as an official religion in Greece

---

17   Konstantinos Tsitselikis, "Greece," in *Yearbook of Muslims in Europe. Volume 5*, ed. Jørgen S. Nielsen et al. (Leiden: Brill, 2013), 309.

but provisions for Muslims only exist in the area of Thrace. Islam is taught in minority schools and there are about 300 mosques in the three provinces of Thrace. Sharia law is also used by the local Muftis to resolve disputes in matters of inheritance or family. However, such provisions are safeguarded by law only in relation to the Muslim minority of the area. In contrast, there are no religious provisions outside of Thrace for the growing numbers of Muslim immigrants in the country. There is no official mosque or Islamic cemetery in Athens at the moment, although there are long-term plans for its construction. Yet, a number of informal prayer halls operate mostly in Athens where the majority of the immigrant Muslim population is concentrated. Many Muslim migrants face serious issues not only in terms of their religious practice but most importantly in relation to their legal status, since it is often difficult and expensive to get residence permits and almost impossible to gain citizenship.

Aside from scattered accounts of travellers and other newcomers connected to British colonies in the Muslim world, Ireland did not serve as a prominent destination for westward bound Muslims until the middle of the twentieth century when students, largely from South Africa, began arriving in Ireland in pursuit of education. Even then, Muslim migration patterns were mainly limited in scope to medical students or other professionals who remained within the country for various reasons after completing their degrees. The Royal College of Surgeons in Ireland played a significant role in facilitating Muslim community development since the 1950s by providing places for students whose prospects of higher education and professional development were otherwise constricted by the apartheid regime.[18]

The steady yet modest growth of Muslims in Ireland was bolstered by population spikes surrounding times of economic prosperity often related to the expansion of niche industries, including aviation and halal meat exports. The larger and more significant spurts in Irish Muslim population growth seem to have taken place since the 1990s, when broader economic gains across the country, especially in urban centres such as Dublin, Cork and Galway provided space for Muslim entrepreneurs and other job seekers from abroad in addition to refugees from the wars in Bosnia and Iraq. This enabled the Muslim population in the Republic of Ireland to grow from 3,875 in 1991, to 19,147 in 2002, until finally reaching 63,443 in 2019.[19] This surge has resulted in the accelerated

---

18   Adil Hussain Khan, "Transnational Influences on Irish Muslim Networks: From Local to Global Perspectives," *Journal of Muslim Minority Affairs* 31/4 (2011): 487–488.

19   James Carr, "Ireland", in *Yearbook of Muslims in Europe*. Volume 10, ed. Oliver Scharbrodt, (Leiden: Brill, 2019), 342–359.

INTRODUCTION

expansion of religious institutions and Muslim organizations intended to cater to relatively diverse Muslim communities across the country, especially in Dublin and its surrounding areas where the largest concentrations of Irish Muslims reside.[20] Today, Irish Muslim communities are comprised of South Asians, Arabs, and Africans from across the continent, as well as Malaysians, Eastern Europeans, and others, including an increasing number of converts.[21]

The appeal of Ireland as an English-speaking country in Western Europe to Muslims of former British colonies is apparent and, in years past, has helped promote its image amongst aspiring residents of Europe as a preferred alternative to Britain due to its different circumstances, employment opportunities, and less restricted policies towards immigration in comparison.[22] The allure of Ireland changed drastically with the economic downturn of 2008 following the collapse of the Irish economy that led to a government bailout in 2010. This decline may have drawn further attention to immigrants in Ireland, including Muslims, who were previously under less scrutiny when populations were smaller and employment opportunities were greater.

Nevertheless, Muslims in Ireland have generally benefited from settling in a country whose historic struggles with religion have in some ways paved the way for better interfaith relations that lead to greater cooperation and encourage the development of a socially cohesive environment.[23] This is particularly true amongst members of the Roman Catholic majority who are often willing to empathize with outsiders who might share a sense of postcolonial camaraderie, such as those arriving from Muslim majority countries. The influence of this background remains strong within the collective memory of the Irish and may have eased certain aspects of Ireland's encounter with Islam while the economy was flourishing, since colonial resistance has firmly been part of Irish national identity for so long. This dynamic lies in sharp contrast from the circumstances that have framed the discourse between Muslims and host communities in Britain, France, and Germany, and has provided a unique context for emerging Muslim communities as they continue to struggle to find their place in Irish society.[24]

---

20   Central Statistics Office, *Census 2011 Profile 7*, 17.
21   Adil Hussain Khan, "Creating the Image of European Islam: The European Council for Fatwa and Research and Ireland," in *Muslim Political Participation in Europe*, ed. Jørgen S. Nielsen (Edinburgh: Edinburgh University Press, 2013), 224.
22   Tuula Sakaranaho, *Religious Freedom, Multiculturalism, Islam*, 270–271.
23   See Sakaranaho, *Religious Freedom, Multiculturalism, Islam*, Chapter 4.
24   Jørgen S. Nielsen, *Muslims in Western Europe* (Edinburgh: Edinburgh University Press, 1995), 1–7.

Portuguese Muslims and Islam are intimately associated with colonial and post-colonial mobilities and later with the globalization of migration flows.[25] The Portuguese colonial experience included Angola, Guinea-Bissau, Mozambique, São Tomé and Principe, Macau and East Timor. The first Muslims in continental Portugal came for educational purposes in the 1950s and the 1960s and they were mostly single male students from Sunni families of Indian origin from Mozambique. During decolonization and due to post-independence Africanization policies and civil war, several Muslim families of Indian and Pakistani background, both Sunni and Isma'ili, moved to Portugal.[26] At the same time a distinct wave of immigration, Muslims and Christians from Guinea-Bissau, gained expression and visibility. They were mainly young male labour migrants who would work in the lower ranks of the Portuguese economy, namely in construction. Soon this new migration flow of Muslims from Guinea-Bissau reached approximately 30,000 persons and represents until today the demographically most important Muslim population in the country.[27]

In the context of the changing position of Portugal vis-à-vis global migration flows (in relation to the democratic transition and the economic development that followed European integration), the late 1980s and the beginning of the 1990s witnessed a significant change in immigration patterns to Portugal, a change that marked the arrival of migrants from countries that had no previous historical links with Portugal. All through the 1990s and 2000s, besides the continuing immigration from Portuguese speaking countries, new migrants arrived from Eastern Europe but also, although in smaller numbers, from Muslim majority countries such as Bangladesh, Pakistan, Senegal and Morocco.[28]

According to representatives from the main Islamic organizations and academic researchers there were between 48,000 and 55,000 Muslims, including

---

25 Jorge Macaista Malheiros, *Imigrantes na Região de Lisboa: Os Anos da Mudança, Imigração e Processo de Integração das Comunidades de Origem Indiana* (Lisboa: Colibri, 1996); Susana Bastos, and José Bastos, *Portugal Multicultural* (Lisboa: Edições Fim de Século, 1999); Nina Clara Tiesler, "Muçulmanos na Margem: A Nova Presença Islâmica em Portugal," in *Sociologia, Problemas e Práticas* 34 (2000): 117–144; Fernando Soares Loja, "Islam in Portugal," in *Islam, Europe's Second Religion*, ed. Shireen Hunter (London: Praeger, 2002), 191–203; Abdoolkarim Vakil, "Comunidade Islâmica em Portugal," in *Dicionário Temático da Lusofonia*, ed. Fernando Alves Cristóvão (Lisboa: Associação de Cultura Lusófona-Instituto Camões, 2005), 186–189; José Mapril, "The New South Asians: The Political Economy of Migrations between Bangladesh and Portugal," *Revista Oriente* 17 (2007), 81–99.

26 Tiesler, "Muçulmanos na Margem"; Vakil, "Comunidade Islâmica em Portugal."

27 Vakil, "Comunidade Islâmica em Portugal."

28 Rita Gomes Faria, "Marroquinos em Portugal: Imigração, religião e comunidade," *Lusotopie* 14/1 (2007): 205–221; Mapril, "The New South Asians."

INTRODUCTION

8,000 Ismaʿilis, in 2019.[29] While it is possible to find Muslims throughout continental Portugal, in Madeira and in the Azores, the majority live in the Lisbon Metropolitan Area, both in the city centre as well as in its suburbs, such as Laranjeiro, Odivelas, Damaia and Cacém.[30] Socio-economically, the Muslim population is very diverse and includes occupations from management and administrative personnel of public and private companies to entrepreneurs and workers in the most under-privileged sectors of the Portuguese economy.

In terms of religious infrastructure, it is possible to find a diverse array of institutions and projects. The first Islamic association, the Islamic Community of Lisbon (ICL), was founded in 1968 by the aforementioned group of Muslim students that came to Portugal to study in the 1950s (most of these were already Portuguese citizens). This institution was of paramount importance for the Muslims that arrived in Portugal after decolonization and the revolutionary period. Today, the ICL is the main institutional representative of Islam in the public space acting as an umbrella association for Sunni Muslims in the country. The ICL also has access to state-owned television and radio channels, where it is responsible for the organization of several programmes together with the Catholic Church and other minority religious groups. Beside the ICL, more recently founded associations have also gained importance such as the Bangladesh Islamic Community and the Multicultural Islamic Community. These new institutions are formally recognized by the Portuguese state according to the new religious law, implemented at the beginning of the 21st century. This law regulates the field of religious groups – the official recognition by the Portuguese state, the celebration of religious holidays, the recognition of marriage and burial, among others – but allows each religious congregation to manage issues on education, ritual, etc., as long as it does not collide with other principles in the public space.[31]

In total, there are more than thirty mosques and prayer halls all throughout the country, including the *Jamatkhana* of the *Shiʾa Imami Ismaʿili Muslim Community*, most of which are located in Lisbon. Their location goes from central areas of the capital, to the suburbs, namely Amadora, Almada and Odivelas. These institutions have very diverse congregations in terms of nationalities (Bangladesh, Pakistan, Portugal and Guinea-Bissau), languages

---

29   José Mapril, Pedro Soares e Laura Almodovar, "Portugal", in *Yearbook of Muslims in Europe.* Volume 10, ed. Oliver Scharbrodt, (Leiden: Brill, 2019), 530–544.

30   Tiesler and Mapril, "Portugal," 517–530. See also McGarrigle's chapter in this book.

31   Fernando Soares Loja, "Islam in Portugal," in *Islam, Europe's Second Religion*, ed. Shireen Hunter (London: Praeger, 2002), 191–203.

(Bengali, Urdu and Portuguese) and doctrinal perspectives (Deobandi, Barelwi or *tarīqas*).[32]

Moreover, several educational infrastructures have emerged in the past years, the most emblematic of which is the *Colégio Islâmico de Palmela*, an Islamic College, with a secular and religious curriculum, that is considered an example of success in the national educational system.[33] Several mosques and prayer rooms also offer initiation to *Qur'anic* classes (informally called *madrassas* or *medersas*) and there are several tutors that organize private classes. Other elements in this infrastructure for Islam in Portugal include halal butchers and sections of cemeteries destined exclusively for Muslims in Lumiar, Odivelas and Feijó.[34]

Having said this, it is important to mention that the privileged relation between ICL and mainstream Portuguese political parties and media is frequently mediated by a discourse that emphasizes the uniqueness of the Portuguese scenario, frequently described as more peaceful and convivial in comparison with other European contexts. This exceptionality is the basis upon which several official and public discourses argue that there is no Islamophobia and racism against Muslims in Portugal, in spite the number of incidents and widespread prejudicial ideas about Muslims, that reveal a kind of banal islamophobia. According to many, this uniqueness is justified by the long historical connection with Islam and Muslims through the colonial/imperial experience and the lusotropical imaginary.

Still in relation to the Portuguese case, it is essential to mention how the Al-Andaluzian references have been increasingly patrimonialized in several parts of the country, through the figures of the Moors and enchanted, saintly, women, but also through medieval markets, touristic routes and archeological findings.[35] Similarly to what is happening in certain parts of Spain,[36] this Al-Andaluzian heritage works ambiguously between the Moor, as the enemy

---

32   See Tiesler and Mapril, "Portugal"; Michele Johnson, *Being Mandinga, Being Muslim: Transnational Debates on Personhood and Religious Identity in Guinea-Bissau and Portugal* (Urbana-Champaign: University of Illinois, 2002).

33   Mapril, José, "'Aren't You Looking for Citizenship in the Wrong Place?' Islamic Education, Secular Subjectivities and the Portuguese Muslim," *Religion and Society* (2014).

34   Loja, "Islam in Portugal"; Tiesler and Mapril, "Portugal"; Clara Saraiva and José Mapril, "Scenarios of Death in Contexts of Mobility: Guineans and Bangladeshis in Lisbon," in *The Power of Death*, ed. Ricarda Vidal and Maria José Blanco (Oxford: Berghahn Publishers, 2014).

35   Cardeira da Silva, Maria, "O sentido dos árabes no nosso sentido," *Análise Social* 173: 781–806.

36   Hirschkind, Charles, 2016, "Granadan Reflections," *Material Religion* 12:2, 209–232.

INTRODUCTION

of the Portuguese hegemonic national identity, and the Al-Andaluz, as a heritage, with its economic value.

It is this complex context that has created the condition of possibility for the emergence of competing and contested ideas about a "Portuguese Islam";[37] ideas that in their multifarious forms persist to this day and led to a dichotomy between "our Muslims," "the good ones" and the "other," "immigrant," "foreigner," Muslim (seen as a possible threat).

So, what do these four cases tell us about European Muslims and Islam?

2 Muslims in the Margins of Europe

The literature on European Muslims and Islam has mainly focused on a fairly small number of Western European countries with large Muslim populations. In these, Islam and Muslims seem to assume an increasing visibility and importance in the public sphere. Revealing, undoubtedly, is the importance of Islam and Muslims in political discourses from all sectors of the political spectrum in these countries. This *Islamization of the public sphere* and *the production of Muslims as a subjectivity* in contemporary Europe has been part and parcel of a political process that began in the mid-seventies and has gained momentum since 9/11. If until the seventies, migrants from Muslim majority countries were mainly thought of as "labour migrants" or members of some ethno-national group, currently it is hardly possible to avoid mentioning their Muslimness.[38] One of the consequences of these processes is that it has essentialized the religious, as if everything could be explained by the simple fact that one is a Muslim.

In spite of this, in the past decades the interest in these topics led to an increasing number of publications and research on the theme, frequently revealing the multiple and complex ways of being European Muslim. This vast literature allows us to de-homogenize, through empirical studies, the ways Muslims are frequently glossed in several political and mediatic landscapes, in which Islamophobia and racism assume central stage.

In a way it is possible to say that ever since the first collective endeavour to study the institutionalization of Islam in Western European countries by

---

37 Vakil, "Comunidade Islâmica em Portugal."; Vakil, Abdoolkarim, Monteiro, Amaro e Machaqueiro, Mário, Moçambique: Memória Falada do Islão e da Guerra (Coimbra: Almedina, 2011).

38 Stefano Allievi, "How the Immigrant has Become Muslim: Public Debates on Islam in Europe," *Revue Européenne des Migrations Internationals* 21/2 (2005): 135–163.

Thomas Gerholm and Yngve Lithman's *The New Islamic Presence in Western Europe* in 1988,[39] the debates coming from the UK, Germany, France as well as the Netherlands have been central to the study of European Muslims. Our aim is to contribute to such literature by focusing, empirically and theoretically, on lesser-known European contexts and see how these cases, with their historical particularities, contribute to the issues, themes and discussions about European Muslims and Islam.

Before proceeding, though, it is important to position our proposal within the now well-established literature on these topics. This is a very vast field of studies and in such a short introduction we do not have the possibility to analyse in detail all its contributions. In spite of this, it is worth mentioning three overarching themes to the study of Islam in Europe / European Islam with which our volume engages. The first one is mainly about the *institutionalization of Islam* in several European contexts and is exemplified by Gerholm and Lithman,[40] Barbara Metcalf,[41] Brigitte Maréchal et al.,[42] among many others. These studies reveal the processes and claims made by Muslims to make space for Islam, including the construction of mosques,[43] the performance of rituals,[44] the institutionalization of Islamic education,[45] the building of Islamic cemeteries[46] and the access and production of mediascapes.[47] These studies show how "migrants of Islamic religion"[48] were in Europe to stay and not simply *birds of passage*, as several mainstream European political parties seem to have expected – see for example, the political discourses about

---

39   Tomas Gerholm and Yngve Lithman, *The New Islamic Presence in Western Europe* (London: Mansell's, 1988).

40   Gerholm and Lithman, *The New Islamic Presence in Western Europe*.

41   Barbara Metcalf, *Making Muslim Space in North America and Europe* (Berkeley: University of California Press, 1996).

42   Brigitte Maréchal, Stefano Allievi, Felice Dassetto, and Jørgen S. Nielsen, ed., *Muslims in the Enlarged Europe: Religion and Society* (Leiden: Brill, 2003).

43   Jocelyne Cesari, "Mosque Conflicts in European Cities: An Introduction," *Journal of Ethnic and Migration Studies* 31/6 (2005): 1015–1024; Marcel Maussen, *Making Muslim Presence Meaningful* (Amsterdam, Amsterdam School for Social Science Research working paper 2005).

44   Pierre Bonte, Anne-Marie Brisebarre and Altan Gokalp, ed., *Sacrifices en Islam: Espaces et Temps d'un Rituel* (Paris: CNRS Editions, 2002).

45   Robert Hefner and Muhammad Qasim Zaman, ed., *Schooling Islam: The Culture and Politics of Modern Muslim Education* (Princeton: Princeton University Press, 2001); Maréchal et al., *Muslims in the Enlarged Europe*.

46   Maréchal et al., *Muslims in the Enlarged Europe*.

47   Maréchal et al., *Muslims in the Enlarged Europe*.

48   Peter van der Veer, "Transnational Religion: Hindu and Muslim Movements," *Global Networks* 2/2 (2002): 95–111.

INTRODUCTION

Turkish migration, *Gastarbeiter*, and the temporary nature of labour produced by certain segments of the German political spectrum.[49] Overall, this large and complex strand of literature reveals how Muslims, with migrant and non-migrant background, feel at home in several European countries, in spite of contexts that persistently treat them as "foreigners" (even if born and raised in Europe).[50]

A second theme with which this edited volume dialogues is *transnationalism and transnational relations and experiences*. This literature reveals and analyses the translocal processes in which Muslims, of migrant and non-migrant background, participate.[51] It implies not only secular processes and fields, such as political participation in the home country and long distance nationalism,[52] but also border-crossing processes of the religious and the ceremonial. As Ralph Grillo[53] has argued, it is possible to identify distinct approaches to the relation between transnationalism and Islam. One is the study of migrant networks and the circulation of tangible and intangible goods (including rituals[54]) in such networks. Examples include the ritualization of transnational space, described by Ruba Salih[55] in the context of weddings between Italy and Morocco, or in the sacrificial rituals performed by Mancunian Pakistanis in Pakistan.[56] A different approach to transnationalism and Islam involves the study of transnational religious movements and their connection with migration. Two emblematic examples are the Mouride networks from Senegal[57]

---

49 Ruth Mandel, *Cosmopolitan Anxieties: Turkish Challenges to Citizenship and Belonging in Germany* (Durham: Duke University Press, 2008).

50 Salmon Sayyd, "BrAsians: postcolonial people, ironic citizens" in *A Postcolonial People: South Asians in Britain*, eds. Ali, N. et al. (London, Hurst & Co. 2006), 1–10; Tariq Modood, *Still Not Easy Being British: Struggles for a Multicultural Citizenship* (London. Thretham Books, 2010).

51 Nina Glick Schiller, Linda Basch and Cristina Blanc-Szanton, "Transnationalism: A New Analytic Framework for Understanding Migration," *Annals of the New York Academy of Sciences* 645 (1992): 1–24.

52 Eva Østergaard-Nielsen, *Transnational Politics: Turks and Kurds in Germany* (London: Routledge, 2003).

53 Ralph Grillo, "Islam and Transnationalism," *Journal of Ethnic and Migration Studies* 30/5 (2004): 861–878.

54 Ralph Grillo and Katy Gardner, "Transnational Households and Ritual: An Overview," *Global Networks* 2/3 (2002): 179–191.

55 Ruba Salih, "Reformulating Tradition and Modernity: Moroccan Migrant Women and the Transnational Division of Ritual Space," *Global Networks* 2/3 (2002): 219–231.

56 Pnina Werbner, *Pilgrims of Love: An Ethnography of a Global Sufi Cult* (London: Hurst & Company, 2003).

57 Grillo, "Islam and Transnationalism"; Bruno Riccio, "Transnational Mouridism and the Afro-Muslim Critique of Italy," *Journal of Ethnic and Migration Studies* 30/5 (2004): 929–944; Ralph Grillo and Benjamin Soares, "Transnational Islam in Western Europe,"

and the Tablighi Jamaat.[58] A final approach focusing on the relation between transnationalism and Islam treats Islam as a universal discursive formation, including discourses about the *umma* as a trans-national, trans-ethnic and trans-class "community" produced by several movements[59] and as a transnational public sphere (in which there are many debates and positions about what is the "correct" ceremonial practices and the "good" Muslim).

Another framework for studying European Muslims/Muslims in Europe focuses on Islamophobia, anti-Muslim racism, governmentality and the making of subjectivities. The studies on Islamophobia have focused on topics such as the prohibitions of the both veil and the construction of Mosques and minarets,[60] the global racialization of Muslims,[61] the progressive incorporation of Islamophobic arguments in several mainstream European political parties,[62] and more broadly on cultural racism throughout Europe and the omnipresence of colonial legacies.[63] One line of research has focused on the way state and civil society institutions in Europe have been engaged in the making of Muslim subjectivities, through Islamic education, the creation and sponsor of umbrella institutions, etc.[64] These initiatives reveal, as several authors have

---

     ISIM Review 15 (2005): 11. Benjamin Soares, "An African Muslim saint and his followers in France," *Journal of Ethnic and Migration Studies* 30/5 (2004): 913–927.

58   Barbara Metcalf, *"Traditionalist" Islamic Activism: Deoband, Tablighis, and Talibs* (Leiden: I.S.I.M., 2005); John Bowen, "Beyond migration: Islam as a transnational public space," *Journal of Ethnic and Migration Studies*, 30/5 (2004): 879–894; Van der Veer, "Transnational Religion: Hindu and Muslim Movements."

59   Grillo, "Islam and Transnationalism"; Stefano Allievi, "Islam in the Public Space: Social Networks, Media, and Neo-communities," in *Muslim Networks and Transnational Communities in and across Europe*, ed. Stefano Allievi and Jørgen S. Nielsen (Leiden: Brill Publishers, 2003), 1–27. Peter Mandaville, *Transnational Muslims Politics: Reimagining the Umma* (London: Routledge, 2001).

60   Cesari, "Mosque Conflicts in European Cities."; Maussen, *Making Muslim Presence Meaninguful.*

61   Abdoolkarim Vakil and Salman Sayid, ed., *Thinking Through Islamophobia* (London: Hurst, 2011); Junaid Rana, *Terrifying Muslims: Race and Labour in the South Asian Diaspora* (Durham: Duke University Press, 2011).

62   Ferruh Yilmaz, "Right Wing Hegemony through the Immigration Debate in Europe," *Current Sociology* 60/3 (2012): 368–381.

63   Annelies Moors and Ruba Salih, "'Muslim Women' in Europe: Secular Normativities, Bodily Performances and Multiple Publics," *Social Anthropology* 17/4 (2009): 375–378; Marcel Maussen, Veit Bader, Annelies Moors, eds, *Colonial and Postcolonial Governance of Islam: Continuities and Ruptures* (Amsterdam: Amsterdam University Press); Ali, *A Postcolonial People: South Asians in Britain;*

64   Nico Landman, "Imams in the Netherlands: Homemade better than Import," *ISIM Newsletter* 2 (1999): 5; Marcel Maussen, *The Governance of Islam in Western Europe* (Imiscoe working paper, 2006).

INTRODUCTION

shown, the complex articulations between morality, citizenship, governmentality, differential inclusion and moral panics in which ideas of the "good" and the "bad" Muslim are thought out and performed.[65] All these governmentalities and techniques are related with the growing role of security issues and the fear of terrorism and radicalization of Muslim populations.[66]

This leads us to ask what aspects differ, if at all, from European countries with smaller and relatively less studied Muslim populations in comparison and what these contribute to the existing literature on the topic. For instance, some of the chapters in this collective volume provide a reminder that not all Muslims in Europe are a phenomenon related to post-WW2 labour migration. Both Greece and Finland have had, since their independence, a permanently settled Muslim minority, whose rights have been taken into account in the shaping the national identity of these nation-states. In Portugal, the first Muslim presence in the former colonial metropolis, Lisbon, is associated with university students who came to study in Portuguese Universities in the 1950s. These Muslims were already Portuguese nationals and comprised the younger generation of middle-class entrepreneurs, of Indian background, in colonial Mozambique, that were later essential to the creation of the main representative institutions of Islam in Portugal. Even in Ireland, early Muslim migrants were students and not labourers.

Second, it is possible to see how distinct models of state–religion arrangements have developed and how these relate to different projects about the making of a place for Islam. For instance, in Portugal the majority Catholic Church continues to have a regime of privilege with the Portuguese state (celebrated in a new concordat in 2004) but it contributed, together with the Islamic Community of Lisbon and other religious groups, to make claims about the space for religious minorities in the public sphere. Such pressure groups were actively involved in the new religious law, approved in 2001, in which several rights of religious collectives are recognized. Likewise, in Finland and Ireland, the majority church also helped the more recently arrived Muslims find their place in inter-religious relations and has supported the inclusion of newcomer Muslims into state–religion relations. For the Greek Muslims of Western Thrace, a modern version of the Ottoman millet system was adopted.

---

65   Mahmood Mamdani, *Good Muslim, Bad Muslim: America, The Cold War and the Roots of Terror*, London, Penguin Random House (2005).

66   Ariane Chebel d'Appolonia and Simon Reich, ed., *Immigration, Integration, and Security: America and Europe in Comparative Perspective* (Pittsburgh: University of Pittsburgh Press, 2008); Jocelyn Cesari, *The Securitisation of Islam in Europe* (CEPS Challenge Programme, 2009), accessed December 9, 2012, http://aei.pitt.edu/10763/1/1826.pdf.

Therefore, focusing on these contexts allows us to extend the comparative outlook between Catholic, Orthodox and Protestant majority countries and raise some questions about the ways, these dominant religious landscapes, together with the different state-religion arrangements, have an impact on the institutional panorama and on the experiences of concrete people.

Third, organizing a book about such contexts allows us to deepen our understanding of historical legacies and the past and present role of Islam in the public sphere. Again, the Portuguese case is quite revealing. During the liberation/colonial wars the Portuguese authorities – *Estado Novo* – was actively engaged in identifying the loyalties of Muslims: were they with the colonialists or were they supporting the independence/liberation struggles? In this context, the Portuguese authorities designed a plan to create a Portuguese Islam – from Minho to Timor with 2 million Muslims.[67] This project implied the co-option of certain Muslim figures, namely institutional leaders of the community in several territories. Other segments of the community, though, made several efforts to build alternative projects to an idea of Portuguese Muslim, an alternative discourse that reverberates today. It is thus possible to say that the idea of a "Portuguese Islam/Muslim," transmitted by certain sectors of Sunni Muslims in Portugal today, is connected with the late colonial period and the ways Muslims were seen with suspicion.[68] It is clear though that such discourses and narratives have been transformed and assume today a totally different meaning and have been used to counter (local and transnational) Islamophobic arguments about the incompatibilities between Islam and a liberal political ethic.[69] The situation is, however, somewhat different in Greece where historical issues related to the Ottoman Empire and Greek national identity have made the issue of Muslim incorporation a much more sensitive topic, also related to the treatment of the Greek minority in Turkey.

Fourth, some of these cases reveal dichotomous and hierarchic discourses, produced by some segments, that performatively produce ideas about autochthone and allochthone ("immigrant," "foreign") religions and religious groups, and this includes Muslims and Islam. In these cases, the "good" and the "bad"

---

67   Abdoolkarim Vakil, Fernando Monteiro and Mário Machaqueiro, *Moçambique: Memória Falado do Islão e da Guerra* (Coimbra: Almedina, 2011).

68   Mário Machaqueiro, "Portuguese Colonialism and the Islamic Community of Lisbon" in *Colonial and Postcolonial Governance of Islam: Continuities and Ruptures*, eds, Marcel Maussen, Veit Bader, Annelies Moors (Amsterdam: Amsterdam University Press, 2011): 211–232.

69   José Mapril "'Aren't You Looking for Citizenship in the Wrong Place?' Islamic Education, Secular Subjectivities, and the Portuguese Muslim," Religion and Society: Advances in Research, 5 (2014): 65–82.

INTRODUCTION 19

Muslim emerge quite strikingly and, in the process, reproduce degrees of alterity and anti-immigration/nativist rhetorics.

And this leads us to a final point: these four contexts allow us to see the transnationalization of global Islamophobia and how its presence is increasingly being felt. How it is, in a way, localized according to specific historic and contextual elements. National historical experiences with Islam and Muslims, including hegemonic national identities and imperial and colonial legacies and its alterities, do seem to matter. But there is also a growing impact of globally shared moral panics – see for instance, global islamophobia – as well as EU-based developments, economic and political (e.g. the reinforcement of right-wing populist parties and movement that mobilize anti-immigration/ anti-Islam-Muslims agendas), that interact in complex ways with the public space in these four countries, when it comes to issues on Islam, Muslimness, citizenship, the place of the religious and the secular, etc.

In sum, on one hand, we argue that the settlement and institutionalization of Islam depends on the historical routes of each of these contexts. We can see how national particularities and histories, as well as different national priorities on what are considered central issues, have an impact of the place for Muslims and Islam. On the other though, it is also clear that national debates and political dynamics are increasingly embedded in a pan-European and global discourses about Islam and Muslims, increasingly influencing national decision-making processes and outcomes, debates in the public domain and the dynamics of recognition. The most obvious of these are related not only with security issues, but also to different forms of governance of Islam and the management of religious diversities, some of which explicitly directed at Muslims and Islam.

3 Governmentalities, Recognition and Mobilities

In order to address the aforementioned ideas and debates, the chapters in this edited volume are arranged according to four major themes, namely: (1) Governing Islam and Muslims; (2) Politics of Recognition; (3) Public Debates and (In)visibility; and, finally, (4) Mobilities and Belonging.

In Part 1, *Governing Islam and Muslims*, and drawing inspiration from the vast array of studies on this topic produced in the past decades, the objective is to explore the ways in which Islam and Muslims have been governed by looking at the institutional configurations of some of these countries. Tuomas Martikainen's Chapter (1) looks at the foundation process of the Islamic Council of Finland, and through that at the relationship of the Finnish State and Muslim organizations. The author researches the role of various actors and interest groups in the establishment of the Islamic Council from 2004 to 2007, including the viewpoints of activists and organizations, including public authorities. This chapter locates the foundation process of the Islamic Council of Finland within the broader context of post-1990 changes in the Finnish welfare state and explores the argument that there is no historical model for the Islamic Council of Finland based on state–church relations, but rather that it is an innovation in the paradigm of New Public Management.

In the next Chapter (2), Luís Pais Bernardo focuses on the state-religion relationships in Ireland and Portugal from 1970 to 2010. Bernardo looks at the role of the Catholic Church in Ireland and Portugal and suggests that Catholicism's "degree of integration largely determines the level of institutionalization of later religious communities and their capacity to claim for rights extension." However, the factual incorporation into political processes of Muslims in Ireland and Portugal also differ. This is due to "a mixture of historically inherited and strategically decided mechanisms of interest intermediation," whereby national models provide the basic institutional framework in which new religions create relationships with the state, but also leaves room for powerful actors (in this case the Irish and Portuguese Catholic Church) to strategically consider how to relate and support the incorporation of new religious actors into existing and new networks. Bernardo also points out the need to forget assumptions of (Muslim) community size and representative organizations, as de facto inclusion into networks is also based on other considerations as in the case of the Isma'ili community in Portugal, where even national business relations have played a role. Bernardo's key point is that, besides taking national differences in state-religion and institutional environments into account, only a diversity of national cases can reveal the full scope of state-religion developments across Europe.

Religious education is a compulsory subject in Finnish primary and secondary schools, and it is provided in the student's own religion in a non-confessional manner by professional religion teachers. Simultaneously with the diversification of the religious field in Finland since the early 1990s, the number of students with minority religion background, including Muslims, has risen. All teaching at school is based on officially approved curricula, which has also been created for minority religions. Tuula Sakaranaho's Chapter (3) looks at how Islamic religious education, including the shaping of its curriculum, is used as a tool for governing Muslims pupils in Finland by way of teaching a "general Islam," not taking into account various national and doctrinal interpretations of Islam. Sakaranaho looks at the process of how an Islamic teaching curriculum was created and how public authorities have aimed to influence Muslims through religious education. Sakaranaho's chapter is a telling example of how new inputs into an existing system are made to conform to national expectations and institutional models, and how Islamic religious education is one tool for governing Muslims in Finland.

Part 2, *Politics of Recognition,* is in clear continuation with the previous theme but gathers a group of chapters more focused on the dynamics of recognition in the public sphere. This second section, although also looking at the institutional scenarios (as in Section one), it is more focused on processes developed by Muslims themselves, in a clear bottom-up way. Adil Hussain Khan, for instance (chapter 4), discusses the development of Irish Muslim institutional frameworks, including the sudden proliferation of mosques, which has been taking place with great urgency in recent years. This has enabled rivalries among Irish Muslims who are struggling to distinguish themselves. This process has led to competition among Irish Muslim community leaders who are trying to gain recognition by attracting certain sections of the Muslim population and by establishing Muslim constituencies as a viable minority amongst the non-Muslim majority. This chapter examines existing power structures within Irish Muslim communities at present. It also compares how different concepts of authority have been evoked by Irish Muslim community leaders to establish unique ideological orientations as representatives of Irish Islam. Khan analyses the influences on Irish Muslim community leadership by identifying key factors impacting power structures in Irish Islam, which largely revolve around issues of funding, internal religious recognition, and public opinion. Ultimately, this study explores the nature of the relationship between religious power and religious truth by showing how contested notions of Islamic authenticity are validated through different conceptions of authority within contemporary Irish Islam.

Venetia Evergeti (Chapter 5) looks at the history of Islam in Greece. The chapter discusses the socio-historical establishment of Muslim minorities in Greece in the context of the construction of Greek national identity and its relationship to (Turkish) Islam. Moreover, it provides an account of recent developments and shifting paradigms amidst the increasing numbers of Muslim immigrants in the country. The focus is on the religious organization, identification and belonging of Muslims, as these developed historically, both in Thrace as well as once they moved to Athens and other big cities.

Finally, Des Delaney's Chapter (6) focuses on young Sunni Muslims in Dublin, Ireland, and discusses how they feel recognized in the spheres of family, community, law and society. Inspired by Axel Honneth's theory of recognition and supplementing it with narrative empirical data, this chapter explores whether the interviewees' perceive positive or negative forms of recognition within multiple spheres of social interaction. The results provide a mixed image of both recognition and misrecognition. Whereas feelings of familial, communal and legal recognition are generally shared among the interviewed youth, societal recognition is lagging behind. The chapter underlines the complexity of feelings of recognition at the individual level while simultaneously noting the role of society at large.

Part 3, *Public Debates and (In)visibility*, focuses on what is made visible/ enunciated and invisible/silenced about Muslims and Islam in some of these countries. In Chapter seven, Stacey Scriver discusses why the use of the "Muslim veil" has received only marginal attention in Ireland. According to her, "a masculinized ethno-nationalism and the historical role of public religion" are the main reasons why the veil is likely not to cause any great controversy even in the near future. However, the same factors "deny Muslims in Ireland the possibility of substantively belonging to the dominant group and thus to the full range of rights and responsibilities of citizenship in Irish society." Scriver's chapter is an analysis of public debates in Ireland from May to October 2008. The chapter argues that even though being religiously different is more acceptable in a more religious society like Ireland, other political processes allow keeping a distance between the non-welcome Others. In Scriver's view, full citizenship is still not possible unless these barriers can be removed.

Next, Nina Clara Tiesler and Susana Lavado argue that, contrary to other European countries, the contemporary Muslim presence in Portugal has not raised major tensions among the population, nor has it called the attention of the media on a regular basis, or been put at the top of the agenda of political negotiations and social research. This eighth chapter analyses this relative silence by looking at some of the recent historic and political factors that may have contributed to this impression of a relative public silence concerning the local Muslim communities in Portugal. In addition, data from the Group-focused Enmity in Europe Project provides the backbone of the analysis on individual attitudes toward Muslims in Portugal and other European countries. Results suggest that there is a discrepancy between the attitudes toward the Muslim community in Portugal and toward Muslims and Islam as a more abstract category.

In Chapter 9, Panos Hatziprokopiou provides a panorama of Islam in contemporary Greece, by looking at its newer Muslim residents, their characteristics and the ways they are portrayed in mainstream public discourses. Hatziprokopiou also shows the challenges in making estimates of the number Muslims by a thorough statistical discussion. Building on a variety of sources, the key issue concerns the growing Muslim presence in the country, due to both a growth of migratory flows involving increasing numbers of immigrants

INTRODUCTION   23

from Muslim majority countries and the rise of migrant Muslim communities in the public sphere with the increasing politization of Islam. Such a growing presence suggests multiple shifts regarding the character of Islam in Greece.

In Part 4, we gathered chapters dealing with *Mobilities and Belonging* and the importance of Islam, national belonging, sectarian divisions and gender to the way our interlocutors think about their worlds in motion. Marko Juntunen (chapter 10), focuses on a complex suburban setting where globally produced sectarian and political discourses intersect with immigrant regimes and multicultural policies. Based on a research on the Iraqi diaspora in Finland, Marko reveals the contrasting religious and political perceptions, the complex personal histories of persecution, and the tense social and symbolic boundaries in such a multicultural suburban context. The Iraqis are caught up in a collision of discourses not only with relation to violence and social fragmentation at home, but they also stand between the increasingly contradictory refugee regime and multicultural social policies that essentialize identities on religious and sectarian terms. Multicultural work attempting to build bridges between diasporic communities and the Finnish state often fails to recognize the internal divisions within the diaspora and thus engenders particular types of responses: silences and forms of silencing that are rooted in cultural and religious practices.

Yafa Shanneik and Marja Tiilikainen's Chapter (11) looks at Somali women in Finland and Sudanese women in Ireland, and how they give meaning to religion and culture in their home surroundings. Using Thomas A. Tweed's concepts, the authors' show how religious and other identities are reproduced in private settings and how they embed cultural meanings. Some differences between the groups of women are apparent. The Sudanese use material goods, whereas the Somali women preserve particular knowledge, for example, of how to organize rituals in a culturally new, non-Islamic environment. The domestic space is a central place for creating identities and offer opportunities for both tradition and change. The chapter illustrates different strategies for preserving religious memory as well as the dynamics of how religious memory adapts to new contexts and changes.

Finally, Jennifer McGarrigle's Chapter (12) explores various elements of the religious spatiality of Muslims in post-colonial Portugal and provides a spatial analysis of religious landscapes, conceived as residence and collective spatial appropriation for worship in the Lisbon Metropolitan Area. The dichotomy of invisibility and visibility in relation to peripheralization and centrality in the city and particular forms of spatial appropriation is discussed. We see here, then, that the "Portuguese Muslim Community" can only be understood in the context of the national and ethnic sub-collective Muslim groups that are represented in different spaces across the city. In general terms, broader trends in the ethnic geography of the city are replicated with a clear central/peripheral pattern that creates both visibility in the city centre and invisibility on the urban margins. Initial settlement was largely driven by structural factors at the time of migration and later consolidated by networking among family, nationality and ethno-cultural groups resulting in differentiated settlement patterns. The adaption of the organizational structures of associations at the local level has carved out an important role for several of the religious communities, particularly those from Western Africa. They mediate between public institutions and the local community and oftentimes represent an access point to public and third-sector resources. In the case of Lisbon, controversies or tensions related to Muslim and non-Muslim relations and the visibility of Islam in territorial terms have largely been avoided.

All in all, the chapters in this edited volume highlight how national contexts, with their particular historical routes, including economic development, colonial legacies and post-colonial dynamics, migrations, church-state relations, secularism(s), the place of the religious and heritage making, influence Muslim experiences and the making of Islam, in its religious and institutional logics. We claim, therefore, that the research about European Islam and Muslims will benefit from these studies, which draw further attention to the varied experiences of diverse Muslim populations around the continent and broaden our understanding of the dynamics of Muslim settlement in different social contexts. Having said this, all the chapters, in one way or the other, highlight the fact that our interlocutors' experiences cannot solely be understood in the light of national particularities. Global mobility flows, global islamophobia and racism, neoliberalism and a changing political economy, among other variables, are all essential elements to take into consideration while analysing the complexities of European Muslims, including those in less studied contexts such as Finland, Ireland, Portugal and Greece. All these chapters highlight dynamics that are simultaneously distinct and similar to the ones analysed in the existing literature on other European countries. Overall, this edited volume will hopefully contribute to a fuller picture of the similarities and differences among Muslims and Islam in their own societies, in comparison with other cases described in the literature, while paying attention to broader European or global tendencies.

PART 1

Governing Islam and Muslims

∴

CHAPTER 1

The Founding of the Islamic Council of Finland

Tuomas Martikainen

The role of national, representative Muslim councils in Western Europe has become a matter of scholarly interest. A common feature of many of these councils is the involvement of public authorities in their creation and support, including funding, interest in agenda setting and establishing a partnership in counter-radicalization and counter-terrorism activities.[1] As Ferrari notes, forming representative organizations for diverse Muslim communities is challenging, as there are few parallels in the Islamic tradition for such institutions.[2] The religious and ethnic diversity of Muslims also creates friction with regard to co-operation and, in some cases, makes it impossible. The founding of representative bodies incorporates elements of negotiation and innovation as well as structural pressure by the majority society. Nevertheless, many national representative bodies have been created in recent decades, including one in Finland since 2006.

The creation of national Islamic councils is part of the legal, political and structural incorporation of immigrant religious traditions into Europe.[3] The impact of historical state–church relationships has been referred to as the central force in shaping contemporary developments on immigrant religious incorporation.[4] This perspective claims that historical arrangements in

---

1   Brigitte Maréchal, "Institutionalisation of Islam and Representative Organisations for Dealing with European States," in *Muslims in the Enlarged Europe: Religion and Society*, ed. Brigitte Maréchal et al. (Leiden: Brill, 2003); Marcel Maussen, *The Governance of Islam in Western Europe: A State of the Art Report* (IMISCOE, 2007), 30–31, accessed November 26, 2013, http://www.iom.lt/documents/GovernanceofIslam.pdf; Jonathan Laurence, *The Emancipation of Europe's Muslims: The State's Role in Minority Integration* (Princeton: Princeton University Press, 2012).

2   Silvio Ferrari, "The Secularity of the State and the Shaping of Muslim Representative Organizations in Western Europe," in *European Muslims and the Secular State*, ed. Jocelyn Cesari and Seán McLoughlin (Aldershot: Ashgate, 2005), 11–23.

3   Maussen, *The Governance of Islam in Western Europe*.

4   Joel S. Fetzer and J. Christopher Soper, *Muslims and the State in Britain, France, and Germany* (Cambridge: Cambridge University Press, 2005); Timothy A. Byrnes and Peter J. Katzenstein, ed., *Religion in an Expanding Europe* (Cambridge: Cambridge University Press, 2006); José Casanova, "Immigrants and the New Religious Pluralism: A European Union/United States Comparison," in *Democracy and the New Religious Pluralism*, ed. Thomas Banchoff (Oxford: Oxford University Press, 2007), 59–83. See also Bernardo's chapter in this book.

state–church relations are the key to explaining the nationally different trajectories that take place among new immigrant religious communities. While there is much insight in this perspective, it can be argued that the model is based too heavily on the historical formation of modern statehood, and that its explanatory power is limited regarding more recent changes in state structures, which also affect the position of religious organizations.

The context of this study, Finland, is often described as a Nordic welfare state, referring to its tradition of state-led social engineering. The Finnish welfare state has, however, gone through major transformations since the 1980s. Finnish social scientists have described the transition as a move from a "planning economy" to a "competition economy,"[5] and described the new type of society as "competitiveness society"[6] and "project society."[7] Risto Heiskala summarizes some central aspects of the transformation as follows: Governmental co-ordination has moved from hierarchical planning to market mechanisms, including network management and privatization. Key developments in the "competitiveness society" include new public management, outsourcing and the privatization of welfare services, and the growth of projects and programmes as new forms of governance. These have replaced top-down bureaucratic mechanisms.[8]

The State's retreat from being the self-evident caretaker of the Finnish society has entailed the growing expectancy of other sectors of society to deliver not only services and goods but also identities and forms of belonging. Consequently, we have witnessed an increase of public debates about social capital and civil society where associations and other voluntary organizations are expected to take a more prominent position than before in creating social cohesion and general welfare. This Finnish restructuring is part of a global trend in neoliberal policies. The growing role of religion as an important factor in civil society has increasingly been noted both internationally and in

---

5 Pertti Alasuutari, "Suunnittelutaloudesta kilpailutalouteen: Miten muutos oli ideologisesti mahdollinen?," in *Uusi jako: Miten Suomesta tuli kilpailukyky-yhteiskunta?*, ed. Risto Heiskala and Eeva Luhtakallio (Helsinki: Gaudeamus, 2006), 43–64.

6 Risto Heiskala, "Kansainvälisen toimintaympäristön muutos ja Suomen yhteiskunnallinen murros," in *Uusi jako: Miten Suomesta tuli kilpailukyky-yhteiskunta?*, ed. Risto Heiskala and Eeva Luhtakallio (Helsinki: Gaudeamus, 2006), 14–42.

7 Pekka Sulkunen, "Projektiyhteiskunta ja uusi yhteiskuntasopimus," in *Projektiyhteiskunnan kääntöpuolia*, ed. Kati Rantala and Pekka Sulkunen (Helsinki: Gaudeamus, 2006), 17–38.

8 Heiskala, "Kansainvälisen toimintaympäristön muutos ja Suomen yhteiskunnallinen murros," 37.

Finland,[9] whereas much less attention has been given to its impact on state–church relations. This chapter will address that lack of reflection.

The aim of this chapter is to describe the organization process of the Islamic Council of Finland (in Finnish, *Suomen Islamilainen Neuvosto*, abbreviation SINE) that took place from 2004 to 2007. It discusses the roles of church–state relations and an emerging neoliberal governance of religion in the organization process. The chapter starts with a brief presentation of Muslims and state regulation of religion in Finland. Then it looks at the founding process of SINE. Next, it analyses this process by looking at the creation of political opportunity structures, Muslims' resource mobilization and the securitization of Islam as explanations. Finally, it concludes that the founding of SINE sits well among broader trends in public administration that are related to changes in the Finnish welfare state, and cannot be understood solely in the framework of historical state–church relations.[10]

In relation to the broader thematic of this volume, the chapter highlights a transition period with Finnish governance of minority religion. While Muslims in Finland initially arrived as internal migrants in the Russian Empire, and their relationship with the independent Finnish State was settled as part of national freedom of religion legislation in the early 1920s, the post-Cold War Muslim organisations in the 1990s and 2000s were increasingly affected by a new rational of governance and influenced by a European and global mediascape of Islam as problematic. Currently, the two governance models work simultaneously, and it remains to be seen to what direction they develop.

---

9   For example, Anders Bäckström and Grace Davie, ed., *Welfare and Religion in 21st Century Europe: Volume 1. Configuring the Connections* (Farnham: Ashgate, 2010).

10   The material of the study has been collected as part of my Academy of Finland funded postdoctoral project "From First to Second Generation Islam: Religious Adaptations in Finnish Mosques and among Muslim Youth" (2007–2010). I conducted semi-structured interviews with representatives of Muslim organizations, individual Muslim activists and public officials in different ministries and governmental bodies during 2008, as well as gathered different kinds of official documents. The quotations in this chapter are from the interviews, and the respondents have had the opportunity to read and comment on the interview transcript. All but one of the interviewees consented to having their real names used in publications, but for this chapter I have decided to refer to their background organization. This does not guarantee their anonymity, since it is likely that people knowledgeable in the field will be able to identify most of them. For this reason, I sent the manuscript of the chapter for comments to all whose interviews are quoted so that they had the opportunity to withdraw their comments.

1 Muslims and State Regulation of Islam in Finland

The dominant religious tradition in Finland is the Evangelical Lutheran Church that grew out of the Catholic Church during the Reformation in the 1520s when Finland was an eastern province of Sweden. As Finland was annexed as a Grand Duchy to the Russian Empire in 1809, the old legislation remained in force, including the prohibition of non-Lutheran religious activity. This system started to change during the 19th century. First by the extension of rights to the Russian Orthodox population that historically inhabited the border region between Sweden and Russia, and later by a growing toleration of other religions, including the legalization of non-Lutheran, Protestant churches in 1889. Moreover, the state-church system was challenged by emergent modernization in the latter half of the 19th century, including changes in social status systems related to early urbanization and industrialization, as well as the secularization of public administration and education. These social changes coincided with great migrations to North America, increased global mobility and trade, and growing religious diversity. New religions, including Catholicism, different Protestant churches, Judaism and Islam, gained a foothold through immigration and conversion. Much of the migration took place within the Russian Empire, from where also the first permanently settled Finnish Muslims community – the Tatars – arrived (see Introduction). In the aftermath of the October Revolution in Russia, Finland declared its independence in December 1917. This was followed by a new, Constitution Act in 1919 and the Law on Religious Freedom in 1922, ending the time of religious restrictions and introducing freedom of religion to the religious and non-religious alike. The Lutheran and (now Finnish) Orthodox Churches gained a special status, later defined as "the two folk churches," but all other religions also had the opportunity to register and gain state recognition.[11]

The role of all minority religions remained peripheral in Finnish society, and did not attract major interest among the majority, even though there were issues of public interest and conflict at times. The situation remained more or less the same through the 20th century, even though religious diversity slowly grew. The Lutheran Church was culturally dominant until the 1960s, when secularization gained strength. Since then the role of the Lutheran Church has slowly weakened, even though it is still a powerful institution in many

---

11   Markku Heikkilä, Jyrki Knuutila and Martin Scheinin, "State and Church in Finland," in *State and Church in the European Union*, Second Edition, ed. Gerhard Robbers (Baden-Baden: Nomos), 519–536.

THE FOUNDING OF THE ISLAMIC COUNCIL OF FINLAND   31

respects.[12] In general, the state has maintained a distance from religious affairs. The largest state intervention in religious affairs was the Finnicization of the Russian Orthodox Church, which became a national, Finnish Orthodox Church in the 1920s.[13] Another example of public intervention, though much smaller in scale, was the effort to control Bible smuggling into the Soviet Union by Protestant Christian groups. This activity irritated Soviet officials and was therefore monitored by the Finnish Security Intelligence Service.[14] Religion as such was not a significant matter of national security.[15]

According to the Law on Religious Freedom of 1922 (which came into effect in 1923 and was amended in 2003), minority religions can be registered as religious community organizations (Finn. *rekisteröity uskonnollinen yhdyskunta*), whereby they can, among others, be entitled to the right to conduct legally approved marriages and have religious education in public schools. Since 2008, communities of this type have also been able to apply for State support, if they have enough members. However, only communities that have a creed, congregation and membership can apply for the status. Many Islamic organizations have taken advantage of the opportunity, which resulted in the founding 25 such organizations by 2007 and even more since. In addition, many communities, as well as other Islamic groups, have organized themselves as registered associations (Finn. *rekisteröity yhdistys*), which is the most common form of civic organization in Finland, even though this does not lead to official recognition as "religion."[16]

Current Finnish public debates on Islam and policy interest in Muslims are inherently tied to post-1990 immigration.[17] These policies and debates

---

12   Kimmo Ketola, "Uskonto suomalaisessa yhteiskunnassa 1600-luvulta nykypäivään," in *Moderni kirkkokansa: Suomalaisten uskonnollisuus uudella vuosituhannella*, Kimmo Kääriäinen, Kati Niemelä and Kimmo Ketola (Tampere: Kirkon tutkimuskeskus, 2003), 17–52.

13   Mika Nokelainen, *Vähemmistövaltiokirkon synty: Ortodoksisen kirkkokunnan ja valtion suhteiden muotoutuminen Suomessa 1917–1922* (Helsinki: Suomen Kirkkohistoriallinen Seura, 2010).

14   Piia Latvala, *Valoa itään? Kansanlähetys ja Neuvostoliitto 1967–1973* (Helsinki: Suomen Kirkkohistoriallinen Seura, 2008).

15   Matti Simola, ed., *Ratakatu 12: Suojelupoliisi 1949–2009* (Helsinki: WSOY, 2009).

16   Tuomas Martikainen, "Muslimit suomalaisessa yhteiskunnassa," in *Islam Suomessa: Muslimit arjessa, mediassa ja yhteiskunnassa*, ed. Tuomas Martikainen, Tuula Sakaranaho and Marko Juntunen (Helsinki: Suomalaisen Kirjallisuuden Seura, 2008), 62–84.

17   Teemu Taira, "Islamin muuttuva julkisuuskuva: Tapaustutkimus Helsingin Sanomista 1946–1994," in *Islam Suomessa: Muslimit arjessa, mediassa ja yhteiskunnassa*, ed. Tuomas Martikainen, Tuula Sakaranaho and Marko Juntunen (Helsinki: Suomalaisen Kirjallisuuden Seura, 2008), 200–224.

do not have a primary background in religious considerations, but rather in immigrant integration, empowerment and social problems, as well as international coverage of Islamic terrorism.[18] Even though Islamic and other religious associations were only part of policy networks to a small extent in the 1990s, their role has risen in the 2000s, when the political implications of 9/11, the Muhammad cartoons controversy (2005–2006), and other similar events manifested themselves. The concern is, of course, fear over Muslim radicalization and Islamic terrorism, which is embedded in more general worries about the marginalization of certain (often Muslim background) immigrant groups and their offspring.[19] In light of this, we have witnessed the emergence of a dual policy towards Islam, which, on the one hand, aims to incorporate and enhance social integration of immigrants (Muslims) and, on the other hand, attempts to prevent Muslim radicalization and Islamic terrorism. This mix of policies on social integration and national security is evident in many public policies towards Islam in Finland, as elsewhere in the Western world.[20] Much of the public discussion and policy development has been related to developments external to Finland, and hence national debates on Islam can only be understood in a broader European and global context.

Whereas the full impact of the immigrant integration–security nexus on religion is only emerging, it does challenge historical state–church relations by introducing new governance structures, as well as implementing new modes of self-governance, into the communities under scrutiny.[21] The general thrust of these changes falls in line with New Public Management, where networks (and markets) have grown in importance, together with contractual

---

18 Pentti Raittila and Mari Maasilta. "Silmäyksiä islamin esittämiseen suomalaisessa journalismissa," in *Islam Suomessa: Muslimit arjessa, mediassa ja yhteiskunnassa*, ed. Tuomas Martikainen, Tuula Sakaranaho and Marko Juntunen (Helsinki: Suomalaisen Kirjallisuuden Seura, 2008), 225–243.

19 Ministry of the Interior, *Safety First: Internal Security Programme. Government Plenary Session 8 May 2008*, Publications of the Ministry of the Interior 25/2008 (Helsinki: Ministry of the Interior, 2008).

20 Cf. Ariane Chebel d'Appollonia and Simon Reich, ed., *Immigration, Integration, and Security: America and Europe in Comparative Perspective* (Pittsburgh: University of Pittsburgh Press, 2008); Sara Silvestri, "Public Policies towards Muslims and the Institutionalisation of 'Moderate' Islam in Europe: Some Critical Reflections," in *Muslims in 21st Century Europe*, ed. Anna Triandafyllidou (London: Routledge, 2010), 45–58.

21 Tuomas Martikainen, "The Governance of Islam in Finland," *Temenos* 43/2 (2007): 243–265; see also Mitchell Dean, *Governmentality: Power and Rule in Modern Society* (London: Sage, 1999); Nikolas Rose, *Powers of Freedom: Reframing Political Thought* (Cambridge: Cambridge University Press, 1999).

agreements as well as various administrative techniques of control.[22] For instance, Miikka Pyykkönen[23] has argued that immigrant associations can be seen as an element of "pan-European paradigms of new governance," whereby the state increasingly uses civil society actors as tools for policy implementation. As I have argued elsewhere,[24] a similar shift in policy paradigms seems to be taking place in state relations with religious associations that have been observed in other policy fields in Finland, including health care and social policy.[25] Unique to Islam is the concern for national security that has been the main factor in raising the importance of religion on the political agenda and has thereby speeded up the process of change. Securitization of religion is part of the broader trend of securitizing social problems whereby it becomes targeted with different kinds of administrative technologies.

The nature and scope of an emerging form of governance of religion in Finland is still difficult to estimate because, on the one hand, it relies on the historical model of state–church relationships and, on the other hand, it is based on new policy networks and other governance techniques. This is a typical feature of neoliberalized public management that blurs path dependence while at the same time introducing new models of rule.[26] As a fuller picture is yet to emerge on the impact of recent policy changes on religion at large,[27] below I will look at the founding process of the Islamic Council of Finland and argue that we are, indeed, witnessing the birth of a new form of governance of religion in Finland.

---

22   Anne Mette Kjær, *Governance* (Cambridge: Policy Press, 2004).

23   Miikka Pyykkönen, "Integrating Governmentality: Administrative Expectations for Immigrant Associations in Finland," *Alternatives* 32/2 (2007): 217.

24   Tuomas Martikainen, "The Global Political Economy, Welfare State Reforms, and the Governance of Religion," in *Post-Secular Society*, ed. Peter Nynäs, Mika Lassander and Terhi Utriainen (New Brunswick: Transaction Publishers, 2012), 71–93; Tuomas Martikainen, "Multilevel and Pluricentric Network Governance of Religion," in *Religion in the Neoliberal Age: Political Economy and Modes of Governance*, ed. Tuomas Martikainen and François Gauthier (Farnham: Ashgate, 2013), 129–142.

25   Risto Heiskala and Eeva Luhtakallio, ed., *Uusi jako: Miten Suomesta tuli kilpailukykyyhteiskunta?* (Helsinki: Gaudeamus, 2006); Kati Rantala, and Pekka Sulkunen, ed., *Projektiyhteiskunnan kääntöpuolia* (Helsinki: Gaudeamus, 2006).

26   Neil Brenner, Jamie Peck and Nik Theodore, "Variegated Neoliberalization: Geographies, Modalities, Pathways," *Global Networks* 10/2 (2010): 182–222.

27   Ville Jalovaara and Tuomas Martikainen, "Suomi maallistumisen jälkeen: Valtiokirkollisuudesta uskontojen markkinoihin," in *Religions återkomst: Brytningspunkter i kyrkan, religionen och kulturen*, ed. Tuomas Martikainen and Ville Jalovaara (Helsingfors: Magma, 2010), 27–39.

2 The Creation of the Islamic Council of Finland

The Islamic Council of Finland was founded on Saturday, 11 November 2006 and officially registered as a voluntary association on Thursday, 1 March 2007. SINE is an umbrella organization, originally with 14 member organizations that had grown to 23 by April 2011. During its first years of existence SINE was involved in arranging many events, taking part in public discussions, and developing a wide variety of activities in its five committees (burial, education, legal, media, youth). SINE is increasingly involved in and co-operating with many religious and administrative networks. It is governed by a Shura representing the member organizations and run by a board that is annually selected by the Shura. Until now, SINE has been financed by the Finnish state. In the following, a description of how SINE came into being will be presented. The following description is based on the interviews conducted as part of my research project unless stated otherwise.

The local organization of newly arrived Muslims started in Finland at the turn of the 1990s, and already by the mid-1990s some Muslims anticipated the need for a common endeavour. A number of Muslim activists had realized that they have common concerns, regarding issues such as Muslim burial, where they would need the negotiation power embedded in a common representative body. The first organization aimed at founding such a body was the Federation of Islamic Organizations in Finland that was registered in April 1997. The federation did not gain a considerable following and has remained of minimal importance to this day. As one of the communities involved states:

> It was in the mid-1990s, actually in 1995, when we started to have more talks about the need for a union. We were there to found the union in Jyväskylä in 1997. However, very soon we learned that the Federation aimed at controlling its member societies. It was evident in the first letter, and we let them know our opinion in writing, and left the union.
> Representative of a mosque association

It became obvious from the interviews conducted that there were conflicts between different Muslim interest groups. The main issues mentioned are concerned with the roles of the central and local associations, as referred to above, but may also have included personal antipathies, as well as unsettled issues about previous misconduct, which was mentioned several times in relation to a failed attempt to create a Muslim graveyard in the Helsinki region in the late 1990s. The shortcoming is reflective on the heterogeneity of the newly arrived Muslim communities and reflects the broader post-Cold War migration dynamics that no longer produce singular communities. Nevertheless, the unsuccessful attempt to found a federation led many communities to focus on developing their own activities. The need for a common platform did not, however, disappear and had apparently resurfaced at regular intervals so that a new effort became timely after the terrorist attacks on New York and Washington DC on 11 September 2001.

> It was again a good chance to attempt cooperation after 9/11. A meeting was arranged and there were also people present from the previous effort in the mid-1990s. A committee was formed. (...) Issues related to Islam and Muslims are many, and grow, and we need to get all Muslims to organize. (...) ETNO had also started its activities.
> Representative of a mosque association

A new meeting was arranged at the Al-Iman (Munkkiniemi) mosque in Helsinki, and later a more controversial one at the Herttoniemi mosque, but the effort soon met with similar difficulties as the earlier attempt. Not all participants shared similar visions, and some of the participants left the group. A committee was nevertheless formed, and slowly started to develop the idea among a smaller group of mosque associations.

Alongside these developments, the Finnish administration was proactive in hearing minority concerns. The Advisory Board for Ethnic Relations (ETNO) had been founded in 1998, and religious organizations also found their way into its activities. Additionally, the Office of the Ombudsman for Minorities was founded in 2002, and has become an important actor in minority related issues in Finland. Both of these governmental organizations had their predecessors, but their scope of activity has been expanded in their transformations to include ethnic and religious matters. In the background of the transformations were new EU directives against discrimination and their implementation in Finland. Actors in the field of minority governance were growing in number at the turn of the 2000s, and these were seen by Islamic organizations as alternatives in promoting their cause.

One reason for the interest of public authorities in Islam was that there had been several issues of public concern regarding new Muslim immigrants. These issues included male and female circumcision, Islamic religious education in schools, Muslim burials, and concerns about mosque premises and the planning of purpose-built mosques, as well as Muslim practices and clothing in working life. These concerns touched many branches of public administration, and finally the Ombudsman for Minorities emerged in 2002 as the key player in solving such problems. Unaware of the on-going internal debates to create an Islamic council among some Muslim communities, the Ombudsman started to consider the need for a representative council.

> It was an exciting process with quite big surprises along the way. It started when I was working for the first year as the Ombudsman for Minorities in 2002. The first issue that opened my eyes was boy's circumcision, and I saw how precarious the position of these people was our in society. I also understood that they have to be involved if we are going to solve these problems. The solution cannot come from above, but it needs to come from the inside. But they also need help, let us say, of a sympathetic partner, as a kind of midwife. I had in the beginning two old Muslim contacts. They helped me out before the communities came into the picture. The process started in January 2004. I was in London at an informal seminar of public authorities and specialized bodies on equal treatment [referring to activities based on EU Directive 2000/43/EC] in Member States. I had asked a colleague of mine to introduce me to someone from the Muslim Council of Britain, as I had heard that such an organization exists. (...) I met this guy and he told me how difficult the process had been, and it took fifteen years for them to create the organization, as there were issues relating to representation of genders and regional balance of the organization, etc. These were the same questions that we later encountered. So, when I returned I wanted to start this process and continued discussing it with my two contacts. (...) The process took longer than expected because at the same time we were amidst the implementation of the Non-Discrimination Act.
>
> Ombudsman for Minorities

The EU anti-discrimination directive and networks born out of that context provided the Ombudsman with the necessary tools to proceed in his effort to further the creation of an Islamic council. The Ombudsman for Minorities was also aware of eventual difficulties experienced in other countries, and considered how to avoid them. His strategy was to position himself as a "sympathetic partner" guiding the process in order to prevent the impression that it is a state-dictated process. The first meeting was organized in September 2005 and it was intended to map the needs and interests of Muslims, but not without surprises.

> Half an hour before the meeting was supposed to start somebody came to me and told me that they already have had extensive negotiations and the statutes were almost ready. I had no idea of this. (...) Well, what was

I supposed to do? I somehow figured out that they were not fully satisfied with the outcome, as they failed to get a broader representation, so we agreed that we would return to mapping the needs [of the Muslim community], and that their proposal could be one alternative in the process. Then we concluded that the idea of a representative council is necessary and that we would see how to take into account the work already done and meet again later in the autumn. At the second meeting we then outlined the basis of the new statutes.

Ombudsman for Minorities

Some fifty people participated in the first meeting to discuss the need for a representative council, and they agreed to continue the process. The participants were put into working groups to discuss various issues. People from the Office of the Ombudsman for Minorities functioned as secretaries for the working groups. In this way they also learned more about the different visions and existing tensions among Muslims. The first meeting also provided the Ombudsman with the surprise that similar plans were active among Muslims. In the words of a Muslim activist: "Then the Ombudsman came up with his suggestion, but he did not know about our efforts. We told him about our efforts, and with just three meetings SINE was born" (Representative of a mosque association).

The founding meeting took place in November 2006. There we encountered the problem that some people wanted to have a completely different proposal regarding the structure of the organization and they put forth an alternative version of the statutes. It had to do with how many votes an organization has, and as there was a group of small organizations of one or two people, a question arose about what kind of communities these are. Then we had to vote on this.

Ombudsman for Minorities

Eventually SINE was founded at a third meeting in November 2006 and officially registered as a voluntary association in the following year. The Ombudsman's vision of SINE's role was "a social, political, not a religious, organization. The intention was not to create a sharia court or anything like that. Of course, doctrinal matters can be discussed, but even that should support these sociopolitical issues." Although SINE was founded, it also needed some funding to get started. The Ombudsman for Minorities was aware of discussions relating to Muslims (the memory of the Muhammad cartoons controversy was still fresh) in the Finnish Government. He informed the Government of the new council and mentioned that it could play an important role in Muslim social integration, but it should be given time to develop its own dynamics. He also mentioned that financial support would be needed to run the organization. This eventually led to the seed funding for SINE that was organized by the Prime Minister's Office.

> As the Islamic community [SINE] had organized, we noticed that there was a lack of cash, which was needed to get things running. Then I petitioned the ministries to provide 10,000 euros each. (...) All of this is based on what I discussed with the Prime Minister at an earlier stage. (...) He told me to take care of the matter, and that is what happened.
>
> Prime Minister's Office

3   Institutionalizing Islam

The previous description of the founding process of the Islamic Council of Finland illustrates some of the aims, intentions and tensions taking place simultaneously. They reflect both the diversity of Muslim aspirations and the interests of Finnish public authorities. Next we shall look in more detail at the process from the perspectives of political opportunity structures, resource mobilization and securitization. These perspectives allow us to see the extent to which a path-dependent explanation based on state–church relations functions, and whether there are other dynamics at play.

3.1   *Opportunity Structures and Coercive Isomorphism*
Collective civic action in Finland is rather difficult without an officially recognized organization, at least if one's objectives include relations with public authorities. The political mobilization of interests needs organizational backing, which is commonly a registered voluntary association in Finland. As both Pyykkönen[28] and Martikainen[29] have noted, public authorities have often been proactive in supporting immigrant organizations in Finland. It is also worth noting that the effort to create a common Islamic representational body on the national level has parallels among other types of immigrant associations. According to Miikka Pyykkönen,[30] public officials supported the foundation

---

28   Pyykkönen, "Integrating Governmentality"; Miikka Pyykkönen, *Järjestäytyvät diasporat: Etnisyys, kansalaisuus, integraatio ja hallinta maahanmuuttajien yhdistystoiminnassa* (Jyväskylä: University of Jyväskylä, 2007).

29   Tuomas Martikainen, *Immigrant Religions in Local Society: Historical and Contemporary Perspectives in the City of Turku* (Åbo: Åbo Akademi University Press, 2004).

30   Miikka Pyykkönen, *Järjestäytyvät diasporat.*

THE FOUNDING OF THE ISLAMIC COUNCIL OF FINLAND 39

of all kinds of immigrant societies during the 1990s, and relatively soon, as the number of such societies grew rapidly, also asked for representative bodies to ease their negotiations. Representational bodies became more sought after during the 2000s. Once they were set up, they gained recognized positions as interlocutors. Hence, the demand for a Muslim representative organization is part of a larger trend in immigrant organization.

The immigrant organizational process is often supported by public authorities whereby certain key individuals function as middlemen. In the case of SINE, it was the Ombudsman for Minorities since such a body would be useful in his work. This is what Paul DiMaggio and Walter Powell have named coercive isomorphism, which "results from both formal and informal pressures exerted on organizations by other organizations upon which they are dependent and by cultural expectations in the society within which organizations function."[31] This may take the form of force, persuasion, or invitation to join, as well as other means. In this case, there are external structural and cultural pressures that asks Muslims follow certain criteria in their organizations, which model their activities in that context. As previous models for similar activities are scarce, the process is in itself culturally innovative. The phenomenon is widely recognized among immigrant congregations,[32] and is implicit in the discussion of Christianization or Protestantization of immigrant religions in the West. In the case of SINE, the organizational process coincided with major transformations in the Finnish welfare state whereby different networks were increasingly required to administer a "neoliberalized" welfare state.[33] As Islam does not have a church type of organization, which is the normative presumption in Finnish state–church relations, representativeness needs to be organized in a different way.

The role of the public authorities in the creation of SINE is many-sided. First, Muslims only became aware of the need for a common representational body when they were asked about it, usually by a public authority. Second,

---

31 Paul J. DiMaggio and Walter W. Powell, "The Iron Cage Revisited: Institutional Isomorphism and Collective Rationality in Organizational Fields," *American Sociological Review* 48/2 (1983): 150–151.

32 For example, R. Stephen Warner, "Immigration and Religious Communities in the United States," in *Gatherings in Diaspora: Religious Communities and the New Immigration*, ed. R. Stephen Warner and Judith Wittner (Philadelphia: Temple University Press, 1998), 3–34; Wendy Cadge, "De Facto Congregationalism and the Religious Organizations of Post-1965 Immigrants to the United States: A Revised Approach," *Journal of the American Academy of Religion* 76/2 (2008): 344–374.

33 Heiskala and Luhtakallio, *Uusi jako*; Rantala and Sulkunen, *Projektiyhteiskunnan kääntöpuolia*.

public authorities have been active in helping Muslims create such organizations. Third, public authorities have provided funding or other resources to these organizations. In other words, public authorities have played a crucial role in creating the political opportunity structure in which Muslims can then mobilize themselves. This is a paradigmatic example of coercive isomorphism.

3.2 Resource Mobilization

The main aim of Muslim organizations in the creation of SINE was to create a collective voice for their concerns and a platform to resolve them. In order to achieve this, they needed to organize themselves and overcome internal differences. According to Fetzer and Soper, "the key features of an effective social movement are, first, a skilled cadre of leaders who can translate the amorphously held values of the group into political capital, and, second, a well-established institutional structure from which group leaders draw resources to form new organizations."[34] The ongoing efforts since the mid-1990s are a powerful reminder of the agency of minority groups to improve their position, but they also reveal the internal tensions as well as the weakness of Islamic solidarity once matters become more practical and down to earth. For the process to be successfully finalized, some actors decided to leave or were excluded. It is also possible, and even likely, that the difficulties in creating a joint council have international dimensions, as some Muslim activists were involved in international Muslim organizations (in this case, at least, the Federation of Islamic Organizations in Europe and an unspecified Pakistan-based organization) that promote different agendas. This aspect requires more study, but, alongside personal quests for status positions, it appears to loom in the background.[35]

Perhaps the creation of something like SINE was just a matter of time, but the active involvement of the Ombudsman for Minorities made a major difference to the outcome. In practical terms, it meant help in arranging meetings, posting invitations and paying travel costs, as well as having access to legal expertise, as the Ombudsman for Minorities and many of his colleagues were lawyers. As the statutes needed to be approved by the National Board of Patents and Registration, which takes care of the registration of voluntary associations in Finland, the process was aided by professional help. The most important role, however, of the Ombudsman for Minorities was his role in merging the

---

34   Fetzer and Soper, *Muslims and the State in Britain, France, and Germany*, 8.

35   For a similar development in Ireland, see: Adil H. Khan, "Transnational Influences on Irish Muslim Networks: From Local to Global Perspectives," *Journal of Muslim Minority Affairs* 31/4 (2011): 486–502.

interests of public authorities and Islamic organizations. Even though this was done subtly, it most likely eased the way to acquiring the finance that gave SINE a head start.

Whereas questions of the representativeness of particular Islamic organizations were a headache before SINE, now public authorities, as well as other organizations, have an organization to turn to. Even though SINE does not represent all Islamic organizations in Finland, it can safely claim to represent the largest and most influential mosque associations. It has also rapidly been included in many central organizations taking care of immigrant integration and interfaith activities, including ETNO and the Cooperation Forum of Religions in Finland. In practice this means that a number of Muslim activists are gradually becoming part of administrative and interfaith networks, which are central to gaining support and legitimacy for their current and future claims.

The foundation of SINE has been a successful case of resource mobilization of Muslim activists in Finland.[36] In public administration, SINE is now seen as a legitimate representative of Muslims. While it is premature to assess its impact on the handling of Muslim-related issues in public administration, it certainly has strengthened the Islamic voice in matters concerning Muslims.

3.3   *Securitization*

Securitization is about how things become matters of security by the objectification of the perception of a threat leading to an exceptional response. The securitization of religion in Europe is intimately tied to questions of immigrant integration and Islam.[37] The main concern for national security in independent Finland has, however, been the Soviet Union followed by Russia, and not immigration. The threat of a Communist takeover was the dominant political concern after the Second World War, which only ended following the dissolution of the Soviet Union. Islam, or more specifically Islamic terrorism, has only gradually emerged as a concern in national security policy in Finland. Already in the 1970s the Finnish Security Intelligence Service (SUPO) was alert to Arab terrorism, even though the issue of religion was not present at the time. However, since then international terrorism has in one form or another been an area of focus in security policy and policing. For instance, international marriages were a worry for the Finnish Security Intelligence Service

---

36   Cf. Fetzer and Soper, *Muslims and the State in Britain, France, and Germany*, 7–10.

37   Barry Buzan, Ole Wæver and Jaap de Wilde, *Security: A New Framework for Analysis* (London: Lynne Rienner Publishers, 1998), 23–24; Jocelyn Cesari, *The Securitisation of Islam in Europe* (CEPS Challenge, 2009), accessed November 26, 2013, http://aei.pitt. edu/10763/1/1826.pdf.; Silvestri, "Public Policies towards Muslims and the Institutionalisation of 'Moderate' Islam in Europe."

from early on since they might lead to the settlement of individuals with links to terrorism.[38]

The role of secret policing in the creation of the Islamic Council of Finland is not clear, but it is certain that SUPO was following it, even though it was not openly present. Also, we can presume that many (if not all) participants were aware that they could be monitored during the process because many of the activists had earlier contacts with SUPO. A major challenge in assessing the role of security concerns on policies relating to Muslim communities is its secretive nature. Documentation of the post-1990 developments in anti-terrorism activities is only publicly available as highly generalized information. However, it is known that the role of monitoring terrorism has risen on the agenda of SUPO during the last two decades. In the 2000s, between one-fourth and one-third of SUPO's resources were used for this purpose.[39] The amount that is devoted to Islamic terrorism is unknown, as are the methods for monitoring and conducting counter-terrorism activities. Nonetheless, both the monitoring of and the cooperation with Finnish Muslim organizations evidently takes place.

One thing is certain, however: that both the spokesmen of SINE and public authorities are wary of the threat of Islamic terrorism and are worried about an eventual radicalization of Muslims in Finland, especially Muslim youth. Even though the anti-radicalization discourse can be seen as a strategy used by SINE to strengthen its status and gain legitimacy as a representative of "moderate" Islam, the concern seems genuine. From the perspective of public authorities, the issue has slowly risen on the agenda. One example of this may be found in the statutes of SINE, which state that it aims to counter radicalization. The same phrase is found in the national curriculum of Islamic religious education in primary and secondary schools, even though such statements are not present in other minority religious education curricula.

4 Path Dependence and Governance of Islam in Finland

The simplest form of a path dependent explanation based on state–church relations does not hold in the case of SINE. The Finnish state has shown an equal level of interference with minority religion affairs only in the case of the nationalization of the Orthodox Church in the 1920s, which was motivated

---

38 Kimmo Rentola, "Suojelupoliisi kylmässä sodassa 1949–1991," in *Ratakatu 12: Suojelupoliisi 1949–2009*, ed. Matti Simola (Helsinki: WSOY, 2009), 9–120.

39 Matti Simola, "Suojelupoliisin organisaatio 1992–2009," in *Ratakatu 12: Suojelupoliisi 1949–2009*, ed. Matti Simola (Helsinki: WSOY, 2009), 269.

both by nationalism and the aim of blocking Soviet influence via the Russian Orthodox Church. Otherwise religion has remained off the agenda as a top political priority. The presence of path dependence can be seen through the incorporation of organizations (coercive isomorphism) in which existing administrative systems "need" organized counterparts in order to fulfil their duty as demonstrated earlier. It is, however, a novelty in minority religions affairs, as far as the active involvement of public authorities is considered, and furthermore the organizational form of SINE as a voluntary association is not part of the historical state–church relations.

What then, if not historical models, prompted the need to support the foundation of SINE? Whereas it could be argued that the personal interests of the Ombudsman for Minorities were central, it does not explain the simultaneous organizational efforts among other types of immigrant communities that were both large scale and far reaching. One explanation can be seen in the policies concerning immigrant incorporation that have been augmented since Finland joined the European Union in 1995. These policies are an expansion of new governing rationales that stem from the ideas of both immigrant emancipation and activation in order to lessen social problems and to improve the position of immigrants in the labour market. As immigrant (Muslim) integration has increasingly become intertwined with security concerns, a need has emerged to treat integration problems as religious matters as well. As no representative bodies were present in Finland, we can argue that there was a demand from the public authorities that was waiting to be satisfied. The exact outcome is necessarily shaped by individual and institutional actors, but the drive for a representative body was inherent in new immigrant integration policies, amplified by security concerns. The novelty of the organizational form can be confirmed in that there was no ready-made governmental grant system that could be applied to SINE, but the money was found on an ad hoc basis from different ministries based in the Prime Minister's Office's initiative. One motivation to provide government funding was that SINE might otherwise have been open to funding from non-national sources whose intentions might be unclear.

Ultimately, the foundation of SINE has its rationale in other fields of public policy rather than historical state–church relations. Instead, it is more closely related to the expansion of the state's interest in using civil society organizations as partners in the spirit of New Public Management. Due to security concerns, the outcome is slightly different than usual because under normal circumstances civil society organizations must compete for resources in an "open market." However, in the case of SINE, funding is used both as an emancipatory effort and a technology of control. Whereas the situation is in many respects unique, several other ongoing changes, including the initiation of state funding of all minority religions since 2008, the growing role of religions in the production of welfare, and the incorporation of minority religious interest groups in administrative networks, are pointing in the same direction, namely that the historical state–church relations are changing and minority religions are finding a new place in society.

Acknowledgement

This chapter has been supported by The Governance of Islam in Finland, Ireland and Canada Project funded by the Academy of Finland (project number 1132479).

CHAPTER 2

State and Religion in Peripheral Europe: State-Religion Relations, Corporatism and Islam in Portugal and Ireland (1970–2010)

Luís Pais Bernardo

Recent studies on the accommodation of Islam point to the need of looking at inherited State-society arrangements in order to ascertain the modes and causes of specific State responses to the emergence of Islam.[1] Many researchers recognize the specific character of each Muslim community, but research on Islam in Europe sometimes defines States as entities without specific legacies and constraints. While reducing European societies to background sketches is not common, it is the case that European States have not been as closely scrutinized in the context of studies on Islam in Europe as they might have been.[2] As suggested in the introductory chapter in this volume, this lack of scrutiny is compounded by a distinct lack of research on contexts beyond France, Germany, the Netherlands and the United Kingdom. In recent years, denser and more frequent research on Italy, Spain and Switzerland has somewhat mitigated the problem. But it remains the case, as also suggested in the introductory chapter, that contexts such as Finland, Greece, Ireland or Portugal, where lower demographic significance of Muslims seems to be linked to perceived lower sociocultural and sociopolitical significance, require further investigation.

---

1 John Madeley, "A Framework for the Comparative Analysis of Church-State relations in Western Europe," in *Church and State in Contemporary Europe: The Chimera of Neutrality*, ed. John Madeley and Zsolt Enyedi (London: Frank Cass, 2003), 23–50; John Madeley, "Unequally Yoked: The Antinomies of Church–State Separation in Europe and the USA," *European Political Science* 8/3 (2009): 273–288; Jonathan Laurence, *The Emancipation of Europe's Muslims: The State's Role in Minority Integration* (Princeton: Princeton University Press, 2012).

2 Examples of research taking the State as a largely undefined background variable are, e.g., Jocelyne Cesari, *When Islam and Democracy Meet: Muslims in Europe and in the United States* (New York: Palgrave Macmillan, 2004); Jocelyne Cesari, "Mosques in French Cities: Towards the End of a Conflict?," *Journal of Ethnic and Migration Studies* 31/6 (2005): 1025–1043; Jocelyne Cesari, "Muslim Identities in Europe: The Snare of Exceptionalism," in *Islam in Europe: Diversity, Identity and Influence*, ed. Effie Fokas and Aziz Al-Azmeh (Cambridge: Cambridge University Press, 2007); Ruud Koopmans, Marco Giugni and Florence Passy, *Contested Citizenship: Immigration and Cultural Diversity in Europe* (Minneapolis: University of Minnesota Press, 2005).

© KONINKLIJKE BRILL NV, LEIDEN, 2019 | DOI:10.1163/9789004404564_004

Not only because further research sheds light on social and political processes, thus enriching existing and future research on better-known contexts, but also because repositioning research into lesser-known contexts enable the questioning of taken-for-granted linkages between demographic and sociopolitical significance. As far as research on the impact of State-religion relations on the accommodation and incorporation of Islam into polities, politics and policy spaces is concerned, this is, we argue, an important argument.

Literature on Islam in Europe tends to bring theoretical depth into its explorations of community politics, as well as discussions on the cultural dimension of contemporary Islam in Europe.[3] Some works engage with institutional problems and conceptualize States as more than monolithic entities,[4] but few studies mention deeper debates about the nitty-gritty of State theory, especially its institution-oriented strand, and how opening a dialogue between both fields would help in shedding light on a number of issues.

The question is therefore not just one of understanding Muslim communities' and representatives' experiences.[5] Recognizing that institutions are produced by their cultural contexts as much as they produce them should not translate into overemphasizing culture (as has been the case with literature on Islamophobia or research inspired by Edward Said[6]) or even religion; institutional conditions are as important as the cultural production and embeddedness of institutions. If we are to focus on institutional conditions, then it follows that contemporary democracies, such as Portugal and Ireland, must be looked at from State-building and State redeployment stages and critical junctures (e.g., the 1822 Liberal revolution in Portugal or the 1922 Anglo-Irish Treaty in Ireland), in order to identify the key conditions (here understood as social institutions, such as religion, or organizations, such as the Catholic Church)

---

3 Yvonne Yazbeck Haddad, *Muslims in the West: From Sojourners to Citizens* (Oxford: Oxford University Press, 2002); Shireen Hunter, *Islam, Europe's Second Religion: The New Social, Cultural and Political Landscape* (Westport: Praeger, 2002); Cesari, *When Islam and Democracy Meet*; Cesari, "Mosques in French Cities"; Cesari, "Muslim Identities in Europe"; Abdulkader H. Sinno, ed., *Muslims in Western Politics* (Bloomington: Indiana University Press, 2009).

4 Jonathan Laurence, "Managing Transnational Islam: Muslims and the State in Western Europe," in *Immigration and the Transformation of Europe*, ed. Craig Parsons and T.M. Smeeding (New York: Cambridge University Press, 2006), 251–273; Jonathan Laurence, "The Corporatist Antecedent of Contemporary State-Islam Relations," *European Political Science* 8/3 (2009): 301–315; Jonathan Laurence, *The Emancipation of Europe's Muslims*; Sinno, *Muslims in Western Politics*.

5 Jørgen S. Nielsen, *Muslims in Western Europe*. Third Edition (Edinburgh: Edinburgh University Press, 2004); Jørgen S. Nielsen et al., ed., *Yearbook of Muslims in Europe. Volume 1* (Leiden: Brill, 2009).

6 Edward Said, *Covering Islam* (New York: Pantheon Books, 1981).

that may have had a long-lasting impact on the politics and policies of the polity. Thereafter, explaining the pool of institutional repertoires at the disposal of policymakers,[7] the operationalization of those repertoires in terms of adaptive strategies to cope with contemporary conditions, and their implementation is the next step.

This chapter compares Ireland and Portugal. "State–religion relations"[8] is the key issue in both countries' State-building processes as far as the contemporary management of religious diversity is concerned, but it is also true that other forms of incorporation of social groups, namely those that were perceived at the time to pose challenges to the hegemonic political order, such as trade unions, Catholics or anarchists, for example, are also inherited and thus we must include forms of interest intermediation into our analysis, as proposed by Jonathan Laurence. The accommodation of Islam in Portugal and Ireland is an effect of available institutional repertoires; taken as ideational constraints, historical legacies and strategic choices, these repertoires define how States and policy makers face, frame and tackle contemporary expressions of Islam. As argued in this study, differences between both cases are due to different State–Catholic Church relational patterns and different patterns of interest intermediation or degree of societal corporatism.[9] These are complementary conditions and, in Catholic contexts such as Ireland and Portugal, they are somewhat entangled: the Catholic Church is the largest and most powerful interest group in both Ireland and Portugal; the structure of social policy subsystems are evidence of this in both cases and underline the Church as a special interest group[10] and its corresponding influence over policy making. Evoking Schattschneider's proposal, bias is mobilized against whichever groups their dominant counterparts decide to exclude from policy venues.[11] Institutional repertoires are also shaped by the ways in which the Catholic Church has behaved over time and how that behaviour has impacted State-religion relations

---

7   Paul Pierson, "Increasing Returns, Path Dependence, and the Study of Politics," *American Political Science Review* 94/2 (2000): 251–268.

8   "State–Catholic Church relations" is the more rigorous definition with relation to Ireland and Portugal, but the general argument is about State-religion relations.

9   Colin Crouch, *Social Change in Western Europe* (Oxford: Oxford University Press. 1999); Colin Crouch and Wolfgang Streeck, *The Diversity of Democracy: Corporatism, Social Order and Political Conflict* (Cheltenham: Edward Elgar, 2006); Philippe Schmitter and Gerhard Lehmbruch, *Trends toward Corporatist Intermediation* (London: Sage Publications, 1979).

10   Carolyn M. Warner, *Confessions of an Interest Group: The Catholic Church and Political Parties in Europe* (Princeton: Princeton University Press, 2000); Anthony James Gill, *The Political Origins of Religious Liberty* (Cambridge: Cambridge University Press, 2008).

11   Elmer Schattschneider, *The Semi-Sovereign People* (New York: Holt, Rinehart and Winston, 1960).

and exerted an indirect effect on the accommodation of Islam. In the chapter, we provide an initial explanatory account of the separate mechanisms through which State-Church relations and corporatism interact.

The second section of this chapter introduces three topics: Islam in peripheral European polities, State-religion relations and State-society relations. In these introductory remarks, we start by trying to put State theory back into research on Islam in Europe. Some research has focused on so-called "host" societies and Muslim communities without enough attention to ongoing debates on State autonomy and contradictory State capacities. We aim to pose the question of whether this makes sense and if, in studying comparatively smaller States, it makes a difference in the analysis of Islam in Europe. The third section of this chapter is an analysis of Portuguese and Irish responses to religious diversity and specifically the functional differentiation of Muslim communities and representatives. As far as we are concerned, policy legacies, in the shape of institutional repertoires, and belief legacies, in the shape of belief structures and the structure of the religious field itself[12] are the most important sets of background conditions. In the final section, I will critically engage with traditional accounts of State-Islam relations in Western Europe, arguing that bias towards large cases (in both community and polity size) has had the consequence of limiting knowledge on the politics of State-Islam relations and State-society relations.

1 Islam and State-Religion Relations in Peripheral Europe

The study of contemporary Islam in European peripheries, namely Portugal and Ireland, needs further development within the literature on Islam in Europe. Choosing peripheral countries nicely supplements traditional case selection procedures: polities with longer histories of migrant inflows, generally stable and pluralist democracies with low or at most intermediate societal homogeneity levels. In the case of Islam in Europe, one should add the number of Muslims (measured as number of foreign-born individuals coming from Muslim-majority countries, usually regardless of subjective religiosity levels or subjective religious identity) to scope conditions for the selection of a case or cases. Researchers often study either traditional national cases (e.g., Germany,

---

12   Pierre Bourdieu, "Genèse et structure du champ religieux," *Revue Française de Sociologie* 12/3 (1971): 295–334; Terry Rey, "Marketing the Goods of Salvation: Bourdieu on Religion," *Religion* 34/4 (2004): 331; Helena Vilaça, *Da Torre de Babel às terras prometidas: pluralismo religioso em Portugal* (Porto: Edições Afrontamento, 2006).

France, the Netherlands or Britain), which may include pairing two or more countries,[13] or employing small-N comparative designs.[14] Recently, Belgium, Spain, Italy and Switzerland have become increasingly common cases. Finland, Greece, Ireland and Portugal, among others (e.g., other Scandinavian countries), have been largely left out on account of insignificant size of Muslim communities or general non-comparability. Also recently, this has started to change, as the *Yearbook on Muslims in Europe*[15] and the *Euro-Islam.info* website, among other examples, have brought other contexts to scholarly attention. More extensive research, such as Michael Minkenberg's work,[16] has put more countries in comparative perspective.

These selective comparative designs pose a number of additional problems. First, most peripheral countries are recent migrant-receiving countries (Figure 2.1), posing questions related to temporality and policy response sets in a continent dominated by transnational policy transfer and learning – for instance, policy responses to Islam in Ireland are partially explained by learning effects from Irish integration into the EU and linguistic linkages with Britain, while policy responses to Islam in Portugal are broadly framed within "intercultural dialogue" as promoted by the Council of Europe, something which may be explained by the admission of Portugal to the EEC. Moreover, traditional migration typologies may or may not apply to more recent migrant-receiving countries. In Ireland, asylum policy has defined much of the public debate on migrant inflows;[17] in Portugal, labour migration from Eastern Europe and

---

13   Adrian Favell, *Philosophies of Integration: Immigration and the Idea of Citizenship in France and Britain* (Basingstoke: Palgrave, 2001); Marcel Maussen, *Constructing Mosques: The Governance of Islam in France and the Netherlands* (Amsterdam: Amsterdam School for Social Science Research, 2009).

14   J. Christopher Soper and Joel S. Fetzer, "Religious Institutions, Church-State History and Muslim Mobilisation in Britain, France and Germany," *Journal of Ethnic and Migration Studies* 33/6 (2007): 933–944; Joel S. Fetzer and J. Christopher Soper, *Muslims and the State in Britain, France, and Germany* (Cambridge: Cambridge University Press, 2005).

15   Nielsen et al., *Yearbook on Muslims in Europe. Volume 1.*

16   Michael Minkenberg, "The Policy Impact of Church–State Relations: Family Policy and Abortion in Britain, France, and Germany," *West European Politics* 26/1 (2003): 195–217; Michael Minkenberg, "Democracy and Religion: Theoretical and Empirical Observations on the Relationship between Christianity, Islam and Liberal Democracy," *Journal of Ethnic and Migration Studies* 33/6 (2007): 887–909; Michael Minkenberg, "Religious Legacies, Churches, and the Shaping of Immigration Policies in the Age of Religious Diversity," *Politics and Religion* 1/3 (2008): 349–383.

17   Piaras Mac Éinri, "Immigration: Labour Migrants, Asylum Seekers and Refugees," in *Understanding Contemporary Ireland*, ed. Brendan Bartley and Rob Kitchin (London: Pluto Press, 2007), 236–248; Piaras Mac Éinrí, *Immigration into Ireland: Trends, Policy Responses, Outlook* (Cork: Irish Centre for Migration Studies, 2001); Bryan Fanning, *Immigration*

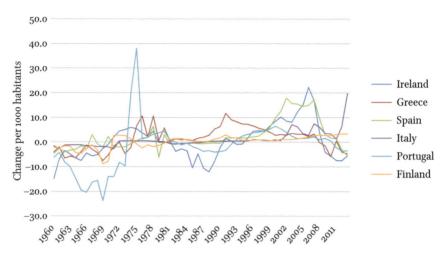

FIGURE 2.1 Crude rate of net migration in Finland, Greece, Ireland, Italy, Portugal and Spain, per 1,000 habitants
SOURCE: EUROSTAT.

migrant inflows resulting from the independence of former colonies on the African continent have defined migration profiles.

While models might apply to more traditionally researched cases, such as guest-worker regimes in Germany and the Netherlands, they may not fit correctly into peripheral cases. Looking at demographic and faith profiles of Muslim communities in Ireland and Portugal, discussions that may apply to France or Germany do not necessarily apply in these cases. In Portugal and Ireland, the distinction proposed by Jonathan Laurence, though controversial and in need of further investigation, broadly applies: "Embassy Islam" and "Political Islam" are two sets that define different phases and engagement strategies. The main difference between Ireland and Portugal is that the "Embassy Islam" stage in Ireland is yet to subside, as Islam in Ireland is clearly more transnationally oriented than Islam in Portugal (with the exception of the Isma'ili community in Portugal – an exception which emerges from historical legacy and an important institutional advantage detailed later in this chapter); in the Portuguese context, Muslim communities seem less differentiated at a representation

and Social Change in the Republic of Ireland (Manchester: Manchester University Press, 2007); Bryan Fanning and Fidele Mutwarasibo, "Nationals/Non-Nationals: Immigration, Citizenship and Politics in the Republic of Ireland," *Ethnic and Racial Studies* 30/3 (2007): 439–460; Ronit Lentin, "Ireland: Racial State and Crisis Racism," *Ethnic and Racial Studies* 30/4 (2007): 610–627; Anthony Messina, "The Politics of Migration to Western Europe: Ireland in Comparative Perspective," *West European Politics* 32/1 (2009): 1–25.

level, depend on networking strategies with other actors in the polity and on a corporatist-style intermediation and institutionalization processes. Recent years have shown rapid change in the Portuguese context, but these crossnational differences are still broadly applicable.

Many peripheral countries show high levels of religious homogeneity. Portugal and Ireland are highly homogeneous in this regard. If we accept secularization as a theoretical starting point,[18] these two countries, along with Poland, are some of the least "secular" countries in Europe. Although José Casanova's theses on differentiation and privatization[19] seem to hold, surveying data on subjective religiosity and church attendance shows that Catholicism remains important as a belief system in both countries (see Figures 2.2–2.3 and Table 2.1), setting the stage for the argument that in looking at religious communities and processes of accommodation, one should be careful not to understate the influence of a monopolistic model and the monopoly agent(s) within.[20]

Patterns of accommodation of non-institutionalized social groups must be accounted for in relation to political structures, namely in terms of how, when,

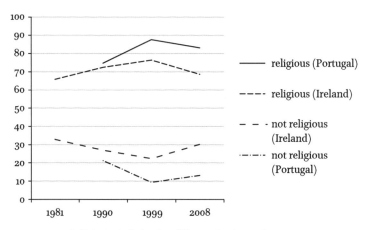

FIGURE 2.2 Religiosity in Ireland and Portugal 1981–2008, per cent
SOURCE: EVS ACCUMULATED 2008.

---

18   Karel Dobbelaere, *Secularization: A Multi-dimensional Concept* (London: Sage Publications, 1981).
19   José Casanova, *Public Religions in the Modern World* (Chicago: University of Chicago Press, 1994); José Casanova, "The Secular, Secularizations, Secularisms," in *Rethinking Secularism*, ed. Craig Calhoun, Mark Juergensmeyer and Jonathan VanAntwerpen (New York: Oxford University Press, 2011), 54–75.
20   Anthony Gill, *The Political Origins of Religious Liberty*.

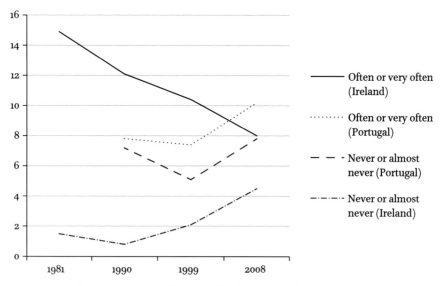

FIGURE 2.3 Religious service attendance in Ireland and Portugal 1981–2008, per cent
SOURCE: EVS LONGITUDINAL DATA FILE.

TABLE 2.1 Denominational belonging in Ireland 1981–2008

	Which religious denomination?								
Country (Year)	Buddhist	Free church/Non-denominational church	Hindu	Jewish	Muslim	Orthodox	Other	Protestant	Roman Catholic
Ireland (1981)	0	1.2	0	0	0.1	0	0.8	1.7	96.2
Ireland (1990)	0.5	0.2	0.3	0	0	0	0.1	2	96.9
Ireland (1999)	0	0.5	0.1	0	0	0.2	1.4	2.1	95.6
Ireland (2008)	0	0	0	0	0.2	0.2	1.4	4.1	94.1

SOURCE: EVS ACCUMULATED 2008.

STATE AND RELIGION IN PERIPHERAL EUROPE   53

TABLE 2.2   Denominational belonging in Portugal 1981–2008

				Which religious denomination?					
Country (Year)	Buddhist	Free church/Non-denominational church	Hindu	Jewish	Muslim	Orthodox	Other	Protestant	Roman Catholic
Portugal (1990)	0	0.1	0	0.1	0	0	1.3	0.3	98.2
Portugal (1999)	0	0	0	0	0	0	2.7	0.3	96.9
Portugal (2008)	0	0	0	0	0.2	0	3	1.6	95.3

SOURCE: EVS ACCUMULATED

why, by whom and on what account opportunities for institutionalization are allocated. For instance, a decentralized political system where local authorities are invested with policy making could theoretically exert a positive effect on the accommodation of Islam, provided that resident Muslim communities have been allocated sufficient resources, given appropriate system-level conditions (i.e., extension of rights to religious communities) to recognize opportunities and benefit from them. This is a consequence of State–religion relations[21] and how the Irish and Portuguese States have historically negotiated religion and religious communities. The position of Catholicism is important: its degree of integration largely determines the level of institutionalization of later religious communities and their capacity to claim for rights extension; we follow the historical legacy of State–religion relations model proposed by Kuru,[22] and it is the case that regulatory and redistributive policies[23] towards Islam in Portugal and Ireland depend upon the degree to which a State promotes secularism as a policy paradigm, which Kuru attributes to elite allegiances in State-building processes.

---

21   Silvio Ferrari, "The Secularity of the State and the Shaping of Muslim Representative Organizations in Western Europe," in *European Muslims and the Secular State*, ed. Jocelyne Cesari and Seán McLoughin (Aldershot: Ashgate, 2005), 11–21.

22   Ahmet Kuru, *Secularism and State Policies towards Religion: The United States, France and Turkey* (Cambridge: Cambridge University Press, 2009).

23   Theodore J. Lowi, "Four Systems of Policy, Politics, and Choice," *Public Administration Review* 32/4 (1972): 298–310.

These three sets of explanatory conditions – migrant-inflow typologies, societal homogeneity and institutional specificities/legacies – help us explain responses to Islam in Portugal and Ireland through societal corporatism and State-religion relations.

2   An Analysis of Portuguese and Irish Responses to Religious Diversity and Islam

The Structured Dialogue with Churches, Faith Communities and Non-Confessional Organizations was set up in 2007 under the aegis of Taoiseach Bertie Ahern (Fianna Fáil) and kept in place by Enda Kenny (Fine Gael) in 2011. The unfolding crisis of the Irish Roman Catholic Church marked an epochal change in Irish society (running contrary to arguments understating Church influence over Irish society in the twentieth century) and it is an interesting case of a corporatist practice interacting with the legacy of State–religion relations. The name itself reveals how the Irish State makes religion legible[24] in the twenty-first century: by detailing "Churches," "Faith Communities" and "Non-Confessional Organizations," including humanists and atheists, Irish policy makers render a complex set of social conditions and interest groups manageable. However, its informal character (as compared to proximate Portuguese counterparts) also advises caution in overdetermining its corporatist character; while post-Celtic Tiger Ireland certainly retains historically inherited arrangements,[25] societal diversity and wider societal responses to migrants have shaped how the State deals with religion.

An interesting policy document, the Intercultural Health Strategy, provides us with trace evidence of the specific ways in which Irish policy makers have made different communities "legible" (Scott 1992, 2003). This policy document employed consultations with many of Ireland's resident minority religious traditions while including some communities that could be construed as ethnic or national, like the Chinese community. The pattern repeats itself across Irish institutions: ethnicity and religion are discernible as separate categories, but are generally conflated – whether one looks at the structure and mission of NCCRI, the defunct Equality Authority or the Equality Tribunal. The accommodation

---

24   James C. Scott, *Domination and the Arts of Resistance: Hidden Transcripts* (New Haven: Yale University Press, 1992); Laurence, *The Emancipation of Europe's Muslims*.

25   Basil Chubb, *The Government and Politics of Ireland* (Stanford: Stanford University Press, 1982); John Coakley, "Society and Political Culture," in *Politics in the Republic of Ireland*, ed. John Coakley and Michael Gallagher (London: Routledge, 2004), 25–49; Diarmaid Ferriter, *The Transformation of Ireland* (Woodstock: Overlook Press, 2005).

of Islam in Ireland has developed within this context and a comparatively rapid internal differentiation among communities, as well as important transnational linkages, have played an important role in defining how accommodation (or lack thereof), as a specific mode of institutionalization, has developed over time. In that respect, the number of different organizations claiming to represent one or more segments of Muslim residents in Ireland has increased to the extent of covering most of the country (there are registered charities or semi-official Islamic communities or associations in Cork, Galway and Limerick, three of Ireland's largest cities) and providing multiple insights into the political life of Islam in Ireland.

The dynamics of interaction and recognition between the Islamic Cultural Centre of Ireland (ICCI) and the Islamic Foundation of Ireland (IFI) show how fluid, as compared to Portugal, Islam in Ireland is. There has been a remarkable transfer of recognition of dominance (in the sense of garnering influence and mobilizing resources) from the IFI to the ICCI. While the IFI is the oldest institution, ICCI is clearly the largest, best-equipped organization to deal with political issues pertaining to Islam in Western Europe. Its representativeness is highly contentious[26] and the perceived growth in its influence has been represented as misconstruing the dynamics of Islam in Ireland. In this sense, it is important to recognize that Sheikh Halawa has become an important figurehead for a new transnational Islam, connected with Muslim-majority contexts that wilfully fund cultural initiatives. The al-Maktoum Foundation is one such example. Another important reference, in this sense, is the European Council for Fatwa and Research; its establishment in Dublin is at once a consequence of the ICCI's resource pool and signals Islam in Ireland as a transnational phenomenon. Islam in Ireland is socio-demographically diverse and its connection with refugee/asylum-seeker inflows is significant. The growth of Islam in Ireland arises from two factors: language and labour. The former refers to the post-colonial character of Ireland and the latter refers to the growth in migrant inflows following the Irish economic boom of the mid-1990s. As a consequence of former British colonial occupation and dominion, English is one of two official languages; 1950s student migration, especially to the Royal College of Surgeons in Dublin from former or soon-to-be former British imperial territories, is best explained by linguistic affinities (i.e., South African students) and the preeminence of South Asian staff in post-war Irish healthcare has been significant enough to merit discussion in policy documents on the accommodation of culturally diverse staff in public health services.

---

26   Mary Fitzgerald, "The Future of Islamic Ireland," *The Irish Times*, February 12, 2011.

These examples are not exhaustive. They stand in contrast to the Portuguese case. Irish responses are explained by institutional constraints on the choices available to actors facing societal change and associated governance challenges. Homogeneity is important to our argument, but only as it is matched with complementary institutional homogeneity, namely a monopoly of the Catholic Church in State-religion relations that crowds out other possibilities. We describe the historical trajectory of Irish (and Portuguese) State-religion relations in the fourth section of this chapter.

Sets of institutional arrangements, which we refer to as repertoires, were available to policy makers and representatives at any given stage of the interaction between Islam and the State. The Catholic Church adopted strategies to maintain its privileged status.[27] Coupled with a historically slow secularization trend[28] and a partially pluralist post-colonial religious field, this has ensured salience and elevated status to religion as a social institution. These pressures towards sustained salience of religion explain why religious communities shifting into interest groups were and are still (partially) salient and influential. Since the Irish State remains a contradictory hybrid of secular and non-secular components operating in a society where religion only recently became a belief system among others,[29] religious interest groups, namely Muslim representatives, have been able to organize and quickly differentiate. The non-secular features of the Irish State, embodied, for example, in the Catholic dominance in primary school governance, introduced a bias in responses towards religious interest groups that allowed for their entry into institutionalized systems. Differences between entry and growth after entry are important: for example whether the North Dublin School effort set the stage for replication and implementation across Ireland. Regarding this particular school, its establishment and operation has been a point of contention. Moreover, the patronage system, while affording benefits to Muslim communities, also entails costs that may be difficult to negotiate by newcomers with enough resources to benefit from opportunities but not enough leverage to build a sustainable base. The interplay between the secular and non-secular components of the State apparatus is important because the Irish Constitution limits hands-on regulation and the State is precluded from enlarging its mandate beyond enforcing

---

27   Grace Davie, *The Sociology of Religion* (Los Angeles: Sage Publications, 2007); Gill, *The Political Origins of Religious Liberty*.

28   This is changing at a rapid pace, but we maintain that trends towards secular dominance remain slow in Ireland as long as a comparative perspective is kept.

29   Charles Taylor, *A Secular Age* (Cambridge: Harvard University Press, 2007).

rights extension.[30] Systems of interest intermediation, or instances of societal corporatism,[31] are weak. There is no formal, much less a recognizable, procedure through which the State makes religious groups readable (in the Scott/Laurence sense) apart from legacy procedures involving the Catholic Church. Institutionalization via structured consultation committees, State-designated representatives at official venues or State-sponsored umbrella organizations has not, thus far, been observed in State–Islam relations in Ireland. Accounts of State–Islam relations posit an either secularist or non-secularist State struggle to identify the causal links behind these formations. Islam in Ireland, as other increasingly differentiated communities that pursue goals as interest groups, faces low entry costs but high maintenance costs in their engagement with policy venues and goal seeking. The monopoly of the Catholic Church exerts paradoxical effects: it lowers entry costs and raises maintenance; interest intermediation disavows any policy responses that would correct these asymmetries.

The Portuguese case stands in contrast to the Irish case. The Roman Catholic Church has never been in a non-dominant situation, either in the structure of the religious field or in terms of political allegiances. Although the Portuguese Constitution asserts non-confessionality, representatives and policy documents usually ascribe an exceptional role to the Catholic Church on the basis of its representativeness.[32] This rhetorical device is in itself evidence of corporatist practice. It is mostly obvious that Portuguese citizens are culturally Catholic and census data show an overwhelming majority of Catholics. But subjective religiosity and church attendance show that Portuguese citizens maintain a diminishing connection with Church structures. Portugal is facing a comparatively slow secularization process but church attendance is remarkably low. The Constitution prevents any mandatory question on religion (taking a cue from French legal tradition), but a question on religious affiliation is included in the census. The State is obliged to maintain non-discriminatory policies, converging with European Union standards since roughly 2001. The Concordat between the Portuguese State and the Vatican, instead of a general law, continues to regulate the religious field, further entrenching the Catholic Church's dominance.

---

30 Tuula Sakaranaho, *Religious Freedom, Multiculturalism, Islam: Cross-reading Finland and Ireland* (Leiden: Brill, 2006).

31 Crouch, *Social Change in Western Europe*; Crouch and Streeck, *The Diversity of Democracy*.

32 Manuel Braga da Cruz and Natália Correia Guedes, *A Igreja e a cultura contemporânea em Portugal 1950–2000* (Lisboa: Universidade Católica, 2001).

Additionally, the 2001 Law on Religious Freedom takes its cues from the Concordat and policy makers accept the preeminence of Church representatives in most instances. There is no process of self-selection among religious communities. Corporatist rules and modes of conduct are dominant. "Acceptable" communities are assigned seats in official bodies, as stated in the 2001 Law. Those rules and modes of conduct show that an account of discrimination or non-pluralism must include New Religious Movements, especially those in which proselytism or heterodox practices are structural to their belief systems. In the Commission on Religious Freedom, which operates as the religious field regulatory agency, there are two representatives from the Sunni and Isma'ili Muslim communities. These representatives enjoy high levels of political trust and are highly embedded in both inter-religious networks and policy issue networks. Exclusionary corporatism is enhanced by the role of the dominant Catholic Church. It has repeatedly entered public discussion warning against influence from aggressively proselytizing movements. The Catholic Patriarch in Lisbon also publicly voiced his concerns on interfaith marriage on account of gender relations in Islam. Regulation-wise, the Catholic Church is therefore a gatekeeper and a field-maker.

The contemporary Portuguese religious field operates under constrains imposed by the Catholic Church. If religious communities operate in such a way that they are regarded as potential coalition partners – as is the case with many smaller communities, such as the Baha'i or Hindus – with non-threatening behaviour, the Church generally operates as a facilitator. As a long-term result from the Second Vatican Council, Church strategies toward variation in religious diversity have become more subtle and less aggressive. Two of those strategies are the cooptation of smaller communities and facilitation of assignment into official venues. Through those strategies, the Church aids the State in maintaining a corporatist grip on religious regulation. Furthermore, organizational bias remains mobilized towards Catholicism as the most representative belief system in Portugal. In contrast to Ireland, where such claims to representativeness are also backed by statistical evidence, there are far fewer (if any) instances where corporatist practice is as evident. The patronage system in primary schools and the general preeminence of the Catholic Church in education and healthcare is significant but there is no evidence that it is a product of active exclusionary practice. These configurations are effects of historical legacies. The logic of low entry costs/high maintenance costs seem to apply. In Portugal, entry costs are also increased by the regulatory environment.

Accounts of Islam in Portugal might then underline the importance of Catholicism in policy venues without discussing its functional and causal dimensions, possibly underplaying how bias is mobilized for or against Islam in

STATE AND RELIGION IN PERIPHERAL EUROPE

policy making. However, there is little evidence of such bias against Islam. The 2001 Law on Religious Freedom does not prevent Muslim communities from registering in the State Registry on Religious Associations (Registo Colectivo de Pessoas Religiosas) and there are few legal constraints on the observance of rituals or seasonal festivities. The two most important communities in Portugal enjoy a level of salience not enjoyed by, for example, New Religious Movements or non-federated evangelical churches. The community built around the Lisbon Central Mosque has been a participant in policy making since the 1990s,[33] after transitioning from an Embassy Islam structure into a rooted religious community, following efforts by two key individuals (Suleiman Valy Mamede and Abdool Vakil) to reestablish Islam in Portugal after 1974. The Islamic Community of Lisbon is an interesting case. As a community, it faces pressures from migration inflows and the needs of representativeness in a corporatist environment. Its leaders are generally highly educated, Mozambican-born individuals of South-Asian (Indian) background. The inflow of West African and South Asian (Bangladeshi and Pakistani) migrants forced change within the community. At the same time, the community also faced the need to represent Islam at specific policy venues, especially in an important committee that decided, in a corporatist style, on public broadcasting rights for religious communities. It became the most important interfaith forum for selected religious traditions, which had the opportunity to broadcast hour-long programmes on their preferred themes. In Ireland, RTÉ did not provide for such opportunities.

The Islamic Community of Lisbon was one of the earlier members. It represented "Islam" to the committee sponsors. The Catholic Church had most of the broadcast timeslots, even though it benefited from live Sunday mass broadcasts and an important Catholic local newspaper network. Communities were selected on the basis of vague criteria: statistics on size were hardly

---

33   Nina Clara Tiesler, "No Bad News from the European Margin: The New Islamic Presence in Portugal," *Islam and Christian-Muslim Relations* 12/1 (2001): 71–91; Nina Clara Tiesler, "Novidades no terreno: muçulmanos na Europa e o caso português," *Análise Social* XXXIX /173 (2005): 827–849; Nina Clara Tiesler, "Islam in Portuguese-speaking Areas: Historical Accounts, (Post)Colonial Conditions and Current Debates," *Lusotopie* 14/1 (2007): 91–101; AbdoolKarim Vakil, "The Crusader Heritage: Portugal and Islam from Colonial to Postcolonial Identities," in *Rethinking Heritage: Cultures and Politics in Europe*, ed. Robert Shannan Peckham. (London: I.B. Tauris, 2003), 29–44; AbdoolKarim Vakil, "Questões Inacabadas: Colonialismo, Islão e Portugalidade," in *Fantasmas e fantasias imperiais no imaginário português contemporâneo*, ed. Ana Paula Ferreira and Margarida Calafate Ribeiro (Porto: Campo das Letras, 2003), 257–297; AbdoolKarim Vakil, "Do Outro ao Diverso," 283–312; AbdoolKarim Vakil, "Comunidade Islâmica em Portugal," *Dicionário Temático da Lusofonia*, ed. Fernando Cristóvão (Lisbon: Associação de Cultura Lusófona-Instituto Camões, 2005), 186–189.

evident from Census data, as most religious traditions were subsumed under an "other" category and thus unquantifiable. Though impossible to determine without further investigation, their willingness to accommodate corporatism as a system of interest intermediation might have been important. Corporatist-style assignment was beneficial to Islam and to other religious traditions elected by both the State and the dominant religious tradition. It allowed those religious traditions to bypass the cost of entering policy making and allowed communities to focus on decision-making, giving those early representatives a significant advantage over other religious traditions. A few years later, the 2001 Law on Religious Freedom established the requirements for registration in the National Religious Association Registry. The Commission on Religious Freedom shows its membership. Sunni and Isma'ili representatives are members. The community represented by the Islamic Community of Lisbon, as stated before, is as much a product of societal change as of the will of Valy Mamede and Abdool Vakil, which have engineered consensus around Muslims in Portugal, although peaceful "coexistence" or "acceptance" should not be overplayed, especially in the wake of 9/11. It is nevertheless the case that Mamede and Vakil, along with the current imam at the Lisbon Central Mosque, Sheikh David Munir have engineered, to a large extent, the frame in which categories such as "Muslims" or "Islam" are perceived in Portuguese society. The broader issue of frame reception and reconfiguration, while relevant to accounts of Islamophobia and bias against specific religious traditions, does not disprove this: Islam in Portugal continues to be framed along specifications initially provided by the abovementioned actors.

The clientelistic character of Portuguese political culture, with its emphasis on personal social capital, has interacted with renewed interest in Islamic heritage, especially as archaeological findings and work produced by two generations of academics have sought to break traditional narratives of "Christian Reconquista" and "Muslim-Christian clashes." These tropes exert little influence in actually existing policy-making processes, as these are better understood in terms of current religious field dynamics. The Isma'ili community is an interesting illustration. It is not large and it does not engage in high-profile religious activities. But it has garnered important State support. It is now the first non-Christian community to enter into a Concordat-style agreement with the Portuguese State. The Isma'ili representative at the Commission for Religious Freedom is also the representative of Prince Karim Aga Khan. His representation is ambassadorial and the agreement is international in scope. Moreover, the Aga Khan Foundation is a powerful civil society organization. It sponsors several projects in vulnerable neighborhoods and has tried to decentre faith-based debates from Catholicism. The Isma'ili community is well connected and its representation at the Commission for Religious Freedom indicates that community size must be weighed against power and the mode of representation itself. In Portugal, for example (in contrast to Ireland), power and representation in policy venues are not necessarily related to representativeness. While State officials justify informal bias towards Catholicism because of its demographic representativeness, such justifications would seem to exclude the Isma'ili community.

The problem of taking the State as a set of arrangements devoid of significant contradictions or internal conflicts emerges when one tries to reconcile a constitutionally non-confessional State with binding agreements such as the Concordat, the embeddedness of religious entities in welfare provision and corporatist practices that are biased towards Catholicism. The membership of the Isma'ili, Hindu and Jewish communities on the Commission support this, as their representativeness is not a plausible reason for membership attribution. Instead, their membership results from the corporatist framework of State-religion relations and the role of the Catholic Church in mobilizing bias in support of its continued dominance. Islam is increasingly institutionalized into policy-making venues through corporatist arrangements, signaling that Laurence's framework applies to Portugal. It does not apply reasonably to Ireland.[34]

The question now is why these arrangements differ across Ireland and Portugal. Portuguese and Irish historical trajectories were sufficiently similar until recently, even if we take into account the 50-year long fascist dictatorship in Portugal. We therefore argue that the current structural and functional environment for religious diversity management is not a product of cultural notions of belonging or national primacy of a given tradition. Rather, current structures and functions are a product of long-term institutional trajectories. This is a counter-intuitive argument: the Portuguese Catholic Church, since 1822, sided with conservative groups to safeguard a specific *status quo* and collect what its representatives saw as just rewards for significant disenfranchisement in the eighteenth century. Most subsequent State–Church relations stem from that foundational choice. In 1974, it was, once more, siding with the losing conservative side of a struggle. In Ireland, the Church was an institution with manifold social and political functions. It was the caretaker of Irish national and republican identity facing colonial occupation and a Northern neighbor. Indeed, Irish republican nationalism is tinged with Catholic tropes, the largest of which is the Church as a monopoly actor in the world of morals and ethics. As an institution, it was perceived to side with nationalists in

---

34   Laurence, *The Emancipation of Europe's Muslims.*

the struggle for autonomy and subsequent independence.[35] It sided with those who fought against the *status quo* and eventually established a new political order in Ireland. The contrast would seem to suggest that the Church in Ireland would be in a much better position to determine whether Islam or other newcomers would be able to enter policy-making venues than in Portugal, but this is disputable. The position of each institution in each country explains, to a large extent, how and why Islam is institutionalized. In Ireland, there are no established procedures and whatever contexts in which Islam or Muslims have managed to venture into. It was mostly established by using own resources and supporting costs which did not automatically translate into institutionalization, whereas in Portugal such costs were bypassed by a highly corporatist procedure which stemmed from the preeminence of the Church in defining which communities were to enter policy making and those that were not. The religious field in Portugal is much more hierarchical than in Ireland and its regulatory framework assigns resources to the Church to such an extent that it is able to decisively influence these patterns of recognition and assignment. In Ireland, no such procedure exists and the Church is quickly becoming disenfranchised, as Tom Inglis has aptly discussed.[36]

Simplistic conclusions (such as those we incurred in a previous study[37]) over degrees of separation or modes of institutionalization of Islam into West European polities need to be put into question. Debates over the usefulness of categories such as State–Church relations and religious diversity should take their place. Islam in Portugal and Ireland is an important comparative case study on both grounds. The analytical concept of State–religion relations is an important tool because it allows us to engage with the structure of the religious field and its power consequences. Among those, we point to why a dominant group exists, how it strategizes and behaves and what are the consequences of its actions. The reversal of migration flows at the end of the 1980s in both countries and the consequential growth in Islam representativeness did not, in our view, create a very large or unwieldy challenge to existing policy subsystems. Those existing systems already had procedures in place to accommodate

---

35   Bill Kissane, "The Illusion of State Neutrality in a Secularising Ireland," in *Church and State in Contemporary Europe: The Chimera of Neutrality*, ed. John Madeley and Zsolt Enyedi (London: Frank Cass, 2007), 73–94.

36   Tom Inglis, *Moral Monopoly: The Rise and Fall of the Catholic Church in Modern Ireland* (Dublin: University College Dublin Press, 1998); Tom Inglis, "Individualisation and Secularisation in Catholic Ireland," in *Contemporary Ireland: A Sociological Map*, ed. Sara O'Sullivan (Dublin: University College Dublin Press, 2007), 67–72.

37   Luís Bernardo, "The Accommodation of Islam in Portugal and the Republic of Ireland: A Comparative Case Study," Unpublished MA Thesis (Lisbon: ICS – UL, 2010).

religious communities and, in the case of Ireland, limited religious diversity, on account of its colonial legacy. The Catholic Church in both instances worked as a facilitator, specifically for Muslim representatives. In both countries, Muslim representatives face the same challenges of other world religious traditions. This is counterintuitive, given widespread perceptions of Islamophobia. But once one shifts the comparison to New Religious Movements, the position of Muslim and Jewish communities, for example, becomes much more nuanced. Demographic representativeness, such as in the case of the Portuguese Jewish and Isma'ili communities, is not necessary to be demographically relevant to be assigned a position in policy venues, since existing corporatist practice ensured that.

3   A Critical Discussion of Traditional Accounts of State–Islam Relations

This problem becomes more important as we move to a very simple quantitative literature survey (limited to the English language).[38] Its results point to the existence of geographic bias with important implications: usual cases (e.g. France, Germany, the Netherlands or the United Kingdom) do not exhaust institutional typologies, historical legacies or societal dynamics. The cases explored in this chapter show as much: although there is potential for comparison between the "usual case" cluster and other, "less than usual" counterparts, establishing baseline comparability drives us to question the extent to which pairing cases across clusters ought to precede initial exploration and comparison between cases at the margin of Europe, as put in the introductory chapter to this volume. Peripheral cases, including Ireland and Portugal, form a cluster within Western Europe because they share several similarities. As Katzenstein points out, smaller polities usually share certain patterns that set them apart from larger cases to some degree[39] (comparing Germany to Portugal with regard to the accommodation of Islam is difficult if we are aiming at a most different systems design, which is a difficult standard to achieve because both Portugal and Germany do have commonalities). Portugal and Ireland may be

---

38   A search expression on Google Scholar (islam AND (germany OR ~britain OR france OR netherlands OR switzerland OR belgium)) returns about 813,000 references, while the same expression with a different geographical descriptor (islam AND (ireland OR spain OR portugal OR italy OR finland OR norway)) brings up about 328,000 references, less than half of the former.

39   Peter Katzenstein, "Small States and Small States Revisited," *New Political Economy* 8/1 (2003): 9–30.

paired for a comparative case study[40] once we clearly establish how and where they are similar. In this sense, the pairing of Ireland and Portugal is adequate. The religious field structure has remained relatively similar over a large time-span. Migrant inflows have increased from the early 1990s, and State capacities have also remained stable.

What explains different modes of institutionalization or accommodation is the legacy of State–religion relations and the power-distributional structure embedded in those relations. Concretely, this is observed in how religious interest intermediation provided or failed to provide opportunities for newcomers, such as Muslim communities, to be assigned positions in policy-making systems. There is a highly restrictive corporatist arrangement in Portugal. It results from the contradictory and evolving relationship between the Catholic Church, which has sided with conservative allies for three centuries and the Portuguese State which has autonomously defined Church deterrence[41] as a priority after confrontations related to heavy-handed regulatory enforcement. While the religious cleavage is important in Portugal, the monopoly of the Church was never contested until the twenty-first century. The structure of the Commission for Religious Freedom illustrates this. It reserves seats for several Catholic representatives based on representativeness criteria. But contradictions are clear as we attempt to understand why representatives from symbolically significant but small communities, such as Islam and Judaism, should be afforded representation at a regulatory venue while leaving out more representative communities, such as the many Protestant traditions. This is an effect of many phenomena: reconfigurations in the religious field, secularization, strategic considerations by religious actors and the role of the State. Once the Catholic Church perceived its role to be diminishing as secularizing tendencies seemed to step in during the late twentieth century, it engaged in strategic allegiance-making with those groups it perceived as traditional and non-threatening religious traditions, so as to exclude "proselytizing" New Religious Movements from policy making. Muslim representatives have benefited from this complex interaction and the emerging but contested understanding of Islam as a core component of the Portuguese historical legacy. As Muslim communities tried to engage with policy, these complex interactions worked in such a way that both representatives affiliated with the Islamic Community

---

40   Alexander George and Andrew Bennett, *Case Studies and Theory Development in the Social Sciences* (Cambridge: MIT Press, 2005); Sidney Tarrow, "The Strategy of Paired Comparison: Toward a Theory of Practice," *Comparative Political Studies* 43/2 (2010): 230–259.

41   Paula Borges Santos, *Igreja Católica, estado e sociedade, 1968–1975 : O caso Rádio Renascença* (Lisbon: Imprensa de Ciências Sociais, 2005).

of Lisbon and the Isma'ili community now stand at the religious regulation agency and are recognized as important policy and societal actors.

The Irish case shows how the interplay of State action and inaction benefit monopolies that might be endangered by changing trends and patterns in society. The Irish State was politically inclined towards the Catholic Church from its early years (1922–1937), but little was done to entrench the role of the Church into the polity. It is appropriate to discuss an Irish Catholic moral monopoly, given that the Irish Catholic Church was the trustee of a specifically Irish republican nationalism. But the Irish Catholic Church was never an overwhelming force in Irish politics. Current institutional disaffection towards the Church (epitomized by Enda Kenny's mercurial speech at the Oireachtas on the Cloyne Report) is partially explained by fewer links between the State and the Catholic Church. This in turn explains the pattern of institutionalization of Islam and Muslim representatives. The State assigned legibility to groups through a deeply rooted system of interest intermediation with important strategic implications. Compared to Portugal, the institutionalization of Islam in Ireland remains fluid. Islam in Ireland is also more diverse. Belief systems, associational patterns and political engagement[42] are more varied than in Portugal. Power is clearly polarized in Dublin; several new organization forms have emerged in other Irish cities, especially Cork and Limerick.

In conclusion, we point to three issues. First, previous debates within the field have been relatively silent on State-theoretical considerations. In order to go further, Kuru and Laurence point in interesting directions. Both authors attempt a more historically grounded and sensitive exploration of the processes of accommodation of Islam. In this regard, this chapter aims to explore contradictions embedded in the State apparatus and how those contradictions might support institutional explanations. Second, the importance of macro-level factors, such as "State-religion relations" or "citizenship models," depends upon linear thinking, both concerning the State and the associational life of Muslims. Cross-national comparisons open the possibility of engaging with the dynamics of Muslim community life in relation to the State and other traditions in the religious field. Previous debates have not focused as much as possible on the importance of the religious field and dominant organizations (in Ireland and Portugal, the Catholic Church) that may offer or withhold support for the assignment of legibility to communities. Third, links between community, representation and power should be questioned. Modes of interest intermediation

---

42   See Oliver Scharbrodt and Tuula Sakaranaho, ed. "Islam in the Republic of Ireland," *Journal of Muslim Minority Affairs* 31/4 (2011) for a relevant in-depth analysis of Islam in Ireland.

could be looked at in more detail, as these structures sometimes redefine and sometimes completely bypass the connection between representativeness and representation. Representativeness may neither be a necessary nor a sufficient condition for representation. Power relations in the religious field and how they translate into specific policy systems may be at least as important as assessing community size and media salience.

CHAPTER 3

The Governance of Islamic Religious Education in Finland: Promoting "General Islam" and the Unity of All Muslims

Tuula Sakaranaho

In December 2011, all the major newspapers and newsrooms in Finland reported an incident where the Finnish Security Intelligence Service (SUPO) intervened in the teaching of Islam at a school in the city of Tampere. According to the Finnish news agency (STT), some Muslim parents had complained about a non-Muslim teacher of Islam who in their opinion did not know or care about Islam enough to teach Islam with the necessary competence and respect. Several meetings had been arranged in order to solve the dispute between the non-Muslim teacher and Muslim parents but without success. Seemingly it was the Islamic Community of Tampere that contacted SUPO for help and it came up with a solution of hiring an assistant teacher who was Muslim and who could take part in the lessons of Islam taught by the disputed non-Muslim teacher.[1]

The involvement of SUPO in a dispute on Islamic education and the subsequent friction between a teacher and parents was met with surprise and even dismay. SUPO's main functions are counterterrorism, counterespionage and security work,[2] whereas the content of religious education in school is generally managed by the Finnish National Board of Education, municipalities, and schools. Disputes between teachers and parents are usually solved on a local level where school principals play a major role. Thus, it is no wonder that

---

1   See for instance, "Supo ratkoi islamin opetuksen kiistoja Tampereella," *Helsingin Sanomat*, December 14, 2011, accessed November 12, 2014, http://www.hs.fi/a1305551334180; "*Supo selvitti uskontoriidan Tampereella: Lapsia ei koulussa opetettu Koraanin mukaan,*" *Aamulehti*, *December 14, 2011,* http://www.aamulehti.fi/Kotimaa/1194710202008; Kaleva, "SUPO ratkoo islamin opetuksen kiistoja Tampereella," *Kaleva*, December 14, 2011, accessed November 12, 2014, http://www.kaleva.fi/uutiset/kotimaa/al-supo-ratkoo-islamin-opetuksen-kiistoja -tampereella/559024; "SUPO puuttui uskontoriitaan Tampereella," *MTV uutiset*, December 14, 2011, accessed November 12, 2014, http://www.mtv3.fi/uutiset/kotimaa.shtml/al-supo -puuttui-uskontoriitaan-tampereella/2011/12/1459836.

2   "The Finnish Security Intelligence Service," Police, accessed May 31, 2012, http://www.poliisi .fi/poliisi/supo60/home.nsf/pages/indexeng.

SUPO's involvement in an intra-school issue on a very practical level was widely publicized and generated heated debates in the social media. SUPO itself did not give any specific justification for its conduct but merely referred to its role in Finnish society as the guarantor of security and social harmony.

Notwithstanding SUPO's reasoning, it is not clear how the above-mentioned dispute on a religious education teacher's ability to teach in a proper manner was a matter concerning national security and harmony – unless any sort of a conflict related to Islam and Muslims can be classified as such. In the current political atmosphere, marked by global anxiety for security, this is exactly how Islam and Muslims tend to be perceived, not only in Finland but in Europe at large. Recent decades have witnessed a change in European governments' policies from benign neglect to active management of religious minorities, of which Muslims are seen as the most challenging for the social order of a multicultural European society.[3] European states perceive Islam very much as a social problem and have developed different tools of management in order to deal with it, for instance, by nominating Islamic councils as representative bodies and as interlocutors with the state.[4] Consequently, there is a growing need not only for studies on religiosity of Muslims but also on the opportunities that societies create or restrict for the development of Islam in Europe.[5]

One important area where Islam has been identified as a social problem concerns Islamic religious education in European state schools.[6] The above-mentioned incident in Tampere was exceptional and the controversy soon abated. However, even as a single case, it raises important questions concerning the governance of Islamic education in Finnish schools. The schools act as barometers of social change and thereby mirror the growing cultural and religious pluralism of a society. Hence, they have become important scenes for cultural encounters and a real testing ground for the multicultural policies of a country.[7] This was also acknowledged in the security programme of

---

3 Bryan S. Turner, *Religion and Modern Society: Citizenship, Secularization and the State* (Cambridge: Cambridge University Press, 2011), 192–193; Jonathan Laurence, *The Emancipation of Europe's Muslims: The State's Role in Minority Integration* (Princeton: Princeton University Press, 2012).

4 See Laurence, *The Emancipation of Europe's Muslims*; Tuomas Martikainen, "The Governance of Islam in Finland," *Temenos* 43/2 (2007): 243–265.

5 Frank J. Bujis and Jan Rath, *Muslims in Europe: The State of Research*, IMISCOE Working Paper No. 7 (Amsterdam: IMES, 2006), 8, accessed June 11, 2012, http://library.imiscoe.org/en/record/314221.

6 Veit Bader, "The Governance of Islam in Europe: The Perils of Modelling," *Journal of Ethnic and Migration Studies* 33/6 (2007): 872.

7 See Tuula Sakaranaho, *Religious Freedom, Multiculturalism, Islam: Cross-reading Finland and Ireland* (Leiden: Brill, 2006), 314ff.

the Ministry of the Interior in 2008, which stated as one of its goals to make a survey on the education of minority religions in Finland and actively seek solutions to its problems. This goal was a part of the Ministry of the Interior's policies in order to improve the security of immigrants and ethnic minorities in this country.[8] Finland, however, is not alone in its worries about security issues. According to Lisa Baughn, "The growth of immigrant Muslim communities and the concerns for the spread of extremism amongst Muslim youth has provided impetus for standardized education programmes in Islam across nearly all of Western Europe."[9]

Developing standardized education programmes can be seen as part of a larger process since the 1970s and especially after 9/11 in which Muslims have being constructed explicitly as religious subjects in different state policies (see the Introduction of this volume). In Finland this process took place rather late in comparison to countries of Southern Europe, for instance, but more or less in parallel with the Republic of Ireland where, in similar fashion to Finland, the change from an emigration to immigration country happened only since the 1990s.[10]

As a result of the rather recent growth of a Muslim population in Finland, no powerful Muslim organizations have developed in the country, unlike ex-colonial countries such as the UK, France and the Netherlands. Even though Finland has had Tatars as a historical Muslim minority for over a hundred years, this ethnic group have made very few public demands, but instead have opted to take care of separate language and religious education within their own community. It is only during recent decades that they have started to come out publicly as representatives of Islam, but there is to date little collaboration between the Tatars and the more recent Muslim arrivals. All in all, the field of Islam in Finland is very heterogeneous and consists of Muslims with many conflicting interests, which makes it difficult to build a functioning representative body for addressing Muslim needs in Finland. This, of course, is a problem faced by the state also in other European countries where the

---

8   Ministry of the Interior, *Turvallinen elämä jokaiselle: Sisäisen turvallisuuden ohjelma* (Helsinki: Ministry of the Interior, 2008), 26–30. However, according to the interim report of the Ministry of the Interior in 2010 nothing had been done on this matter. See: Ministry of the Interior, *Sisäisen turvallisuuden toimeenpanon ohjelma. Väliraportti 1/2010* (Helsinki: Ministry of the Interior, 2010), 50. The Internal Security Programme of 2012 does not refer to this issue; see: Ministry of the Interior, *A Safer Tomorrow – Internal Security Programme* (Helsinki: Ministry of the Interior, 2012).

9   Lisa Baughn, "Islamic Education in Europe," *Euro-Islam.info*, accessed March 19, 2012, http://www.euro-islam.info/key-issues/education.

10 Sakaranaho, *Religious Freedom, Multiculturalism, Islam*, 8–9.

state has taken an active role in setting up such bodies among Muslims.[11] In similar fashion, the establishment of the main Finnish representative body of Muslims, namely the Islamic council of Finland (SINE), was the initiative of a Finnish state agency (see Martikainen in this volume) and the state has also been active in respect of Islamic religious education in schools.

In Finland, Islamic education programs are incorporated into the public school system.[12] The manner in which this takes place in practice reveals a kind of dynamism of inclusion and exclusion of Muslims in relation to Finnish school education in need of a study. In addressing the issue of Islamic education in Finland, this chapter takes part in the rapidly expanding field of research about the ways that Muslim needs are accommodated and regulated in Western European countries and hence on the measures of creating or hindering opportunities for establishing Islam in a multicultural European society. In the main, European states have addressed Muslim needs in education mainly in two ways, namely by financing separate Islamic schools, as in Ireland, or by organizing Islamic Religious Education as a part of the general school curriculum, as in Finland.[13] These arrangements are linked to specific historical relations between state and church in each country.[14]

Theoretically, the chapter will employ the perspective of governance, which to date has gained little attention in studies on Muslims in Finland.[15] It will first address the traditional modes of governance, such as state legislation as well as national rules and regulations concerning religious education in Finland. Second, it will address the ways that the current system in Finland engages education authorities, schools, teachers and pupils of Islam in different processes of regulation, steering and accommodation of Islamic education in Finland.[16] As noted by Maussen, this kind of approach "creates opportunities for a type of analysis that goes beyond the study of (formal) legal

---

11 See Laurence, *The Emancipation of Europe's Muslims.*

12 For other European countries that have opted for the same system, see Baughn, "Islamic Education in Europe."

13 See Marcel Maussen, *The Governance of Islam in Western Europe: A State of the Art Report*, IMISCOE Working Paper No. 16 (Amsterdam: IMER, 2007), accessed June 11, 2012, http://www.iom.lt/documents/GovernanceofIslam.pdf; Bujis and Rath, *Muslims in Europe.*

14 See Tuula Sakaranaho, "Encountering religious diversity: multilevel governance of Islamic education in Finland and Ireland," *Journal of Religious Education* 66 / 2 (2018), 111–124.

15 See Martikainen, "The Governance of Islam in Finland."

16 Maussen, *The Governance of Islam in Western Europe*, 5; Bader, "The Governance of Islam in Europe," 872.

arrangements, and also looks at practices of application, implementation and interpretation."[17]

With respect to governance, the distinction by Bader between external and internal governance will be loosely employed.[18] Consequently, this chapter will look at the governance of Islamic religious education in Finland on three levels of administrative hierarchy starting with the state as a creator of legal opportunity structures, then proceeding to curriculum as a site of external regulation, and, finally, to teachers as actors in internal regulation. To start with, however, the development and challenges of Islamic religious education in Finland will be briefly outlined.

1 The Growing Demand for Islamic Religious Education in State-supported Schools

The aim of the Finnish state is to develop a pluralistic and a multicultural society that is based on the reciprocal respect of different cultures and religions. The policies of multiculturalism in Finland emphasize the right of society members to individual cultural identity, and encourage full participation in society, irrespective of one's cultural identity. Thus, various Finnish governmental action plans on ethnic discrimination and racism emphasize the constitutional right of different ethnic groups in Finland to maintain and develop their own language and culture.[19] However, the Finnish policies go even further than just hoping to preserve different languages and cultures. When certain requirements are fulfilled, Finnish schools offer classes conducted in their own language to pupils speaking minority languages in addition to normal curriculum subjects. The same affects minority religions. Consequently, an increasing number of languages and religions are taught in Finnish state schools. In this respect, Finland is undoubtedly quite exceptional among European countries.[20]

According to Finnish law, pupils are entitled to education in their own religion at school, provided that certain criteria for this education are met. Hence, as a result of growing religious pluralism in Finland, the number of

---

17 Maussen, *The Governance of Islam in Western Europe*, 5.

18 Bader, "The Governance of Islam in Europe," 873–874.

19 Sakaranaho, *Religious Freedom, Multiculturalism, Islam*, 52–54.

20 See Finnish National Board of Education, *National Core Curriculum for Basic Education Intended for Pupils in Compulsory Education* (Helsinki: National Board of Education, 2004); Tuula Sakaranaho, "Religious Education in Finland," *Temenos* 49/2 (2013): 9–35.

pupils availing themselves of the right to religious education at school is increasing rapidly.[21] This is particularly so in the case of Islam where the number of Muslim pupils in the metropolitan area of Helsinki is constantly increasing. The expanding ranks of Muslim pupils indicate the general increase in the numbers of Muslims, which started to grow rapidly at the end of the 1980s and especially at the beginning of the 1990s when the Somali refugees started to arrive. Till then, the Muslim population mainly consisted of a small community of Turkish Tatars and some independent immigrants mainly from the Middle East and North Africa. The estimated number of Muslims at present is somewhere around 60,000. Unlike in many other European countries, in Finland no ethnic group of Muslims dominates the community living in the country. Thus, irrespective of a rather small number, Muslims in Finland constitute a very heterogeneous population with various ethnic, linguistic and religious differences.[22]

Along with the rapid growth of the number of Muslims in general, and Muslim pupils in particular, the organization of Islamic religious education has become a pressing issue for municipalities and schools. Children of the previous generations of Muslims, belonging to Tatar or Arab families, attended the Lutheran religious education or were exempted from it in order to participate in religious classes provided by a religious community. This situation prevailed in Helsinki until the middle of the 1980s when Islamic religious education was introduced in state-supported schools. The first and only teacher at the time was the imam of the Tatar community, who used the book *Islamin opin perusteet* (Basic Teachings of Islam), published in the 1980s by the Islamic Congregation of Finland. At this stage there were only a few Muslim pupils, who were gathered together from different schools. Beginning in 1994, a second teacher was employed for teaching Islam, and he circulated among three schools, with a couple of pupils in each school. In Espoo and Vantaa, Islamic religious education started after the middle of the 1990s when the overall number of Muslims began to grow rapidly.[23]

In Helsinki, the number of pupils attending Islamic education more or less doubled at the beginning of the 21st century. In 2001, there were around four hundred Muslim pupils in the schools of Helsinki, while in 2003 it was over

---

21   Tuula Sakaranaho and Eero Salmenkivi, "Tasavertaisen katsomusopetuksen haasteet: Pienryhmäisten uskontojen ja elämänkatsomustiedon opetus Suomessa," *Teologinen Aikakauskirja* 114/5 (2009): 450–470; Sakaranaho, "Religious Education in Finland."

22   See Tuomas Martikainen, "Finland," in *Yearbook of Muslims in Europe. Volume 3*, ed. Jørgen S. Nielsen et al. (Leiden: Brill, 2011), 187–196.

23   Sakaranaho, *Religious Freedom, Multiculturalism, Islam*, 352.

nine hundred. By 2004, the number had already reached 1,200.[24] According to the most recent estimates in September 2011, the number of Muslims pupils in Helsinki schools was over three thousand (3,077), whereas in Espoo the number was 1,064 and in Vantaa 1,216.[25] Thus, the overall number of pupils participating in Islamic education in the metropolitan area of Helsinki is already over 5,000.[26] These numbers do not include all Muslim pupils, even though the general school policy is to direct all Muslim pupils to Islamic religious education. Moreover, these figures represent the metropolitan areas, whereas the number of Muslim pupils is much smaller in other parts of Finland. Nonetheless, these figures show the change that has taken place during recent decades with respect to the visibility of Islam and Muslims in Finnish schools. It also helps explain the challenges faced by the municipalities and schools in organizing their teaching. In 2011, there were around 25 teachers of Islam in the schools of the metropolitan area of Helsinki.[27]

Since Islam is such a new subject in Finnish schools it has not, naturally enough, been established in the same manner as the Lutheran religious education, where teacher training is organized by three different universities, and textbooks and teacher guides abound. Due to being such a recent subject, Islamic religious education is also more disadvantaged in comparison with Orthodox and Catholic religious education. In consequence, there are several problems involved in teaching Islam: the lack of qualified teachers is acute, very few textbooks or teacher guides are available,[28] classes are very heterogeneous, and the number of pupils attending class is often too large for a single teacher to manage the diversity for such numbers.[29] An additional problem is the language. Religious instruction is given in Finnish, which is usually not the mother tongue of most pupils or teachers, except in the case of converts. Moreover, since pupils usually have only from one to two hours of religious

---

24 Sakaranaho, *Religious Freedom, Multiculturalism, Islam*, 352–355.

25 Tuulia Tikkanen, email message to Nina Maskulin, May 15, 2012; Anuleena Kimanen, email message to Nina Maskulin, May 14, 2012; Irja Reinikainen, email message to Nina Maskulin, May 15, 2012.

26 Suaad Onniselkä, "Islamin opetus koulussa," in *Mitä muslimit tarkoittavat? Keskustelua islamilaisista virtauksista Suomessa ja Euroopassa*, ed. Tuomas Martikainen and Tuula Sakaranaho (Turku: Savukeidas, 2011), 122–138.

27 Tikkanen, email; Kimanen, email; Reinikainen, email. See also Onniselkä, "Islamin opetus koulussa," 135.

28 The Finnish National Board of Education is in charge of a working group presently preparing textbooks of Islam for the primary and secondary schools, which should help relieve the situation soon.

29 Sakaranaho, *Religious Freedom, Multiculturalism, Islam*, 373–382.

education per week, teachers of minority religions are compelled to rotate among numerous schools in order to fill in full-time schedules.[30]

Most teachers of Islam are not formally qualified and therefore earn a minimum salary, which has been an ongoing problem recognized by both teachers and municipalities alike.[31] The problem prevails even though the University of Helsinki started a training program for teachers of Islam in 2007. In order to take part in the studies of teacher education, however, a person needs to be either a student of the University of Helsinki or have a suitable Master's Degree. In addition, she or he has to have excellent command of the Finnish language. These two matters have proved to be a serious obstacle for current teachers of Islam whose level of education and command of the Finnish language varies greatly.[32] In order to ease their situation, however, education authorities of different municipalities have appointed a person who operates as a contact teacher for teachers of different (minority) religions, and the municipalities also organize regular education for their teachers. These measures, however, do not solve the basic problem concerning the formal competence of the teachers of Islam. It remains to be seen whether the Ministry of Education and Culture will address this problem in due course. In sum, Muslims in Finland are entitled to Islamic religious education in school, even though many practical problems still exist more than twenty years after the program was started. It is this entanglement of legal rights and practical implementation that constitutes the context for the governance of Islamic religious education in Finland.

2   Legal Opportunity Structure: The Right to Islamic Religious Education

Finland is a welfare state that promotes the equality of the members of its society before the law. This principle of equality is also a guiding principle in

---

30   Hanna Karvonen, "Salaam Aleikum: Islamin opettajien käsityksiä omasta työstään ja uskonnonopetuksesta Helsingin kouluissa" (minor thesis, University of Helsinki, Department of Teacher Education, 1998), 24; Hennariikka Lempinen, "'Pitäisi olla taikuri.' Islamin opettajien käsitykset islamin uskonnon opetuksesta peruskoulussa" (master's thesis, University of Helsinki, Faculty of Theology, 2002); Tuula Sakaranaho et al., "Religion in Migration. Studies on Muslims in Finland," in *New Challenges for the Welfare Society*, ed. Vesa Puuronen et al. (Joensuu: Publications of the Karelian Institute, University of Joensuu, 2004), 124–139.

31   Sakaranaho, *Religious Freedom, Multiculturalism, Islam*, 375.

32   See Sakaranaho and Salmenkivi, "Tasavertaisen katsomusopetuksen haasteet."

relation to religious rights and their implementation in Finnish society. Finnish legislation concerning freedom of religion and conscience, most recently articulated in the Freedom of Religion Act, grants the right of children belonging to different religious communities to receive education "in accordance with their own religion" (Finn. *oman uskonnon opetus*) as a part of the school curriculum.[33] For those pupils who do not wish to attend religious education, schools are obliged to organize classes in Ethics.[34]

Thus, the organizers of comprehensive and general upper-secondary education[35] (i.e. municipalities) are obliged to arrange religious education for the majority. Since 75 per cent (2013) of the Finnish people are members of the Evangelical Lutheran Church of Finland, it is Lutheran religious education that, in practice, is predominant in Finnish schools. This predominance is strengthened by the fact that attending Lutheran religious education is obligatory for those pupils who are members of the Lutheran Church. Hence, Lutheran pupils do not have the right to attend education in other religions, nor education in Ethics, even if their parents should so wish. The only exception to this rule involves students of the upper-secondary school, who start their studies when they are over 18 years of age and, hence, are legally adults. These students can choose between religious education and education in Ethics. However, pupils belonging to some other religious community, or no religious community at all, are allowed, if their parents so wish, to participate in Lutheran religious education. It is interesting to note that of the Finnish Muslims, some Tatar pupils have availed themselves of this right and participated in Lutheran religious education for the simple reason that it is practical when taking the matriculation exam where one is able to choose Lutheran religion, Orthodox religion, or Ethics.[36]

The aforementioned provision on religious education also states that the municipalities are obliged to organize religious education for at least three pupils or students belonging to the Evangelical Lutheran Church or to the

---

33   *Perusopetuslaki* 6.6.2003/454: 13 §, *Lukiolaki* 6.6.2003/455: 9 §, Finlex – Valtion säädöstietopankki, accessed July 7, 2013, http://www.finlex.fi/; see Anu Koikkalainen, *Uskonnonopetus ja ihmisoikeudet* (Helsinki: Ihmisoikeusliitto, 2010), accessed June 13, 2012, http://ihmisoikeusliitto.fi/images/pdf_files/uskonnonopetus.pdf.

34   *Uskonnonvapauslaki* 6.6.2003/453, Finlex – Valtion säädöstietopankki, accessed July 7, 2013, http://www.finlex.fi/.

35   Comprehensive school refers to nine years of compulsory education. After that a student can choose between general upper-secondary school (i.e. high school) and vocational upper-secondary school, both lasting three years.

36   Personal communication of the author with a member of a Tatar community, December 12, 2003.

Orthodox Church of Finland, not attending the religious instruction of the majority. Due to the clear majority position of Lutheranism, this provision, in practice, concerns the Orthodox pupils and students. With regard to the Orthodox Church, its status as the second folk church in Finland is obvious from the provisions required for the arrangement of Orthodox religious education. In contrast to other minority religions, municipalities are obliged to arrange Orthodox religious education as soon as they have three Orthodox pupils or students, and no request from the parents or students is needed.

For members of religious communities other than those of the Lutheran or Orthodox faiths, municipalities are obliged to organize religious education if there are at least three pupils or students in the area of a municipality belonging to a particular registered religious community, and if the parents of these pupils, in the case of comprehensive schools, or students themselves in the case of upper-secondary school, so request. Thus, in contrast to the compulsion of the Lutheran education, education in the minority religions, other than that of the Orthodox, is distinctly voluntary and is, at least in principle, left to the initiative of the parents or students themselves.

In addition to religious education, municipalities are also obliged to organize education in Ethics (Finn. *elämänkatsomustieto*) for those pupils who are not members of any religious community and who do not participate in Lutheran education. The minimum requirement of pupils is three, but the request of parents is required only in cases where a pupil is a member of a religious community but the municipality does not organize education in her or his religion. Therefore, education in Ethics has the same standing as the Orthodox religious education where the number of three pupils is necessary but no request from the parents or students is needed.

Reading the above-mentioned provisions, it is obvious that they base the right to religious education first and foremost on membership of a religious community. Pupils who are not a member of a registered religious community can, at the request of their parents, take part in religious education in line with their upbringing or cultural background where such education is available. However, the "rule of three" does not concern non-members of a religious community, no matter how strong their religious identity might be, and, therefore, the municipalities are obliged to arrange religious education only for pupils with registered membership in a particular religious community.

It is interesting to note that the new law gives the largest range of choice in religious education to those pupils and students whose families adhere to some minority religion but who are not members of any registered religious community. Thus, for instance, un-registered Muslim pupils or students can choose

Lutheran or Islamic religious education, or Ethics. Since only around ten per cent of Muslims are registered members of an Islamic community, most of them in actual fact belong to this particular category.

In terms of governance, the current legislation in Finland on religious education gives Muslims considerable freedom of choice, which in turn makes possible some sort of self-regulation in this matter. The choices that Muslim parents make concerning their children's education have a direct impact on the municipalities as providers and schools as organizers of religious education. Naturally, any sort of self-regulation demands that the parents are familiar with the Finnish system and know how to implement their freedom of choice in practice. Unfortunately, there is no precise information available concerning how and why Muslim pupils and their families make their choices in this respect.

In any case, the number of pupils attending Islamic religious education at least in the metropolitan area of Helsinki is steadily growing and the schools clearly aim at directing pupils to education in line with their family's religious background, especially in the case of Muslims. The municipalities have also received support from the Muslim associations and parents who have expressed a concern for Muslim pupils attending Ethics when, in their opinion, they should take part in Islamic religious education. In 2003, the City of Espoo received letters from a group of Muslim parents, from the Somali Federation of Finland (*Suomen Somaliyhdistys ry*), from the Finnish League of Muslim Youth (*Suomen Musliminuorten Liitto*), and from the teachers of Islam in Espoo, supporting the obligation of Muslim pupils to attend Islamic religious education at school. All these letters shared a common concern for not allowing Muslim pupils to attend education in (secular) Ethics, when they should be receiving education in Islam. Sending such letters and hence making one's voice heard is an example of the ways that Muslim parents and associations can exert influence on the regulation of religious education in schools.

In any event, fostering plurality of religious education is seen, from the state point of view, as a benevolent gesture of recognition towards different religious communities – and, indeed, it is very much accepted as such from the latter's point of view. Moreover, some sort of an obligation of Muslim pupils to attend Islamic religious education in schools is defended with the principle of similar treatment concerning all pupils irrespective of their religious differences.[37] At the same time, however, the policy of directing all pupils with Muslim

---

37   Marita Uittamo, *Uskontojen ja elämänkatsomusaineiden opetuksesta Espoossa* (Espoo: Espoon kaupunki, 2001), 9–11; cf. Sakaranaho and Salmenkivi, "Tasavertaisen katsomusopetuksen haasteet."

background to Islamic religious education is riddled with the same problem as the obligation of pupils belonging to the Lutheran Church to participate in the Lutheran religious education, namely a failure to recognize the diversity within this group of pupils.[38] In treating pupils with any sort of Islamic cultural background as a unitary religious whole, this kind of educational policy glosses over the ethnic, cultural and religious heterogeneity of these pupils. In so doing, it falls into the "religionization"[39] of these pupils and thereby can enforce an essentialized and stereotypical view of Islam and Muslims that is otherwise familiar to us from the media treatment of Islam. Perhaps, one can observe here something that has been called "the reification of collective identities" which according to Martikainen is a by-product of the special type of governance characteristic of the New Public Management prevailing in the age of Neoliberalism.[40]

The need for recognition of different kinds of Islamic orientation among pupils and their families might, however, come up in due course. The obvious outcome of the above-mentioned provisions, fostering a "denominational pattern"[41] of religious education in Finnish state-supported schools, is a growing plurality of the religions taught in class. Followed to its logical conclusion, the law in its present form could lead to a situation where, in similar fashion to Christianity, religious education is not only provided in different religious traditions, such as Islam and Buddhism, but also in different schools of these traditions. If Muslims follow suit, Finnish municipalities could feasibly end up in a situation where members of around twenty registered Islamic communities each demand Islamic religious education in accordance with their own

---

38 See Martin Scheinin, "Koulujen uskonnonopetus ihmisoikeuksien näkökulmasta," *Teologinen Aikakauskirja* 106/6 (2001): 515–517.

39 Bhikhu Parekh, "Religion and Public Life," in *Church, State and Religious Minorities*, ed. Tariq Modood (London: Policy Studies Institute, 2007), 16–22; Sakaranaho, *Religious Freedom, Multiculturalism, Islam*, 68–71; Tuula Sakaranaho, "Islam ja muuttuva katsomusaineiden opetus koulussa," in *Islam Suomessa: Muslimit arjessa, mediassa ja yhteiskunnassa*, ed. Tuomas Martikainen, Tuula Sakaranaho and Marko Juntunen (Helsinki: Suomalaisen Kirjallisuuden Seura, 2008), 173–176; Anuleena Kimanen, "Voimaa tiedosta: Islamin kouluopetuksen merkitys eräille espoolaisille musliminuorille" (minor thesis, University of Helsinki, Department of Teacher Education, 2011), 4, 18, 20.

40 Tuomas Martikainen, "Reframing Islam and Muslim Identities: Neoliberalism, Minority Governance and the Welfare State in Finland," in *Living Islam in Europe. Muslim Traditions in European Contexts*, ed. Dietrich Reetz (forthcoming).

41 Markku Holma, "Finland," in *Religious Education in Europe: A Collection of Basic Information about RE in European Countries*, ed. Peter Schreiner (Münster: ICCS / Comenius-Institute, 2000), 38.

interpretation. In practice, this will not be the case, not on this scale at least, for the simple reason that these registered Islamic communities should have a national curriculum of Islamic tradition authorized by the National Board of Education, with suitable teachers, and so forth. These practical problems notwithstanding, one should not forget that recent years have shown a development whereby the Shi'a Muslims in Finland have increasingly started to organize themselves into separate mosque communities and make their voice heard, for instance, via a monthly journal *Salam*.[42] Consequently, it might be just a question of time before they start to make demands for their legal rights and express their separate needs for Islamic religious education in Finnish schools.

3 External Governance: The Curriculum and "General Islam"

According to Thomas Popkewitz, we can view curriculum as an "invention of modernity" that "involves forms of knowledge whose functions are to regulate and discipline the individual."[43] Thus, the curriculum is an important tool of social regulation and power, which is used by the state in order to manage individuals' interpretation of social reality and the manner of their actions. This regulation takes place in two different ways: first, it defines the boundaries of desired knowledge that the schools should transmit to their pupils, and, second, it sanctions the ways that individuals should understand the world and construct their identity as a member of society. Popkewitz maintains that what we learn in school is more than just about what to think and how to act. It is also about learning dispositions, awareness and sensitivities towards the world we live in.[44]

Against this background, offering a particular kind of Islamic religious education in Finnish schools can be seen "as a clear form of social regulation, which is built into the Finnish curriculum" and hence "as an act of controlling Islam and Muslims" living in Finland.[45] In practice, every curriculum reflects its time

---

42   See http://www.resalat.fi; http://www.shiaislam.info.

43   See Thomas S. Popkewitz, "The Production of Reason and Power: Curriculum History and Intellectual Traditions," *Journal of Curriculum Studies* 29/2 (1997): 131, 140. Popkewitz's thinking is influenced by Michel Foucault's ideas about "governmentality" (see pp. 141, 147), but he does not develop this theoretical perspective any further.

44   Popkewitz, "The Production of Reason and Power," 139, 144.

45   Inkeri Rissanen, "Teaching Islamic Education in Finnish Schools: A Field of Negotiations," *Teaching and Teacher Education* 28/5 (2012): 747.

and social context and is produced in a process of negotiation and interaction between different social actors. It is therefore important to pay attention to how and by whom a curriculum is drafted and authorized. An equally important question concerns the way that teachers understand the curriculum and implement it in class.

In Finland, it is the duty of the Finnish National Board of Education to draft the national curricula of religious education for comprehensive and general upper-secondary schools.[46] At present, the aims of religious education in general include, first, information on one's own religious tradition and, second, information about other religions and world-views.[47] In other words, the aim of religious education in school is a broad, all-round education of different religions and outlooks on life. The justification for this sort of religious education is the necessity to bring up young people who, as members of a pluralist society, should be able to make independent value judgements, carry social responsibility, and to participate in cultural interaction. Pupils and students should have a good command of "cultural literacy" (Finn. *kulttuurinen lukutaito*) concerning religions, and understand the importance of religion for individuals, societies and cultures.[48]

The National Board of Education published in 2005 Overall Curriculum of the Lutheran and Orthodox religious education and those of the "other religions," including Islam, in 2006.[49] The first Overall Curriculum of Islam was drafted by a small group of Finnish administrators and members of Muslim communities, which was authorized by the National Board of Education in May 1995. It is stated in a letter of decisions accompanying this document that the basic contents of this Curriculum of Islam for comprehensive and upper-secondary school are in line with the proposal made by the Finnish Islamic communities. The Muslim communities listed in the letter of decision concerning the 1995 Overall Curriculum of Islam include only the Tatar communities in Helsinki and Tampere. At the time, there were also some immigrant-based

---

46   For a description of the process, see Annukka Jamisto, "Opetussuunnitelman valmisteluprosessi ja monikulttuurinen koulu," in *Monikulttuurisuus ja uudistuva katsomusaineiden opetus*, ed. Tuula Sakaranaho and Annukka Jamisto (Helsinki: University of Helsinki, 2007), 117–120.

47   See the 10 October 2003 memorandum of the Finnish National Board of Education, *Perusopetuslain muutosten vaikutukset uskonnon ja elämänkatsomustiedon opetukseen sekä koulun toimintaan* (Helsinki: Finnish National Board of Education, 2003).

48   Juha Seppo, *Uskonnonvapaus 2000-luvun Suomessa* (Helsinki: Edita, 2003), 180.

49   See Finnish National Board of Education, *Perusopetuksen opetussuunnitelman perusteet* (Helsinki: Finnish National Board of Education, 2004); Finnish National Board of Education, *Perusopetuksen muiden uskontojen opetussuunnitelman perusteet* (Helsinki: Finnish National Board of Education, 2006.)

THE GOVERNANCE OF ISLAMIC RELIGIOUS EDUCATION IN FINLAND 81

Islamic communities in operation, but there is no mention of their input in this matter.[50]

The 1995 Overall Curriculum of Islam listed the aims of Islamic religious education for primary, secondary and general upper-secondary schools. Islamic education in the primary school, in accordance with the 1995 Curriculum, focused on socializing children in their own religious tradition. This aim was also shared by teachers of Islam (interviewed in 1998) who to some extent introduced children to religious practice, such as greeting in the Islamic way, learning how to prepare oneself for prayer, and conducting prayer in a proper manner. Some of them asked for permission from the school principle to conduct prayer with the pupils during the school breaks, and some conducted prayer in class.[51] In secondary school, the aim of the Islamic education was to widen the scope of teaching so that it also covered important moral issues and helped pupils take personal responsibility for the choices they make.[52]

The 1995 Curriculum of Islam was clearly confessional. The contents of teaching focused almost entirely on Islam, with the aim of educating Muslim pupils so that they would actively adhere to their religion. By placing importance on the transmission of its own tradition, the aims of Islamic education in the 1995 Curriculum closely corresponded with those of Catholic and Orthodox education.[53]

The Overall Curriculum of Islam, in accordance with the Freedom of Religion Act of 2003, was confirmed by the National Board of Education in May 2006. The 2006 Overall Curriculum of Islam differs fundamentally from that of 1995. First, the drafting process of the 2006 curriculum was different in the sense that it was not produced in close cooperation with Muslim communities as was done previously. The 2006 Curriculum of Islam was partly based on the curriculum of Islam drafted in the City of Espoo where a teacher of Lutheran religious education functioned as a consultative teacher of minority religions and actively took part in drafting a local curriculum of Islam with the help of teachers of Islam.[54] Even though it was written with the Islamic perspective in mind, the general outline and vocabulary closely followed the curriculum of

---

50 See *Islamin uskonnon opetussuunnitelman perusteet peruskouluun ja lukioon* 3/430 (Helsinki: Finnish National Board of Education, 1995); Sakaranaho, *Religious Freedom, Multiculturalism, Islam*, 357–358.

51 Karvonen, "Salaam Aleikum," 17–18.

52 See *Islamin uskonnon opetussuunnitelman perusteet peruskouluun ja lukioon*.

53 Markku Pyysiäinen, *Tunnustuksellinen, tunnustukseton ja objektiivinen uskonnonopetus: Opetussuunnitelma-analyysi Suomen ja Ruotsin peruskoulun uskonnonopetuksen tavoitteista ja sisällöstä* (Helsinki: Kirjapaja, 1982), 24.

54 Kimanen, "Voimaa tiedosta," 22.

Lutheran religious education.[55] This draft was then worked on by the National Board of Education together with a working group that consisted of school representatives who were familiar with the education of minority religion and of teachers of Islam who represented different orientations of Islam working in the metropolitan area of Helsinki.[56]

According to Pekka Iivonen, who was in charge of the drafting process in the National Board of Education, the curriculum of Islam was among the curricula of "other religions" that was "easiest to draft." He said that the education of Islam in Finland is now fairly well established and that there are many teachers of Islam who are familiar with the Finnish school system and could therefore help with the process. In his experience, moreover, the basic tenets of Islam are fairly uniform and the contents of the education of Islam uniformly accepted by Muslims all around.[57]

The form of Islam taught in Finnish schools is entitled "general Islam" and its main content is explicated in the 2006 Overall Curriculum of Islam included in the overall curriculum for "other religions" by the National Board of Education.[58] According to the 2006 Overall Curriculum of Islam, the purpose of Islamic education is to strengthen the Islamic identity of a pupil. Pupils, moreover, are aided in understanding the significance of Islam for oneself and for society at large. In addition to these aims with a focus on Islam, pupils are also taught to understand and interact with people who think and behave differently. In similar fashion to the Overall Curriculum of Religion in general, the Islamic education also aims at the overall education of religions and outlooks on life.

The 2006 Curriculum of Islam mentioned above clearly avoids confessional language in a theological sense. Instead, it refers to the "Islamic identity," which is constituted in interaction with others. The reference to "identity" is also systematically repeated in the curricula of other minority religions. All in all, the term "identity" seems to constitute the catchword of the recent curricula of religions, which thereby employ the terminology characteristic of

---

55   Sakaranaho, *Religious Freedom, Multiculturalism, Islam*, 367–372; Sakaranaho, "Islam ja muuttuva katsomusaineiden opetus koulussa," 173–174; cf. Tuula Sakaranaho, "Pienryhmäisten uskontojen opetus ja monikulttuurisuuden haasteet," in *Katsomusaineiden kehittämishaasteita: Opettajankoulutuksen tutkinnonuudistuksen virittämää keskustelua*, ed. Arto Kallioniemi and Eero Salmenkivi (University of Helsinki: Department of Teacher Education, 2007), 3–16.

56   Jamisto, "Opetussuunnitelman valmisteluprosessi ja monikulttuurinen koulu," 122.

57   Jamisto, "Opetussuunnitelman valmisteluprosessi ja monikulttuurinen koulu," 122.

58   Finnish National Board of Education, *Perusopetuksen muiden uskontojen opetussuunnitelman perusteet*. See also Sakaranaho, *Religious Freedom, Multiculturalism, Islam*, 359–365; Kimanen, "Voimaa tiedosta," 25–29.

non-confessional religious education.[59] The non-confessional emphasis in the new curricula is even more accentuated with the prohibition of introducing religious practice in class.

Both of the aforementioned overall curricula of Islam for comprehensive and upper-secondary school entail an understanding of Islam as a universal tradition, without paying much attention to the variety of interpretations that abound about Islam, not only among Muslims worldwide but also among Muslims in Finland. In a sense, the Finnish Curriculum of Islam seems to correspond with the curricular programs of the Islamic Religious Community of Austria (*Islamische Glaubensgemeinschaft in Österreich*), which attach great importance to "consensus elements" constituting "a common denominator that can serve as a basis for relations among Muslims."[60]

A clear difference in the recent Curriculum of Islam in comparison to the 1995 curriculum is the aim to learn "to accept and respect people with different beliefs and outlooks on life." This wording actually provoked discussion in the aforementioned seminar organized by the Board of Education in November 2004 on the education of minority religions. Some Muslim participants voiced concerns about why the Curriculum of Islam speaks of "acceptance" and "respect" while the curricula of other religions simply refer to the "familiarization with" other religions and outlooks on life. It was noted that "acceptance" of other religions and outlooks of life implies much stronger commitment than simply getting to know them. In this respect, it would seem that the expectations for Muslims are far greater than for adherents of other religions. One can only conclude that the negative publicity of fundamentalist tendencies in Islam have resulted in the overt emphasis on "tolerance" in the Curriculum of Islam, which in itself is yet another example of how security concerns direct the governance of Islam in Finland.[61]

4 Internal Governance: Teachers and Teaching of "True Islam"

The discrepancy between theory (curriculum) and practice (class room) is one of the main challenges in the governance of religious education. It seems that there was and is a fairly wide consensus among administrators and teachers of

---

59   Peter Schreiner, "Introduction," in *Religious Education in Europe: A Collection of Basic Information about RE in European Countries*, ed. Peter Schreiner (Münster: ICCS / Comenius-Institute, 2002), 7–11.

60   Irka Mohr, "Islamic Instruction in Germany and Austria. A Comparison of Principles Derived from Religious Thought," *Cahiers d'études sur la Méditerranée orientale et le monde turco-iranien* 33 (2002): 161.

61   See Martikainen, "The Governance of Islam in Finland," 249–250.

Islam about the necessity to teach "general Islam" in Finnish schools, but it is in the classroom that this conviction is put into practice. Apart from a few studies on the education of Islam in class,[62] we have very little information on what is taking place in teaching Islam in practice and how well aware teachers of Islam are of the content of the Curriculum of Islam.

Teaching "general Islam" creates a situation in a classroom where the teacher and pupils might speak different languages, come from different countries and belong to different orientations of Islam, but who nonetheless need to find a way to coexist together. What this system does is to force Muslims to overcome their differences and find a balance between different interested parties. While teachers of Islam might warmly support the idea of "general Islam" in the curriculum and consider its teaching unproblematic, in practice they face many challenges in teaching it in class. For instance, the teaching should be suitable for both Sunni and Shi'a Muslims, and a teacher should be impartial in dealing with different orientations of Islam. In practice, however, this does not always take place. Most of the teachers of Islam are Sunni, which of course reflects the general numbers of Muslims of whom only 5 to 10 per cent are Shi'a. As noted by Onniselkä, not all of the teachers are able to keep to the spirit of "general Islam" and do reveal some prejudice against the Shi'a.[63] Teachers also have to deal with conflicts, which at times erupt among pupils with different cultural backgrounds representing different strands of Islam. However to some extent they allow pupils to explain about different Muslim conventions and hence express their separate ethnic identities. At the same time, teachers of Islam strictly control the expressions of differences between Muslims and try to avoid any conflict that may arise. They prefer common education for all Muslims for the simple reason that in their view it promotes peaceful coexistence of Muslims not only in school, but also in Finnish society in general.[64] In addition to pupils, teachers of Islam also have to deal with parents who do not necessarily understand the Finnish school system in general and teaching "general Islam" in particular. They need to convince Muslim parents that they

---

62 Lempinen, "Islamin opettajien käsitykset islamin uskonnon opetuksesta peruskoulussa"; Karvonen, "Salaam Aleikum"; Rissanen, "Teaching Islamic Education in Finnish Schools"; Kimanen, "Voimaa tiedosta"; Leena Maijala, "Islamin opetus kouluissa – oppilaiden puheenvuoro," last modified January 13, 2009, accessed December 1, 2014, http://www.teologia.fi/opinnaytteet/pro-gradut/414-islamin-opetus-kouluissa-oppilaiden-puheenvuoro.

63 Onniselkä, "Islamin opetus koulussa," 126.

64 Rissanen, "Teaching Islamic Education in Finnish Schools," 745–746; see also Kimanen, "Voimaa tiedosta," 37–38.

are teaching the right kind of Islam to their children. In addition, teachers often have to act as a negotiator between parents and school.[65]

A recent study by Rissanen on the teachers of Islam reveals an interesting strategy that they use in order to solve the problems attached to teaching "general Islam": teachers of Islam argue for "true Islam," which is cleansed of ethnic and cultural differences. They hence try "to balance between presenting the existing differences as belonging to the scope of acceptable Islamic diversity or declaring them as un-Islamic in order to emphasise the universal nature of Islam."[66] In doing so, they use the category of culture to both condemn and legitimize the differences, and, in both cases, their purpose seems to be to strengthen the ideal of commonality among Muslims. Consequently, they tend to circumvent anything that could be seen as a threat to Islamic unity in their teaching.[67] Thus, the curriculum term "general Islam" changes into "true Islam" in the vocabulary of the teachers, who promote the idea of the universal nature of Islam and the unity of all Muslims.

Part of this regulation also concerns the way teachers of Islam perceive the identity of their pupils as Finnish citizens. In addition to supporting Islamic identity, the teachers claim that the education of Islam can enhance the pupils' integration into Finnish society. The aim is to encourage their pupils' commitment to and active participation in Finnish society as Muslims. In this respect, the teachers of Islam reiterate the Finnish ideal of multiculturalism, which defines integration as a reciprocal process where one is allowed to keep one's culture and religion but is also encouraged to participate as a full member of Finnish society. Surprisingly perhaps, the reciprocity is made possible according to the teachers of Islam by adhering to "true Islam," whose values are in congruence with the values of Finnish society. For instance, they claim that "tolerance" is an Islamic virtue because there is no compulsion in Islam. In addition to tolerance, they also include in Islamic virtues honesty, reliability, fairness and peacefulness, which undoubtedly are accepted as main values in Finnish society at large. Being a "good Muslim" entails respect for others.[68] Thus, teachers of Islam actively take part in the governance of Islam by the regulation of the content of Islamic education in class in accordance with

---

65   Sakaranaho, *Religious Freedom, Multiculturalism, Islam,* 381–382; Rissanen, "Teaching Islamic Education in Finnish Schools," 747; for the experiences of the pupils in between their parents and the education of Islam in school, see Kimanen, "Voimaa tiedosta," 39–40.

66   Rissanen, "Teaching Islamic Education in Finnish Schools," 745.

67   Rissanen, "Teaching Islamic Education in Finnish Schools," 745.

68   Rissanen, "Teaching Islamic Education in Finnish Schools," 743–747.

the main values and principles of liberal, secular society, even if they articulate it in terms of "true Islam."

With the change of vocabulary from "general Islam" to "true Islam," and avoidance of conflicts arising from the heterogeneity in class, as well as supporting the identity of Muslim pupils as Finnish citizens, teachers of Islam can be seen to conduct a kind of internal governance of the education of Islam. First, they put in practice the legal opportunity structure of religious education provided by the state; second, they develop their own interpretation of "general Islam" outlined in the curriculum of Islam; and third, they are key figures in integrating Islamic education into the practice of the Finnish school system.

5 Challenges of Islamic Religious Education

It is obvious from the discussion above that teachers of Islam have a crucial role to play in the governance of Islamic education in Finnish schools. They are the ones who put into practice the legal provisions of religious education and interpret the Curriculum of Islam in class. They also operate as mediators between their pupils, parents and school, as well as between pupils and Finnish society. These various functions can be seen as part of the internal governance of Islamic education. This internal governance is made possible by the fact that all teachers of Islam involved in the studies mentioned above were Muslims who held a double role both as a teacher and as a Muslim.

Muslim teachers of Islam warmly support the present system of religious education in Finland. In their view, this system should be preserved since it best guarantees the interests of both the religious majority and minorities, which enhances the sense of religious minorities being respected by the wider society. They also see that the gradual process for establishing Islamic education in schools can advance the integration of Muslims into Finnish society.[69] Teaching one's own religion in school "indicates that religious minority groups are recognized and their identities legitimized in Finnish schools." Consequently, teachers of Islam "represent a legitimate Muslim identity in school."[70]

The picture, however, is very different when a teacher of Islam is not a Muslim, as in the conflict at Tampere mentioned at the beginning. The case of Tampere reveals one of the sore points in the new provisions concerning religious education in Finland. According to the recent Freedom of Religion

---

69 Lempinen, "Islamin opettajien käsitykset islamin uskonnon opetuksesta peruskoulussa," 120.

70 Rissanen, "Teaching Islamic Education in Finnish Schools," 748.

Act (2003), and the subsequent provisions concerning education, teachers of religion no longer need to be members of a registered religious community nor adhere to the religion they teach. The rationale behind this policy is that the quality of a religious education teacher's training is more important than personal conviction. According to this line of thought, training and qualification as a teacher guarantees a teacher's ability to teach fairly the religious traditions other than one's own.[71] It is here that a problem arises. As mentioned above, most Muslim teachers of Islam are not formally qualified, whereas there are non-Muslims who are, and municipalities prefer to hire qualified rather than non-qualified teachers.

The case of non-Muslims teaching Islam in school is but one example of the contradictions that the current system of religious education in Finland is riddled with. For instance, pupils are entitled to education in their "own religion" but its teaching should not be confessional. Moreover, pupils are directed to a certain religious education according to their membership in a registered religious community. At the same time, however, teachers who are teaching them their "own religion" are not necessarily members of the very same religious community. This might not be a problem with Lutheran religious education but it certainly is a matter of friction for religious minorities.[72]

What we can learn from the discussion above is that the main challenge in organizing religious education in Finland from the governance point of view concerns its internal governance, especially in the case of religious minorities such as Muslims. Islam taught by Muslim teachers creates an opportunity structure where they can be active participants in the Finnish school system and thereby fulfil the aims of the Finnish policy of integration as a reciprocal process. At the same time, current legal provisions concerning teachers of religious education seem to thwart this opportunity structure and pave the way for an organization of religious education that does not leave any room for its internal governance by members of religious minorities. Thus, the current system of religious education in Finland is riddled with contradictions as mentioned above. Perhaps, hiring an assistant teacher who was a Muslim and who took part in the lessons on Islam taught by a non-Muslim teacher in Tampere was a kind of Solomon's judgement by SUPO for the reconciliation of conflicting interests in a secular, multicultural Finland.

In sum, looking at the way that Islamic religious education is organized in Finnish state-supported schools, it is obvious that there are similarities but also clear differences when comparing Finland to other European countries.

---

71   Sakaranaho and Salmenkivi, "Tasavertaisen katsomusopetuksen haasteet."
72   Sakaranaho and Salmenkivi, "Tasavertaisen katsomusopetuksen haasteet."

Finnish schools provide Muslim pupils with Islamic religious education in a similar fashion to Austria, for instance, but not in a confessional manner. Moreover, in Finland the teachers of Islam are not necessarily Muslims, which is usually the norm in other European countries where Islam is taught in school. Thus, the way that Islamic religious education is organized in Finland does not seem to fit any of the models that are functioning in other European countries. Why this is so is a topic in need of further research.

PART 2

Politics of Recognition

∵

CHAPTER 4

Concepts of Authority in Irish Islam

Adil Hussain Khan

1 Background and Scope

The growth of the Muslim population in Ireland since the 1990s has led to the expansion of Muslim organizational structures across the country. This has resulted in Muslim organizations vying for authority by seeking recognition from both insiders and outsiders. This represents a unique step in the history of Islam in Ireland, since Irish Muslims are beyond the initial stages of community formation but have yet to cement their positions within Irish society. The provisional administrative structures that currently exist within Irish Islam are still developing with few exceptions. Likewise, no organization has the capability of presenting itself as a longstanding representative of Irish Islam, since all existing organizational structures within Ireland's Muslim communities are relatively new. The case of Ireland sheds light on the initial stages of forming Muslim organizations and the dynamics of internal competition among Muslim immigrants that has taken (and is currently taking) place in countries across Europe.

The research for this study was carried out alongside first-hand observations of influences on developing Irish Muslim power structures. Many aspects of this study represent personal reflections on the development of Irish Muslim institutions, such as mosque administrations, and their struggle to establish authoritative positions in Irish civil society. This study attempts to discern a line of inquiry that was initially posed by Talal Asad in his critique of the assumptions made by Clifford Geertz about religious symbols, but it does so from within an Irish Muslim context. Asad raised a fundamental question in his book *Genealogies of Religion* by asking what can be said about religious symbols without considering how these symbols have come to be authorized.[1] Asad also identified the importance of looking more broadly at the complex relationship between religious power and its ability to create religious truth.[2] This chapter attempts to pursue Asad's line of questioning by looking at the relationship between Irish Muslim power structures and their influence on

---

1 Talal Asad, *Genealogies of Religion* (Baltimore: The John Hopkins University Press, 2003), 53.
2 Talal Asad, *Genealogies of Religion*, 33, 45.

© KONINKLIJKE BRILL NV, LEIDEN, 2019 | DOI:10.1163/9789004404564_006

representations of Irish Islam, as a means of considering how different conceptions of Irish Muslim authority relate to different conceptions of Irish Islam. In other words, this chapter is as an attempt to show how religious power and religious influence in Ireland is shaping religious truth in Irish Islam.

There are a number of challenges in establishing Muslim agency in European countries like Ireland that are not limited in scope by their effect on particular segments of the Muslim community. This has forced community leaders to formulate justifications for the relevance of their positions or for the standing of their organizations through creative means. We shall see how Muslims have appealed to different channels at their disposal and have used different mediums to establish authoritative positions in Ireland. However, since Islam is not an institutionalized religion with a formalized religious hierarchy or a single representative body, there is considerable leeway to negotiate the boundaries of what authority in Islam actually means, especially in a contemporary European context.

There are different spheres of authority based on different criteria for how organizational outlooks may be interpreted. For example, one Muslim organization may focus on political objectives abroad while another focuses on religious education in local communities or on women's rights. Each organization might attain a position of authority within its respective genre in its own right. This occurs when different groups with specialized interests concentrate efforts on niche segments of the Muslim population for different reasons, which makes evaluating the extent of an organization's authority contingent upon its own unique circumstances. This also means that one organization may exercise authority over a particular group of Muslims but not over others. For our purposes, authority has largely been equated to an organization's ability to represent sections of the Muslim community of Ireland in the public sphere, whereas the impact factors discussed below represent elements in Irish Islam affecting those influences.

Considering that Muslim organizations are geared towards particular segments of the Muslim population, it may be useful to present an outline of distinctive communities of Muslims in Ireland today. Defining these communities explicitly, however, is problematic for a number of reasons, not least of all because many communities are still in the process of coming together. For this reason, there will be no rigorous breakdown of each community subset in an attempt to retain the dynamic characterization of Ireland's newly organized Muslim communities altogether. We shall attempt instead to discern common trends appearing to transcend the particularities of various Irish Muslim organizations by affecting the broader Muslim population of Ireland as a whole. This will enable us to identify major influences on an organization's authority and its longevity without being distracted by a particular organization's developmental dilemmas. We shall now turn our attention to the most important factors impacting the authority of organizational structures in Irish Muslim communities today.

2 Influences on Authoritative Structures

2.1 *Funding*

The primary and most evident factor impacting the ongoing contestation between Irish Muslim organizations today is money. The organizations that are currently taking the lead in presenting themselves as representatives of Irish Islam are the major mosque organizations with the greatest abundance of financial resources at their disposal. All of these organizations, to some extent, receive support stemming from the same donor, even though the allocation of funds is uneven. The largest mosque in Ireland, the Islamic Cultural Centre of Ireland (ICCI) in Clonskeagh, Dublin 14, has the strongest link and most direct connection to the al-Maktoum family of Dubai, the largest financiers of Islam in Ireland.[3] The collective philanthropic endeavours of members of the al-Maktoum family are often publicized in Europe under the banner of the Maktoum Foundation, which in actuality represents a vast network with extensive resources worldwide.[4] Within this network, it appears as though the primary sponsor of Irish mosque organizations is His Highness Sheikh Hamdan bin Rashid al-Maktoum (b. 1945), the Deputy Ruler of Dubai and the Minister of Finance and Industry of the United Arab Emirates. One of Sheikh Hamdan's best known humanitarian projects in European Islam is the al-Maktoum College of Higher Education (formerly known as the al-Maktoum Institute) in Dundee, Scotland, which provides fulltime courses in language instruction and Islamic Studies.[5] The Maktoum Foundation has also funded a number of

---

3 See the official website at http://islamireland.ie (accessed December 2017).

4 This is not to be confused with the Mohammed bin Rashid al-Maktoum Foundation, which was founded in 2007 by His Highness Sheikh Mohammed bin Rashid al-Maktoum (b. 1949), who is the head of Dubai's ruling family as well as the Vice-President and Prime Minister of the United Arab Emirates. See the official website of the Mohammed bin Rashid al-Maktoum Foundation at www.mbrfoundation.ae (accessed December 2017). Although both brothers are known for their philanthropy, Sheikh Hamdan seems to be the primary sponsor of Irish mosque organizations, perhaps even due to altruistic concerns, such as a genuine personal interest in the advancement of European Islam.

5 These courses are now accredited by the Scottish Qualifications Authority (SQA) but were previously validated by the University of Aberdeen. See the official website at www.almcollege.org.uk (accessed December 2017).

mosques and Islamic centres throughout Europe, including in Ireland, in accordance with local needs.

One of these projects is the Essalam (*al-salām*) mosque of Rotterdam, which opened in 2010. The Maktoum Foundation has fully funded the construction and day-to-day operation of this mosque, including its extensive administrative staff, in much the same way it has funded the Islamic Cultural Centre of Ireland (ICCI) since its opening in 1996. The institutional autonomy resulting from the ICCI's financial stability has facilitated Dublin's transformation into the international headquarters for the European Council for Fatwa and Research (ECFR), headed by Sheikh Yusuf al-Qaradawi.[6] Accordingly, the Maktoum Foundation covers the ordinary expenses of the European Council for Fatwa and Research. The Maktoum Foundation also offers annual subsidies to five other major mosque organizations in Ireland, including: (i) the Islamic Foundation of Ireland, which runs the Dublin Mosque in Dublin city centre; (ii) the Muslim Association of Ireland, which runs the Tallaght mosque in Dublin 24; (iii) the Cork Muslim Society, which runs Cork's main mosque; (iv) the Galway Islamic Cultural Centre, which runs both major mosques in Galway; and (v) the Islamic Cultural Centre of Cavan, which runs the – comparatively smaller – local mosque of Cavan.[7] The implications of this financial network are significant, considering the relatively modest size of Ireland's Muslim population and the limited number of mosque organizations across the country. Moreover, the Maktoum Foundation generously provides financial support to additional mosques throughout Ireland on a case-by-case basis as needed.[8]

No other countries or transnational organizations have funded mosques in Ireland since the early 1990s in a capacity comparable to the Maktoum family of Dubai. Notwithstanding these contributions, certain embassies have demonstrated a willingness to make irregular contributions in support of Irish mosques, especially those with fulltime imams or their expenditures.[9] The Emirati contributions to Irish Islam remain unmatched, bearing in mind that they are primarily appropriated through the Maktoum Foundation as opposed

---

6 See Jakob Skovgaard and Bettina Gräf, ed., *Global Mufti: The Phenomenon of Yusuf al-Qaradawi* (London: C. Hurst & Co, 2009).

7 Personal communication with the executive director of the ICCI, Dr. Nooh al-Kaddo, at his office in Clonskeagh (February 2011).

8 This includes partial funding for the Ahl al-Bayt Islamic Centre in Milltown. Personal communication with Ali al-Saleh (February 2011).

9 See Adil Hussain Khan, 'Transnational Influences on Irish Muslim Networks: From Local to Global Perspectives,' *Journal of Muslim Minority Affairs* 31/4 (2011), 492, 494–495; see also Jonathan Laurence, *The Emancipation of Europe's Muslims: The State's Role in Minority Integration* (Princeton: Princeton University Press, 2012), 30–69.

to other embassy channels. National competitors include Kuwait, Saudi Arabia, and other Gulf States (such as Qatar and Bahrain), as well as Iran, and – until the revolution of 2011 – Libya. This has created an imbalance in the power relations between mosque organizations based on financial leverage, which favours the ICCI in Clonskeagh. The pressure exerted by administrative executives of the Islamic Cultural Centre of Ireland has developed into an implicit hierarchy of Irish mosque organizations, which is not present within the Muslim community itself. This structure of authority is a direct consequence of the ICCI's financial advantage in relation to competing mosque organizations, which rely heavily upon the discretion of ICCI administrators with regard to the management and distribution of Maktoum Foundation funds.

The Maktoum Foundation's patronage of Islam in Ireland is controlled almost in its entirety at the national level by the ICCI's executive, owing to the special relationship between the two organizations rooted in their historical connection. It is possible to illustrate the influence of privileged access to the primary source of revenue by highlighting the most publicized positions of authority in Irish Islam. These include the resident imam of the ICCI's mosque in Clonskeagh (the largest mosque in Ireland), the chair of the Irish Council of Imams (Ireland's national umbrella organization for imams), and the general-secretary of the European Council for Fatwa and Research. All three positions are occupied by the same person and consistently receive public exposure in Irish Islam. This type of institutional efficiency has facilitated the creation of a public image that portrays a uniform expression of Irish Islam at the local, national, and international levels. This enables the ICCI's executive, as influential intermediaries between the Maktoum Foundation and local Irish Muslims, to embody a distinct sense of authority, even though the roots of this authority are contingent upon the proximity of the ICCI's executive to its Maktoum Foundation funders.

The resulting hierarchy of Irish mosque organizations is exaggerated by outsiders who misinterpret its role by attributing a disproportionate religious significance to the ICCI's imam and his personal views, based on the presumption that the imam's personal opinions are somehow representative of Irish Islam.[10] The staff of the ICCI benefit from this attention, and seem to take pride in having an opportunity to host high profile events involving a variety

---

10   For one example, see the article 'If there is any terrorist trend amongst Muslims in Ireland, the Muslim community will take every step to stop it,' *Irish Independent* (23 September 2006), where Sheikh Hussein Halawa is declared to be the 'leader of Ireland's Muslims'; it may also be useful to note the implicit presumptions made by the discussion in John Downes, 'Council of Imams to Help Integrate Muslim Faithful into Society,' *Irish Times* (16 September 2006).

of dignitaries and key figures in Irish politics, who range from local councillors to foreign diplomats, and even heads of state, such as the *Taoiseach* (Prime Minister) and President of Ireland.[11] Interestingly, administrators at the ICCI frequently deflect concerns about the imbalance of power and the misrepresentation of their roles as representatives of Irish Islam as a means of quelling internal disputes. This is done by drawing parallels between their personal roles at the ICCI and those of corporate employees with limited power who may be dismissed from their posts at any time, despite the Maktoum Foundation's utter disinterest in micromanaging the internal politics of the Irish Muslim community, or any other European Muslim community for that matter.

2.2 *Community Leadership and Internal Religious Recognition*

This brings us to the second factor impacting Irish Muslim authoritative structures, namely the establishment of religious recognition among Muslims in Ireland. Establishing religious recognition in Ireland is a complicated process, since Irish Islam may be seen in recent years to represent a microcosm of the global *umma* in its diversity of religious and cultural expressions. This is due in part to the boom in Ireland's Muslim population since the 1990s,[12] which has brought together a variety of Muslims from a diverse range of lifestyles and socio-economic backgrounds in comparison to other countries with gradually developing Muslim populations or shared colonial histories. For the time being, no ethnic group has established a clear role of dominance, which will one day become inevitable as the Muslim population continues to grow. This means that religious representation and religious sympathies are diverse but still consistent with recent trends of Islamic thought, since important movements from the Muslim world and expressions of contemporary Islam are visibly represented in Ireland, including those found in South Asia, the Middle East, and Africa.

---

11 The mosque's inauguration was attended by Irish President Mary Robinson and Sheikh Hamdan al-Maktoum on 16 November 1996. For other examples, see also the Taoiseach's Speeches Archive, available at www.taoiseach.gov.ie (accessed December 2013), which includes 'Speech on the occasion of visit to the Islamic Cultural Centre' (1 October 2001); see also 'Remarks by the Taoiseach, Mr Bertie Ahern TD, on meeting with members of the Irish Islamic community on the 10th anniversary of the opening of the Islamic Cultural Centre of Ireland at Clonskeagh, Dublin' (2 November 2006); see also Press Release, 'Minister Mary White, T.D., visits the Islamic Cultural Centre of Ireland in Clonskeagh today' (29 June 2010), which is available through the website of the Office for the Promotion of Migrant Immigration at www.integration.ie (accessed December 2017).

12 For example, the census returns of 1991 indicate that only 3,875 Muslims were living in Ireland at the time. See Government of Ireland, *Census 1991: Volume 5 – Religion* (Dublin: Government of Ireland, Stationery Office, 1995), 22.

This raises the question of how to identify influential spokespersons regarded internally as representatives of their respective communities. The Muslim scholars of Ireland who resemble some vague notion of Irish 'ulamā, are typically those associated with the larger mosques. The presumption, however, that mosque representatives function in accordance with widespread public approval is wrong, since nearly every major mosque in Ireland, at least for the time being, relies heavily on external funding, which directly impacts an organization's exposure both within and beyond Irish Muslim communities. There are a number of smaller mosques and Muslim organizations emerging from local and private sources, but their future is uncertain in relation to the larger more established venues. This makes the relationship between mosque representatives and their Irish Muslim constituencies complicated by the fact that the general perception of religious recognition is correlated with an organization's publicity and therefore its access to funding, as opposed to public approval. As a result, the reputation of Muslim community leaders amongst outsiders can be attributed neither to religious recognition of insiders nor to a religious movement's popularity within Irish Muslim communities. This is because many Muslims simply make use of whichever venues are the nicest or most accommodating in terms of providing access to facilities, and not necessarily as a means of expressing support for the administrators or imams who maintain those facilities. Outsiders may look at larger mosque venues, however, and falsely presume that insiders share religious sympathies with the leadership of these organizations.

For this reason, outside perception of organizational success is related to financial leverage, since the largest mosque organizations with the best sources of funding seem to have the most impressive facilities. In turn, spokespersons of these organizations portray themselves as representatives of large segments of the Muslim population. Furthermore, Muslim institutions appear to hire those who share similar views and are willing to cooperate with the organization's religious objectives, in contrast to hiring those who better understand local constituencies or express a desire to address local concerns. For example, the imams and administrative staff of the four largest mosques of Ireland since the 1990s have tended to share sympathies with the Muslim Brotherhood (*al-Ikhwān al-Muslimūn*). This is not the result of widespread support for the Muslim Brotherhood in Ireland, but rather a result of external factors that have enabled its sympathizers to become concentrated in important positions of authority that oversee the allocation of funding. It is pragmatically beneficial for financiers to support more institutionalized movements, such as the Muslim Brotherhood, due in part to its organized structure, network of resources, and general stability as a transnational movement. These movements serve as safer investments for those wishing to support Muslims in Europe. The Muslim Brotherhood in this respect is among the best organized Muslim organizations in Ireland. This has facilitated the establishment of the headquarters for the European Council for Fatwa and Research (ECFR), which once again is headed by the spiritual figurehead of the Brotherhood, Sheikh Yusuf al-Qaradawi, at the ICCI in Dublin.[13] Other Islamist organizations, such as the Jamaʿat-i Islami of South Asia, do not have as much influence in Ireland at this time, and hence do not draw the same level of external support, despite having an institutionalized framework. These dynamics of course could change rather quickly in favour of other movements, such as Tablighis, Salafis, the Gülen movement, or some other group in Ireland, based on access to financial resources as opposed to shifts in Muslim public opinion. Such an action could not be taken to mean that Irish Muslims who frequent these mosques suddenly changed their ideological orientations in accordance with mosque administrators or financiers.

With this in mind, religious recognition of Muslim scholars in Ireland is often reduced to public perception of the institutions to which an individual scholar or imam belongs. This is the reality of developing Muslim communities in Europe which distinguishes them from more established Muslim communities in other parts of the world. Hence, imams stationed at major mosques in Ireland are known largely by their institutional affiliations rather than being known independently for their religious reputations or scholarship. This enables the spokespersons of the largest mosques or Muslim institutions in the West to benefit from institutional prominence, particularly among non-Muslim observers who unassumingly ascribe religious authority to them.[14] Unlike Europe, local imams in the Muslim world are not regarded as regional authorities of Islam whose views must be expressed in public discourse as a means of voicing Muslim public opinion. Rather, religious recognition can be established independent of mosque affiliation, which enables scholars to serve, work for, and form private centres of learning, worship, or charity that are free from institutional restrictions or objectives. Accordingly, one must question whether Irish Muslims would support the religious views of local imams if their pulpits were dissociated from the major mosques that provide them with a public platform, especially since these platforms are bolstered by

---

13   See Adil Hussain Khan, 'Creating the Image of European Islam: The European Council for Fatwa and Research and Ireland,' in *Muslim Political Participation in Europe*, ed. Jørgen S. Nielsen (Edinburgh: Edinburgh University Press, 2013), 215–238.

14   See Martin van Bruinessen, 'Producing Islamic Knowledge in Western Europe: Discipline, Authority, and Personal Quest,' in *Producing Islamic Knowledge: Transmission and Dissemination in Western Europe*, ed. Martin van Bruinessen and Stefano Allievi (London: Routledge, 2011), 5–9.

financial support from foreign donors whose interests are shaped by concerns that revolve around finding the safest spokespersons for their investments. This is done by funding institutionalized movements, such as those favouring political Islam, which are not openly hostile – as others might be – to promoting notions of Westernized Islam, such as the Brotherhood in this case. This means that large mosque organizations must strike a balance between serving the interests of local Muslims and those of their non-Muslim hosts in order to establish institutional longevity and promote financial efficiency, instead of funding an otherwise unorganized congregation of local Muslims of different ethnic and socio-economic backgrounds who might simply desire better access to religious facilities. The problem with this approach in terms of establishing religious representation is that it creates the false perception of community leadership, even though local Muslims would likely continue making use of the best facilities available, irrespective of whomever happens to be leading the prayer. This is different from traditional conceptions of religious authority rooted in more conventional indicators of Islamic scholarship, such as peer recognition, public approval of one's scholarly abilities, or displays of personal piety, which often precede the reputations of the most eminent religious scholars in Muslim majority countries.

2.2.1 Religious Education and Irish Imams

The path to religious scholarship in the Muslim world has typically begun with a solid grounding in a traditional Islamic education. Since the advent of modernity, changes in both Islamic education and conceptions of Islamic scholarship have dramatically altered the criteria against which scholars may be measured.[15] Nonetheless, the centrality of religious education in establishing scholarly recognition in the Muslim world still creates certain expectations of religious authority in Irish Islam. The historic connection alone between religious education and religious authority seems capable of justifying a comparison between the educational backgrounds of Irish imams with what might be considered more traditional standards. This comparison illustrates the complexities of attaining religious recognition in Ireland and the unique standards upon which Muslim religious authority in Ireland is based. It also shows how an imam's status within a local community, and his recognition beyond it, is not simply a product of educational background.

---

15   See Malika Zeghal, 'The "Recentering" of Religious Knowledge and Discourse: The Case of al-Azhar in Twentieth-Century Egypt,' in *Schooling Islam*, ed. Robert W. Hefner and Muhammad Qasim Zaman (Princeton: Princeton University Press, 2007), 107–130.

With regard to Islamic education and training, there are only a small number of imams who currently have completed extended courses of study that amount to little more than foundational survey courses comparable to Western equivalents at the undergraduate level. A handful of imams have completed advanced degrees worthy of further discussion in relation to their authority. The most notable of them is the resident imam of the ICCI, Sheikh Hussein Halawa, who initially studied at al-Azhar University in Cairo before completing advanced degrees in Pakistan.[16] His educational background represents a considerable accomplishment within the Irish context in comparison to most imams. Many Irish imams at smaller mosques have only pursued programs of religious study retrospectively through correspondence courses, after already having acquired positions at local mosques. Altogether, the majority of fulltime imams who are permanently stationed at Irish mosques have limited religious education and minimal spiritual training. There are also a few Salafi (meaning Wahhabi in this case) preachers who have undergone periods of semi-formal study in Saudi Arabia and elsewhere, but they are not affiliated with major mosques and usually focus on *da'wa* (proselytization) activities.

Within the mosque framework, the most highly educated imam in Ireland is Ali al-Saleh (or Abu Hassan as he is commonly known) of the Ahl al-Bayt Islamic Centre in Milltown, Dublin 14.[17] He is not only a qualified physician, who holds a medical degree from the Royal College of Surgeons in Ireland, but an accomplished student of Islamic Studies.[18] Ali al-Saleh completed a number of programs of study at the Hawza in Qum from 1988 to 1997 before returning to Ireland from Iran. His numerous *ijāzas* (traditional certifications) from most major *marāja'* of Shi'i *'ulamā* (religious authorities) in Najaf, however, do not translate into religious authority amongst Sunnis. In addition, unrelated factors, such as ethnic background and cultural differences, present a challenge to imam Abu Hassan's otherwise uncontested standing within Ireland's Shi'i community. Similar disputes based on ethnic and cultural differences have manifested themselves among Ireland's Sunni Muslims in recent years. This has led to the formation of independent mosque organizations for South Asian Muslims and for Africans, mainly from Nigeria.

Beyond the ICCI's mosque network in Ireland, there are a few notable imams whose educational achievements stand out. Firstly, there is Shaheed Satardien who studied Islam in South Africa prior to settling in Ireland. Satardien also

---

16   Adil Hussain Khan, 'Narratives of Muslim Migration to Ireland,' *The Muslim World* 107/3 (2017): 414–415.

17   Adil Hussain Khan, 'Narratives of Muslim Migration to Ireland,' 411–413.

18   See the official website at www.shiamuslimsinireland.com (accessed October 2014).

holds advanced degrees from Islamic University of Medina and Umm al-Qurra University in Saudi Arabia.[19] He has served as the Director of Ideal Business College in Dublin, and is therefore known by various titles, such as 'Doctor' – in reference to his Ph.D. – and 'Professor' in addition to the more traditional 'Sheikh.' Sheikh Dr Shaheed Satardien is best known within the Muslim community for his public opposition to the ICCI's platform, which at times has heightened the aura of controversy surrounding his reputation in a way that is consistent with Muslim rivalries in contemporary Islam. Though Satardien's influence does not necessarily represent a counterbalance to the ICCI's network in Ireland, he has certainly excelled in developing a plan of action tailored towards his own religious objectives, including hosting events that promote better interfaith relations between Muslims and non-Muslims, to the ICCI's chagrin.

Among the better known imams who cater to South Asian communities in Dublin is Isma'il Kotwal, who only received limited training through preliminary programs affiliated with Dar al-'Ulum, Karachi, the major Deobandi organ of Pakistan. Kotwal's standing amongst South Asian Muslims in Ireland, however, is largely attributed to the support of his affluent financiers, as opposed to his education or personal achievements, as seen with Satardien. Kotwal's support stems from his connections to a prominent Dublin based family of entrepreneurs that has graciously provided him with mosque space to preach to South Asian immigrants for the time being. His ability to converse in both English and Urdu is often presented as his greatest credential by supporters, which provides a sense of the overall expectations of Irish imams. Kotwal has attempted to portray himself in a more traditional role by adopting the title '*muftī*,' which might offer an indication of his self-image within the context of the broader Irish Muslim community, despite the deficiencies in his educational background. It also illustrates the techniques employed by marginal imams attempting to establish themselves as religious authorities among the developing Muslim communities of Ireland by cementing career paths with credentials.

The final Irish imam worth considering in this context is Sheikh Dr Allama Umar al-Qadri, a native of Pakistan who grew up in Holland before relocating to Ireland.[20] Umar al-Qadri holds advanced degrees from Minhaj University in Lahore (the leading institution of the Minhaj al-Qur'an movement founded by Tahir-ul-Qadri) as well as a Ph.D. from Open University in Holland. Although Umar al-Qadri initially established the Clonee mosque upon his arrival in

---

19 Adil Hussain Khan, 'Narratives of Muslim Migration to Ireland,' 425–427.
20 Adil Hussain Khan, 'Narratives of Muslim Migration to Ireland,' 428–429.

Ireland, he now runs the al-Mustafa Islamic Centre in Blanchardstown, Dublin 15. Umar al-Qadri, has a modest but loyal following beyond Ireland due to his personal and religious affiliations, which enables him to make regular appearances on Noor TV, a Muslim satellite channel based in Britain.[21] This suggests that Umar al-Qadri might have a broader reach than other Irish imams, even though his age and lack of resources place him at a disadvantage in comparison to those with more experience and financial support. Umar al-Qadri has demonstrated promise in other areas, including community building and dialogue, since his communication skills distinguish him from those who lack proficiency in European languages, especially English. His youth and inexperience may detract from his ability to command a strong sense of religious authority at this time, even though he has the potential to develop further his reputation and a greater sense of religious authority in the future.

When taken together, Ireland lacks a large group of resident scholars with extensive educational backgrounds in traditional programs of study beyond the minimal qualifications for an average neighbourhood imam. Within this context, the practice of adopting multiple accolades to prefix one's name has likely developed as a conscious effort to bolster perceptions of religious authority, both within and beyond the Muslim communities of Ireland. This desire could be driven by the fact that most Irish imams would experience much more difficulty distinguishing themselves from their counterparts in Muslim majority countries, where mosque imams are commonplace and prominent *ulamā* have often made lifelong commitments to religious education and scholarship. The contributions of contemporary *ulamā* would, of course, be made alongside conventional responsibilities associated with mosque imams, especially at the beginning of one's career. The lack of diversity of Ireland's Muslim leadership has enabled a flattening of the normative hierarchy of religious authority that exists within Muslim majority countries, such that mosque imams and religious scholars (*ulamā*) in Ireland are effectively treated as if they were the same. Irish imams are consequently expected to perform the complete range of religious services for community members as needed, which inevitability hampers attempts at specialization. This also makes it difficult for Irish imams to command respect among local Muslim communities and further develop religious credentials, which might enable them to establish themselves as religious authorities among the more learned members of the Irish Muslim population.

This means that most imams in Ireland must resort to external sources of knowledge for spiritual guidance and moral support by redirecting difficult

---

21   See the official website at http://thenoor.tv (accessed December 2017).

questions to prominent scholars (*ʿulamā*) abroad. Although these scholars abroad might mirror a particular Irish imam's personal persuasions, they lack first-hand experience of religious life and civil society in Ireland. This type of religious hierarchy may be characterized by an informal network of friends and colleagues based primarily in the Middle East and South Asia, who make themselves available as 'reference points' for addressing sensitive questions as they arise.[22] By establishing an *ad hoc* process of channelling tricky questions abroad, transnational links are strengthened between European countries, like Ireland, and the Muslim World, which retains pre-existing dominions of authority in Muslim majority countries. The process itself of outsourcing religious expertise, however, diminishes religious authority of Irish imams by drawing attention to educational deficiencies at the local level and highlighting the discrepancy between Irish imams and traditional Muslim scholars abroad. Ironically, by regularly turning to foreign scholars to strengthen religious authority, Irish imams affirm their role in Irish society as non-authoritative actors. For this reason, the link between religious authority and religious education and training is contingent upon endorsements that are imported and then publicized internally through precarious means. This enables individual imams to disseminate personal views of religion and politics in a nominally partisan fashion while promoting their own transnational network of scholars or private institutions of study as if it were a franchise.

It may be important to reiterate here that religious education does not necessarily translate into religious authority at the local level. In addition, an imam's religious authority within a particular segment of the Muslim community may not depend upon direct community support, since some imams have established themselves as proxy representatives of various movements or institutions abroad. With this in mind, challenging a particular imam's authority is often perceived as challenging the ideologies of a particular institution or movement, which is certainly not the case in other Muslim societies that are characterized by larger Muslim populations and a more established religious infrastructure. This suggests that Irish imams become better situated to sustain positions of authority as community leaders by closely aligning themselves with familiar figures abroad. This is different from developing personal standing in local communities through other means, such as community

---

22   This terminology is borrowed from Brigitte Maréchal who uses it in a similar context to describe scholars and other religious authorities, such as the ECFR, who serve as religious references to the Brotherhood's sympathizers in Europe. For example, see Brigitte Maréchal, *The Muslim Brothers in Europe: Roots and Discourse* (Leiden: Brill, 2008), 89, 237–239, and Chapters 7–8.

service, outreach projects, or counselling services, as well as spiritual development programmes, which would usually stem from previous education and training. Religious education and training in this sense appears insignificant in comparison to other factors impacting religious authority.

2.2.2 Different Criteria for Different Communities

Imams catering to particular segments of the Muslim community are held to standards unique to that segment. For example, the tenure of Sheikh Hussein Halawa of the ICCI is equally contingent upon a number of unrelated circumstances, including his current role as general secretary of the European Council for Fatwa and Research (ECFR), his proximity to Sheikh Yusuf al-Qaradawi, and the prestige of his al-Azhar education. These credentials are most relevant, however, within Ireland's *Ikhwānī* population and would not carry the same weight among Irish Pakistanis, irrespective of their religious sympathies, whether Sufi, Deobandi, Jamaʿat-i Islami, or some other expression of Islam aside from the Brotherhood. This is due to the fact that the South Asian community has its own criteria for establishing religious authority, which corresponds to the expectations of South Asian Muslims with regard to education, spiritual lineage, and linguistic proficiency.

In the case of South Asian Muslim communities in Ireland, an imam's authority might rest upon a unique set of figures or institutions recognisable to South Asians. Importantly, these criteria are only loosely connected to religious knowledge, spiritual training, or outward expressions of personal piety. This also means that an Irish imam is responsible for promoting his own brand of Islam in order to fulfil the expectations of his constituency, where relevant characteristics need not represent adherence to fixed ideologies, as in the case of rigid forms of sectarianism. Instead, the arrangement entails that an imam must be versed in a number of religious and cultural conventions familiar to his congregation. Once an Irish imam becomes established within a local community, his position appears to be secure, since there is little competition between imams within niche segments of an Irish Muslim community. Still, religious education and training could play a greater role in establishing religious authority if multiple candidates vying for the same position were juxtaposed. In the limited context of Ireland, however, there is typically only one imam per community subset, with the exception of the *Ikhwānī* imams, who seem, at least for the time being, to be coordinating their efforts.

Although it is important for imams to gain acceptance from congregations, it is more important for them to find support from financiers to convey a sense of legitimacy as representatives of particular expressions of Islam. Accomplishing this is more problematic for imams beyond Ireland's network of Maktoum mosques, since non-network imams experience comparatively greater difficulty in securing external sources of funding. It may be useful to note here that many mosques in Ireland initially started out as private homes or commercial warehouses first rented by local members in order to establish venues for niche congregations. As temporary mosque venues were established, aspiring imams were recruited from abroad to fulfil specific needs of segments of a local Muslim community. It was only after their arrival that many of these professional imams set out to augment their congregations by rallying support around themselves, which eventually led to the development of more permanent mosque structures. This was only possible after members of a local community became sufficiently capable of supporting a full-time imam.

Some professional imams in Ireland have taken a different route to establishing spaces for themselves, which developed as a consequence of personal circumstances connected with their unsolicited arrivals in the country as ordinary Muslim immigrants. Professional imams who belong to this category independently migrated to Ireland for unrelated reasons. Upon arrival, they began preaching as a means of earning a livelihood by making use of private residences at prayer time or by personally renting warehouses for Friday services. Gradually, this attracted local congregations capable of supporting monthly expenditures when solicited for donations. This arrangement instantly legitimized a temporary platform for professional imams – who may have found themselves residing in Ireland unexpectedly – by co-opting temporary prayer facilities or by opening what effectively amounted to private mosques situated in one's personal home, which could then later be expanded as congregations grew. Once a venue had been procured for religious activities, the imam's stature as an Irish Muslim community leader became sufficiently established.

Thus, there are three types of imams functioning in Ireland at present: (i) the fully funded imam, (ii) the co-funded imam, and (iii) the non-funded or privately funded imam. The fully funded imam has a purpose-built mosque and needs no community support to bolster his authority, such as the imam of the ICCI. In this case, as with others, Muslims would likely continue visiting the ICCI's mosque irrespective of the imam leading the prayer, since they are drawn to the religious services provided by the mosque venue as members of the Irish Muslim community. The second category corresponds to partially funded or co-funded imams and their mosques, such as those associated with the Islamic Foundation of Ireland (IFI) or the Muslim Association of Ireland (MAI), both of which rely to some extent upon community support for meeting annual budgets in varying measure.[23] The third and final category corresponds

---

23   See the official website at http://www.islaminireland.com (accessed December 2017); see
      also www.mai-ireland.ie (this site seems to have replaced but was accessible prior to 2011),
      a replacement site seems to be http://maionline.ie/ (accessed December 2017).

to numerous Irish imams who lack outside investors to support their cause. These imams must foster the growth of congregations out of necessity and rely upon community support or personal contacts for provisions. This category would include Sheikh Shaheed Satardien or Allama Umar al-Qadri, and might help to explain why their mosques are regarded as being more accommodating to both insiders and outsiders.

It is interesting to note the discrepancy between the financial resources of contemporary imams in Ireland and those of traditional ʿulamā whose livelihoods were supported by endowments established for the pursuit of independent religious scholarship and services.[24] The situation in Ireland gives way to a different type of competition based on the need to establish oneself both within a local community and with potential funders. This ultimately encourages Irish imams to distinguish themselves by adopting stances in opposition to each other, instead of promoting each other's excellence and contributions to Irish society. For example, the situation makes it necessary for a Sufi imam to be seen as a representative of Sufism, and a Salafi imam to be seen as representative of Salafism, whereas in reality most ordinary Muslims in Ireland take on hybrid identities. This not only creates a false image of Irish Muslim religiosity but also widens the gap between local imams and their congregations. It is also clear that other factors including language, culture, and socioeconomic background play an important role in identity formation for Muslim communities in the West.[25]

2.3 Grassroots Movements and Public Opinion

This brings us to the third factor influencing authority in Irish Islam, which may be described as the collective voice of ordinary Irish Muslims or local Muslim community opinion. The most active grassroots movements have managed to develop social programs autonomously by remaining free from the aforementioned spheres of external influence, including the circles of international funders that continue to shape the agendas of career imams. Although few grassroots movements exist at this time, ordinary Irish Muslims possess the

---

24 For example, see Gregory C. Kozlowski, 'Imperial Authority, Benefactions and Endowments (Awqāf) in Mughal India,' *Journal of the Economic and Social History of the Orient* 38/3 (1995): 355–370; in contrast, see Ann Lambton, 'Awqāf in Persia: 6th–8th/12th–14th Centuries,' *Islamic Law and Society* 4/3 (1997): 298–318.

25 See Marcia Hermansen, 'Hybrid Identity Formations in Muslim America: The Case of American Sufi Movements,' *The Muslim World* 90/1–2 (2000): 158–197; see also Peter Holtz, Janine Dahinden and Wolfgang Wagner, 'German Muslims and the 'Integration Debate': Negotiating Identities in the Face of Discrimination,' *Integrative Psychological & Behavioral Science* 47/2 (2013): 231–248.

latent potential to take control of representations of Islam being advanced by Irish Muslim spokespersons on their behalf. This would provide Irish Muslims with a greater sense of self-determination. There are a limited number of grassroots movements that have been founded largely in opposition to traditional structures headed by career imams affiliated with major mosque organizations. There are also a number of student societies catering to youth and women's groups that actively organize events or social functions around the country, even though they are not necessarily seen as representative of Islam.

Beyond the realm of student organizations, the most influential grassroots movement in Ireland is the Arab Communities Forum, a non-profit organization founded by Abderrazak Zeroug who coordinates its activities.[26] Zeroug chose the term 'Arab' for his organization, instead of an overtly Islamic title, as a means of ducking criticism from imams who felt threatened by the challenge it posed to their authority.[27] As such, the Arab Communities Forum may continue its activities unopposed without attracting negative attention from perturbed Muslim rivals who claim to represent the voice of Irish Islam. Officially, the Arab Communities Forum is an open forum for anyone interested in issues pertaining to the Arab world, irrespective of their ethnic background, religious beliefs, or nationality. Though in actuality the organization is dominated by Arab and North African Muslims alongside Muslim students of South Asian descent.

The Arab Communities Forum resembles a Muslim advocacy group whose fluid objectives revolve around providing a range of specialized services on a case-by-case basis on behalf of disenfranchised Muslims who lack adequate space within existing mosque frameworks or Irish society. The Arab Communities Forum also arranges support for immigrant families who require assistance navigating the pitfalls of Irish civil society on account of various hardships, including language barriers, legal complications, medical illness, or any of the many immigration hurdles which may, and often times do, arise. In addition, the Arab Communities Forum has hosted cultural events, such as private *'aqīqa* (first haircut ceremony) parties for new-born infants, discussion forums intended to address current events, and at times *tajwīd* (recitation) classes geared towards English-speaking Irish Muslims interested in learning how to read the Qur'an in Arabic properly. The open atmosphere has attracted Muslim youth from student organizations who feel disillusioned by the administrations of the main mosques. This has allowed the Arab Communities

---

26   See the official website at www.arabcommunityireland.com (accessed May 2012); see also Adil Hussain Khan, 'Narratives of Muslim Migration to Ireland,' 422–425.

27   Personal communication with Abderrazak Zeroug, 2009 to 2011.

Forum to generate support both internally, within the Muslim community, and externally, with city councillors, media representatives, and members of the *Gardaí* (police), amongst others. The Arab Communities Forum hardly ever hosts events on local mosque grounds and rarely involves central figures affiliated with the administrative offices of the main Maktoum mosques.

The Arab Communities Forum might seem similar to other non-profit grassroots organizations, with the exception of its founder's credentials, since Abderrazak Zeroug holds advanced degrees in traditional Islamic Studies from respected institutions in the United Arab Emirates and Saudi Arabia. In this sense Zeroug possesses similar credentials and religious qualifications to the most learned imams in Ireland. Remarkably, he is not regarded as a 'Sheikh' by local Muslims and does not present himself as a 'Muslim' community leader before the general public. This makes it easy for Muslims who are sceptical of Irish imams to accept Zeroug's services since he is not openly affiliated with any major scholars, institutions, or ideologies. This has enabled Abderrazak Zeroug to build trust among Muslims and become a key figure in strengthening community relations between Muslims and non-Muslims in Ireland, especially among branches of government that deal with ethnic minorities, immigration, and incoming refugees.

In terms of religious services, some groups loosely affiliated with the Arab Communities Forum have set up unofficial tribunals, which focus on aspects of Muslim family law in Ireland. Although legal services are not advertised, these tribunals regularly help couples in crisis or Muslims with complicated issues that otherwise would not find adequate recourse within the mosque network for various reasons, such as when people fear the social stigma attached to activities frowned upon by mainstream members, or when people are afraid of potential legal repercussions under Irish law. Examples of these could involve Muslims seeking religious advice while managing polygamous marriages or those confronting the challenges of obtaining refugee status with Irish authorities.

The response of some Irish Muslims, particularly youth, is to treat the Arab Communities Forum and its activities as if they represent authentic Islam in Ireland. This places grassroots organizations, such as the Arab Communities Forum, on equal footing with numerous other competing brands of Islam within the country, including those limited by culturally specific expressions of religiosity, such as the Deobandis, the Muslim Brotherhood, Barelwis, or others. This is not to suggest that the type of Islam being promoted by the Arab Communities Forum is representative of Islamic liberalism, since Zeroug's personal views might appear rather traditional, if not conservative, to outsiders even though his organization is neither sectarian nor obtuse. This makes

Zeroug rather different from Irish imams associated with major mosques. To illustrate this point, the Arab Communities Forum even welcomes disgruntled members of the Shiʻi community experiencing similar problems as their Sunni counterparts in expressing dissent to community leaders who occupy positions of authority within the organizational structure of the Ahl al-Bayt Islamic Centre.[28]

In terms of authority, grassroots movements, like the Arab Communities Forum, are influential at the local level, especially in Dublin where most are based. This results from limited organizational infrastructure, which – at least for the time being – may delay further growth nationally, even though grassroots organizations will likely expand their activities beyond the local level one day. This raises questions regarding the scope of influence of Irish Muslim organizations, since most existing movements have concentrated efforts at either local, national, or international levels. This implies that the regional spheres of influence are mutually exclusive, resulting in a situation where the most active international Muslim bodies in Ireland, such as the European Council for Fatwa and Research, have little influence at the local level. Likewise, grassroots movements that function successfully at the local level in major Irish Muslim centres, such as the Arab Communities Forum in Dublin, have little influence nationally or internationally. The impact factors influencing Irish Islam are interconnected, which at times makes it difficult to distinguish financiers from those they finance or from ordinary Muslims participating in the development of Irish Islam, even though each is separate and reflects different interests.

3   Implications and Prospects

There is tension between three different authoritative structures in Irish Islam: (i) the mosque organizations, (ii) the financiers of mosque organizations, and (iii) the independent grassroots organizations comprised of ordinary Irish Muslims. Grassroots movements focus on the immediate context of Islam as a new religious phenomenon in Ireland. They are flexible in terms of combining different ideologies in order to accommodate Irish Muslims at the local level by incorporating Muslims from a variety of backgrounds and age groups and by often providing a platform for Irish Muslim women. In contrast, mosque organizations are run primarily by career imams trying to impose sectarian-style ideologies on constituencies who do not necessarily share a similarly uniform Muslim identity. These imams appeal to personal networks of scholars and

---

28   See the official website at www.shiamuslimsinireland.com (accessed October 2014).

institutions to promote narrow interpretations of Islam and instantly connect Irish Muslims with broader movements worldwide. In doing so, they appeal to local Muslims for support of the struggles of fellow Muslims abroad and press local politicians to take action on areas of international concern, which have become increasingly common in an era of globalization.[29] Lastly, there are funders of mosques in Ireland, such as the Maktoum Foundation, which are looking for ways to support religious initiatives of European Muslims while concurrently establishing better relations with European governments as an indirect means of furthering diplomatic ties and business partnerships. In smaller European countries, such as Ireland, where the Emirati embassy in Dublin only opened in 2010, mosque organizations that receive annual support from the Maktoum Foundation fulfil this role by strengthening public relations. In addition, the non-profit status of mosque organizations or their affiliates provides an outlet for carrying out charitable work as a means of acquiring tax relief for foreign companies doing business in Ireland.

This process of institutionalizing Muslim communities as a means of gaining recognition is unfolding in the Irish context uniquely in comparison to other European countries. The different circumstances in Ireland and the much more recent timeframe in which these processes are taking place will allow for interesting comparisons between other Western European countries with larger Muslim populations, such as France, Germany, and Britain, which went through their own processes of institutionalization as Muslims populations first grew. In these countries, it has become clear that certain religious or ethnic minorities have come to dominate the way in which the politics of recognition has played out, unlike Ireland, which still lacks a clearly dominant religious or ethnic group of Muslims for now, which might still allow for a change in course one day as Muslim communities continue to grow.

The different factions of the Muslim population in Ireland have different interests in establishing distinctive identities that represent Irish Islam. The competition for recognition has brought some of these differences to light, as interests advanced under various banners are taken up to symbolize the values of each particular faction. As a result, some have come to see Islam in Ireland as a religion of prosperity with lavish facilities and an institutionalized infrastructure that maintains the spectacle of an idealized image on public display. In other cases, Islamic authenticity is defined by imams who present their own

---

29   See Pnina Werbner, *Imagined Diasporas Among Manchester Muslims: The Public Performance of Pakistani Transnational Identity Politics* (Oxford: James Currey, 2002); see also Peter Mandaville, *Transnational Muslim Politics: Reimagining the Umma* (New York: Routledge, 2001).

credentials as the standard of excellence by which religious piety in an Irish context ought to be measured. Finally, there are others who present Islam in Ireland as a product of Irish Muslim volition. The most authentic Muslim community leaders in this case are those who are willing to engage with ordinary Irish Muslims on a personal level by addressing and resolving everyday concerns. In each of these instances, Irish Muslims appeal to different conceptions of authority to bolster their claims and gain favour both inside and outside localized communities.

This has enabled complex structures of power to develop whose relationships shape the expansion of narrowly defined conceptions of Islam in Ireland, by guiding the direction of Muslim organizations along a particular path in the country, and by providing a context in which all Irish Muslims will be forced to operate for the foreseeable future. These contested notions of authority will determine, to some extent, the course of the debate on Islamic authenticity in Ireland, which shapes the trajectory taken by Irish Muslims, if only by diminishing the likelihood of developing prospects antithetical to these influences. Thus, the current processes of forging power structures within an Irish Muslim context has already put into motion a mechanism by which religious power is being utilized to shape religious truth. This provides at the very least an insight into how the critique proposed by Talal Asad, as mentioned above, might be applied to an Irish context, especially when one looks back at the development of Irish Islam.[30] This shows that the factors impacting these developments reflect contested modes of authority in competition for strategic recognition.

Acknowledgements

The research for this study was carried out as part of a postdoctoral research project investigating the history of Islam in Ireland at University College Cork from 2009 to 2011. It was funded by the Irish Research Council for the Humanities and Social Sciences (IRCHSS), which since 2012 is simply known as the Irish Research Council (IRC), and also by the Department of *An Taoiseach*.

---

30 Talal Asad, *Genealogies of Religion*, 33, 45–46.

CHAPTER 5

Nation-state, Citizenship and Belonging: A Socio-historical Exploration of the Role of Indigenous Islam in Greece

Venetia Evergeti

The presence of Islam in Europe today results mainly from large numbers of workers and other migrants from the Middle East and former colonial rule in Africa, Asia and the Caribbean. Although the overwhelming majority of European Muslims are living in Western European countries, there are significant pockets of indigenous Muslim populations in the European periphery and especially the Balkans. Regardless of their long history and the important role that such communities have played in the formation of a notion of "European Islam," they attract proportionally much less academic and media attention than the more recent Muslim migrant communities.

Greece is a country that provides a very interesting case in the study of European Islam, not only because of the large numbers of newly arriving Muslim immigrants but more importantly due to the existence of a small but socially significant indigenous Muslim minority within its borders. What is known as the "Muslim minority of Greece" is a diverse population of approximately 120,000 people who live in the north-eastern part of Greece in the area of Thrace. Although officially recognized as a homogeneous community under the umbrella of its common religion, the ethnic definition and recognition of its name has always been a contested issue. Within the context of newly emerging migrant Islam in the country (which is explored thoroughly in Chapter 12 of this collection), there has been a significant political and academic shift in recent years in the way Islam is viewed, portrayed and studied in the country.

In contrast to "migrant Islam," which includes people from diverse ethnic groups, the historical Muslim presence in the Greek national context is strongly interrelated to Ottoman history and the Greek revolution (1821) against the Ottoman Empire.[1] In this respect, the Greek national identity was officially constructed against the Ottoman ruler, which resulted in the formation of hegemonic perceptions of Islam as a religious and national other. What makes

---

1 Konstantinos Tsitselikis, "The Legal Status of Islam in Greece," *Die Welt des Islams* 44/3 (2004): 402–431.

© KONINKLIJKE BRILL NV, LEIDEN, 2019 | DOI:10.1163/9789004404564_007

Greece interesting as a case study of Islam in a European country is this particular history and the fact that some elements of the Ottoman millet system have survived when it comes to the Muslim communities in Greece today.[2] Furthermore, Orthodoxy played an important role in the way Greek nationalism developed and even today the Orthodox Church continues to be the pillar of Greek nationalism. In this respect, Greece offers a very unique case which shares some similarities and differences with the other three countries explored in this volume. Firstly, Greece has a different colonial history to Portugal. Similarly to Ireland and Finland it was occupied by an imperial power but unlike Portugal, there are autochthonous Muslims in Greece whose citizenship rights are governed by international treaties and similarly to Finland their presence has shaped the national identity discourse.

Focusing on the indigenous Muslims, the aim of this chapter is twofold. Firstly, the discussion will trace the socio-historical establishment of the Muslim minority in Greece in the context of the construction of Greek national identity and its relationship to (Turkish) Islam. Secondly, it will provide an account of recent developments and the shifting paradigms amidst the increasing numbers of Muslim immigrants in the country. The focus here is on the religious organization and ethnic identification and belonging of the indigenous Muslims as this developed historically, both in their "home" area of Thrace and once they move to Athens and other big cities.

1   Greek National Identity and the Minority Issue in Greece

Anastasia Karakasidou, a Greek anthropologist specializing in the – officially unrecognized – Slavo-Macedonian minority in Greek Macedonia, has suggested that minority problems in Greece lie with determining what constitutes ethnicity and what constitutes nationality.[3] She sees this problem as having its basis in the process of nation-building in Greece at the beginning of the 1900s. She argues that the Greek state had to redefine ethnicity as nationality in order to bring together, under a common national consciousness, all the various ethnic groups that inhabited the country after the four-centuries-long Ottoman rule. Therefore, after Greek independence in 1830, "in addition to the

---

2 Konstantinos Tsitselikis, "The Pending Modernisation of Islam in Greece: From Millet to Minority Status," *Südosteuropa* 55/4 (2007): 354.

3 Anastasia Karakasidou, "Vestiges of the Ottoman Past: Muslims Under Siege in Contemporary Greek Thrace," *Cultural Survival* 19/2 (1995), accessed November 17, 2014, https://www.culturalsurvival.org/ourpublications/csq/article/vestiges-ottoman-past -muslims-under-siege-contemporary-greek-thrace.

inevitable problems attaching to the creation of the basic infrastructure of a state where none had previously existed, there was also the pressing need to create a shared sense of Greek identity."[4]

This became the task of Greek intellectuals at the time. To them the Greek nation-state could only be the continuation of Hellenism that had been disrupted by the Ottoman invaders. However, the progression of classical antiquity to the present had to be reinvented. Indeed, it was at the very beginning of the establishment of the new nation that the nationalist intelligentsia selectively rejected any connections with the Ottoman legacy, any oriental elements like folklore, customs and traditions, in an attempt to rediscover the "idealized" point of origin. This intellectual wave is known as the "Greek Enlightenment" and was highly influenced by the fact that the language, culture and thought of the ancient Greek world were highly valued throughout Europe (especially in the movement of European Enlightenment) during the crucial decades of the national "awakening."[5]

Moreover, Greek scholars have maintained that the determining characteristic of the Greek nation during the Ottoman period was the Orthodox religion, along with language and a common national consciousness.[6] Although, a Greek nation was non-existent at the time, it is true that all Orthodox people were unified (regardless of language) under the Orthodox Church in Constantinople.[7] Thus, modern Greek nationalism started with Greek independence in 1830, and in the words of Adamantia Polis "... it was spurred ideologically by the role ascribed to ancient Greece by the Renaissance [and European Enlightenment] ... Consequently, the revival of a modern Greek nationality necessitated a return to the classics, a purification of the language and the spread of education in order to recapture the intellectual primacy of ancient Greece."[8]

---

4 Richard Clogg, *A Concise History of Greece* (Cambridge: Cambridge University Press, 1995), 47.

5 Clogg, *A Concise History of Greece.*

6 See, Anna Triantafyllidou, "National Identity and the Other," *Ethnic and Racial Studies* 21/4 (1998): 593–612; John S. Koliopoulos and Thanos Veremis, *Greece: The Modern Sequel. From 1821 to the Present* (London: Hurst & Company, 2002); Georgios Mavrogordatos, "Orthodoxy and Nationalism in the Greek Case," *West European Politics* 26/1 (2003): 117–136.

7 Under the Ottoman administration the different ethnic groups were divided through the *millet* system, which defined them according to their religion rather than their ethnic origin. Therefore, the Orthodox Christians belonged to the Orthodox Christian *millet* and were subject to the administration of the Greek Patriarchate in Istanbul, regardless of the fact that apart from the Greeks it also contained other ethnicities. Moreover, the fact that the Ottoman Turks referred to the Orthodox *millet* as the *millet-i Rum* or "Greek" *millet* imposed a notion of Greekness to all Orthodox people at the time. For an analysis of the millet system, see Stefanos Katsikas, "Millets in Nation-States: The Case of Greek and Bulgarian Muslims, 1912–1923," *Nationalities Papers* 37/2 (2009).

8 Adamantia Polis, "Notes on Nationalism and Human Rights in Greece," *Journal of Modern Hellenism* 4 (1987): 148–149.

NATION-STATE, CITIZENSHIP AND BELONGING

Further, the link between antiquity and the present was Greece's medieval Byzantine past. However, it is not surprising that this connection with "past glories" had developed, since during the years of the war of independence there was a need to formulate a distinct collective element for which the people would fight to liberate from the "Ottoman yoke" as it was called. Therefore, in this newly constructed identity, there was no room at all for the legacy of the 400 years of Ottoman rule. On the contrary, this heritage was discharged as non-appropriate.[9] Indeed, Adamantios Korais (one of the most prominent Greek scholars at the time of the revolution, whose written work constitutes an important component of the national heritage and is therefore part of the school curriculum today) "declared in his autobiography that in his vocabulary 'Turk' and 'wild beast' were synonymous."[10]

In this respect, within Greek reality, national identity – and therefore the conception of Greekness – is understood "as an organic whole in which Greek Orthodoxy, the *ethos*, and the state are a unity."[11] However, the importance of the Orthodox religion has yet another implication. The Ottoman rule had the effect of isolating the Greek world from the great historical and intellectual movements that were so influential in the evolution of Western Europe. However, the Orthodox clergy further reinforced this isolation. This had its roots in a strong bitterness at the way in which Catholic Europe had tried to impose papal supremacy as the price of military help for the Byzantine Empire when the latter was threatened by the Ottoman Turks. The fall of Constantinople to the Ottoman Turks is still felt as "a national trauma, a calamity that annihilated Greek culture...."[12] It is not accidental that it is Tuesday the 13th (and not Friday, as it is in the western world) that is considered a day of ill omen in Greece today. That was the day (Tuesday 13th May 1453) that the πόλη (*poli*) "city," as it is known in the Greek world, was captured.

---

9   Jusdanis explores the ways through which early Greek literary historians aimed at showing how "Turkey could not produce culture but destroyed literature" and through the Ottoman rule "plunged the country into cultural and economic poverty." He also argues that this was a selective process by historians and literary critics (which coincided with the rise of the Greek state) who emphasized "both the ethnic integrity and occidental character of Greek literature in order to promote Greece's identity against the 'Turkish other'" (Gregory Jusdanis, "East is East – West is West: It's a Matter of Greek Literary History," *Journal of Modern Greek Studies* 5 [1987]). Also, for a further analysis of how Greek cultural continuity was constructed by the elite scholars, see Michael Herzfeld, *Ours Once More: Folklore, Ideology, and the Making of Modern Greece* (Austin: University of Texas Press, 1987).

10   Clogg, *A Concise History of Greece*, 3.

11   Adamantia Polis, "Greek National Identity: Religious Minorities, Rights and European Norms," *Journal of Modern Greek Studies* 10 (1992): 171.

12   Jusdanis, "East is East – West is West," 1.

However, in redefining ethnicity as nationality "the Greek state created the contradictions that form the basis of the minority issue in Northern Greece today."[13] Tracing the history of the development of the Greek nation-state, Baldwin-Edwards examines the construction of a common Greek identity and its relation to the many non-Greek speakers (Vlachs, Slavs and Albanians) that took part in the Greek revolution. Within a few decades after its establishment, the Greek nation state managed to incorporate all the different ethnic and linguistic groups residing in Greek territory under a "constructed imagined community with a shared belief in its common history and roots, albeit with a large dose of imagination."[14] The Muslim community of Western Thrace has always remained an exception to this "homogenizing" process as it presents a highly problematic situation where a local group has a different religion and ethnic consciousness despite their officially recognized Greek nationality. Since nationality, religion and ethnicity are seen as a unity, to hold Greek citizenship (or Greek nationality) is not enough for full social acceptance in the nation if one's religion and ethnicity differ from the dominant ones. Furthermore, the indigenous Muslims of Thrace have often been seen as an enemy within because of their affiliation with the Ottoman Empire/Turkey and Islam, an ethnic and religious category that still represents *Otherness* in modern Greece. Although there are parallels with the migrant Muslims here in terms of such constructions of "*Otherness*," an interesting distinction relates to the ways in which Muslim migrants in Greece are also often associated in the public perception with Ottoman/Turkish Islam which is understandably rejected by migrant organisations (see for example Chapter 12 in this volume).

2   **Balkan Islam and Minorities in Greece**

The Balkans, also known as the peninsula of Aimos, have repeatedly been turned – in the past but unfortunately still today – into a battlefield of bloody conflicts due to the opposing nationalisms and the inevitable creation of national borders in a way that left minorities within the respective countries. It is true that these minorities have suffered and still are suffering discrimination within the host countries because they are almost always considered as

---

13   Karakasidou, "Vestiges of the Ottoman Past," 5.

14   Martin Baldwin-Edwards, "Immigrants in Greece: Characteristics and Issues of Regional Distribution," *Mediterranean Migration Observatory Working Paper* 10 (Athens: Panteion University, 2008), 14, accessed October 17, 2014, http://www.mmo.gr/pdf/publications/mmo_working_papers/MMO_WP10.pdf.

the "Trojan Horse" of the respective, most of the times neighbouring, "mother" country. In this sense, geography has played an important role since the "motherland" of most of the minorities in the Balkans is almost always a neighbour of the host country.[15] Therefore, politically and militarily speaking, they are considered as a threat to the security and the borders of the host country.

Moreover, the issue of Muslim minorities in the Balkans has been compared with the presence of Islam in Europe; a subject that has become very popular in academic research, and which is informed by the debates surrounding the problematics of Muslim minority communities within the Western world.[16] The emergence of Muslims in Europe has been largely connected with early Muslim migration in industrialized Western European countries, and therefore conceived as a migrant population coming from a "rival civilization" or "victim side" which depicts the colonial nature of migration. Lately, Muslim minority populations have been seen as a threat or challenge to Western societies. Much of this debate arose from the 1979 Iranian revolution and religious militancy in various Muslim countries; however, more recently it has been reinforced by the 9/11 and other, more recent, terrorist attacks and the resurgence of Islamic extremism within Europe and in the Middle East.

Although the above highlights the situation in most of Western Europe, it is important to emphasize the difference in Eastern Europe. In the former, the migration process was the predominant (if not the only) factor that helped in the creation and the establishment of Muslim minorities. On the contrary, in Eastern Europe, and specifically the Balkan Peninsula, there was constant movement of the populations that resulted in the mixing of different races, religions and languages, a process that continued till recently. In many cases the different groups did not assimilate, either because of their temporary position or because of the politics followed by the dominant population. For many groups, the meaning of ethnicity that prevailed at that point was connected with the determination of ethnic, religious and linguistic relations without necessarily having a connection with geographical space. In this respect, there are those "indigenous" Muslim populations in the area that social research and demographic statistics, predominantly occupied with Muslim migrants in Europe, have largely excluded.

---

15 For an elaborated discussion on minorities in the Balkans, see Hugh Poulton, *The Balkans: Minorities and States in Conflict* (London: Minority Rights Publication, 1995). Poulton provides extensive coverage of the history of the area and its respective states and minorities.

16 Tariq Modood, Anna Triandafyllidou and Richard Zapata-Barrero, ed., *Multiculturalism, Muslims and Citizenship: A European Approach* (London: Routledge, 2006).

Not unlike the case of the Finish Tatar Muslims and their connection to Russian imperialism, the indigenous Muslims in Greece became the "remnants" of the Ottoman Empire in the newly established nation-states after the creation of their borders. What is of great importance, however, is to recognize the difference in that these populations did not become minorities through migrating which is another significant reason why they cannot be studied in the same way as the immigrant Muslim population in Europe. These indigenous Muslims, once part of the Ottoman Empire were given the status of a minority within the different countries that accommodate them through conventions and treaties between the newly established countries. Today, some of these groups are identifying themselves with Turkey as far as it is seen as the remainder of the old Ottoman Empire, or at least the closest country to their own Islamic traditions. Such is the situation with the Muslim minorities in Bulgaria and Greece.

Although Greece (compared to other Balkan and European countries) is largely homogeneous, it has always been host to a number of ethnic, religious, and linguistic groups that are qualified as minorities under international law. Today, contrary to what is commonly assumed, in Greece there are more indigenous minorities than the Muslim one: there are Vlachs and Slavophones, Tsamides, Catholics, Protestants and several other religious and ethnic groups, such as small numbers of Evangelicals and Jews.[17]

Of all these groups, it is mostly the Muslims of Thrace that have received political and media attention. Even the recent academic interest in the minorities of Greece tends to reinforce the idea that apart from the Muslim minority in Thrace there are no other "indigenous" – meaning old, non-migrant – minorities in Greece, as it concentrates on the newly emerging immigrant communities. This is because the issue of the minority in Western Thrace has played a significant role in the developments of Greek-Turkish relations. Also, the area of western Thrace has a strategic military position and Greece has often expressed her fears that a Muslim minority, so close to the borders of Turkey and with a Turkish ethnic consciousness, could result in a situation similar to the one of Cyprus. Therefore, the Greek authorities adopted an assimilation policy towards this heterogenic population that lives across the Greek frontier because it was (and still is) considered as a constant threat in the area. As revealed in the previous section, this view is also connected with the important

---

17   For an exploration of the different minority groups in Greece, see Lena Divani, *Greece and Minorities* (in Greek) (Athens: Nefeli, 1995) and Richard Clogg, ed., *Minorities in Greece: Aspects of a Plural Society* (London: Hurst and Company, 2002).

role traditional Greek Orthodoxy has played in the construction of the modern Greek national identity.

3   The Area of Western Thrace

What was centuries ago known as the area of Greater Thrace is now divided among Greece, Bulgaria and Turkey. The Greek part of Thrace, widely known as Western Thrace (where the Muslim minority lives today), lies in the north-eastern part of Greece. In the north it borders on Bulgaria along the ridge of the Rhodope Mountains, in the south on the Thracian sea, in the west on the Greek part of Macedonia along the Nestos River, and in the east with Turkey and the area of Eastern Thrace along the Evros River. As mentioned above, the history of Western Thrace is connected with the history of the Balkans. The numerous invasions of Celts, Bulgarians, Serbs, Romans, Turks and other peoples during the Middle Ages had as a result the alienation of biological and cultural characteristics of the indigenous population. However, the complete invasion by the Ottomans after the fall of Constantinople in 1453 was one of the most crucial points in the history of Thrace because of the spread of Islam in the area. Like the rest of the Balkan Peninsula, Thrace comprised part of the Ottoman Empire for almost 400 years.

In 1908 the Bulgarians took advantage of the revolution of the Neo Turks and established in the area of Thrace an independent state. After the Balkan wars (1912–1913) the Turks took back the Thracian parts under Bulgarian occupation (both Eastern and Western); however, under the treaty of London (1913) the Western part of Thrace was ceded to Bulgaria. After the end of the First World War (1919) most of Thrace (both Eastern and Western) was occupied by the Greek army. It officially became part of Greece in 1920 when it was ceded by Bulgaria in a treaty concluded at Sèvres on 20 August 1920 and was then divided into 6 provinces. According to the first official census of 1920, the Muslim population constituted the majority of the Thracian population, amounting to 103,000 people. However, the Treaty of Lausanne, signed in July of 1923 and the exchange of populations that followed changed the demographic landscape of Thrace, as well as the rest of Greece.

Given the significance of these treaties and the historical events during which they were signed, it is necessary to look at them in more detail. The attempt here is to illustrate the important role they played in the general attitude adopted by the Greek state towards its minorities and as a consequence the present position of the Muslim minority in Western Thrace.

4　From the Protocol of 1830 to the Treaty of Lausanne

The first ever minority protection agreement Greece signed was in the Protocol of London in 1830. That was also the first recognition from the Great Powers of the political independence of Greece after the Greek war of independence.[18] The agreement concerned the Catholics in Greece and assured their religious and political equality regardless of their faith. In 1881, the Greek-Turkish treaty of Constantinople (by which Thessaly and part of Epirus came under the rule of the Greek state) safeguarded the religious freedom and autonomy, within their communities, of the Muslim populations of the newly attached territories.[19] However, it was in the Peace Treaty between Greece and Turkey of 1913 that we had more guarantees for the protection of the Muslim communities in the "New Countries." In particular, in article 11 it was stated that, "the life, the property, the honour, the religion and the traditions of the people of the newly attached territories in Greece should be precisely respected." In the same article the duties of the muftis (the religious leaders of the community) were for the first time mentioned. Their jurisdiction was defined, strictly over the religious affairs of the community and the administration of the *vakoufia* (religious settlements, gained through charity and used as schools, hospitals, etc.).[20]

Yet the problem of Muslim minorities in Greece emerged after the Balkan wars with the massive movements of populations in the area. The League of Nations, in an attempt to safeguard both the welfare of the minorities that were emerging, and the international peace, encouraged the adoption of a series of

---

18　The Greek war of independence did not result in the liberation of the Greek people but only in the creation and recognition of a small kingdom of Greece. In the London Protocol the borders of Greece were defined to what was later known as Central Greece, the Peloponnese and the Greek islands of the Cyclades. At that time quite a large part of the Greek world, such as Thessaly, Epirus, Macedonia and Thrace and the Greek islands of the Aegean and the Ionian Sea was not included in the new state. This is quite important because for almost one hundred years after the first recognition of that small part of Greece, the Greek people were passionately attached to a goal inspired by the Megali Idea (The Great Idea), which meant the independence and unification of all the Greeks under Ottoman rule. This goal kept the Greeks together and reinforced an even stronger sense of a unified national identity. For more details, see Harry J. Psomiades, *The Eastern Question: The Last Phase* (Thessaloniki: Institute for Balkan Studies, 1968).

19　Clogg, *Concise History of Greece*.

20　The conditions of both these treaties were later replaced by the general stipulations regarding the protection of minorities of the Sèvres Treaty of 1920. For details on all these treaties and agreements, see Clogg, *A Concise History of Greece* and Psomiades, *The Eastern Question*.

agreements and declarations for the protection of minorities in "certain newly reconstituted or significantly enlarged states." Greece belonged to this category and, as I mentioned above, became party to a number of such agreements. However, the most important of these agreements (and for the purposes of the examination of the historical position of the Muslim minority) were the Sèvres treaty, for the protection of minorities in Greece, and the treaty of Lausanne, which settled the final borders between Greece and Turkey.

The treaty of Sèvres was signed on 10 August 1920, between the British Empire, France, Italy and Japan, on the one hand, and Greece on the other. The conditions of the treaty provided for a zone of Greek influence in Smyrna (Izmir), which would eventually lead to the annexation of that area to Greece and also allotted to Greece the whole of Thrace (Eastern and Western). Most of the minority protection stipulations concerned the area of Thrace, and started as follows:

> Whereas since January 1, 1913, large accessions of territory have been made to the Kingdom of Greece, and whereas the Kingdom of Greece, which has given to the populations included in its territories, without distinction of origin, language or religion, equality of rights, is desirous of conforming these rights and of extending them to the populations of the territories which may be added to the Kingdom, so that they shall have a full and complete guarantee that they shall be governed in conformity with the principles of liberty and justice ...

This was also the first time that the element of language had been taken into account in the protection of minorities in Greece. However, the special convention on the protection of minorities "... shall come into force at the same time as the treaty finally regulating the status of Thrace," as was stated at the end. This happened with the treaty of Lausanne.

The harsh terms of the treaty of Sèvres encouraged the growth of the new Turkish nationalist movement, which was led by Mustafa Kemal Atatürk. The Nationalists with Kemal as their leader, rebels in the eyes of the Ottoman Government in Istanbul, set as their aim the defence of the territorial integrity of the Turkish portion of the Ottoman Empire, namely Anatolia and Eastern Thrace. Kemal in *The Speech* (a well-known Turkish national document) was speaking of the formation of a "Turko-Mohamedan community that would include western Thrace."

Thus, after the defeat of the Greek army by Kemal in Asia Minor in 1922, it has been reported that Turkey went to the conference of Lausanne as a winner.[21] The main issue to be resolved was the ability of Greece and Turkey to arrive at a mutually acceptable boundary settlement. The main zones of conflict were Eastern and Western Thrace. Consequently, the Lausanne conference opened with a discussion of the Thracian frontier between the two countries. After extensive negotiations, the peace treaty of Lausanne was signed on 24 July 1923 between the British Empire, France, Italy, Japan, Greece, Romania, and the Kingdom of the Serbs, Croats and Slovenes, on the one hand, and Turkey on the other. By the terms of the treaty, Greece lost all that she had gained at the treaty of Sèvres: the Smyrna enclave, eastern Thrace and the islands of Imvros and Tenedos. The Maritsa (Evros) River was defined as the border between Greece and Turkey, thus dividing Thrace between them.

At the end of January 1923 a separate convention on an exchange of populations was signed between Venizelos and Inonu, the Greek and Turkish representatives respectively. This provided that there should be "a compulsory exchange of Turkish nationals of the Greek Orthodox religion, established in Turkish territory, and of Greek nationals of the Muslim religion established in the Greek territory." Around 1,300,000 Greek refugees from Asia Minor and eastern Thrace were allowed to settle in western Thrace and other parts of Greece, while some 500,000 Turks settled in eastern Thrace. This has been characterized as the most drastic remedy that was prescribed at Lausanne for reducing the potential for future friction between Greece and Turkey.[22] It was hoped then that the transfer of populations not only would serve to transform Greece and Turkey into homogeneous national states but it would also help to lessen future conflict over the minorities excluded from the exchange. However, there are quite diverse opinions on that. Divani, for example, argues that, "in vain they tried to carve a map on ethnic and national lines. New states were established, there were geographical and territorial reformulations, we even had exchanges of populations; however the ideal 'one state, one nation' was not feasible. The newly established states were also 'multi-ethnic' in one way or another."[23]

Haralabidis shares the same view: "The Lausanne treaty is one of the unique and outstanding examples in the history of treaties that proves what the Great Powers are capable of doing when they do not take into consideration the interests of people."[24] On the other hand, Clogg states that: "Despite its fearful

---

21   Divani, *Greece and Minorities*, 63.
22   Rene Hirschon, "The Consequences of the Lausanne Conventions: An Overview," in *Crossing the Aegean: An Appraisal of the 1923 Compulsory Population Exchange between Greece and Turkey,* ed. Rene Hirschon (Oxford: Berghahn Books, 2003), 13–20.
23   Divani, *Greece and Minorities,* 26 (my translation).
24   Michael Haralambidis, *National Issues* (in Greek) (Athens: Gordios, 1994), 46.

consequences in terms of human misery there was probably no realistic alternative to such an uprooting. The events of the previous years (before the exchange) the cycle of atrocity and revenge, had destroyed beyond repair the possibility of the peaceful symbiosis of Greek and Turk."[25] However, the truth remains that the issue of the minority in Thrace was in many cases, and still remains, a cause of dispute between the two countries.

The only exceptions to the exchange were the members of the Greek population of Istanbul and the Muslim population of western Thrace, who could prove that they were established in the respective areas prior to October 1918 (hence the term *etablis*). The convention imposed upon Turkey a number of minority obligations that Greece, too, had to respect vis-à-vis the Muslim minorities found in its territories. This meant that there was a condition of mutuality for the protection of minorities in the two countries. Many people adopting a defensive attitude when asked about the rights of the Muslim minority in Greece, attempt to compare Greece's record with the records of the neighbouring country. In this respect, it is not accidental that many earlier studies and reports on the position of the minority were comparisons between the latter and the Greek minority in Turkey. The truth is that the Greek minority in Turkey is now only 2,500 people from the 100,000 that it was after the signing of the Lausanne treaty.

Articles 38 to 44 of the convention defined the rights of the minorities living in each country. For example, article 39 stated that, "Turkish nationals of non-Muslim minorities will enjoy the same civil and political rights as Muslims. All the inhabitants of Turkey, without distinction of religion, shall be equal before the law...." Also, articles 40 and 41 provided for the right of non-Muslim minorities to establish and run at their own expense any religious and social institutions or schools where the instruction will be in their own language. Finally, article 45 provided that "the rights conferred by the provisions of the present section on the non-Muslim minorities of Turkey will be similarly conferred by Greece on the Muslim minority in her territory." The government of Venizelos also re-enforced Decree 2345 that was voted in 1920. Under the decree the minority's institutions, such as the mosques, the educational establishments and pious foundations (*vakoufia*) would be headed by the muftis, religious leaders responsible for the regulation of administrative issues who would be elected by the Muslim minority itself.[26] Moreover, Decree 2345 safeguarded the civil and

---

25   Clogg, *A Concise History of Greece*, 101.

26   Today there is much debate around the issue of the mufti and his duties. For an exploration of the topic from a legal perspective, see Zafirios Mekos, *The Responsibilities of the*

political rights of the minority as they were defined by article 39 of the Lausanne treaty. Further, in 1930 a Turkish Consulate was established in Komotini.

5 Greek-Turkish Relations and the Muslim Minority from the Lausanne Treaty to Today

It is very difficult to find exact figures for the ethnic composition of Thrace before the Lausanne settlement. The figures given by both the Turkish and the Greek side, as Psomiades argues, "are somehow controversial and vary considerably from year to year. Those persons recorded as Turks or Muslims included, besides Turks, many Bulgarians, Albanians, Bosniaks and others. Many of these peoples had fled to Thrace as a result of the turmoil in the Balkans from 1908 to 1914."[27]

In a similar way the figures given for the Greeks in Thrace included Bulgarian, Albanian, Armenian and other Eastern Orthodox Christians. As mentioned above the exchange of the populations has been interpreted as an attempt to eliminate the existence of such a mixture of minority ethnic groups in the respective countries, something like a "non-violent ethnic cleansing." Nevertheless, from the Greek point of view the "move of the Turkish Muslims from Greece would help to re-establish the Greek refugees."[28]

The fact remained though that there were those non-exchangeable minorities which after the settlement amounted to 118,903 Muslims in western Thrace and 125,046 Orthodox Christians in Istanbul.[29] Thus, according to most of the sources cited here, since the signing of the treaty of Lausanne, the position of the minority has been influenced by three main elements: First of all, political and historical developments in Greece; second, the modern reforms and the establishment of the Turkish Republic by Kemal, and, finally and most importantly, by the developments in Greek-Turkish relations.

Thus, it is argued that the Greek-Turkish rapprochement of the 1930s resulted in the improvement of the position of the minority. The Muslim community was concentrated in three provinces (Komotini, Xanthi and Didimotiho), the administration of which was organized by three "conservative" muftis, who were generally opposed to the rapid reforms Kemal was imposing on the

---

Mufti and Greek Legislation (in Greek) (Athens: Sakkoulas, 1991) and Tsitselikis, "The Legal Status of Islam in Greece."

27 Psomiades, *The Eastern Question*, 45.
28 Venizelos as cited in Psomiades, *The Eastern Question*, 65.
29 Psomiades, *The Eastern Question*, 69.

NATION-STATE, CITIZENSHIP AND BELONGING   125

neighbouring Turkish society at the time. The muftis were elected by the minority, and in each *muftiyya* (the mufti's administrative offices) there was a
committee responsible for the appointment of teachers in the Muslim schools,
the administration of the *vakoufia*, the allocation of financial resources etc.
Apart from administrative matters the three muftis were also responsible for
legal issues concerning the minority (which they were resolving on the basis
of Islamic law). Although the members of the minority had the right to choose
Turkish citizenship and move to Turkey (as was stated by the treaty of Sèvres),
there were only 200 persons who chose to do so during that decade.[30] This was
taken as a sign of the good relations between the minority and the Greek state
at that point.

However, it has been said that there existed discontent in the higher social
ranks of the urban Muslim population, especially those living in Komotini.[31]
The more prosperous members of the minority in the big cities, were not very
pleased with the religious administration of the minority affairs because they
were ideologically identifying themselves with the Kemalist reforms as opposed to those living in villages in rural areas who were leading a more traditional and religious way of life. This separation and tension between the "Old
Turks" and the "New Turks" as they have been called, was apparent throughout
the years that followed the treaty of Lausanne and the establishment of the
Turkish Republic, up to even today. The term "Old Turks" refers to those who
were more attached to the old religious traditions as they had been established
through the Ottoman legacy, whereas the "New Turks" were those who would
advocate Kemalism, seeing religion and state (or administration of the community's affairs in their case) as two different things.[32] Especially after the establishment of the Turkish Consulate in Komotini in 1930, there was a constant
tension between the Kemalists in the Consulate and the muftis. The modern
reforms of Kemal, which included the abolition of the religious schools (*iero-
didaskalia*), the state's control of religious movements, the adoption of Swiss
civil law and generally the exclusion of religion and the adoption of foreign –
and mainly opposed to Islamic tradition – cultural practices,[33] were met with

---

30   The number that was given by the Ministry of Foreign Affairs in 1928, as quoted by Divani,
      Greece and Minorities, 176.
31   See Feathertsone et al., *The Last Ottomans: The Muslim Minority of Greece, 1940–1949*
      (Basingstoke: Palgrave Macmillan, 2011).
32   See Divani, *Greece and Minorities,* 176–177.
33   For more information about Kemal's reforms and the establishment of a modern Turk-
      ish Republic, see Feroz Ahmad, *The Making of Modern Turkey* (London: Routledge, 1993),
      52–71. On Islam in Ottoman society and its later development through the establishment
      of the Republic, see Bernard Lewis, *The Emergence of Modern Turkey: Studies in Middle*

opposition and fear from the minority. Besides, we should not forget that the treaty of Lausanne, which safeguarded the rights of the minority, had characterized it as a religious (Muslim) minority. This was often used by the religious leaders, who were afraid that any deviation from the articles of the treaty would result in the further loss of their rights (such as the establishment of religious schools, and the autonomous administration of the minority by the muftis). In other words, there was the fear that any elimination of the religious component of the minority would immediately allow more state control. Such an intervention was unfavourable not only as a matter of religious principle, but also because it would mean that it would be easier for the Greek authorities to intervene in the minority's affairs and therefore to promote an assimilation program. On the other hand, the minority's Muslim leadership regarded the Kemalist reforms as irrelevant and detached from their own reality. There was no guarantee that the modern reforms would not result in the loss of their old (Islamic) traditional roots. Their commitment to their religion provided personal security, but also guarded the coherence of their community. Initially, the Greek state tried to keep a neutral position. However, in 1929 (and after the request by the Turkish government and the pressure of the Kemalists in Thrace) the Greek state introduced the new Turkish script (with Latin characters) into the schools of the minority.

The outbreak of World War II resulted in the predicament of the position of Greece as a whole. In addition, the German-Bulgarian occupation of western Thrace during 1941–1944 involved considerable suffering for the local population.[34] As a result many Muslims sought shelter in neutral Turkey. Migration to Turkey continued after the war because of the civil war that broke out in Greece in 1944. The mountains of western Thrace became one of the main theatres of the war during which both sides tried to win over the Muslim minority.[35] Thus, from 1947 to 1949 the Greek Communist Party (KKE) published a special pamphlet called *Savas* (which means war in Turkish) which was addressed to the minority, promising the improvement of its position after the assumption of power by the KKE. On the other hand, *Ellinikos Voras* (Greek North), a newspaper published by the Royal Army was claiming that the communists were taking measures against the minority. In the period from 1939 to 1951, therefore, 20,000 Muslims left western Thrace for Turkey. Migration to

---

Eastern History (Oxford: Oxford University Press, 2001) and Binnaz Toprak, *Islam and Political Development in Turkey* (Leiden: Brill, 1981).

34 For a detailed exploration of the position of the Muslim communities during this turbulent period, see Featherstone et al., *The Last Ottomans.*

35 See Clogg, *A Concise History of Greece* and Featherstone et al. *The Last Ottomans.*

Turkey continued until 1988 when the Turkish government in an effort to restrain the migrant tendency of the minority initiated a law under which those who wished to migrate to Turkey had to live for ten years in settlements in the least developed provinces of Anatolia which are mainly inhabited by Kurds.[36] Migration, therefore, seems to be the main reason that the size of the Muslim minority has remained more or less stable since 1923.

New developments in Greek-Turkish relations between 1950 and 1955 signalled the mutual improvement of the position of the Greek and Muslim minorities in the two countries. In 1951 an agreement was signed concerning the education of the minorities in each country. This provided for the exchange of teaching staff and the establishment of Turkish schools in western Thrace (as well as Greek schools in Istanbul). The books, journals and other teaching material in the minority schools were to be published and sent from Turkey to Greece and vice versa (see specifically articles 1, 2 and 7 of the 1951 Greek-Turkish agreement). Following this agreement the first Muslim Lyceum was established in Komotini, under the name of "Djelal Bayar" (he was the president of Turkey from 1950 to 1954). Furthermore, the Greek government accepted in 1954 the Turkish request, as it was expressed by the Turkish ambassador in Athens, Cemal Taraj, to replace the adjective Muslim with that of Turkish minority. Thus, on 28 January 1954, the chief administrator of western Thrace, G. Fessopoulos sent a note to the officials of the Thracian municipalities and communities by which he ordered them to use the adjective Turkish instead of Muslim in titles denoting associations and locations.[37] However, this initiated more tension within the minority and was a cause of misunderstanding between the two countries.[38] The Greek state was once again accused of supporting those who were in favour of the Kemal reforms against others who were for the maintenance of the Muslim traditions to which mostly the Pomaks (one of the ethnic subgroups of the minority) are attached.

---

36   Ahmad, *The Making of Modern Turkey.*
37   This initiative on the part of Greece has been repeatedly characterized as dangerous and resulting in a series of problems with the neighboring country. Andreades notes that "this change of names is contrary to the explicit formulation laid down in the treaty of Lausanne which refers to 'Muslims' and not 'Turks.' Aiming at the substitution of the term 'Turkish' for 'Muslim' the Turkish Government thought to obtain recognition of a national minority in Greece despite of (*Sic*) the fact that all the so-called Turks are Greek citizens. Nevertheless, legally the character of this minority continues to be religious and not national..." Kostas G. Andreades, *The Moslem Minority in Western Thrace* (Amsterdam: Adolf Hakkert 1980), 14–16.
38   In April 1953, handwritten proclamations were posted in some Mosques in Komotini proclaiming that the "insulters" of Islam would be punished by death. For an extended reference on the incident, see Andreades, *The Moslem Minority in Western Thrace*, 47–49.

On the 6th of September 1955 violent riots erupted in Istanbul aimed at the Greek community, which at that time consisted of 100,000 people. The houses, shops and cemeteries of the minority were burned and destroyed, and since then the number of the Greek population in Istanbul has been falling – it is no more than 3,000 people today.[39] Thus, these violent events against the Greek minority in Istanbul, and even more so the dispute over Cyprus, led to a further deterioration of the position of the Muslim minority in Thrace. From 1956 onwards there have been mounting complaints of discrimination. With section 19 of the 1955 Code of Citizenship, the state allowed the withdrawal of Greek citizenship from persons of non-Greek ethnic origin who have left the country "with no intention of returning." Of course this was freely interpreted according to the situation at the time by the respective officers (i.e., whether a person from the minority had any intention of returning or not after a visit to Turkey). This was used extensively during the period of the military dictatorship in Greece (1967–1974), which in any case worsened things even more for the minority. Members of the Muslim community were dismissed from positions in public offices and replaced by governmental appointees.[40] Also, the employment of teachers from Turkey to minority schools in western Thrace stopped after 1967, and in 1968 the military government established the Special Pedagogic Academy in Thessaloniki, whose graduates were the only qualified teachers to teach in the minority schools. Subjects like religion, mathematics, natural sciences, music and gymnastics were taught in Turkish, while the subjects of history, geography and political science were taught in Greek. This caused complaints by the Turkish Government that the Greek state tried to impose a Hellenized education system in western Thrace, which was isolating students from their modern Turkish culture.[41] The military government also initiated the expropriation of Muslim land for public use without giving adequate compensation.

In spite of the restoration of democracy in 1974, the violations of human rights of the minority continued. It has been argued that the Turkish invasion in Cyprus made the situation even worse. Since 1977 all Turkish geographical names in Komotini have been replaced by Greek names. The use of any Turkish names in official documents and in print has also been prohibited and is under penalty of fines and imprisonment. Moreover, mention of the Turkish name in parenthesis after the Greek names has also been forbidden. In addition, the

---

39   For more details of these events, see Alexis Alexandris, *The Greek Minority of Istanbul and the Greek-Turkish Relations 1918–1974* (Athens: Centre for Asia Minor Studies, 1978).

40   See Poulton's discussion on the issues of the minority during that period. Poulton, *The Balkans,* 185–187.

41   Poulton, *The Balkans.*

NATION-STATE, CITIZENSHIP AND BELONGING

use of the adjective Turkish in titles referring to associations or foundations, such as the "Turkish Teachers Association" or the "Turkish Youth Union of Komotini" has been also prohibited by a decision of the Athens High Court on 28 July 1987. In its decision the court stated that

> the use of terms like Turks, Turkish etc. characterise not only different nationality, language and religion, but also and most significantly foreign citizens ... which creates confusion as regards the citizenship of the members (of the association) and whether they are Muslims of Greek citizenship or of Turkish nationality and citizenship ... This gives the impression that within the Greek state there is a union of foreign and even more Turkish citizens, whereas in reality they are Greek citizens ...[42]

Furthermore, the court argued that the use of the word Turkish to describe Greek Muslims could endanger public order.

Today, the major problem regarding the administration of the Muslim institutions and foundations is the election of the mufti. The problem emerged in July 1985 when the mufti of Komotini died. The government replaced him with a governmental appointee who resigned almost immediately because of strong protests, but he was also replaced by another governmental appointee. This appointment was also followed by protests which became more intense in the summer of 1988 when a large demonstration by Muslims in Komotini was followed by two explosions – one in the central Mosque and one in a cemetery. In 1990 the government established a new law regarding the "Muslim religious leaders." In article 1 the law states the procedure for the appointment of the mufti and the skills that one needs in order to apply for the position. Also, according to the law (article 5) the duties of the mufti are restricted to the religious affairs of the minority. Furthermore, any "doubtful" decisions of the mufti cannot be executed without the contest of the Greek courts. Finally, with article 9 of the same law, Decree 2345 of 1920 was abolished, which mainly meant that the religious leaders (recognized as *topotirites*, "local supervisors") could no longer be elected by the minority but had to be appointed by the government under the stated procedures. In 1991 the replacement of the mufti of Xanthi elected by the Muslims with a government-selected candidate led to serious protest in which thirteen people were injured and on 26 August the Mosque in Komotini was bombed. Today the problem still remains and in many instances has resulted in conflicts within the minority. In 1990 unofficial

---

42 Translated from the decision of the High Court of Athens (no. 1729/1987, 3), which regarded the operation of the Union of Turkish Youth of Komotini.

elections were organized that resulted in the election of two "independent" muftis for the areas of Komotini and Xanthi in addition to the three appointed by the state.[43]

Political developments in Greece and the turbulent relations between Greece and Turkey have always had a noticeable impact on Greek minority policies and the research produced within this context. A major shift, both in terms of policies and in academic research, came in the early 1990s when the political and academic promotion of multiculturalism in Europe resulted in increased European pressure to respect minority rights in Greece.[44] This had a positive impact on the general status but more importantly on the education of the minority.

Since the 1990s, Muslims of Greek citizenship have had increasing access to tertiary education, thanks to an affirmative action policy enacted by the Greek Ministry of Education, which reserves 0.5% of admission slots at universities and institutes of higher technical education for the minority.[45] One of the biggest reforms in minority education came in 1997 with the Programme for the Education of Muslim Children (known in Greek as PEM).[46] This programme was initially introduced in order to improve Greek language skills among pupils in Muslim minority schools, and therefore facilitate their integration within the wider Greek society. Since its beginnings, it has employed more than 100 experts from a variety of disciplines who have organized and implemented training seminars for minority teachers, rewritten Greek textbooks for minority high schools, and sought to take seriously into account the needs of the children of the minority whilst attending to their diverse linguistic and cultural identities.

A recent visit (December 2017) of the Turkish President to Athens proved that the minority's socio-political representation and the legal protection of

---

43 For details, see Tsitselikis, "The Legal Status of Islam in Greece."

44 For a discussion of the language rights of the minority, see Katerina Mantouvalou, "Equal Recognition, Consolidation or Familiarisation? The Language Rights Debate in the Context of the Minority of Western Thrace in Greece," *Ethnicities* 9/4 (2009). For an exploration of the regional policies in Thrace, see Dia Anagnostou, "Breaking the Cycle of Nationalism: The EU, Regional Policy and the Minority of Western Thrace, Greece," *South European Society and Politics* 6/1 (2001).

45 Angeliki Ziaka, "Muslims and Muslim Education in Greece," in *Islamische Erziehung in Europa/Islamic Education in Europe*, ed. Ednan Aslan (Vienna: Bohlau, 2009), 149.

46 For details of the programme and information on the education system of the minority, see Thalia Dragonas and Anna Fragoudaki, "Educating the Muslim Minority of Western Thrace," *Islam and Christian Relations* 17/1 (2006) and Thalia Dragonas and Anna Fragoudaki, ed., *Addition, not Subtraction/Multiplication, Not Division* (in Greek) (Athens: Metehmio, 2008).

its rights are important issues that still define Greek-Turkish relations. During his visit, the first such visit of a Turkish leader to Greece in 65 years, Erdoğan insisted that the rights of the Muslim minority of Thrace should not be locked in the Treaty of Lausanne which he said was anachronistic and needed to be replaced. Whether some aspects of the treaty need replacing or not, this still remains an important international treaty that defines many aspects of the relations between the two countries including land and sea borders and their respective minorities' rights in Greece and Turkey. Furthermore, Erdoğan's characterisation of the minority as an ethnic (Turkish) one failed to take into account the ethno-linguistic composition of the minority and the important differences that exist between the three different groups that comprise it. This is a theme that will be explored in the next section.

6 The Ethno-linguistic Composition of the Minority: Turks, Pomaks and Roma

For many years, following the treaty of Lausanne, the indigenous Muslims in Thrace have been characterized as a "religious minority" and at the same time they are considered as a homogeneous community in terms of language and origin, a fact that is seen as specifying the group's cultural unity. Nevertheless, the minority is divided into three different ethno-linguistic groupings: the Muslim population of Turkish origin (to whom I mostly referred in the historical review above); the Pomaks, a Slavic group; and a third Roma group that is mostly referred to as the Muslim Gypsies. The formation of their diverse identities has not been without tensions and conflicts, especially for the Turks, part of whom (especially the educated elite) identify with the secularism of Kemalist Turkish politics. The question of whether the Muslim minority of Thrace should be viewed as a homogeneous religious community or as a set of diverse ethno-linguistic groups has been debated for many decades in Greece.[47]

The ethnic composition of the minority is one of the most extensively covered issues in Greek, but also Turkish and Bulgarian studies. It is also the most controversial topic within academic and political circles in Greece, at both a local and a national level. Thrace has often been described as a politically and

---

47 On the subject, see in particular the works of Christina Borou, "The Muslim Minority of Western Thrace in Greece: An Internal Positive or an Internal Negative Other?," *Journal of Muslim Minority Affairs* 29/1 (2009); Venetia Evergeti, "Boundary Formation and Identity Expression in Everyday Interactions: Muslim Minorities in Greece," in *Crossing European Boundaries: Beyond Conventional Geographical Boundaries*, ed. Jaro Stacul et al. (Oxford: Berghahn Books, 2006).

nationally sensitive area by both academics and politicians.[48] The presence of a Muslim minority close to the Turkish border has been seen as problematic and the two countries have striven to present it under two antithetical homogenizing titles: as "a unified Muslim minority" according to the Greek official discourse and as "one Turkish minority" according to the Turkish discourse.[49]

Political factors as well as issues related to language, ethnicity, and religious practice are all intertwined, making this a very complex situation. The ethnic Turks are the dominant group within the minority not only because of their number (56,000) but also because of the socio-historical and political developments in the area. The Pomaks (38,000) and the Roma (18,000) thus face the problem of being a minority within a minority. For the Pomaks, this problem became apparent during the Greek civil war when they were regarded as "the fifth column of Bulgaria and of Communism."[50] This image of them was probably wrong, as many Pomaks were persecuted by Bulgaria and supported the Greek annexation of Thrace.[51]

In general, the Pomak population is concentrated in the mountainous regions of Rodopi and Xanthi, while the Turks live in the plains, and the Romas mainly in villages around the urban centres. Most members of the Muslim minority are farmers, employed in agriculture (mainly tobacco) or raising livestock. Despite the fertile soil, the region remains one of the least developed in the EU. This underdevelopment has led to an "internal migration" towards the major cities of Athens and Thessaloniki, where the Muslims (mainly from the Pomak and Roma groups) find work as labourers, technicians, and street vendors.[52]

Recent ethnographic studies in Thrace have shown that there exists an inner hierarchy among the Muslim populations of the area. Those who claim to have a Turkish origin often look down on the other two groups and try to impose a unifying Turkish ethnic origin on the entire minority. The Pomaks come second. They are often seen as the most religious of the three groups and have a very traditional lifestyle. Ethnographic work has confirmed that religion is one of the most important elements in their self-definition and that, in

---

48   Borou, "The Muslim Minority of Western Thrace in Greece."

49   Evergeti, "Boundary Formation and Identity Expression in Everyday Interactions."

50   Ulf Brunnbauer, "The Perception of Muslims in Bulgaria and Greece: Between the 'Self' and the 'Other,'" *Journal of Muslim Minority Affairs* 21/1 (2001): 48.

51   Featherstone et al., *The Last Ottomans.*

52   On the internal migration of indigenous Muslims from Thrace to Athens see Venetia Evergeti and Panos Hatziprokopiou, Performing and Practicing Islam in the Orthodox City in Fouskas, T. and Tsevrenis, v. (eds.) *Contemporary Immigration in Greece: A Sourcebook.* (Athens: EPLO, 2015).

NATION-STATE, CITIZENSHIP AND BELONGING

the remote Pomak villages, their dress remains religious, with headscarves for young girls and women and the small white cap for boys and men.[53] The Roma come third in the "hierarchy" and are in many instances socially excluded from the other two groups.[54]

The origin of the Pomaks is obscure and has been interpreted differently by Bulgarian, Greek, and Turkish historians,[55] reflecting the fact that each country has tried to claim the "origin" of this Slavophone group. Anthropological research has shown that Pomak-ness is generally attributed to the Muslim populations of the Rodopi Mountains.[56] However, as Demetriou has argued "... it is the move out of the mountain and into the valley villages that caused Pomaks to become differentiated."[57] In other words, their difference gained historical and ethnic substance and became more apparent once they started moving away from their remote villages in the mountains of Rodopi and mixing with the Turkish part of the minority in the urban areas of Thrace. Some members of the minority's Turkish political elite have even accused the Greek state of trying to weaken the Turkish presence in the area of Thrace by dividing the minority into these three ethnic groupings and by "celebrating" the Pomaks' distinct culture and language. Pomak origin and language is often seen by leading members of the Turkish community as a sign of inferiority. Anthropological studies have shown that many Pomaks will subsequently try to diminish or deny their Pomak identity when interacting with Turkish members of the minority.[58] Their public denial is the result of years of ridicule that they have experienced, coming mainly from local Turkish urbanites.[59]

---

53   For detailed work on the Pomaks, see Sevasti Troubeta, *Constructing Identities for the Muslims of Thrace: The Example of Pomaks and Gypsies* (in Greek) (Athens: Kritiki, 2001). Also, for an anthropological exploration of the identity of the Pomaks, see Domna Michail, "From 'Locality' to 'European Identity': Shifting Identities among the Pomak Minority in Greece," *Ethnologia Balkanika* 7 (2003): 140–157.

54   See the work of Mavromatis for an in-depth exploration of the stigmatized identity of the Roma community in Thrace. Georgios Mavromatis, *The Children of Kalkantza: Education, Poverty and Social Exclusion in a Muslim Community of Thrace* (in Greek) (Athens: Metehmio, 2005).

55   On the different national(ist) views on the Pomaks' origin, see Tatjana Seyppel, "Pomaks in Northeastern Greece: An Endangered Balkan Population," *Journal of Muslim Minority Affairs* 10/1 (1989).

56   See in particular the work of Olga Demetriou, "Prioritizing Ethnicities: The Uncertainty of Pomak-ness in the Urban Greek Rhodope," *Ethnic and Racial Studies* 27/1 (2004) and Ioannis Fragopoulos, "Mosque, Square, Coffee-Shop: Social Mobility and Spatial Organization in a Mountainous Minority Community of Thrace," (in Greek) *Ethnologia* 13/5 (2007).

57   Demetriou, "Prioritizing Ethnicities," 104.

58   Michail, "From 'Locality' to 'European Identity.'"

59   Demetriou, "Prioritizing Ethnicities."

Ethnographic research indicates that Pomak identity is largely locally-specific and gains rigidity in social interactions with other members of the minority, thus resulting in boundary formations and constant negotiation of what comprises Pomak-ness.[60] This negotiation is in fact quite complex. For example, in their social encounters with urban Turks, many Pomaks define themselves as Turks instead of Pomaks;[61] on the other hand, anthropological studies of the Pomak mountainous villages[62] and recent studies on Pomaks who have migrated to Athens[63] show that when among themselves, Pomaks display their Pomak-ness openly. Although the whole of the minority is unified under the umbrella of Sunni Islam, studies focusing on religious trends in Thrace have shown that many Pomaks follow the Bektashi mystical order.[64] The secularist, Kemalist leanings of the Turkish state have not always sat well with Muslims (especially Pomaks) in Thrace, who tend to be conservative and traditional.[65]

Antoniou confirms that the three ethnic categories are not clearly defined. He points out that "most Pomaks and Roma usually view themselves as Turks and state that they belong to the Turkish ethnic group because, for these Pomaks and Roma, Turkish identity offers a higher social status."[66] He allows that this tendency may be partially driven by the minority education system, which prioritizes Turkish over Pomak. Michail makes a similar point about the Pomaks, suggesting that "their Muslim religion, their Slavic language, their socio-economic marginalization over a long period of time, and the fact that they have ethnically been claimed by three different countries, have created a rather movable situation and a flexible ethnicity, which adapts to a variety of inter-group interactions and corresponding changes in their environment."[67]

The Muslim Roma, also referred to as Gypsies or Athiganoi in academic and public discourse, are primarily a nomad group, moving from town to town depending on seasonal agricultural work in the fields. This being said, there are also permanent Roma settlements around the town of Komotini. Their inhabitants speak the Greek and Turkish languages together with their own dialect

---

60   Evergeti, "Boundary Formation and Identity Expression in Everyday Interactions."
61   Demetriou, "Prioritizing Ethnicities."
62   Michail, "From 'Locality' to 'European Identity'" and Fragopoulos, "Mosque, Square, Coffee Shop."
63   Evergeti and Hatziprokopiou, *Islam in Greece*.
64   For an exploration of Bektashism in Western Thrace, see Eustratios Zenginis, *Bektatism in Western Thrace: Contribution to the History of the Distribution of Islamism in the Greek Space* (Thessaloniki: IMXA, 1988).
65   Michail, "From 'Locality' to 'European Identity,'" 141.
66   Dimitris Anoniou, "Muslim Immigrants in Greece: Religious Organisation and Local Responses," *Immigrants and Minorities* 22/2–3 (2003): 155.
67   Michail "From 'Locality' to 'European Identity,'" 144.

of Romany. They are considered to be the least religious of the three groups of the minority and have been subjected to racial prejudice both from within the minority and from the wider Greek society. It was very rare for early research on Thracian Muslims to include a detailed study of the Roma group. This is because, in contrast to the Pomaks, there was very little national interest in superimposing an ethnic origin on the community of the Muslim Roma. Although there are no systematic surveys on discrimination, current research has revealed that due to prejudices and stereotypes, the Roma are one of the most marginalized and socially excluded groups in Greece.[68] This exclusion has created a culture of low educational achievement and of lifelong unemployment. In his study of Kalkantza, a small settlement of Roma people outside the town of Komotini, Mavromatis examined how the educational system reinforces the multiple layers of exclusion experienced by children and young people from the community.[69]

The Roma ethnic identity is very fluid. In an attempt to escape the negative stereotypes and social exclusion that it attracts, Roma display multiple or plural identities, often claiming an ethnic Turkish identity and/or a dominant Greek one depending on the social context. In comparison to the other two groups, their relationship with their religion is not strong. Recent research of Thracian Muslims in Athens has shown that, whereas Pomaks have strong community networks that are reinforced through their religious organization, Muslim Roma in Athens have little knowledge of their religion and very rarely practise it.[70]

7   Conclusion: Constructing Fluid Identities

In the above discussion I have tried to provide an insight into the socio-historical processes through which the Muslim minority was established in Thrace. Thus, the Muslim populations of Western Thrace became a minority due to the outcome of the First World War as well as the outcome of the Greek-Turkish war. Therefore, Greece's indigenous Muslims resided in the area of Thrace before the signing of treaties and agreements that granted them their minority status. Furthermore, their history is very much connected with the Ottoman Empire and in some respects with the outcome of that empire, which is what constitutes modern Turkey which makes the case of the Greek

---

68   Troubeta, *Constructing Identities for the Muslims of Thrace.*
69   Mavromatis, *The Children of Kalkantza.*
70   Evergeti and Hatziprokopiou, *Islam in Greece.*

indigenous Muslims quite unique in relation to both Muslim migrants in Greece and the other Muslim communities covered in this volume.

Quite often the issue of the position and the rights of the Muslim minority in Greece has been addressed in comparison to the Greek minority in Turkey. The reason for this is the condition of mutuality in the Treaty of Lausanne concerning the two minorities. It is quite interesting, however, that although many people, especially from the political and academic world in Greece, wish to deny the Turkish ethnic origin (an origin which is true for at least part of the minority) they still look at the issue through the lens of Greek-Turkish relationships. However, this denial is questionable, especially, if we take into account that the establishment of the Muslim minority in Greece owns its existence to the treaty of Lausanne; a treaty that was signed between the two countries and, as mentioned earlier, is the basis of mutuality for the respective minorities in the two countries.

Nevertheless, the point to be made here is not a "political" one on whether the Muslim minority in Thrace has, as Turkey claims, or has not, as Greece claims, a Turkish origin, but rather the recognition of the three distinct groupings within the Muslim minority and the way Muslim people in Thrace reflect and communicate not only the small but crucial differences between them but also the way they define themselves vis-à-vis the above political situation. In addition, the diachronically conceived range of cultural identities for each minority is more salient for a subtle and better-formed historical understanding. Exploring these relatively small but significant pockets of indigenous Muslim populations in the European periphery provides not only a clearer appreciation of the history of Islam in Europe, but also gives an important conceptual and political context within which to understand current developments of Muslim immigration and settlement in Europe.

CHAPTER 6

Perceptions of Mis/Recognition: The Experiences of Sunni Muslim Individuals in Dublin, Ireland

Des Delaney

Over the last twenty years, spurred on by the economic boom of the late 1990s and by economic globalization generally, the population demographic of Ireland has noticeably changed.[1] This process has moved the country from being a predominantly homogeneous society, dominated by a conservative Catholic ethos, to one of increasing plurality in terms of racial, religious and cultural heterogeneity.[2] An indication of this gradual transformation can be viewed in the increase of new religious and non-religious communities within the state.[3] This is exemplified by the growth of a diverse Islamic community, particularly in the capital city, Dublin.[4]

As the Muslim population has increased and its presence become more visible, a small cohort of academics in Ireland and abroad have acknowledged the importance of such social transformations and initiated research into the dynamics of Muslim communities in Ireland. Such studies have focused on a variety of topical issues such as Islamophobia; the position of Islamic education and finance; the experience of converts to Islam and the public image of the Islamic religion in Ireland.[5] As the other contributions to this anthology show, peripheral European countries like Ireland share commonalities such as a history of colonialism; having an initial status of immigration; the relatively

---

1   Throughout the rest of the chapter, the term "Ireland" refers not to the whole island of Ireland but only to the Republic.

2   Eoin O'Malley, *Contemporary Ireland* (Dublin: Palgrave MacMillan, 2011).

3   Olivia Cosgrove et al., *Ireland's New Religious Movements* (Newcastle: Cambridge Scholars Publishing, 2011).

4   Although Catholicism is still the religion of the majority, the 2011 census indicates that the Muslim population now officially stands at 49,204 or 1.1 percent of the total population. This is a 51.2 percent change since the previous census of 2006. See Central Statistics Office (CSO), *Profile 7: Religion, Ethnicity and Irish Travellers. National Census* (Dublin: Government of Ireland, Stationery Office, 2006). For an historical outline of the growth of the Muslim population in Ireland, see Kieran Flynn, "Understanding Islam in Ireland," *Islam and Christian-Muslim Relations* 17/2 (2006): 223–238.

5   Saleha S. Mahmood, "A Word about Ourselves," *Journal of Muslim Minority Affairs* 31/4 (2011): 467–468.

© KONINKLIJKE BRILL NV, LEIDEN, 2019 | DOI:10.1163/9789004404564_008

late immigration of Muslims; a mediatized environment about Muslim presence; and lastly, being positioned in a marginal research agenda within the wider European Muslim studies literature. With such macro-sociological characteristics held constant, this chapter aims to shed light on the everyday micro-sociological issues that impact Muslims lives in the Irish context. This chapter makes the argument that the majority of research so far conducted on Muslim communities in Ireland can be traced back to the primary ontological issue of recognition; yet to date, no study has formally attempted to apply and ground recognition dynamics in relation to a particular Muslim population in Ireland or Europe for that matter.[6] This work attempts to fill this gap but also to promote continued research on the lived experience of Muslim communities within nation states on the periphery of Europe.

The aim of this chapter is to gain a detailed understanding of how a selection of individuals (n = 25) belonging to the Sunni Muslim community in Dublin perceive how they are recognized or misrecognized in their everyday lives.[7] Utilizing Axel Honneth's theory of recognition and synthesising it with narrative empirical data, this work aims to explore if the interviewees perceive positive or negative forms of recognition within multiple spheres of social interaction i.e., within their family; their Muslim community; the legal sphere; and lastly, within the wider societal sphere. Such subjective narratives give a

---

6 By stating that recognition is an ontological concept, I am referring here to the argument emanating from Hegelian philosophy that recognition of either people; institutions; or states is fundamental to bringing these entities into "being." Laitinen clarifies the ontological relevance of recognition by stating that 'it might seem puzzling how recognition might play a role in the ontology of persons. But if we accept that human beings are *potential* persons when born, and acquiring the relevant capacities is dependent on recognition; or if we accept that being recognised is one constitutive aspect of being a person, [then] there is no puzzle.' See Arto Laitinen, "On the Scope of 'Recognition': The Role of Adequate Regard and Mutuality," in *Philosophy of Recognition: Historical and Contemporary Perspectives*, ed. Hans-Cristoph Schmidt am Busch and Christopher Zurn (Plymouth: Lexington Books, 2010), 319–342. For a deeper analysis on the ethical and ontological importance of recognition, see Heikki Ikäheimo and Arto Laitinen, ed., *Recognition and Social Ontology* (Leiden: Brill, 2011).

7 It is important to distinguish between cognition and mis/recognition. On one hand, cognition is an elementary form of visible identification of an object (whether that is a person; a group; institution; or a state). On the other hand, *an expressive act of recognition is an assessment of worth* that signals future action towards a particular object. Thus, an expressive act of misrecognition refers to an object, which, although visible, is ignored, overlooked, made socially invisible i.e., a misrecognised person is someone who perceives that they are not perceived by others as they feel they should or ought to be. Using the example of Ralph Ellison's novel *Invisible Man*, Honneth has clarified that "invisibility" represents the epistemology of recognition. See Axel Honneth, "Invisibility: On the Epistemology of Recognition," *Aristotelian Society* 75/1 (2006): 111–126.

rich and nuanced understanding of the everyday struggles that Muslim individuals' encounter within a small country located at the margins of Europe. After grounding and refining the research question theoretically, the narrative data analysis will be presented in two sections. Firstly, I will count and tabulate the interviewees' perceptions of recognition and misrecognition for each sphere, and then secondly, I will give a detailed narrative account of the perceptions solely related to misrecognition. Lastly, the conclusion will readdress the initial aims, summarise the main findings and identify potential directions for future research to explore.

1 The Struggle for Recognition

The theoretical frame to be employed is Axel Honneth's theory of recognition, which reconstructs Hegel's early Jena writings and builds upon Jürgen Habermas' theory of communicative action.[8] Honneth, who represents the third generation of the Frankfurt School tradition,[9] has developed a systematic typology that explains the development of a social struggle for recognition.[10] Honneth's theory is built on the main premise that the misrecognition of an individual's normative expectations creates negative moral feelings of injustice within the individual, which are then semantically shared with others enabling the formation of collective struggles of resistance to reclaim recognition. For Honneth, recognition from others is a pivotal intersubjective necessity because it is integral to identity formation and the ability to actualize individual freedom. The theoretical framework revolves around three spheres of recognition: (1) *love relations* between immediate family members, friends and erotic lovers, which equips individuals with emotional support and a basic level of self-confidence;

---

8   Jürgen Habermas, *The Theory of Communicative Action. Vol. 1 & 2* (Boston: Beacon Press, 1984 &1987).

9   Joel Anderson, "Situating Axel Honneth in the Frankfurt School Tradition," in *Axel Honneth: Critical Essays: With a Reply by Axel Honneth*, ed. Danielle Petherbridge (Leiden: Brill, 2011).

10   Axel Honneth, *The Struggle for Recognition: The Moral Grammar of Social Conflicts* (Polity Press, 1995). Importantly, Tariq Modood has advocated strongly for the recognition of ethno-religious hybridity that is a constitutive element of Islamic communities in Europe. See Tariq Modood, "Anti-Essentialism, Multiculturalism and the 'Recognition' of Religious Groups," *The Journal of Political Philosophy* 6/4 (1998): 378–399. In terms of specifically applying a recognition framework, Yer advocates that Honneth's theory can be developed to understand the recognition struggles of Muslim communities within European states. See Majid Yer, "Honneth and the Communitarians: Toward a Recognitive Critical Theory of Community," *Res Publica* 9/2 (2003): 101–125.

(2) *legal relations*, in which the state recognizes the individual as a morally responsible person and provides a person with self-respect; and (3) *societal relations*, in which people receive social esteem for their particular traits and abilities that contribute to the wider societal sphere. Consequently, as presented in Table 6.1, this theory is commonly associated with three modes or spheres of intersubjective bonding: love, respect and esteem. However, slight amendments and additions have been made to Honneth's modes of recognition. Firstly, in the love sphere, this study returns to Hegel's emphasis on the institution of the family. Furthermore, out of necessity, a community sphere has been added. This sphere is larger than the intimate sphere of familial relations but small enough to be differentiated from interactions within the wider societal arena.

TABLE 6.1   Honneth's recognition typology

Recognition theme	Love	Legal	Societal
Mode of recognition	Emotional support	Cognitive respect	Social esteem
Dimension of personality	Needs and emotions	Universal moral responsibility	Particular traits and abilities
Forms of recognition	Primary relationships (family; friends; lovers)	Legal relations (rights; obligations)	Societal relationship (solidarity; societal value and merit)
Relation-to-self	Basic self-confidence	Self-respect	Self-esteem
Forms of disrespect	Abuse and rape	Denial of rights; exclusion	Denigration; insult
Personality threat	Physical integrity	Social integrity	"Honour"; dignity
Public/private	Private	Public	Public
Social justice	Neediness/care	Equality	Achievement

SOURCE: AXEL HONNETH, *THE STRUGGLE FOR RECOGNITION* (CAMBRIDGE: POLITY PRESS, 1995), 129. THE LAST TWO ROWS OF THE TABLE ARE ADDITIONS MADE TO HONNETH'S ORIGINAL TABLE BY THE AUTHOR.

In practical terms, when an individual's normative expectations (of being justly treated in terms of emotional neediness, equality or achievement) are recognized and respected within a specific sphere, an individual's identity is confirmed and a positive relation-to-self i.e., a person's self-worth, is validated.[11] In contrast, Honneth defines misrecognition of an individual's normative expectations, through various forms of disrespect (whether that is by the disrespect of physical integrity through rape or abuse in the love sphere; or the disrespect of social integrity by the denial of rights or exclusion within the legal sphere or the disrespect of an individual's "honour" or dignity by denigration or insult within the more expansive societal sphere) as a personality threat that affects a person's individual relation-to-self i.e., a person's self-worth, that is reflected in a reduction or even eradication of self-confidence in the love sphere, self-respect within the legal sphere and self-esteem within the societal sphere.

It must be noted that for Honneth, negative recognition i.e., misrecognition, is important in that it enables an individual to realize, through a web of moral feelings, that their normative expectations of social justice have not been respected by others. Such feelings alert the individual to the importance of taking action (whether individually or collectively), commonly through a struggle for recognition to regain a positive relation-to-self and to affirm identities integral to being.

It is imperative now to correlate the theoretical framework with the aims of this particular inquiry. Overall, it can be concisely determined that Honneth's typology is primarily concerned with three elements. These are: (1) the nature or form that mis/recognition takes; (2) the moral feelings created by the experience of misrecognition; and lastly, (3) the action or struggle for recognition that individuals and/or collectives take part in. It must be stated that it is beyond the scope of this inquiry to apply Honneth's vast paradigmatic theory to its fullest extent. Instead, this paper will only try to elaborate element (1), which relates to the nature or form that mis/recognition takes. By isolating one particular aspect of the theoretical frame, the research question can be refined and demarcated into two distinct queries:

(a)　Do the interviewees perceive themselves to be either recognized or misrecognized within the different spheres of everyday life?

(b)　If misrecognition is perceived, how does such disrespect manifest itself within a particular sphere i.e., what is the nature or form of misrecognition?

11　For the link between recognition and social justice, see Axel Honneth, *The Pathologies of Individual Freedom* (Princeton: Princeton University Press, 2001).

2 Perceptions of Mis/Recognition

2.1 *Overview of the Narrative Data*

This section of the analysis will analyse query (a) by providing a count of the number of positive and negative perceptions of recognition for each sphere.[12] To compile Table 6.2 below, each interviewee was asked the question of interest, which specifically asked whether they perceived that their normative expectations of recognition were unfulfilled within the various spheres of everyday life. The narrative replies were then categorized into one of two codes: "Recognition Perceived" or "Misrecognition Perceived." The question of interest was worded as follows:

> There are three different types of recognition, which I would like your opinion on. The first is love recognition, which is given by your family or within your Muslim community; the second is legal recognition, which is given by the state, especially in terms of citizenship; and the third is societal recognition for who a person is, for their traits and abilities that they bring to society. Out of these types of recognition, in your opinion, which is unfulfilled?

As Table 6.2 concisely illustrates, a substantial majority of the interviewees perceived that their normative expectations of recognition are fulfilled within their familial unit, their Muslim community and within the legal sphere. Correspondingly for the same three spheres, perceptions of misrecognition are low. Overall, the most striking result relates to the broader societal sphere, in which people are esteemed – or not – for their traits and abilities that they contribute to society; in other words, that their particular "way of life" is

TABLE 6.2   Interviewees' perceptions per sphere of everyday life

Sphere of everyday life		Family	Community	Legal	Societal
Perception n = 25	Recognition perceived	84%	68%	80%	28%
	Misrecognition perceived	16%	32%	20%	72%

---

12   Each interview was conducted in Dublin, digitally recorded and transcribed verbatim by the author. The names of all interviewees have been anonymised and replaced with pseudonyms. In some instances, descriptive information that may identify participants has been either amended or deleted in order to secure anonymity.

PERCEPTIONS OF MIS/RECOGNITION   143

recognized as benefiting the value horizon of society. The results pertaining to
the last sphere are in opposition to the first three spheres in that 72 percent of
interviewees' vocalized narratives that their normative expectations of recognition went unfulfilled within the broader societal sphere. Let us now move to
a more detailed examination of the narrative data relating to the four recognitive spheres of interest.

2.2   *Family Misrecognition*

First, it must be stated that the majority of the interviewees vocalized positive
perceptions of recognition in relation to the familial sphere. Notably, 84 percent of the interviewees perceived recognition to be fulfilled whilst 16 percent
perceived misrecognition within their familial sphere. For example, a first-
generation Muslim,[13] Nabeel, discussed the generational tensions that exist
by articulating that the relationship between "the father and the son."[14] For
this interviewee intra-familial recognition is important. It is the "top recognition" that is an ideal to be strived for or as he states "that we have to dream of,
you see ... but still we are well away [from it]."[15] The next three interviewees
give examples of various subtle forms of familial disrespect that are related to
generational tensions. Kaleem, a convert, discussed the negative impact that
his abusive father had on him as a child and in later life.

> After living my life here [in Dublin], you know, I probably had an average
> of upbringing, you know, my father drank a little too much and then he
> really drank [low tone] and uh, because of that I think we all suffered,
> you know, from an early, from the earliest memories I have, yeah I've got
> memories of my father, you know, really good memories, we used to go to

---

13   In this study, the first generation is defined as Muslims who are aged over 37 years.
      The majority are immigrants who were born and raised outside Ireland. This category
      also includes converts to Islam. The second generation is defined as Muslims, aged
      between 18 and 36, who were either born in Ireland or were born in a foreign country
      and have grown up within and spent the majority of their lives in Ireland. The author
      acknowledges that it is hard to define with precision the age requirements that constitute
      the first and second generations. This study has followed the sampling formula set out
      by Pędziwiatr, who, in his sociological study of young Muslim elites in Europe, defined
      his second generation interviewees as 'men and women who described themselves as
      Muslims, had lived their formative years in Europe and were between 18 to 36 years old.'
      See Konrad Pędziwiatr, *The New Muslim Elites in European Cities: Religion and Active Social
      Citizenship amongst Young Organized Muslims in Brussels and London* (Germany: VDM
      Verlag, 2010), 128–129.
14   Nabeel (First Gen, Male, Denizen), March 13, 2012.
15   Nabeel.

[the] Phoenix Park, we used to take a bunch of kids from the area out to Portmarnock, yeah. All these memories, you know, lovely ones, go shopping with them or whatever but as soon as I came to my understanding, 8, 9, 10 years of age, I realized that when he came back from being out late he was different, you know, not good, yeah, silly with drink, and uh, [there was an] amount of trouble in my house in my teenage years.[16]

To remedy the experience of suffering familial misrecognition and to find his true identity the interviewee established a stable form of recognition to God and a strong identity in the Islamic religion. He states emphatically about his conversion: "I actually really did find out who I was."[17] In other words, he came to a self-realization about himself by developing an abstract spiritual recognition to God, or as he terms it, when he became "a servant of God."[18]

The next two respondents belong to the younger generation and both describe the tensions that they perceive exist between the first and second generations within their families. First Isra, a young female denizen[19] with a strong Islamic identity, expresses her general opinion about the experience of young Muslim women who take off their hijabs to socialize with friends within Dublin city's renowned nightlife. She states that "they know that they are Muslim, and they know that they believe [in the Islamic religion] but at the same time again, they are also trying to integrate [into] the society as well."[20] This statement expresses the unique experience of young Muslim women who are caught in a recognition dilemma between two love relationships – the need to be recognized by their friends and by their immediate families who adhere to and recognize Islamic religious traditions and practices i.e., a social unit in which God is recognized through particular behaviour. It becomes apparent through the narratives that Muslim youth in Ireland are struggling to create a balance between recognition spheres in order to maintain respectful relationships to others while also continuing to develop and realize their own individual identities. This dilemma is reiterated by Isra, when she reflects on her own experience:

---

16   Kaleem, (First Gen, Male, Citizen), December 17, 2011.

17   Kaleem.

18   Kaleem.

19   Thomas Hammer categorized resident third-country nationals who enjoy civic and social rights yet limited political rights within a host country as a new form of social status known as "denizenship." See Thomas Hammer, *Democracy and the Nation State: Aliens, Denizens and Citizens in a World of International Migration* (Aldershot: Ashgate, 1990).

20   Isra (Second Gen, Female, Denizen), November 29, 2011.

PERCEPTIONS OF MIS/RECOGNITION

For example, if my family see me not wearing a scarf and going around and wearing trousers it will cost me problem because I can lose the relation [between] myself and my family because of my dress and all that and again when I see in my friend[s], they all dress and they look nice. I like the fashion, the way they are. I will try to be like the way they are and then again, at the same time, I have to hide it. So, it's really a big problem between the family [and] the new generation [of young Muslims].[21]

Similarly, Azad expresses the generational difficulties that he has experienced within his familial environment. He perceives himself to be different from others in his family: "[I] kinda find sometimes I live in my own other world compared to what folks at home are living in."[22] This disconnection is not of a physical nature but is one of ideas and perceptions that relate directly to conceptions of identity. Like many young European Muslims, Azad conceives of his form of Islam as universal. In other words, it is an Islam that aims to return to the meaning of the Islamic sources – to the Qur'an and the Sunna; an Islam that is not influenced or tainted by particularistic ethno-cultural or nationalistic identities; an Islam that has a strong civic component that is legitimized by the past actions of the Prophet Muhammad during his exile in the multicultural city of Medina.[23] On the other hand, Azad's family elders, who are immigrants to Europe, are viewed in a negative light in that they have a cultural form of Islam in which home-country ethnic traditions have merged with and impact how they practise their Islam in everyday life. The interviewee expresses this disconnection as follows:

You see like I have parents, and uncles, the older guys but the way they kinda view things is quite very different to the way I see them. So, in a way, like kinda sometimes I feel like I'm just living my own [way]...in terms of ideas, or when it comes to ideas or some things, I just find myself, way, a bit out from m[y relations], their own way of thinking...so, it's a bit different because at the same time you don't want to draw yourself into these

---

21   Isra.

22   Azad (Second Gen, Male, Citizen), November 23, 2011.

23   There has been a growing interest in how the second generation Muslim youth in Europe are negotiating identity issues. See Tariq Ramadan, *To Be a European Muslim* (Leicester: Islamic Foundation, 1999); and also Karen Phalet et al., "Ways of 'Being Muslim,'" in *The European Second Generation Compared: Does the Integration Context Matter?*, ed. Maurice Crul et al. (Amsterdam: Amsterdam University Press, 2012).

conflicts so you can keep quiet on certain aspects even if you don't agree with what they say or what they do.[24]

With the above examples in mind, it becomes apparent that when we speak of disrespect within the immediate familial structure the negative recognition spoken of is not a reduction in or a loss of familial love as such; instead as Paul Ricoeur has stated, such misrecognition is related to a lack of approbation i.e., approval.[25] Taken from this vantage point, it can be inferred that the tension that exists between the generations within the Muslim family (and every family for that matter) is related to the recognitive granting (or not) of approval for established and newly evolving conceptions of identity.

2.3   Community Misrecognition

It must be acknowledged that a majority of interviewees – 68 percent – perceived internal community recognition to be fulfilled. On the other hand, 32 percent perceived recognition within their Muslim community to be unfulfilled. These narratives covered a variety of personal experiences, such as the negative impact related to generational tensions within the Muslim community, a lack of community leadership and representation, a lack of support for women's civic action within the community, and lastly, a lack of acceptance towards and support for converts to Islam. Two young interviewees, Isra and Azad, commented that the generational tensions that impact the familial sphere also permeate internal relations within their Muslim community. Isra discusses forms of community rejection experienced by other young Muslim women, like herself, who want to participate in communal social activities, such as sports and the arts, but are prohibited by familial and community norms in which such acts when conducted by females are viewed as a form of spiritual misrecognition. She states that

> a lot of young people they really want to get involved but again, and let's say [for example], we did an acting class within groups and there was some young Muslim girls who was taking part and then, you know, they were told that they cannot do it because of the religion and stuff like that... it's a problem, it's really [a] problem. A lot of young Muslim

---

24   Azad.

25   Ricoeur defined approbation as 'to mutually approve each other's existence.' Paul Ricoeur, *The Course of Recognition*, trans. David Pellauer (Cambridge: Harvard University Press, 2005), 188–196.

women they want to take part [in] football and stuff like that [sport] but they were rejected because of the community, because of their family and they were told 'ah um, you cannot do this because of this way and this way' and again sometimes it's actually for, as we say [the] new generation citizen, their brain can actually think that the family are forcing [them] to have this religion and they're thinking 'oh, I don't really know what religion I have now because if I'm a Muslim I was told I cannot do this, I cannot do that, I cannot and I don't know what to do,' that's why you see some people they don't really care about the family, they just go and do their own thing.[26]

Azad also vocalizes how generational differences permeate community relations. His opinion is that young Muslims are "frustrated" and "lack somebody to look up to."[27] This interviewee has negative feelings towards the home-country mentality of the first generation and how such traditional acts of recognition isolate Muslim youth who are growing up with a different mentality in a different context i.e., within the European environment.

So in a sense, if you go to the mosque ... you'll find most of the time the old people will be there, and not so much of the young people and part of it is maybe language barriers as well because the old folks they speak maybe Arabic of which the [young] guys here, they don't and if they're to have, let's say, lecturers or something [are invited] from there [outside Ireland], and all be towards, give towards Arabic kinda thing of which the young guys kinda feel left out. So you can't really do much of the things. So in a sense, the issues they face, we face most of the time, it's, it's alot of issues but the main one, is to be like, being left out, like not being part of the whole, [the] whole process because of the old guys, the old guys with their own mentality and then the young guys coming up kinda caught in the mix.[28]

In terms of a lack of leadership and representation, three interviewees mention how they felt inappropriately represented by one of the largest mosque organizations in Ireland. Such representational misrecognition has also been identified by Adil Khan, who researched the disconnection between the large mosque

---

26 Isra.
27 Azad.
28 Azad.

organizations and the grassroots of the community.[29] In parallel with practical recognitive disagreements related to better media representation and which language should be used in mosques, two interviewees perceive that they are not recognized by the mosque leaders due to differences related to ideological positioning.[30] Both of these interviewees criticize the main mosques in Dublin as promoting an Islamist interpretation of Islam, which does not leave room for opposing interpretations from other members within the diverse Muslim community. Another interviewee – Akhtar – perceives that he is not represented by the leaders of the Sunni Muslim community in Dublin. In addition to viewing the main mosque establishments as undemocratic and not representative of the grassroots, he is highly critical of the presiding Imams, who have a low proficiency in the English language. Akhtar states his concerns as follows:

> Within the community, yes, the people who are representing us, they're not elected. They are [representing], for some reason, because they speak louder, or because they've got more money or because they've got ... They can quote you this *fiqh* and that rule, Islamic rule – they are deemed to be leaders and they may not be really representative. They just might be proactive and for that reason they might be considered as leaders. They're really not representative.[31]

Female interviewees Dahlia and Safeerah continue the criticism but focus specifically on community support. Both interviewees express, as members of a female Islamic civic group, their struggle to gain support for charitable work conducted in their local district. As Safeerah states, the group's struggle for the recognition of Islam's civic and contributory potential, resulted in "fighting both"[32] i.e., the generalized perceptions that exist broadly within the expanse of Irish society but also within their Islamic community.

The last example of community misrecognition comes from a recent convert to the Islamic religion. Adam narrates his personal struggle to be recognised – "for who he is" – within his newly adopted religious community. Gaining recognition does not come easily for the interviewee but is a struggle in which personal communication is a tool that is utilized to obtain trust, acceptance

---

29   Adil H. Khan, "Transnational Influences on Irish Muslim Networks: From Local to Global Perspectives," *Journal of Muslim Minority Affairs* 31/4 (2011): 486–502.

30   Sayyid (First Gen, Male, Dual Citizen), October 17, 2011 and Adeeb (First Gen, Male, Citizen), October 27, 2011.

31   Akhtar (First Gen, Male, Denizen), October 10, 2011.

32   Safeerah (First Gen, Female, Dual Citizen) and Dahlia (First Gen, Female, Citizen), December 1, 2011.

PERCEPTIONS OF MIS/RECOGNITION   149

and a deeper level of respect from others in the community. For this interviewee, levels of support for new converts to the Islamic religion could be constructively improved by the Muslim community itself. This experience is narrated as follows:

> As a new Muslim especially, you know, I would give '*al-salāmu 'alaykum*' to almost any Muslim I see and 9 out of 10 of them would ignore me. Even if I'm dressed in a long shirt, you know, I'm obviously Muslim from how I dress today, you know, and they will ignore you. I think, I think we need to build on that within the community ... in the Muslim community yeah there's a little bit of a struggle for recognition, you know (low tone). It takes me an hour to get in there [to the mosque], so I'm not in the mosque at the time [I should be], you know, so there is that sense of like wariness and like 'oh, who's he?' and stuff like that but you know, you have to fight for it, to gain recognition you just say 'hello, my name is X,' you know.[33]

By looking back through the narrative data of perceived disrespect within the community sphere, two general themes emerge – a lack of representation and a lack of community support.

2.4   *Legal Misrecognition*

A large majority of interviewees – 80 percent – perceived legal recognition to be fulfilled. In contrast to this majority, 20 percent vocalized a negative perception of legal recognition. These perceptions varied from statements about the denizen experience to a citizen perceiving herself to be unequal to others due to her "foreign" traits and, finally, to opinions that the Irish Constitution and its respective laws should reflect a deeper respect for the Islamic religion and basic human rights generally.

The experience of denizens is important within this section because they do not have full legal recognition, which may limit the length of their residency and impedes their level of political participation.[34] It is therefore interesting to view how this group perceives legal recognition, particularly in terms of civic status. In total, six denizens were interviewed yet only one denizen and one citizen mention negative experiences of recognition associated with the status of denizenship. A citizen, Nurdeen, highlights the difference that separates a

---

33   Adam (Second Gen, Male, Citizen), December 10, 2011.
34   For a further discussion about "denizenship" status, see Ludvig Beckman, *The Frontiers of Democracy: The Right to Vote and its Limits* (New York: Palgrave MacMillan, 2009).

citizen from a denizen. He states concisely that "in terms of legal recognition, if you're an Irish citizen you can't be kicked out of the country."[35] Through first-hand experience of denizenship, Aziz, a second-generation Muslim, outlines his difficulties and highlights the struggles encountered by his parents in obtaining Irish citizenship.

> In terms of legal recognition, I have been here for 10 years and I still have not gotten citizenship. My flatmate [who is also Muslim] and his whole family have been here for 11 years, and they have the same problems as us [in obtaining citizenship]. The thing is you can't follow up on the application, which is annoying.
>
> Researcher: Why do you think you've had to wait this long to receive citizenship?
>
> I've no idea, [I] can't follow up on it. I really have no idea.
>
> Researcher: Do you feel that you want to have Irish citizenship?
>
> Yes, it makes things a lot easier. For example, when going through security at airports and when I travel I have to sort out a visa, which is a hassle. I also have to pay €10,000 in university fees each year and my brother is coming through to university now and he will have to pay the same, which is a big burden on my parents.[36]

While it was assumed that denizens would vocalize experiences of legal disrespect more often than citizens, the narratives do not verify this presumption. In actuality, more citizens – four in total – expressed perceptions of legal misrecognition. This is exemplified by Furat, a young female Muslim who shares dual citizenship with the Republic of Ireland and a Middle Eastern country. She feels that her ethnic and religious traits – her "foreignness" – negatively impact how she perceives her legal and civic equality to others in Irish society. In the following statement, she expresses her fear that her particular difference from the identity standard or norm of "Irishness" causes her to rethink how she acts as a universal citizen of Ireland.

> Legal recognition … myself, personal opinion, is that you always have to think twice about what you are doing legally because you always feel like as if because I'm a foreigner how will they treat me, you know, so say, say for example, I was in a situation where somebody else was in the wrong but I'd be, I'd feel like I wouldn't be able to bring [it] up because it's not

---

35   Nurdeen (Second Gen, Male, Citizen), December 5, 2011.
36   Aziz (Second Gen, Male, Denizen), November 2, 2011.

going to be dealt with that way, that person's the Irish person, I'm the Muslim, you know, the foreigner. Uhhmm, which side will they take, so you kind of, you'll always have that fear, the constant background fear of 'is there a point or is there not a point [to speaking out].'[37]

Interviewees Firaq and Kaleem perceive legal misrecognition to be correlated with a lack of protective guarantees within Irish law and by how the law is enforced in practice by the national security services. They both stress the need for the Irish Constitution and its respective legal system to engender respect for all people within the state and to be cognizant of the claims of minorities. They call for Irish law to respect religion and human rights. Firaq makes the point of how acknowledgement of and respect for Islamic holidays remains absent within the Irish Constitution and its respective laws. He states in relation to Islamic holidays that "it's very difficult to deal with them [because they] are not recognized in any constitution or law."[38] He continues by stating that respect for all people should be an essential element of Irish jurisprudence. In his opinion, recognition should be regulated by the overarching neutral framework of the law. On this point, Firaq remarks that:

> It [respect] should be ingrained into the law that you must respect others. You know, not specifically, I don't think it should specifically mention the Muslims or Catholics or whatever. In general, these are human, basic human rights that they should be provided.[39]

The same interviewee also expressed a highly critical opinion of the work undertaken by the national security services. While understanding the reason and need for such work i.e., investigating people suspected of being involved in terrorist activities or criminal offenses, he vocalizes concern about the way in which such investigations are conducted and criticizes the detrimental impact such actions have on a suspect's immediate family.[40]

> I think the way they [the security services] deal with it [the security issue], they deal with them [the alleged suspects] as if they were in a third world country. Um, with quite a disrespect to many of the laws here

---

37 Furat (Second Gen, Female, Dual Citizen), November 21, 2011.
38 Firaq (First Gen, Male, Dual Citizen), October 19, 2011.
39 Firaq.
40 To understand the construction of Muslim individuals as "suspect", see Mary J. Hickman et al., *'Suspect Communities'? Counter-Terrorism Policy, the Press, and the Impact on Irish and Muslim Communities in Britain* (London: London Metropolitan University, 2011).

[in Ireland] of freedom. They use threatening tones. They, possibly, even physically threaten these people. They [the security services] ... of what I hear, they actually arrive unannounced, late at night, they conduct raids and these people would have families and children who would suffer, and you know, [it] would be very unfair for a little girl to see her dad being shoved down on the ground and treated, mistreated! When really there is nothing [no evidence]. Um, you know ... even if you need somebody it could be done in a different way, uh, in a more civilized way. You can take them, arrest them, deal with them – not in front of their families.[41]

The forms of legal disrespect expressed by the interviewees can be thematically generalized as a lack of protection. This is exemplified by denizen fears about residential insecurity within the Irish state: a fear of voicing civic concerns due to the feeling of being viewed as "foreign" and the perception that the law and its enforcers do not protect Muslim individuals in a respectful manner. Furthermore, by focusing on legal misrecognition, it is possible to identify an overlap that exists between different spheres of recognition. In other words, that legal misrecognition has ramifications in other recognitive spheres that together comprise everyday life. For example, two interviewees claim that legal misrecognition through limited citizenship status negatively impacts an individual's familial life. Also, a female citizen expressed how she felt her equal citizenship status was impeded by the perception of her personal traits as being different from or "foreign" to what is viewed as the dominant "Irish" identity standard. Furthermore, two interviewees linked legal misrecognition back to the familial sphere by emphasizing how legally legitimated security measures can have a negative impact upon a suspect's familial environment.

2.5 Societal Misrecognition

The wider societal sphere is the form of intersubjective bond in which a minority (28 percent) of interviewees perceive recognition to be fulfilled whilst a 72 percent majority perceive societal recognition to be unfulfilled.[42] In line with Honneth's theory, which emphasizes societal respect as related to the recognition of an individual's traits and abilities that contribute to society, many

---

41   Firaq; Kaleem makes a similar criticism based on first-hand experience.

42   Certainly, such perceptions of misrecognition are not exclusive to individuals within the Muslim community. For example, the Travelling community in Ireland also suffers forms of wider societal disrespect. See Jane Helleiner, *Irish Travellers: Racism and the Politics of Culture* (Toronto: University of Toronto Press, 2000). See also Robert McVeigh, "'Ethnicity Denial' and Racism: The Case of the Government of Ireland Against Irish Travellers," *Translocations* 2/1 (2007): 90–133.

PERCEPTIONS OF MIS/RECOGNITION

interviewees referenced various forms of societal misrecognition related to local community relations, discrimination within the public sphere and general misconceptions about the Islamic religion and its adherents within Irish society.

There were numerous direct statements emphasizing societal misrecognition as an issue of concern. Three interviewees stated the following in this regard: "the society one of course";[43] "in terms of societal recognition, I think there's a lot of work to be done";[44] "Yes, there is a concern – I would put this definitely, there is a concern."[45] Akhtar defined his concern as "a question of acceptability, whether by the wider society or the media," which he determines will have an impact on future generations. From his standpoint, it is a question of whether the wider Irish society and media representations "accept them [the Muslim youth] for the way they are or cast them aside as foreigners, as children of foreigners."[46] The importance of societal recognition as compared to legal forms was stressed highly by Adeeb, who stated that the most important issue facing the Muslim community "is [their] identity [and it is] very important that any recognition, not recognition such [as] an official [legal] recognition – only as on paper – but recognition as part of the society, part of the whole community."[47] However, the narrative responses gathered suggest that being "Othered" by Irish society generally is a strong perception amongst the interviewees, regardless of generational, gender or citizenship attributes.[48] This is exemplified by a concise statement made by Ayyub, who has the perception that he does "not remotely"[49] have societal recognition but rather he feels that what he receives from Irish society is "at the best of times, probably pity" for being "who he is."[50]

---

43   Safeerah.

44   Daleela (Second Gen, Female, Citizen), November 16, 2011.

45   Akhtar.

46   Akhtar.

47   Adeeb (First Gen, Male, Citizen), October 27, 2011.

48   The concept of being "Othered" or "Othering" has been defined by various academics from many different intellectual traditions. The following is a comprehensive definition, stated by Jensen, who defines "Othering" as 'discursive processes by which powerful groups, who may or may not make up a numerical majority, define subordinate groups into existence in a reductionist way, which ascribe problematic and/or inferior characteristics to these subordinate groups. Such discursive processes affirm the legitimacy and superiority of the powerful and condition identity formation among the subordinate.' Sune Qvotrup Jensen, "Othering, Identity Formation and Agency," *Qualitative Studies* 2/2 (2011): 63–78.

49   Ayyub (Second Gen, Male, Citizen), October 23, 2011.

50   Ayyub.

Three of the interviewees, who are of the first generation, reference a lack of societal recognition in terms of relations with their non-Muslim neighbours. These interviewees perceive that they are not accepted in full for "who they are," for their traits and abilities, by the people they live beside. Hakim suggests that while "societal recognition from the local community is not forthcoming … [it] will come with time."[51] Other perceptions are more pessimistic. Akhtar, whose family has experienced discrimination, feels "a sense of rejection"[52] from his own neighbours. He mentions that his young daughter has asked questions about the relationship that exists with the neighbours: "why don't they like us next door, why do they call us 'Pakis,' why are they rude to us?"[53] Another interviewee views such discriminatory acts as likely to increase the larger the Muslim population grows within the Irish state. He states:

> as the population increases, recognition by neighbours, recognition is not there in the sense that they are now beginning to view [Muslims] not as students anymore but [as] that somebody who has come to take their job away.[54]

Of the 72 percent who perceived societal misrecognition, just over half gave direct expressions of discrimination that they experienced or of discrimination that they are aware of around them.[55] References were made to various forms of discrimination engaged in by neighbours,[56] by people in the street,[57] towards Muslim women wearing the hijab,[58] within the medical profession,[59] and even familial disapproval towards a family member who converted to the Islamic religion. As Akhtar states about the experience of women, who have converted to the Islamic faith:

> Irish women born and raised here who embrace Islam, if [they] decide to wear the scarf, or dress like [a] Muslim they will be cast aside or they will

---

51   Hakim (First Gen, Male, Citizen), October 17, 2011.

52   Akhtar.

53   Akhtar.

54   Yaseen (First Gen, Male, Citizen), October 26, 2011.

55   Some interviewees did not voice their personal subjective experiences but instead vocalised narratives of societal misrecognition that had been experienced by people within their love sphere i.e., family members or friends.

56   Akhtar; Hakim; Yaseen.

57   Furat; Aamil (Second Gen, Male, Citizen), November 18, 2011.

58   Akhtar; Daleela; Furat; Mazhab (First Gen, Male, Citizen), October 18, 2011.

59   Yaseen.

be considered as foreigners even though they might have an Irish accent, an Irish [ethnic] heritage, 100%. So, they become foreigners in their own country and that is prevalent, that is definitely prevalent in Irish society, unfortunately.[60]

However, such discriminatory practices can be complex and hard to define by the victim leading to doubts about the motivation behind such acts i.e., is the discriminatory act stimulated by Islamophobic, racial, ethnic, cultural, or gender intolerance – or by a combination of these.[61] In relation to this doubt, Daleela states that "you can never know why you didn't get the job, it could be you [a lack of merit or ability required to obtain a job position] or it could be the first impression they are going to get of your culture or [religion]."[62]

A recurring theme that emanates from all the interviews is the persistent struggle against stereotypes and misconceptions. Such narratives revolve around the role of media representations in perpetuating a negative image of Islam and are viewed as having a detrimental impact on Muslims within Irish society. Safeerah expresses her viewpoint that the media is consistently "speaking something bad about Muslims, it's very rarely that they [the media] speak good about us."[63] In terms of action, three interviewees – Ayyub, Furat and Nazir – emphasized that a way to counteract such stereotypes and misconceptions is through intersubjective communication with others. For example, interviewee Nazir states the following experience:

Some people thinking that maybe [Muslim] people are going to the mosque, they are learning how to kill non-Muslim and most of the people are thinking about it – 'what are they doing in this mosque?' I saw one [person], he was angry and he asked me 'what are they doing there, learning something?' [I said to him] 'No, that is not [what you

---

60   Akhtar.
61   For many of the interviewees, Islamophobia exists in the Irish Republic and is an issue of concern. To understand the need to recognize the "new reality" of Islamophobia, see Chris Allen, *Islamophobia* (Farnham: Ashgate, 2010).
62   Daleela.
63   Safeerah. Within the interviews, criticisms related to negative media portrayals of Muslims and Islam within Irish and international media were prominent. Notably, academic research on this topic is extensive. See Elisabeth Poole and John E. Richardson, ed., *Muslims and the News Media* (London: I.B Tauris, 2006). Jack G. Shaheen, *Reel Bad Arabs: How Hollywood Vilifies a People* (Northampton: Olive Brach Press, 2009). See also Kim Knott et al., *Media Portrayals of Religion and the Secular Sacred* (Farnham: Ashgate, 2013).

think], this is ... religion, it is a way of life, [it's] how we live, so this is not [what you think]'.[64]

Nabeel highlights the mutual responsibility of both individuals within Irish society and within the Muslim community, particularly the younger second generation, to develop a better understanding and recognition of the true picture of the Islamic religion by emphasizing the role that personal intersubjective communication and learning processes will play in the future:

> It will be from the other side [the wider Irish society] also to understand but that will come [with] the more understanding of Islam because our understanding of Islam, in general, is what the media is talking about the problems, sometimes Muslims here [in Ireland] or there [outside Ireland], have and show the, unfortunately, ugly picture of Islam or [not] any true picture of Islam but I believe that it [the ugly picture of Islam] will be changed [by] these things, especially with the coming generation.[65]

The many forms of societal disrespect expressed by the interviewees may be thematically generalized as related to a lack of acceptance and understanding. This is exemplified by the numerous accounts of societal misconceptions about the Islamic religion and of discrimination that Muslims encounter in their everyday lives. This lack of understanding within Irish society ensures that Muslims are not recognized for "who they are" within their own society – for their traits and abilities that they bring and that contribute to the value horizon of society as a whole. To counteract this, some of the Muslim interviewees express the view that one-to-one personal communication is the tool through which they can defend "who they are" and correct any misunderstandings and misconceptions. Consistently throughout many of the interviews, the role of the media is referenced as the main medium that maintains and propagates the negative image of Muslims and their religion thereby influencing non-Muslim individuals within Irish society to misrecognise Islam and its adherents. Furthermore, a link and overlap between spheres of recognition is present. Such forms of societal misrecognition such as discrimination, which is legitimized and reinforced by negative media portrayals, can detrimentally impact a person's individual relation-to-self, family, or local community, resulting in significant emotional and psychological distress.

---

64   Nazir (First Gen, Male, Dual Citizen), October 21, 2011.
65   Nabeel.

3   A Facilitating Environment as an Ethical Goal

With macro-sociological commonalities shared by peripheral countries held constant, this chapter provides a *space* for Sunni Muslim individuals living in Dublin to vocalize their subjective micro-sociological experiences of misrecognition within four spheres of everyday life. Thus, this research provides a grounded insight into the perceptions of an understudied religious minority living at the margins of Europe.

In terms of empirical findings, the research shows that family, community and legal recognition are perceived by the majority of interviewees as being fulfilled; however, a minority of interviewees perceive the opposite i.e., that recognition within these three spheres remains unfulfilled and that subtle pathologies of disrespect continue. These forms of misrecognition were generally categorized as being related to a lack of identity approval within the familial sphere; a lack of leadership and support within the community sphere; and a lack of protection within the legal sphere. Despite macro-sociological characteristics shared by peripheral countries that have the potential to foster and enhance more favourable societal recognition and intercultural integration of Muslims in Ireland, such as a history of colonialism, having an initial status of immigration, the relatively late immigration of Muslims, the most illuminating result showed that the wider societal sphere of everyday life is the intersubjective arena that is perceived by a large majority of interviewees as being recognitively unfulfilled. In terms of the nature of such disrespect, the research exposed perceptions of societal discrimination encountered by Muslims in their everyday lives – from neighbours or the local community, in the workplace or on the public street. These forms of disrespect were generally categorized as being related to a lack of understanding about Muslims and Islam. The analysis also verifies how a significant majority of the interviewees view the media as causally linked to the distortion of Muslim identity within Irish society. Overall, it can be stated that the majority of Sunni Muslims interviewed perceive and feel that they are not recognized fully for "who they are" within the wider Irish social sphere.

In terms of the implications for the theory of recognition, this chapter attempted to show the link and overlap between recognition spheres i.e., that disrespect within one sphere may have a negative impact on other spheres of everyday life. Although this argument was tentative, it may prove to be an arena for further empirical investigation. While this research focused on the level and nature of recognition, through a numerical and narrative analysis, future research should aim to understand how recognitive experiences affect an individual's relation-to-self and how negative emotional feelings create action with moral and transformative intent.

To conclude, an important question must be asked: how can forms of disrespect within various spheres of everyday life be reduced? Social-critical theorists have attempted to answer this question by stressing the importance of mutual intersubjective relationships. Similarly, the last quotation in this chapter, by Nabeel, reiterates this crucial point by determining that it will be up to individuals both within the wider Irish society and within various Muslim communities to develop a shared sense of mutual responsibility towards each other in order to come to a better understanding and recognition of each other.

To accomplish this, intersubjective communication is vital, yet its volatility and unpredictability will inevitably lead to further struggles for recognition. What is important, however, is whether struggles for recognition within all interactive spheres will be given a degree of respect leading to tolerant consideration. If this *ethical* stance is adopted and people begin to learn about themselves by recognizing the normative expectations of others, social justice within each sphere of everyday life will have found firmer ground to take root and grow. Such reflection will give a higher degree of freedom to individuals to self-realize "who they are" within their own lived experience that is interwoven with and traverses a variety of complex intersubjective spheres on a daily basis. In Honneth's opinion, ongoing recognition struggles towards an ethical life will expand the realms of social justice and open up *a space for all* to obtain a higher degree of individual autonomy.[66] The creation of such a *facilitating environment* opens up the potentiality for individuals to self-realize the complex dynamics of their own identities and to tolerate the identities of others.

Acknowledgements

This chapter is dedicated to the memory of my father, PJ Delaney, as well as to my children, Daniel and Phoebe.

---

66   Honneth, *The Struggle for Recognition,* 171–179.

PART 3

Public Debates and (In)Visibility

∴

CHAPTER 7

Explaining the Absence of a Veil Debate: The Mediating Role of Ethno-nationalism and Public Religion in the Irish Context

Stacey Scriver

This chapter assesses public discourse in relation to the Islamic veil debate in Ireland. In particular it questions why the Islamic veil did not emerge as a serious point of contention or an issue requiring legislative action, as it did in other European states including the UK and France. Using opinion pieces and readers' letters, the chapter assesses the confluence of Irish perceptions of gender roles, religious expression and national identity to deepen understanding of reactions (or lack thereof) to the Islamic veil. Such an approach permits consideration of the ways in which factors such as gender norms, ethno-nationalism and the historical context of public religion may at once moderate attitudes towards the wearing of the veil while also intensifying exclusionary attitudes and practices. This chapter thus uses the particular case of Ireland – a small, post-colonial state on the geographical margins of Europe with a very small Muslim population (1%) – to better understand the emergence of alliances in the state-faith nexus that at once perceive the right to wear the veil as a religious freedom requiring protection, and yet an othering symbol that signifies Islamic subjectivity as outside the boundaries of possible Irish identity.

1 The Emergence of a Veil Debate in Ireland

While debates surrounding the Muslim headscarf have been evident in Europe for a decade or more[1] and have been 'embedded in discussions on national identity, secularization and modernity,'[2] Ireland's engagement with this issue was marginal and generally reactive to events occurring in other states prior to 2008. Indeed, even the events of 9/11, which galvanized negative reactions

---

1 Sevgi Kiliç, 'The British Veil Wars,' *Social Politics: International Studies in Gender, State & Society* 15/ 4 (2008): 397.

2 Ayşe Saktanber and Gül Çorbacıoğlu, 'Veiling and Headscarf Skepticism in Turkey,' *Social Politics* 15/4 (2008): 519.

© KONINKLIJKE BRILL NV, LEIDEN, 2019 | DOI:10.1163/9789004404564_009

towards Muslims in much of Western Europe,[3] elicited little attention towards Muslim women in Ireland. Newspaper reviews of this period indicated only a minor increase on reportage of the Islamic veil and while the National Consultative Committee on Racism and Integration did report an increase in racist assaults against Muslims in the months following 9/11 they were of a limited nature, uncoordinated and isolated,[4] while the 7/7 bombings in London did not elicit a noticeably increase in racist assaults against Muslims in Ireland.[5]

Muslims in Ireland make up just over 1% of the population. In stark contrast, Catholics account for 84% of the population. Between 2006 and 2011, Islam was a moderately growing religion, growing by 51%. Although this is a considerably faster growth rate compared to Catholicism, which grew by 5%, it is much less than the growth rate of Orthodox (117%), Hindu (75%), Apostolic (73%) or of the growth of Atheists (320%) and Agnostics (132%).[6] Muslims in Ireland are therefore considerably in the minority. However, the presence of Islam in Ireland is not a new phenomenon; a small Muslim population having been evident in Ireland from the 1950s.[7] By 1991, Muslims appear on the Irish Census for the first time.[8] Although in small number, Muslim women wore the veil in Ireland for numerous decades without attracting public attention and Irish public schools have generally accommodated girls who wished to wear the veil with the common clause of requiring the veil to be in the same colour as the school uniform.[9] The constitution provides formal recognition, legitimacy and respect to all religions and specifically does not endow any one religion above others.[10] There has been relatively little public concern in Ireland regarding Muslim immigrants, particularly in comparison to non-Muslim

---

3 Chris Allen, 'Justifying Islamophobia: A Post-9/11 Consideration of the European Union and British Contexts,' *American Journal of Islamic Social Sciences* 21/3 (2004): 4–5, accessed November 12, 2014, http://i-epistemology.net/attachments/847_Ajiss21-3%20-%20Allen%20-%20Justifying%20Islamophobia.pdf.

4 National Consultative Committee on Racism and Interculturalism, *The Muslim Community in Ireland: Challenge some of Myths and Misinformation* (Dublin: National Consultative Committee on Racism and Interculturalism, 2008), 8.

5 National Consultative Committee on Racism and Interculturalism, *The Muslim Community in Ireland.*

6 Central Statistics Office, *Census 2011. Religion, Ethnicity and Irish Travellers. Statistical Tables* (Dublin: Government of Ireland, Stationery Office, 2012), 48.

7 'History of Muslims in Ireland,' islaminireland.com, accessed November 12, 2014, http://www.islaminireland.com/site/assets/files/1001/history_of_muslims_in_ireland.pdf.

8 Central Statistics Office, *Census 2011*, 48.

9 Kieran Flynn, 'Understanding Islam in Ireland,' *Islam and Christian-Muslim Relations* 17/2 (2006): 234.

10 *Constitution of Ireland* (1937): Article 44, accessed November 12, 2014, http://www.taoiseach.gov.ie/eng/Historical_Information/The_Constitution/.

EXPLAINING THE ABSENCE OF A VEIL DEBATE

eastern European and African immigrants who have been common targets of anti-immigration rhetoric.[11] What is known is that prior to 2008 concerns over veiling were limited and polls suggest that Muslims generally felt accepted within Ireland.[12]

However, events in 2008 brought forth a wide range of opinion regarding the veil, Muslim women, immigration and citizenship. Shekinah Egan was a 14 year-old, hockey-playing school girl living in the small town of Gorey, Co. Wexford, in the east of Ireland, when in 2008 she became the centre of nation-wide attention. The daughter of Liam Egan, an Irish-born convert to Islam, and Beverly Egan, a British-born immigrant to Ireland, Shekinah had already been wearing a headscarf at school for a year when her parents wrote to the secondary school she was due to attend the following September to ensure that Shekinah would be welcomed while wearing the hijab. The School Board, tasked with the management of the school on behalf of the patron (usually a Catholic order) confirmed that Shekinah would be allowed to wear a veil; however, the principal of the School, Nicholas Sweetman, wrote to the Minister of Education to ask for clarification on regulations regarding such attire. Explaining his decision, Sweetman argued, the government

> should be offering guidance so that we don't have a situation where in this school the child is allowed to wear the hijab, and another school down the road will say, we don't allow that' and further that, 'it's fine for me to say as principal of this school that it's grand for a girl to wear a hijab, but supposing a child comes wanting to wear the full veil. Do I say yes or do I say no? And why do I say yes or no?'[13]

The government declined to offer guidance or legislate on the issue, referring the decision back to individual school boards. Shekinah continued to wear her veil to school and schools around Ireland continued to issue their own policies regarding religious attire. Within one year, the veil debate that surfaced through the case of Shekinah Egan had largely evaporated. Yet, in the months that followed the circulation of this story, a public debate about the wearing of

---

11 Ceri Peach, 'Britain's Muslim Population: An Overview,' in *Muslim Britain: Muslim Communities under Pressure*, ed. Tahir Abbas (London: Zed Books, 2005), 29.

12 Ciaran Byrne and Shane Doran, 'Muslims Give their Blessing: Vast Majority Here Very Happy, Says Poll,' *The Independent*, December 19, 2006, accessed November 12, 2014, http://www.independent.ie/national-news/muslims-give-their-blessing-vast-majority -very-happy-here-says-poll-65184.html.

13 'Veil raises issues at Gorey School in Gorey Echo,' *Gorey Echo*, May 22, 2008, http://www .goreyecho.ie/news/story/?trs=cwsnmhmhmh&cat=news.

the Islamic veil in Ireland's public institutions, that intersected with wider debates on gender rights, immigration and religion, appeared in the news media. Such debates provide a method for analysing Ireland's relationship to gender norms, national identity and the dominant Catholic religion, while also shedding light on why Ireland has had such a muted reaction to the Islamic veil in comparison with other Western European states.

2   Researching the Veil through News Media and Public Opinion

How the veil is perceived is shaped by the cultural context in which it is worn, ideological traditions and the prevailing perceptions, not only or even mostly of Islam, but also of women, of 'foreigners' and of religion generally. Implicit within the opinions expressed in Ireland are also nationalized notions of gender and the nature of Ireland, Irishness and Irish values. Using opinion pieces and reader letters from popular, quality newspapers, this chapter examines the various themes that have emerged through this debate including those of protection, preservation and contestation and has teased out existing and changing attitudes towards gendered constructions of Irish nationality and citizenship.

The Irish Times is considered to be the 'newspaper of record' for Ireland and has a reputation for being balanced, authoritative and socially, if not economically, liberal. *The Irish Independent* is Ireland's largest selling daily newspaper and its sister paper, the *Sunday Times* is the top-selling paper in Ireland. These newspapers are considered to be 'opinion leaders' in Irish public and political life and are well positioned within the Irish media market.[14] Furthermore, it is 'also assumed that they are regularly read by other media and elites in Ireland' and thus, act to establish the broad contours of public opinion.[15] These papers were thus used in this paper to analyse public opinion. While research has intensively examined the ability of the news media to influence public discourse, it is also important to recognize that the public is not a passive spectator in this process. Opinion pages and reader letters offer an outlet for the public to engage with public debate and influence which topics are represented in the paper and what aspects of such topics receive attention. It was thus deemed important to examine such publications within the quality broadsheets

---

14   Mary O'Regan, 'Explaining Media Frames of Contested Foreign Conflicts: Irish National "Opinion Leader" Newspapers' Frames of the Israeli-Palestinian Conflict (July 2000 to July 2004),' in *Networking Knowledge: Journal of the MeCCSA Postgraduate Network* 1/2 (2007): 13.

15   O'Regan, 'Explaining Media Frames of Contested Foreign Conflicts.'

EXPLAINING THE ABSENCE OF A VEIL DEBATE

considered in order to gain an appropriate sample of public attitudes towards the Islamic veil.

This chapter uses thematic content analysis to reveal dominant themes in relation to the wearing of the Islamic veil in Ireland. Analysing opinion pieces, editorials and reader letters provides an opportunity to gain insight into attitudes and perceptions of the Islamic veil in Ireland, and how they reflect gendered perceptions of nationhood, identity and citizenship and the role of religion in the public sphere. Common themes emerged in which discourses of protection of women, preservation of the national identity and contestation over religious control infused the debate on the veil. Critical discourse analysis provided the method through which to examine variations within the themes and an intertextual approach, described by Kristeva as 'the insertion of history (society) into a text and of the text into history,'[16] allowed for consideration of how the construction of the signifiers of gender, nation, and ethnicity in Ireland within this debate relate to social organization, including tolerance for multiculturalism. This approach thus aims to 'render social phenomena intelligible'[17] and connect such phenomena to the construction and reproduction of gendered and nationalized power-relations in Ireland.

3 Nation as Protector: Debating the Meaning of Rights

Nira Yuval-Davis has argued that 'women's citizenship ... is usually of a dual nature: on the one hand they are included in the general body of citizens; on the other hand there are always rules, regulations and policies which are specific to them.'[18] The veil debates are but one aspect of such regulations and prohibitions that are unique to women and act to define notions of national identity and citizenship. Perceptions of citizenship are influenced by concepts of national identity: in an ideological sense, citizenship refers to the capacity of the individual to belong to the state by embodying the national identity. In a practical sense, the rights and responsibilities of citizenship are not equally distributed amongst all those who formally hold citizenship: as Yuval-Davis has explained, rules, regulations, policies and importantly practices are directed differently towards different groups of people and thus delimit the extent to

---

16   Julia Kristeva, 'Word, Dialogue, and Novel,' in *The Kristeva Reader*, ed. Toril Moi (Oxford: Basil Blackwell, 1986), 39.

17   Majia Holmer-Nadesan, 'Organizational Identity and Space for Action,' *Organization Studies* 17/1 (1996): 50.

18   Nira Yuval-Davis, *Gender and Nation* (London: Sage Publications, 1997), 24.

which some groups and individuals can access the rights and responsibilities of full citizenship. How such 'rights' are understood and conferred also has the potential of articulating the 'dominant' group, defined as capable of protecting the rights of others, and the minority group who are construed as dependent on the protection of the majority group: in other words, who are *tolerated* by the dominant group while never being fully part of the dominant group.[19]

This notion of the dominant Irish granting and protecting the rights of 'Others' was a significant theme within the hijab debate of 2008. 'Rights' were frequently mentioned in reader letters and opinion pieces within the Irish newspapers that were examined to defend or reject the wearing of the hijab in public schools in Ireland. Although the notion of 'protecting' Muslim women has been used by both those who support the veil in public schools and those who oppose its presence, it was more often used to pose the veil as oppressive to women. To understand this discourse of protection as it is enacted within Ireland, one must consider Ireland's colonial legacy and the discursive construction of national identity that linked masculinized ideals such as strength and independence to 'Irishness' and thus full, substantive citizenship.

The vociferousness of Ireland's nationalist discourse is not out of keeping with that of other post-colonial nations. Amrita Basu has argued that 'nationalism that seeks inspiration from an imaginary past usually advocates re-domesticating women and gaining control over their sexuality.'[20] This is a particularly accurate comment in relation to Ireland, where

> Colonial powers identif[ied] their subject people as passive, in need of guidance, incapable of self-government, romantic, passionate, unruly, barbarous – all those things for which the Irish and women have been traditionally praised and scorned.[21]

Stevens et al. describe how Ireland was visualized within English discourse as 'a weak, ineffectual woman that needed to be controlled by a strong, resolute man (Britain).'[22]

---

19   Wendy Brown, *Regulating Aversions: Tolerance in the Age of Identity and Empire* (Princeton: Princeton University Press, 2008), 178.

20   Amrita Basu, 'Introduction,' in *The Challenge of Local Feminisms*, ed. Amrita Basu (Boulder: Westview Press, 1995), 6.

21   Geraldine Meaney, *Sex and Nation: Women in Irish Culture and Politics* (Cork: Attic Press, 1991), 53.

22   Lorna Stevens, Stephen Brown and Pauline Maclaran, 'Gender, Nationality and Cultural Representations of Ireland: An Irish Woman's Place?,' *European Journal of Women's Studies* 7/4 (2000): 408.

To reclaim autonomy, in both a political and symbolic sense, Irish nationalists needed to re-conceptualize the Irish as strong, capable, independent and fierce – all characteristics associated with the masculine. The nation-building project in Ireland relied upon a mythical and masculinized 'Celtic' past in which the Irish people could locate glory, prestige and power. When Ireland's autonomy was realized, with the considerable help of women revolutionaries and revolutionary groups, women as political actors and social agents were largely written out of history and the Irish nation became one of acting men and symbolic women. In the Republic of Ireland, women were given few opportunities for self-expression or agency within this rewritten past but were rather relegated to 'hearth and home.'[23]

Thus, while Ireland is constituted as essentially feminine, the Irish nationalist discourse also constitutes the Irish people as masculine, as the sons of Mother Ireland, whose love and sense of duty requires her defence. In this way Irish nationalism of the late 19th and 20th century articulated an alternative history that contested the colonial perceptions of the Irish identity, and constructed a new, invigorated, but masculine identity for the Irish nation. While this identity did provide a basis for unity it also disenfranchised half the population from full citizenship. Irish women, as active political agents, were sacrificed to the new ideal of the assertive, independent (and male) Irish citizen. To be an active Irish citizen in the new Republic thus required taking on these 'masculine' traits. This history continues to influence understandings of Irishness and Irish identity, as can be identified in the veil debate that emerged in Ireland in 2008, by structuring the relationship between the 'Irish,' defined along these masculinized ethnic lines and 'Others' conceived in opposition as dependent, feminized and in need of protection. The veiled woman becomes the example par excellence of such a view.

Irish Independent columnist Martina Devlin asserts that the veil is inherently oppressive and argues that 'if we accept [the hijab] in schools, we open the door to other practices in the Muslim world even more repressive to women, among them arranged marriages and female circumcision.'[24] Similarly, Eilis O'Hanlon wrote in a more moderate piece in the *Irish Independent* three days later that Muslim girls whose parents do not wish them to cover, 'can frequently be bullied and made to feel inferior and ashamed by those who wear the

---

23   Maryann Valiulis, 'Gender, Power and Identity in the Irish Free State,' *Journal of Women's History* 6/4, 7/1 (1995):118.

24   Martina Devlin, 'If Muslim Men Like the Veil So Much, Let Them Wear It,' *The Independent*, May 22, 2008, accessed November 12, 2014, http://www.independent.ie/opinion/columnists/martina-devlin/if-muslim-men-like-the-veil-so-much-let-them-wear-it-1382759.html.

hijab.'[25] Emer O'Kelly, writing in 2006 noted the increasing presence of veiled women (including those wearing the *niqāb*) in Ireland and states that 'I do not welcome the veil, and I do not believe it is racist to say so. Rather, I believe that to talk about embracing and welcoming what it stands for is to deny equality to women, even when the wearing is merely symbolic.'[26]

Such arguments invoke the image of the veiled Muslim girl/woman as oppressed by a patriarchal religion and/or culture. Letter writer Ruth Dudley Edwards, for instance, argues that allowing the hijab denies the possibility of Muslim girls to contest paternal authority and equates the hijab with child abuse.[27] Within this discourse of protection it is perceived as Ireland's duty, as an enlightened and liberal nation, to counter such tendencies by, for instance, banning the veil from schools. Indeed, *Irish Independent* columnist Sinead Ryan argues that 'we simply cannot have liberal equality laws and continue to pander to repressive minority customs.'[28] Thus the discourse of protection is equated here with the promotion of gender equality through the protection of Islamic girls and women from oppressive and patriarchal foreign cultural practices.

This discourse of protection undermines the veiled woman as a valid, autonomous political agent and relegates her to a special category of woman in need of the state's protection. Her own personal desires and aspirations are discounted as they become connected to an oppressive structure that is seen as limiting her thought. This argument has been expressed within numerous settings, including the European Court of Human Rights where it was asserted that the headscarf appears 'to be imposed on women by a religious precept that is hard to reconcile with the principle of gender equality.'[29] Rottman and Ferree argue that support for Government intervention in women's personal decisions 'can be framed as necessary ... [only] because "Muslim culture" is framed

---

25   Evelyn O'Hanlon, 'Why We Must Say No to the Veiled Threat in Our Schools,' *The Independent*, May 25, 2008, accessed November 12, 2014, http://www.independent.ie/opinion/analysis/why-we-must-say-no-to-the-veiled-threat-in-our-schools-1386365.html.

26   Emer O'Kelly, 'Time to Lift the Veil on Myth of 'Celebrating' Difference,' *The Independent*, June 18, 2006, accessed November 12, 2014, http://www.independent.ie/opinion/analysis/time-to-lift-the-veil-on-myth-of-celebrating-difference-131318.html.

27   Ruth Dudley Edwards, 'Wearing the Hijab at School,' The Irish Times, June 4, 2008, accessed January 12, 2010, A17.

28   Sinead Ryan, 'An Insult to Our Values,' *The Independent*, May 23, 2008, accessed November 12, 2014, http://www.herald.ie/opinion/columnists/sinead-ryan/an-insult-to-our-values -1384214.html.

29   Hege Skjeie, 'Headscarves in Schools: European Comparisons,' in *Religious Pluralism and Human Rights in Europe: Where to Draw the Line?*, ed. M.L.P. Loenen and Jenny E. Goldschmidt (Antwerp-Oxford: Intersentia, 2007), 130.

as oppressive' to an extent that European culture is not.[30] The perception that Muslim women require the protection of the state from patriarchal authority figures with antiquated and misogynistic attitudes within the Muslim community poses the debate as a conflict between opposing value systems,[31] reifying an 'us' vs. 'them' scenario that undermines the possibility for both peaceful, *equal*, co-existence and for the development of an inclusive, equal conception of citizenship and identity.

In a state where the national identity is connected to masculine traits including strength, offering 'protection' to women defines relations of power. Protecting the 'weak,' deemed to be Muslim women at the mercy of religious and cultural oppression, strengthens the discursive connection between those offering protection and the masculine, dominant, Irish identity. Lister explains that 'the greater or lesser ability of certain groups to act as citizens and the degree to which they can enjoy both formal and substantive rights as citizens depends on where they stand on a continuum of inclusion and exclusion.'[32] The fact that Irish women embrace the role of protector, offering protection to the weak resituates the Irish woman opposing the veil as the powerful member capable of offering protection to the weaker, illegitimately Irish, Muslim woman while also reinforcing the boundaries of belonging to the nation. Indeed, veiled Muslim women are excluded from full belonging through the discursive separation of those who offer protection, 'the Irish,' and those deemed in need of protection.

Although the discourse of protection can also be directed towards the protection of rights including the 'freedom to believe and express a belief and the principle of gender equality,'[33] this view was expressed by a minority of letter writers and opinion pieces within the examined newspapers. Breda O'Brien of *The Irish Times*, for instance, regards the demand to wear the veil in Irish schools as an indication of Muslim women's autonomy, stating 'a girl who makes the request to wear [the hijab] in school is likely to have thought about it and be clear about what it means to her. She is doing something brave and counter-cultural' and questions why society should be so concerned

---

30 Susan B. Rottman and Myra M. Ferree, 'Citizenship and Intersectionality: German Feminist Debates about Headscarf and Antidiscrimination Laws,' *Social Politics* 15/4 (2008): 498.

31 Skjeie, 'Headscarves in Schools,' 130.

32 Ruth Lister, 'Citizenship: Towards a Feminist Synthesis,' *Feminist Review* 57 (Autumn 1997): 36.

33 Aart Hendriks, 'Dealing with Different Religious Convictions and Practices,' in *Religious Pluralism and Human Rights in Europe: Where to Draw the Line?*, ed. M.L.P. Loenen and Jenny E. Goldschmidt (Antwerp-Oxford: Intersentia, 2007): 154.

'with young girls from a different background asserting their right to dress modestly.'[34] However, this view was distinctly in the minority and does not appear to have been highly influential in directing the terms of the debate. Rather, the government's refusal to make definitive judgements in relation to wearing the veil in public schools appears as one of the most significant factors in abating this debate. This decision in fact preserves the concept of autonomy – both in relation to individual schools and for individual women; the absence of legislation ensures that the decision on whether to veil is not foreclosed and thus remains a legitimate choice. Such a stance creates difference and debate and contributes to the 'vibrant clash of political positions and an open conflict of interests' that is essential for a thriving democracy.[35]

4   **Preserving the Nation: Diversity, Assimilation and the Irish Way**

Diversity, accommodation, integration and assimilation have become increasingly important notions in European states in recent years. However, recent trends have shifted towards an assimilationist stance in multicultural policy.[36] Khiabany and Williamson assert that in the UK, 'it has now become a new orthodoxy to insist that cultural diversity is a threat to national cohesion and British values, and the veil has become a key visual sign of that "threat."'[37] While Ireland has over the past decades professed a spirit of integration through accommodation and tolerance, the perception of multiculturalism as a threat to the Irish way of life was expressed by Ruairi Quinn, then Labour Party Spokesman on Education and Science, and Brian Hayes, his Fine Gael counterpart, during the summer of 2008 in relation to the Islamic headscarf. Quinn asserted that 'if people want to come into a western society that is Christian and secular, they need to conform to the rules and regulations of that country'[38] and added that 'nobody is formally asking them to come here. In the interests of

---

34   Carl O'Brien, 'Pupils' Right to Wear Hijab is Backed by Almost Half Surveyed; Wearing of Headscarves or Hijabs by Muslim Students,' *The Irish Times*, June 9, 2008, 14.

35   Chantal Mouffe, *The Return of the Political* (London: Verso, 1993), 6.

36   Ellie Vasta, 'From Ethnic Minorities to Ethnic Majority Policy: Multiculturalism and the Shift to Assimilationism in the Netherlands,' *Ethnic and Racial Studies* 30/5 (2007); Christian Joppke, 'The Retreat of Multiculturalism in the Liberal State: Theory and Policy,' *The British Journal of Sociology* 55/2 (2004).

37   Gholam Khiabany and Milly Williamson, 'Veiled Bodies – Naked Racism: Culture, Politics and Race in the Sun,' *Race & Class* 50/2 (2008): 73.

38   Patricia McDonagh, 'Muslim Anger at Opposition Calls for School Ban on Hijab,' *The Independent*, June 2, 2008, accessed November 12, 2014, http://www.independent.ie/national-news/muslim-anger-at-opposition-calls-for-school-ban-on-hijab-1394321.html.

integration and assimilation, they should embrace our culture.'[39] Brian Hayes backed Ruairi Quinn's views and gave his support for the banning of the veil in public schools.

The assimilationist approach does however pose particular problems within a state that is largely defined through reference to a shared ethnicity and history. Assimilation occurs in reference to a stable identity, or as Schneider and Crul explain, '[t]he term assimilation linguistically implies a referent to which immigrants and/or their offspring can become similar.'[40] In contrast to states such as France where assimilation is proposed through the adoption of the national language and adherence to the ideals of the nation, the possibility of assimilation is a factual impossibility in Ireland where the nation is defined by ethnic belonging. The assimilationist position then effectively ensures the exclusion of incomers who are visually different from the majority Irish, due to their skin colour or the wearing of culturally and/or religiously distinct garb. Such a position maintains a continued distinction between the Irish nation and 'Others' living within the state, regardless of their official citizenship status. In the short term such a differentiation may in fact help to quell disquiet over immigration – rather than fearing for the loss of authentic Irish identity, the existence of Others within Ireland actually strengthens Irish ethnic identity. Indeed, reader letters and opinion columns in the foremost newspapers in Ireland expose the separation of veiled Muslim women from the larger Irish polity, as will be examined shortly. Perceiving those who wear the veil as 'outsiders' and even 'visitors' to Ireland, permits their tolerance by Irish society while never granting them the status of belonging.

The shift from multicultural tolerance and accommodation towards assimilation has been justified, in Ireland as elsewhere, by the dual threat of Islamist terrorism and Islamist colonization. The perception of an unwillingness to integrate and the potential danger of a religiously divided society (a danger that Ireland knows well) is represented within the veil debates, indicating the existence of Powellian/Thatcherite 'new racism'[41] in Ireland, in which "culture" and "tradition" become essentialized and bioligized[42] into notions of genealogical "difference" and lie at the heart of the 'fear of being swamped by immigrants.'[43]

---

39   McDonagh, 'Muslim Anger at Opposition Calls for School Ban on Hijab.'

40   Jens Schneider and Maurice Crul, 'New Insights into Assimilation and Integration Theory,' *Journal of Ethnic and Racial Studies* 34/4 (2010): 1144.

41   Martin Barker, *The New Racism: Conservatives and the Ideology of the Tribe* (London: Junction Books, 1981).

42   See, for instance, Michael Omi, '"Slipping into Darkness": The (Re)Biologization of Race,' *Journal of Asian American Studies* 13/3 (2010): 343–358.

43   Yuval-Davis, *Gender and Nation*, 32.

In Austria, which demonstrates a comparatively tolerant approach towards religious expression and practice, an absence of legal restrictions or regulations on the veil is contrasted by the development of restrictive immigration and integration policies and anti-immigration right wing parties,[44] indicating that the absence of regulation on this issue does not denote a multicultural or culturally tolerant approach but may be, rather, the result of the acceptance of religion generally within the public sphere. Ireland has similarly displayed a growing resentment towards immigrants, as practised through the removal of 'jus soli' constitutional rights to citizenship and the restriction of welfare and entitlement rights to EU migrants,[45] while formally defending the right to religious conviction and expression. This suggests that in Ireland the primary concern is the loss of 'Irishness' through the dilution of Irish culture and its perceived ethnic purity. Yet, the very difference expressed by the veil acts to dilute the fear of such acculturation by maintaining the distinct separation between those identified as 'Irish' and those who are not.

One letter writer to the *Irish Independent* expressed a concern that 'non-ethnic Irish women who have citizenship by birth or naturalisation will take up positions in the public service. I do not want, as a woman, to see religion or symbols of religion as the face of public service.'[46] Malone concludes that 'once one leaves or escapes the land of one's birth and enters a new society with a different culture and beliefs, one must adapt to existing values inherent in the new nation.'[47] Although this letter is an oversimplified representation of such views, it nonetheless lays bare a number of issues that go to the heart of the accommodation/assimilation debate.

There is an evident conflation between the notions of 'ethnic' Irish and Christian expressed in the above view. 'Ethnic' Irish may also be Muslim, as indeed was the father of Shekinah Egan, the Irish Muslim school girl whose headscarf sparked the debate in the summer of 2008. Within the discourse of preservation of the nation, the veil is clearly related to ethnicity and 'foreignness.' In an Ireland that used the imagined Celtic past as a foundation for the construction of Irish identity, the production of an ethno-nationalist discourse

---

44 Nora Gresch, Leila Hadj-Abdou, Sieglinde Rosenberger and Birgit Sauer, 'Tu felix Austria? The Headscarf and the Politics of "Non-issues,"' *Social Politics: International Studies in Gender, State & Society* 15/4 (2008): 411.

45 Brian Fanning and Fidele Mutwarasibo, 'Nationals/Non-Nationals: Immigration, Citizenship and Politics in the Republic of Ireland,' *Ethnic and Racial Studies* 30/3 (2007).

46 Vaun Malone, 'Burka Ban Must be Imposed Immediately,' *The Independent,* June 29, 2009, accessed November 12, 2014, http://www.independent.ie/opinion/letters/burka-ban-must-be-imposed-immediately-1795578.html.

47 Malone, 'Burka Ban Must be Imposed Immediately.'

EXPLAINING THE ABSENCE OF A VEIL DEBATE

is standard ideological fare. The utilization of binary divisions between 'us' and 'them' not only disadvantages 'them' ensuring that Muslim women are divorced from legitimate citizenship, but also solidifies the Irish identity – proposing it as under attack and requiring defence. Tohidi and Bayes note that 'in both Catholic and Muslim postcolonial contexts, women are blamed for failing to preserve the native culture and old traditional orders.'[48] Here, the conflation between imagined ethnic nation and religiosity construes the veiled Muslim woman as symbolic of the (potential) loss of 'Irishness' and Irish values – displayed by the letter above, as fear of a foreign face in a familiar, Irish context. This potential, however, as will be seen, is offset by another factor, namely that the very 'Otherness' of veiled women negates a serious challenge to Irish national identity.

Furthermore, there is an assumption that there is a unitary and unique Irish Nation and cultural values that are accessible and imitable. This is by no means unproblematic. As Ging and Malcolm argue, a myth of Irish homogeneity has been consolidated that is 'central to the ideology of the nation-state [and] denies the ethnic and religious diversity that has existed in Ireland for many years.'[49] This un-problematized notion of the Irish is expressed by one letter writer who collapses the Irish Christian way of life into a normative view of 'humans.' He writes 'immigrants to this country who accept the western way and may I say so the Christian way of life and who contribute positively to our society are welcome ... the Irish nation has the ways and means to maintain our ethos and show Muslims that we want integration, absorption, and not separation. People who wear Islamic dress in Ireland (or elsewhere) are seen as Muslims. We should see people as humans first.'[50] This view clearly indicates the myth of neutrality: the majority ethnic group (and their practices, beliefs and attitudes) are universalized and perceived as the 'one shared by everyone.'[51] In the letter, 'others' are clearly defined as non-Christians and their presence is permitted on the condition that they behave and dress according to the

---

48   Nayereh Tohidi and Jane H. Bayes, 'Women Redefining Modernity and Religion in the Globalized Context,' in *Globalization, Gender, and Religion: The Politics of Women's Rights in Catholic and Muslim Contexts*, ed. Jane Bayes and Nayereh Tohidi (New York: Palgrave, 2001), 38.

49   Debbie Ging and Jackie Malcolm, 'Interculturalism and Multiculturalism in Ireland: Textual Strategies at Work in the Media Landscape,' in *Resituating Culture*, ed. Gavan Titley (Strasbourg: Council of Europe, 2004), 126.

50   Michael McCullagh, 'Time for Muslim Debate,' *The Independent*, December 9, 2007, accessed November 12, 2014, http://www.independent.ie/opinion/letters/time-for-muslim-debate-1241710.html.

51   Kiliç, 'The British Veil Wars,' 441.

standards of the Western Christian nation of Ireland and 'contribute positively,' revealing a boundary to acceptance in line with Yuval-Davis' argument that 'multi-culturalism always has limits set by the hegemonic collectivity.'[52] Again, this argument limits full belonging to Christian Irish with non-Christians being accorded limited ideological citizenship 'on-condition' that they 'integrate.' Difference is thus accorded only formal tolerance, which is confined to the private sphere and certainly kept from the 'public.'[53] Thus for non-conforming groups to achieve even partial acceptance requires the denial of a fundamental aspect of one's identity; as An-Na'im persuasively argues, for genuine integration to occur 'it is necessary to respect the cultural and religious right to self-determination, for example, to avoid requiring Muslims (or other immigrants) to abandon or renounce their own identity in order to be accepted as citizens or non-citizen residents of the country.'[54] This argument is doubly resonant where it concerns veiled Muslim women who face discrimination on multiple fronts within Ireland.

Finally, the desire to avoid 'religion, and symbols of religion, in the public services' would construct a public service that is un-representative of the people that it serves. However, this view is echoed within other contexts. Hans Werdmolder, for instance, has argued that 'the freedom of wearing a head-scarf can be considered or imply an infraction of the freedom of other involved persons' and further asserts that 'the State has a special responsibility to demonstrate its impartiality by adopting and enforcing a neutral, and sometimes uniform, dress code for all civil servants in its public education institutions.'[55] This view has been contested by others where it is argued that 'a general prohibition of religious attire is not only difficult to reconcile with the core values of a democratic society, but is neither necessarily favourable for gender equality or the promotion of other rights.'[56] Indeed, not only would such a position exclude a growing number of women from a major employment sector, but it provides a false picture of who the 'Irish' are. Furthermore, as argued above,

---

52 Yuval-Davis, *Gender and Nation*, 56.

53 Bhikhu Parekh, 'British Citizenship and Cultural Difference,' in *Citizenship*, ed. Geoff Andrews (London: Lawrence & Wishart, 1991); Anna Elisabetta Galeotti, 'Citizenship and Equality: The Place for Toleration,' *Political Theory* 21/4 (1993): 585–605.

54 Abdulla Ahmed An-Na'im, 'Global Citizenship and Human Rights: From Muslims in Europe to European Muslims,' in *Religious Pluralism and Human Rights in Europe: Where to Draw the Line?*, ed. M.L.P. Loenen and Jenny E. Goldschmidt (Antwerp-Oxford: Intersentia, 2007), 5.

55 Hans Werdmölder, 'Headscarves at Public Schools: The Issue of Open Neutrality Reconsidered,' in *Religious Pluralism and Human Rights in Europe: Where to Draw the Line?*, ed. M.L.P. Loenen and Jenny E. Goldschmidt (Antwerp-Oxford: Intersentia, 2007), 165.

56 Hendriks, 'Dealing with Different Religious Convictions and Practices,' 154.

Ireland is not a neutral state. Christianity, and particularly Catholicism, has been integrated into the fabric of Irish society resulting in the disavowal of the religious nature of many of the practices and expressions common in Ireland, which entails that denying the right to religious expression impacts Muslim women unequally and indefensibly.

The arguments examined above, while also implicitly reproducing an ethnic- and gender-specific Irish identity, provide some evidence of why the veil debate in Ireland was limited in both duration and intensity: the ethno-nationalist nature of Irish identity permits tolerance of 'Others' so long as they do not challenge membership within the nation. As a constructed emblem of Otherness, the veil demarcates the limitations of Irish identity and thus does not provide a significant challenge to Irishness. In its visibility, it renders *Irish* Muslim women invisible. Thus, arguments that present the veiled woman as a threat to Irish national cohesion are untenable. So long as identity is constructed along ethnic lines, visibly 'foreign' women pose little threat to national identity.

5   Contesting the Religious: Secularism vs. Faith in the Islamic Veil Debate in Ireland

As this chapter has detailed, the veil debate is not just about religion, since a nuanced analysis of the debate must consider the social, cultural and political aspects of the debate. However, it is *also about religion*, about faith and about how religious convictions are expressed. Unlike France or Turkey where the state has consciously been constructed as secular, Ireland has always enjoyed a close relationship with religious institutions, notably the Catholic Church, resulting in a 'close identification between loyalty to the nation and loyalty to the church.'[57] This special history has resulted in rather unique arguments both for and against the veil, as secular and faith-based interest groups use the veil debate to negotiate rights of and limitations on religion in the public sphere.

Philip Watt of the now-defunct National Consultative Committee on Racism and Interculturalism argued that those who advocate 'a ban on the hijab might or might not have fully considered the consequences of such a ban in respect of all religious symbols and obligations in the schools,'[58] indicating that

---

57   Kevin Williams, 'Faith and the Nation: Education and Religious Identity in the Republic of Ireland,' *British Journal of Educational Studies* 47/4 (1999): 317.

58   Zainab Hemani, 'Opposition in Ireland Calls for Headscarf Ban,' *The Muslim News* 330, June 27, 2008, http://www.muslimnews.co.uk/paper/index.php?article=3580.

banning the icons of Christianity may not be the desired outcome of many who oppose the veil in public schools. It is likely that he is correct. Brian Hayes, then opposition spokesman for Education and Science, is reported as stating that 'parents are entitled to send their children to religious schools but those who opt for state education should expect that there won't be "any huge, demonstrable evidence of religiosity."'[59] This apparently overlooks the fact that 92% of state sponsored primary schools are Catholic and devote a considerable period of time to Catholic activities, particularly first communion, confirmation and religious holiday celebrations such as the Christmas pageants (RTE, 2009). As Catholicism is the hegemonic belief system in Ireland it is perceived as the normal way of life and associated with secularism. This view posits Islam as the opposite, as ideological and backward and thus 'divisive' and 'exclusionary.' There is a strong suggestion within this opinion that it is not a religion under attack by those who demand the veil be banned from schools to limit the presence of religious symbolism, but rather the presence of cultural and ethnic 'Others.' Such initiatives would support the continued domination of the normative, Catholic culture in Ireland by delineating what religious symbolism and expression is normal and acceptable to the nation.

Nevertheless, other letter writers have used this debate to make exactly this criticism: that Ireland *is* a Christian nation and cannot make a pretence of secularism by denying other religions while maintaining its Christian heritage. The authors conclude that schools should actually be secular and ban all religious symbolism. *Irish Times* letter writer Sarah Groarke argues that 'in a post-modern, multicultural Ireland, the time has come to remove religious teaching from our state education system'[60] and explicitly includes Catholicism within this argument. Similarly, a recent *Irish Times* article argues that Ireland's system of Catholic state schools could force government to accept other religious schools that may undermine democratic principles. The author advocates that 'the State ... realise that the publicly funded education system is no place for the promotion of particular religions. Only a religiously neutral State education system can protect the education system from becoming a vehicle through which democratic values are undermined.'[61] The shift in the

---

59   Ruadhan MacCormaic, 'Looking Beyond the Headscarf; For Many, the Wearing of the Hijab is a Simple Declaration of Faith; for Others, it is a Symbol of Religious Oppression. Has the Time Come for an Official Hijab Policy?,' *The Irish Times*, June 14, 2008.

60   Sarah Groarke, 'Letters to the Editor: Wearing the Hijab in School,' The Irish Times, June 13th, 2008, accessed January 14, 2010, from ProQuest Historical Newspapers *The Irish Times* (1859–2008).

61   Ronan McCrea, 'State-funded Schools must be Separate from Religions,' *The Irish Times*, December 17, 2009, http://www.irishtimes.com/newspaper/opinion/2009/1217/1224260833016.html.

debate from one about the right to veil to a debate around the role of religion within public life more generally does not denote growing recognition of minority rights; rather, such an appropriation of the veil debate which emerged in 2008 denotes an internal contest of differing opinions within the dominant Irish cultural majority. In fact, within this shift, the interests of the minority ethnic and religious groups are excluded and made invisible as the debate becomes colonized, that is, taken over by the dominant group, who redefine it in their own terms, and the significant role of gender in structuring the debate on the veil is lost.

The argument that religion has no place in the public sphere further discounts the reality for many women that their faith is an essential and indivisible aspect of their identity.[62] Banning religious symbolism and education from schools has little effect for Christian students, whose identity as Christians is enshrined in every aspect of Irish life, while for non-Christians such a ban forces a visible separation between internal values, beliefs and convictions, and external affiliation as citizens or residents of a Western, Christian nation. Such a proposal is unlikely to ease religious and cultural tensions (if they exist) within schools or other public institutions, but rather to simply exclude those who occupy non-normative identities from full civic acceptance, as they are taught through such policies that only some aspects of their identity are compatible with *being* Irish.

The special role of Catholicism in Ireland may provide more insight as to why the debate on the veil never flourished in Ireland. Herbert and Fras have argued that in Western Europe religion has largely been privatized, relegated to the private sphere and perceived as an aspect of individual choice and individual belief.[63] In comparison, in Communist Eastern Europe, religion was not privatized but excluded, leading to a process of re-publicization whereby 'religion emerges in shared social life' in the present.[64] In Ireland religion was never denied and never privatized, but has been part of the everyday fabric of daily life and routine, performed and celebrated collectively within public institutions such as state education. While the dominance of Catholicism has witnessed a decline, particularly in relation to Mass attendance, faith and religious belief remain important in Ireland.[65] Rather than being more tolerant

---

62   Lori Peek, 'Becoming Muslim: The Development of a Religious Identity,' *Sociology of Religion* 66/3 (2005).

63   David Herbert and Max Fras, 'European Enlargement, Secularisation and Religious Re-publicisation in Central and Eastern Europe,' *Religion, State and Society* 37/1–2 (2009).

64   Herbert and Fras, 'European Enlargement, Secularisation and Religious Re-publicisation in Central and Eastern Europe.'

65   Tom Inglis, 'Catholic Identity in Contemporary Ireland: Belief and Belonging to Tradition,' *Journal of Contemporary Religion* 22/2 (2007).

of difference, it may be that the Irish simply see less difference in the presence of the veil in public spheres than do other European States that have been through a more thorough process of secularization. This suggests that Muslim women may be seen as 'Other' because of the discursive association between Islam and 'foreignness' rather than because of their religious identity.

6 Ireland in the European Context: Equal or Exclusive?

Through an examination of the veil debate that emerged in Ireland in the summer of 2008, several factors are revealed that have restricted the development of a more vigorous debate on the veil and related multicultural conflicts. The refusal of the Irish government (through the Department of Education) to issue guidelines or legislate on the wearing of the veil within public schools leaves the issue open to personal and institutional choice. This allows both schools and girls who veil a variety of options and the possibility of negotiation, thus preserving a sense of autonomy that averts direct confrontation between individual rights and institutional and national norms. This decision largely reflects disinterested public attitudes towards the veil debate in Ireland and shows that the issue of the veil has simply not gathered the momentum in Ireland that it has elsewhere. This chapter has identified two primary reasons why the veil debate in Ireland never flourished. Firstly, the construction of national identity along masculinized ethno-nationalist lines forecloses the possibility of a threat to Irish identity by veiled women. The 'difference' and 'foreignness' associated with the veil in fact reinforces exclusive Irish identity, thus averting (for now) multicultural conflict. Secondly, the public nature of religion in Ireland has meant that the veil is seen less as an intrusion than a continuation of the normalized practice of religion in Ireland.

These conditions establish a very different context from the one seen in France, the UK, Germany or Belgium where multicultural conflict has been much more significant and the veil debate has been one of the most visible loci for such conflict. Rather, the case of Ireland contributes to the view expressed by Sevgi Kiliç[66] that state-church relations have a significant impact on the development and direction of debates around the veil. The Irish case is rather more similar to that of Austria whereby an ethno-cultural understanding of identity is mediated by religious pluralism resulting in an absence of a veil debate despite restrictive policies towards immigration.[67] This chapter argues

---

66   Kiliç, 'The British Veil Wars,' 401–402.
67   Gresch et al., 'Tu felix Austria?,' 426.

that in Ireland, the historical acceptance of religion in the public sphere acts in collusion with ethno-nationalist ideals of citizenship and identity to produce, on the one hand, a tolerance of 'Others' that offsets multicultural conflict in the short term, but, on the other hand, leads to a refusal to recognize such 'Others' as full members of the nation by the dominant group, rendering them invisible, and thus powerless to disrupt the discursive construction of the Irish nation.

This analysis does not, however, contrast states, such as Germany, France and the UK which exhibit greater public and political contention around the issue of the veil, with a tolerant, equitable Ireland. Rather, the debates that played out over the summer of 2008 reveal discourses that are highly exclusive and unequal and have the potential to result in significant multicultural conflict and gender inequality. Indeed, if Ireland is to avoid the kind of multicultural conflict that has characterized much of Western Europe in recent years and yet recognize the rights of all women, it is necessary and pressing for conceptualizations of the Irish, Irishness and Irish values to be more inclusive and built on the foundations of equality, autonomy and justice.

CHAPTER 8

Muslim Migration Intelligence and Individual Attitudes toward Muslims in Present-day Portugal

Nina Clara Tiesler and Susana Lavado

Nowadays, and for the last 30 years, Muslims are the largest non-Christian religious group in Portugal, a country where the overwhelming majority of the population (about 80%) self-identifies as Catholic.[1] On viewing Muslim-related discourses from outside Portugal, the question arises why the Muslim presence in this context has not created the "pressure points" that have been frequent in the interaction between Muslims and non-Muslims in Western Europe. It is important to keep in mind that this question derives from a comparative European perspective, from a research agenda that over the past decades[2] started putting Muslim communities in Western Europe at the top of the agenda,[3] not exclusively, but also as a reaction to a new public interest in a climate shaped by discrimination and polemic media framing. A closer look to the framing of Islam- and Muslim-related issues in the Portuguese press before 9/11 revealed that the basic patterns of prejudice as reflected in the media were quite similar to those in other European countries.[4] And still, the simple fact that Muslims are part of the society and are religiously active, dedicated citizens and engaged in Muslim matters and community work did not lead to what became known elsewhere as pressure points between the so-called majority and minority populations (the latter, however constructed). We will take a risk and ask why. Methodologically, this is a risky venture because the question derives from an external research agenda – it did not emerge as relevant from the field itself. As brought to the case from the outside, it sets a frame for our analysis that is alien to the case. We will try to meet this challenge by pointing out

---

1 Statistics Portugal. 2011 Census data.

2 More precisely since 1989, when events like the end of the Cold War, the Rushdie Affair and the first French Headscarf Affair constituted turning points in the research agenda.

3 Nina Clara Tiesler, "Muslim Transnationalism and Diaspora in Europe: Migrant Experience and Theoretical Reflection," in *Transnationalism: Diasporas and the Advent of a New (Dis) Order*, ed. Eliezer Ben-Rafael and Yitzhak Sternberg (Leiden: Brill, 2009), 417–440.

4 Eva-Maria von Kemnitz, "Muslims as Seen by the Portuguese Press 1974–1999: Changes in the Perception of Islam," in *Intercultural Relations and Religious Authorities: Muslims in the European Union*, ed. W.A.R. Shadid and P.S. van Koningsveld (Leuven: Peeters, 2002), 7–26.

© KONINKLIJKE BRILL NV, LEIDEN, 2019 | DOI:10.1163/9789004404564_010

several particulars of the Portuguese case that should be taken into account when approaching this question.

Besides pointing out some political aspects, historical developments and demographics, we will shed light on two further dimensions, namely individual attitudes towards Muslims on the one hand, and the characteristics, social capital and skills of the Muslim population and its representatives on the other.

As in other European countries, Muslims are active in Portuguese society, taking part in social, cultural and religious issues. However, they appear to have been somewhat consistently overlooked on the agenda of the media, social research, and political negotiations. The experience of the encounter between Muslims and non-Muslims in Portugal seems to lie not in what we see but in what we do not see: no controversial issues in parliament, in local administration or in the media, very few public demonstrations against opening mosques, no debates on official recognition or standards of secularism, and no academic discourse on "anti-Muslimness," "Islamophobia" or the role of Islam in processes of social marginalization of ethnic minorities. Why is this relation between Muslims and non-Muslims so void of tensions? What makes it so unnoticed, so silent?

The most immediate answer to this question is numeric: the Muslim community in Portugal is indeed very small. Results from the 2011 Portuguese census suggest that of the almost 9 million people over 15 years old currently living in Portugal, only 20,640 are Muslim.[5] The census numbers are imprecise, as the question about religion is not mandatory and almost 745,000 people preferred not to answer. Estimates from Muslim communities themselves and researchers suggest between 48,000 and 55,000 Muslims in Portugal, mainly in the Lisbon area. But even these larger numbers (that, if anything, tend to decrease)[6] are still very small compared with other European countries.

However, in our perspective, the numbers do not tell the whole story: the smaller size of the community in Portugal compared with other European countries is not the only and perhaps not the most important explanation for the "silence" that seems to surround Muslims in Portugal. This silence seems to have been crafted both by Portuguese distinct socio-historical developments and by specific conditions, abilities and preferences of the Portuguese Muslim community. We will explore these factors in the next sections.

---

5   Statistics Portugal. 2011 Census data.
6   Nina Clara Tiesler and José Mapril, "Portugal," in *Yearbook of Muslims in Europe. Volume 4*, ed. Jørgen S. Nielsen et al. (Leiden: Brill, 2012), 469–480.

1 Out of the Portuguese Research Agenda Spotlight

The contemporary Muslim presence in Portugal is largely the result of post-colonial movements in the 1970s. Mainly after the end of the Portuguese colonies, large groups of Isma'ili and Sunni middle-class families with an Indian or South Asian background came from Mozambique, followed by Fulas and Mandingas who arrived from Guinea-Bissau some years later. Because they arrived as part of a much larger influx of postcolonial settlers, returnees, and refugees, they got "lost in the crowd." In the diversified group of Black African migrants, the percentage of Muslims was very low, and the focus of minority politics and social research was directed primarily at numerically stronger groups, such as Cape Verdians. Muslims were a very small minority within the larger minority of settlers, and they were overlooked amidst the turbulence of the post-revolutionary years. In addition, contrasting with the situation in other European countries, the main protagonists of emancipation of religious minorities in the Portuguese context were not the Muslims, but the Protestants. The religious diversity increased abruptly after the revolution of 1974, but much more attention was given to Protestant denominations (such as Brazilian Pentecostal Churches), New Religious Movements, esoteric cults and some Asian schools of thought.

While academic research in other European countries emphasized the "religious factor," particularly when dealing with immigrant groups with a Muslim background, the majority of Portuguese studies on immigrant groups adopted an "ethnicity" perspective.[7] The 9/11 disaster brought some change to this reality, providing academics with more research funds to study issues related to "Muslims," especially at the European level and in the USA. However, there is not necessarily a linear relation between the sudden increase of research activity and an explosion of scientific knowledge concerning the experience of Muslims in contemporary societies in this specific historical context. Rather, the entanglement of political interests under the heading of "security" with the increase of research interest and possibilities often leads to a mutual production of a hegemonic language that tends to determine the research questions in dominant discourses.

The establishment of this hegemonic language is also exemplified in the design of grand quantitative surveys at the European level, while at the same time these surveys are considered an important tool to alert policy makers about prejudices and anti-Muslim sentiments. Portugal is sometimes included

---

7 Nina Clara Tiesler, "No Bad News from the European Margin: The New Islamic Presence in Portugal," *Islam and Christian-Muslim Relations* 12/1 (2001): 71–91.

in such surveys, and the quantitative data analyses are usually not combined with qualitative insights that might help in putting the former into context. Our decision to discuss survey data in this chapter derives from the experience of academic debates where such data was presented. Data on the Portuguese case usually highlights that respondents in Portugal are "more tolerant" or "open-minded," and are "embracing religious diversity" more than other Europeans when it comes to Islam and Muslims. Vague assumptions, mainly outside Portugal, are then discussed, such as that a higher acceptance of the "religious other" derives from Catholicism ("the overall Catholic population"), or that multiculturalism works smoothly in Portuguese society due to the long history of Portuguese Empire(s). We do not believe that these paths of inquiry (alone) would lead to an enlightened bigger picture because they omit the role of the Portuguese Muslim population as engaged citizens and socially and religiously active subjects in the societal encounter. Describing this role is the contribution of this chapter, even if it is fairly limited in the sense that it focuses nearly exclusively on the period after arrival in Portugal, while the history and experience of Portuguese Muslims starts in colonial times and lacks an in-depth description here.

2   A Smoother Insertion into Society

The Muslim communities in Portugal have demonstrated remarkable potential and abilities that, from a comparative, European perspective, played an important role in the establishment processes of both the local Islamic communities and the umbrella institution CIL (Islamic Community of Lisbon). Some of these abilities stem directly from the fact that the major cause of Muslim migration was the decolonization process of Mozambique and Guinea-Bissau.

Because they had been living under Portuguese colonial rule, the overwhelming majority of Muslim postcolonial settlers were already familiar with the Portuguese language when they arrived. The ability to speak Portuguese made the fundamental problem of obtaining citizenship or a temporary and renewable legal status less critical and favoured insertion into the labour market. Above all, many among those who arrived from Mozambique already held Portuguese nationality.

Life in Mozambique and Guinea also prepared the community to adapt to a new social context in two other important ways. First, Muslims arriving in Portugal already had the experience of living as a minority in a culturally different dominant society. This experience made them more prepared to cope with an establishment and community building process in a new societal setting compared to Muslims who hailed from Islamic majority countries and settled in other European countries. Second, the majority of Muslims in Portugal, namely those of Indian origin, had been established in tertiary sectors of employment in Mozambique. They coped quite well with re-establishing themselves in their occupations (mainly as traders) in Portugal, a process to which the familiarity with the language also contributed.

In addition, Muslims who arrived in Portugal as part of the huge post-revolutionary influx had the advantage of having the support of a small group of elite Muslims who had settled in the country some years before for educational purposes. This group had the intellectual and social capabilities, as well as the useful social connections, needed to build religious and cultural infrastructures that could help in integrating the new arrivees. These were small infrastructures, but served as an anchor for thousands of Muslims arriving among hundreds of thousands of other people who came/returned from the colonies during the post-revolution period. Today, the Central Mosque and local Islamic communities continue to be at the top of the address-lists of Muslims who have recently arrived in the country and are trying to find their way through the bureaucratic jungle of registration.

3   The Central Role of Institutional Representation

The Islamic Community of Lisbon (Comunidade Islâmica de Lisboa – CIL) was created in 1968 by an elite group of Sunni Muslims who came from Mozambique to Portugal to study. CIL (along with other smaller Islamic communities and other religious minorities) began to be recognized as a religious community in 2006, the year of the implementation of the Religious Freedom Act (which was approved in 2001). This new legal status, equivalent to the one of the Catholic Church, allowed CIL to conduct marriages and to benefit from the voluntary consignment by individual tax payers of 0.5% of their income tax. Importantly, the Religious Freedom Act also allowed Islamic instruction and training; the right to practice Islam in special situations such as in prisons or military service; and the absence from school or work to celebrate Islamic festivals or holy days (and granted similar rights to other religious minorities).[8]

Although there are other organized communities in the country, CIL acts as an umbrella organization for different Islamic groups, especially due to

---

8   For further details on the impact of the Religious Freedom Act and information about its practical implications, see Nina Clara Tiesler, "Portugal," in *Yearbook of Muslims in Europe. Volume 3*, edited by Jørgen S. Nielsen et al. (Leiden: Brill, 2011), 447–458.

the small number of Muslims in Portugal and the leadership abilities of its representatives. Thus, in Portugal the CIL is a central Muslim voice, playing a fundamental civic and political role, while in some other European countries the lack of representation may hinder the relations between state and Muslim organizations (and within the latter).

Muslim representatives have played a fundamental role in enhancing the establishment process of religio-cultural infrastructures and in managing the public image of the communities. These Muslim leaders who had studied at the Faculties of Economics, Law and Medicine in Lisbon before decolonization side by side with upcoming non-Muslim political leaders had still experienced the power relations under Portuguese colonial rule in Mozambique. They connected closely with the upcoming Portuguese *classe politique* and could count on informal networks. In their public voice, they have always opted for a rather non-political discourse, which avoided characteristics of "claims-making" and voicing complaints. This is a finger pointing to how to approach the issue of Islamophobia in its Portuguese variety, which certainly has to be traced back to colonial times and beyond.

In addition, because Muslims arrived in Portugal more than ten years later than in other European countries, their elite representatives had been aware of pressure points in other European contexts.[9] The enormous efforts to respond to hegemonic imperatives of "integration" and respective discourses displayed by the Muslim voice in Portugal can be seen as grounded in these two socio-historic factors.

To the present day, the policy of the Islamic community in Portugal has been rather non-political, always very open and positively oriented towards their surroundings (despite sufficient incidents of harassment that could have been raised), with a harmonizing, "low profile" discourse. Although they have had (and will have) to cope with the usual internal struggles every democratic community is facing,[10] members and leaders of the communities have ensured

---

9   Among other instances, this awareness was shown in public in the opinion piece "O Islão e Europa" (Islam and Europe) written by the first president of the Islamic Community of Lisbon, Suleyman Vale Mamede and published by the leading Portuguese (middle class) daily newspaper, *Diário de Notícias*, on June 22, 1990. It is no coincidence that such an opinion piece was published in 1990, as the so-called pressure points were in general only interpreted as being related to "Islam" and/or "Muslimness" since the turning point of 1989 (followed also by the Cultural Turn in the academies) when postcolonial settlers, immigrants and refugees were no longer categorized according to their nationality of origin (such as Turks) or legal status (e.g., refugees from Iran) or economic function (e.g., guest workers) but in terms of religious affiliation.

10   The most publicized internal struggle occurred in the 1985 election for the presidency of CIL. For further details, see Tiesler "No Bad News from the European Margin," 71–91.

a positive image, if noticed at all, in the Portuguese public sphere. This is also due to the kind of activities organized by the Islamic communities, and primarily by the umbrella organization CIL, which is highly active regarding humanitarian aid, welfare and social support programmes (for Muslim and non-Muslim populations) as well as in bringing different religious actors together for dialogue and debate.[11]

In addition, Muslim representatives have maintained strong diplomatic relations with state figures. For instance, whenever the main Islamic communities celebrate an anniversary or special occasion, the Portuguese State is often represented at the highest level; former and present Presidents of the Republic have been given the status of Honorary Members of CIL; and the current CIL President was one of the consultants to the President of the Republic during his visits to India, Turkey and other countries. CIL also had an important diplomatic role by hosting a huge interreligious meeting and inviting the Dalai Lama to be the guest of honour at a time when the Portuguese government had been facing the same problems as other governments regarding their official relations with China.

Nevertheless, it is the strong civic engagement of the community that has gained visibility over the last decades. CIL has made large efforts to educate Muslims for an active citizenship, and civil education is an important part of their religious education curriculum. CIL also encourages Portuguese Muslims and Muslims in Portugal to be aware of both their Muslimness and their Portugueseness, arguing that it is this dual belonging and self-understanding that allows the development of being liberal political subjects.[12]

4   Public Image of the Portuguese Muslim Community

Generally speaking, the media has treated the Muslim community in a fair way, with few exceptions. Symbolically, it is interesting to note that the relationship between the community and the Portuguese media started on the right foot, as one of the first news pieces about the community, published in 1979, mainly highlights the potential advantages of the Muslim presence for the country. Thus, Muslims were not pictured as a threat, but as a positive factor for Portugal.[13]

---

11   Tiesler, "Portugal" (2011), 447–458.
12   José Mapril, "'Bons' muçulmanos: educação islâmica e cidadania na Área Metropolitana de Lisboa," in *Religião em Movimento: Imigrantes e diversidade religiosa em Portugal e Itália*, ed. Helena Vilaça and Enzo Pace (Porto: Estratégias Criativas, 2010), 37–54.
13   Tiesler, "No Bad News from the European Margin," 71–91.

The Muslim representatives have frequently been invited to explain or comment on relevant events related to the "Islamic world." The community leaders generally take this opportunity to give their opinion in an enlightening fashion, contributing to a positive image of the Muslim community.[14] The media also regularly covers special occasions (such as anniversaries and notable visitors to the communities) and festivities (mainly the end of Ramadan). The Muslim community also participates in two television shows dedicated to the different religious communities, broadcast on a not very popular public channel, and in a similar programme on a public radio station. In all these programmes, the time is allocated according to the numerical strength of the community, and so the "lion's share" goes to the Catholic Church, followed by Protestant and Pentecostal Churches.

The public image and visibility of the Muslim community suffered some changes after the events of 9/11, which brought more curiosity and questions about Islam and Muslims. Since then, most of the time, the media approached the question not by analysing and presenting the current Muslim presence in Portugal but rather by presenting Islam as something foreign and very distant from everything that is familiar. For example, a special issue published by a Portuguese magazine dedicated to "Islam" right after 9/11 failed to make any reference to the contemporary Muslim presence in Portugal – focusing exclusively on conflicts and the "Muslim world."[15]

The rhetoric of the "war on terror" put Portuguese Muslims in a very strange situation, leaving them quite alienated in response to questions arising from a new kind of public interest. This rhetoric was dealt with by the Portuguese Muslims and their spokesmen in their normal, utterly calm and patient way. Researchers and Muslims know about harassment. But the Muslim voice in Portugal always stresses: "Muslims in Portugal are not suffering discrimination. They are well integrated citizens and members of society." Still, on one of the rare occasions when the Portuguese Muslim community actually became part of a (polemic) public debate they found support at least from the majority of online readers. It occurred on a TV talk show program at the beginning of 2009. The emeritus Cardinal Patriarch of Lisbon, José Policarpo, addressed Portuguese women, advising them to "think twice before marrying a Muslim man, because that is getting into a whole lot of trouble." The echo reached international scale when *USA Today*, *the International Herald Tribune* and *the Daily Mail*, among others, reported on it. The leading Portuguese newspapers

---

14 For more details about the Muslim community in the media, see von Kemnitz, "Muslims As Seen by the Portuguese Press 1974–1999," 7–26; Tiesler, "No Bad News from the European Margin," 71–91.

15 *História* XXIVIIII (2002), 41.

commented critically on this scandalous comment and provided space for Muslim voices (representative and others), which, as usual, did not reply in a polemic or aggressive way, but expressed their disappointment.

In the previous sections, we have outlined various developments and factors that have shaped the historical recent encounter of Muslims and non-Muslims in present-day Portugal. Before turning to individual attitudes towards Muslims, a note on visibility should be added. One the one hand, Islamic communities gain visibility via civic engagement concentrated on welfare and religious dialogue that is of a rather non-political nature. On the other, the Muslim subject him- or herself is little visible in Portuguese society. Muslims of African background do not dress very differently from other people of African background. Many Muslims have Indian roots or family relatives with Indian roots, but this holds true for huge parts of the general population in the metropolis of the former Portuguese Empire. Very few women wear a headscarf or dress in a way that could be identified as "Islamic" in the eyes of the non-Muslim Portuguese public. This is due to a widespread interpretation of the respective Coranic Sura on the "modesty of women," which is here not translated into specific dress codes but related to modest behaviour in a more general sense.

Understanding Portuguese individual attitudes toward Muslims may help to complete the "puzzle" of why the community has been overlooked in recent years, even by public opinion.

5　　Individual Attitudes toward Muslims

Attitudes toward groups (i.e., prejudice) have been shown to predict behaviours toward those groups, realized in, for example, discrimination in the access to jobs or other resources, support (or lack of it) for immigration or naturalization policies, and even violence and crimes. Even if the relation between the two is not automatic, attitudes generally supply the norms and the rationale for behaviour.[16]

The relative absence of tensions between Muslims and non-Muslims in Portugal may be a consequence of better general attitudes toward the community, resulting in fewer public displays against the Muslim presence in the country compared to other European countries. However, and especially after 9/11, an image of Muslims and Islam as something foreign and distant,

---

16　For a review of the relation between stereotypes, prejudice and discrimination, see John Dovidio et al., "Stereotyping, Prejudice and Discrimination: Another Look," in *Stereotypes and Stereotyping*, ed. C. Neil Macrae, Charles Stangor and Miles Hewstone (New York: Guilford, 1996), 165–208.

and as a potential threat to the country (and to Europe in general) was also conveyed. This image may have influenced Portuguese individual attitudes toward Muslims, making them at least as negative as the attitudes of people in other countries.

We have, then, two different possibilities: on one hand, the particular conditions of Muslim settlement and the Muslim migration intelligence in Portugal may have been able to generate more positive attitudes toward Muslims compared to other European countries. On the other hand, Muslims in Portugal may be seen as a foreign group (albeit they are not, given that the overwhelming majority are Portuguese citizens) that has very different values from the Portuguese (albeit they do not[17]), which generally leads to more negative attitudes.

To explore attitudes toward Muslims in Portugal and other countries, we will use a European comparative survey – the Group-Focused Enmity in Europe (GFE-E). We do acknowledge the limitations inherent in surveys like this one – they tend to consider social groups as a "monolithic entity," asking only a small number of questions that participants should answer selecting a number from a scale. By doing so, surveys like this force social categories or representations onto their respondents, like the idea that there is a homogeneous group of people that we can label "Muslims," or "Portuguese," and that this dichotomy even exists.

However, to some extent, most people use categories such as these to navigate their social world,[18] and if people have more differentiated views on the groups, those tend to be reflected in more positive attitudes toward the group in general in their survey answers. We emphasize that this data should be interpreted carefully, but we also believe this survey constitutes an informative first step in understanding individual attitudes toward Muslims in Portugal compared with other European countries.[19] A more quantitative approach can and should be integrated with more qualitative data, benefiting both fields by suggesting different ways to look at reality and new research questions.

---

17   See Nina Clara Tiesler and David Cairns, "Across Difference: Portuguese Muslim Youth as Portuguese Youth?," in *Youth on the Move: European Youth and Geographical Mobility,* ed. David Cairns (Morlenbach: VS Verlag, 2010), 107–115; Nina Clara Tiesler and David Cairns, "Representing Islam and Lisbon Youth: Portuguese Muslims of Indian-Mozambican origin," *Lusotopie* 14/1 (2007): 223–238.

18   See, for example, Susan T. Fiske et al., "A Model of (Often Mixed) Stereotype Content: Competence and Warmth Respectively Follow from Perceived Status and Competition," *Journal of Personality and Social Psychology* 82/6 (2000): 878–902.

19   It should be noted that these data should always be interpreted in a comparative, between countries perspective. Further information about GFE-E can be obtained at http://www.uni-bielefeld.de/ikg/zick/gfe_project.htm.

6   Data from Group-Focused Enmity in Europe

The Group-Focused Enmity in Europe (GFE-E) is a cross-national comparative survey that analyses prejudiced attitudes toward different groups in Europe. Eight countries took part in the project: France, Germany, Great Britain, Hungary, Italy, the Netherlands, Portugal and Poland. In each country, probabilistic representative samples of 1,000 people aged over 16 were interviewed. The interviews were conducted by telephone in the fall/winter of 2008.[20] Items that aim to analyse attitudes toward "Muslims" were not asked to participants who self-identified as "Muslim" in a previous question.

It is interesting to note that the Muslim communities in these countries are varied in terms of size, allowing us not only to compare Portuguese individual attitudes toward Muslims with the "core" European countries with a larger Muslim population, but also to compare them to countries that have similar percentages of Muslims.[21]

To analyse individual attitudes toward Muslims, an indicator that measures attitudes toward Muslims was computed. It consists of three items ("Islam is a religion of intolerance," "Muslims in [country] are too demanding," "There are too many Muslims in [country]";[22] α scores ranged from .64 to .81; the items were answered on a 4-point scale, where 1 = strongly agrees and 4 = strongly disagrees). The items were later reversed so that higher values represented more negative attitudes toward Muslims.[23]

The descriptive statistics for each country in this scale are presented in Table 8.1. Results show that Portugal has significantly more positive attitudes toward Muslims than Germany, Hungary, Italy and Poland, while no significant

---

20   The project was coordinated by Dr. Andreas Zick (Bielefeld Institute for Interdisciplinary Research on Conflict and Violence, University of Bielefeld). In Portugal, the person responsible for the project was Dr. Cicero Pereira (Institute of Social Sciences, University of Lisbon).

21   Estimates indicate that France has the largest Muslim community, with about 10% of the population being Muslims, followed by Germany and the Netherlands, which have around 5–6% Muslims. The United Kingdom has around 4% and Italy has around 2% Muslims; in Portugal, Poland and Hungary the number is under 2%. Houssain Kettani, "World Muslim Population: 1950–2020," *International Journal of Environmental Science and Development* 1/2 (2010).

22   In Poland and Hungary, the last two questions were formulated as "There are too many Muslims in Europe" and "Muslims in Europe are too demanding."

23   In France, the question was formulated as "Islam is a religion of tolerance," and so the item scale was not reversed.

MUSLIM MIGRATION INTELLIGENCE AND INDIVIDUAL ATTITUDES 191

TABLE 8.1   Means and standard deviation for attitudes toward Muslims, perception of Muslims as terrorists and perceptions of Muslims as a threat to the country's culture, by country.

	Attitudes toward Muslims	Perceptions of Muslims as terrorism supporters	Perception of Muslims as a threat to country's culture
	Mean (SD)	Mean (SD)	Mean (SD)
Great Britain	2.50 (0.87)	2.07 (0.93)	2.77 (0.86)
Germany	2.50 (0.75)	1.90 (0.87)	3.05 (0.70)
Hungary	2.60 (0,92)	2.09 (1.10)	3.05 (0.99)
Italy	2.72 (0.85)	1.85 (0.97)	2.95 (0.78)
Netherlands	2.46 (0.79)	1.95 (0.89)	2.79 (0.80)
Portugal	2.41 (0.53)	2.09 (0.63)	2.53 (0.69)
Poland	2.76 (0.76)	1.96 (0.89)	3.01 (0.71)
France	2.42 (0.76)	-	2.49 (0.86)
Total	2,54 (0.79)	1.99 (0.91)	2.83 (0.83)

Note: Higher values represent more negative perceptions of and attitudes towards Muslims.

differences were found between Portugal and the remaining countries.[24] It is also noteworthy that Portugal, the Netherlands and France are the only countries with results below the mean point of the scale. It seems, then, that individual attitudes in Portugal are at least not unfavourable toward Muslims, and are more positive than in other European countries, giving partial support to the idea that the particular establishment process of Muslim communities in Portugal may be reflected in the individual attitudes toward Muslims.

A more detailed analysis of the individual items included in the Attitudes toward Muslims scale reveals a more complex picture, however. The more positive Portuguese attitudes in this scale seem to be mainly due to the results in two of the items – "there are too many Muslims in [country]" and "Muslims in [country] are too demanding." In the former item, the Portuguese results are significantly more favourable (i.e., express more positive attitudes towards

---

24   We ran a Univariate analysis of variance (ANOVA) using country as the independent variable. There are significant differences between countries, $F(7, 6932) = 14.97$, $p < .001$; Post-hoc analyses reveal that Portugal significantly differs from these four countries ($p < 0.001$) but not from any other country ($p > .10$).

Muslims) than all countries except France and the Netherlands. In the latter, Portugal has the lowest mean, significantly expressing more favourable attitudes than all the remaining countries.[25] These positive attitudes toward the community can be a result of either the effectively small number of Muslims in Portugal or their lack of visibility, and are consistent with the silence surrounding the community, and its capacity to manage relations with non-Muslims in Portugal.

The Portuguese results on the third item of the scale, "Islam is a religion of intolerance" are not that positive. Portugal has significantly more agreement with this item than the Netherlands and Great Britain; no significant differences were found between Portugal and the remaining countries. That is, in this item, Portugal has the same or more unfavourable attitudes toward Muslims than the other European countries.[26] These results suggest that there is a discrepancy between the attitudes toward the weight of the Muslims in Portugal and beliefs about Islam as a religion that supports values different from what the respondents consider Portuguese values.

To further analyse attitudes toward Muslims, a second scale was created that measures the extent to which people perceive Muslims as Terrorism Supporters and is constituted of 2 items ("Many Muslims perceive Islamic terrorists as heroes" and "The majority of Muslims find Islamic terrorism justifiable"; the items were answered on a 4-point scale that was reversed such that 1 strongly disagrees and 4 strongly agrees; α scores range from .69 to .86). France was not included in this analysis, as one of the questions was not asked to the French sample.

As also shown in Table 8.1, Portugal, Great Britain and Hungary are the countries that most perceive "Muslims as supporters of Islamic terrorism."[27]

---

25   Results were obtained with an ANOVA using country as the independent variable. We found significant differences between countries both for the first item, $F(7, 6066) = 20.25$, $p < .001$, and for the second item, $F(7, 6306) = 20.35$, $p < .001$. For the first item, post-hoc analyses revealed significant differences between Portugal and all the remaining countries ($p < .001$) except France ($p = .954$) and the Netherlands ($p = .121$). For the second item, post-hoc analysis revealed significant differences between Portugal and all countries ($p < .001$).

26   We ran an ANOVA using country as the independent variable. There were significant differences between countries, $F(7, 6282) = 6.44$, $p < .001$. Post-hoc analysis revealed that Portugal had significant higher means than the Netherlands ($p = .003$) and Great Britain ($p = .021$), but did not differ from the remaining countries ($p > .800$).

27   We ran the same ANOVA using country as the independent variable. We found significant differences between countries, $F(6, 6157) = 9.88$, $p < .001$; Post-hoc analyses reveal that these three countries significantly differ from all the other countries (p-values range from $< .001$ and $= .057$) but not from each other ($p = 1.00$).

It is noteworthy that a third of Portuguese respondents agree that "Muslims perceive terrorists as heroes" and that more than a quarter agree that "the majority of Muslims believe terrorism is justifiable." These results, in line with the ones obtained in the item that measured perceptions of "Islam as a religion of intolerance," suggest that non-Muslim respondents in Portugal believe that Muslims and Islam support acts that go against their own values; and that Portuguese respondents have more negative attitudes than other European countries when asked more general questions about Muslims and Islam.

Are the more positive results obtained in the items of the first scale pertaining to Muslims in Portugal exclusively due to the small size of the community, then? Not necessarily. Perceptions of Muslims as a threat to the country's culture (measured by the item "The Muslim culture fits well into [country]"; the item was answered on a 4-point scale ranging from 1 = strongly agrees and 4 = strongly disagrees, such that higher values represented a higher level of perceived threat) support the idea that the capacities for integration shown by the Muslim community are reflected in more positive attitudes of non-Muslim respondents in Portugal, in line with the results obtained in the first two items of the general attitudes toward Muslims scale. As shown in the last column of Table 8.1, Portugal and France were the countries that least agreed that Muslims are a threat to the country's culture (both countries had about 50% of respondents agreeing that Muslims are a threat, while this percentage ranged between and 61 and 83% in the other countries).[28] Answers to this item seem to suggest that Portuguese people do not think that Muslims are a very distant, very different group – the respondents believe that Muslims have values and traditions that are similar to those they believe are the values and traditions of the Portuguese. Therefore, the presence of the Muslim community in Portugal seems not to be perceived as a threat to the "country's culture," whatever the respondents' conception of that may be. It is problematic, in our opinion, that the survey did not provide respondents the option to include Islam and "Muslim cultures" into the imagined European ones.

However, there seems to be a paradox. Non-Muslim Portuguese people believe that the Muslims in their midst do not represent a strain for the country: "they are not too many" or "too demanding" and they fit well into the country's culture. At the same time, they believe that "Muslims support terrorism" and "Islam is a religion of intolerance." This paradox is also shown in the correlations between the scales considered in this chapter as presented in Table 8.2.

---

28   An ANOVA using country as the independent variable was significant, $F(7, 6713) = 64.05$, $p <.001$. Post-hoc analyses revealed that Portugal's results are different from the results of all other countries ($p < .001$) except France ($p = .977$).

TABLE 8.2   Correlations between attitudes toward Muslims, perception of Muslims as terrorism supporters and perceptions of Muslims as a threat to the country's culture, by country

	Attitudes toward Muslims and perception of Muslims as terrorism supporters	Attitudes toward Muslims and perception of Muslims as a threat to country's culture	Perceptions of Muslims as terrorism supporters and perceptions of Muslims as a threat to country's culture
	r	r	r
Great Britain	0.52[a]	0.56[a]	0.36[a]
Germany	0.23[a]	0.37[a]	0.13[a]
Hungary	0.09[b]	0.04	0.08[b]
Italy	0.13[a]	0.28[a]	0.16[a]
Netherlands	0.39[a]	0.55[a]	0.27[a]
Portugal	0.12[a]	0.13[a]	0.02
Poland	0.02	0.27[a]	−0.10[a]
France	–	0.39[a]	–
Total	0.22[a]	0.36[a]	0.13[a]

a $p < 0.01$;
b $p < 0.05$.

The correlations between the scales in Portugal are small, much smaller than the correlations in countries such as Germany, the Netherlands or Great Britain.[29] Especially noteworthy is the absence of correlation between the extent to which respondents in Portugal perceive "Muslims as supporters of terrorism" and the extent they believe an Islamic presence constitutes a threat to their view of a "Portuguese culture." One would expect that if people believe Muslims support terrorism, they would also believe that Muslim values and traditions are in contradiction with their own; this seems to not be the case.

---

29   Please note that the small correlations in Poland and Hungary may be due to different formulations of the question in these countries (see note 13 and 16).

In sum, these results are consistent with the discrepancy between the public image of Islam conveyed in Portugal as something foreign and the low-profile, reconciliatory image transmitted by the community on a more day-to-day basis. This difference between attitudes may be explained by the heterogeneity of the "Muslim" psychological category. It is possible that people are thinking about different sub-categories of "Muslims" when answering. For some questions, the respondents may be thinking about the Muslim community in Portugal, while some other questions evoke images of Muslim groups generally associated with terrorism and extremist beliefs and behaviours. To answer the questions we put at the beginning of this chapter, it seems that the particular conditions and abilities of the Muslim community in Portugal were able to generate positive attitudes toward Muslims, but that Muslims in general are seen as a foreign group whose values differ from Portuguese values.

7   Muslim Communities in Portugal: Negotiating between (Lack of) Tensions and In-visibility

In this chapter, we have argued that the establishment process of the Muslim community in Portugal developed differently from those in other European countries with the result that there are almost no pressure points, very few controversial issues, and an almost total absence of public voices against the community. Muslims in Portugal have largely been overlooked by researchers, the media and the general public, due not only to the socio-historical characteristics of the time of arrival of a large part of the community but also (and, in our opinion, especially) because of the characteristics of the community itself and its elite representatives. Up to today, the community has shown a remarkable ability to melt into Portuguese society and to deal successfully with issues that could raise tensions. Besides the fact that the Muslim population in Portugal is very small, the particularities of the Portuguese case are rooted in the colonial past (where Muslims of Indian background represented a middle class ethnic minority in Mozambique), in the specific political and historical context of Portuguese decolonization (when small scale Muslim and Hindu minorities had not been an issue in the huge migratory flow of "white Catholic" refugees/returnees from the colonies), and derive from the remarkable social capital and intellectual capacities of these postcolonial people, which are mainly the community leaders of Indian background who came to Lisbon from Mozambique before decolonization. Furthermore, when the immigration patterns had changed in Portugal in the early 1990s, this is to say, when the "country of emigration" had for a short period changed into a "country of immigration," again, the number of Muslims among the "new immigrants" (now without colonial linkage) was very small (see Mapril in this volume on Bangladeshi and Pakistani Muslims).

The silence surrounding the Muslim community in Portugal seems to be reflected in the Portuguese individual attitudes in the form of a discrepancy between the specific attitudes towards the Portuguese Muslim community and towards Muslims and Islam more generally. Thus, on one hand, the results of GFE-E seem to suggest that the individual attitudes specifically towards Portuguese Muslims and Muslims in Portugal may be, in fact, more positive than the individual attitudes in other European countries, probably due to the specific characteristics of the community in Portugal; on the other hand, the results also suggest that this positive image is not extended to attitudes toward Muslims and Islam as a broader category, which is seen as a threat due to the perceived intolerance and connections with terrorism.

As mentioned before, the data from GFE-E is obviously limited, not least due to the nature of the questions and the limited options for the respondents where, as in so many other surveys, a logic of difference and distance is reproduced. Nevertheless, it raises important questions: Do Portuguese people generally think of the Portuguese Muslim community when asked about "Muslims" or does the silence around the community make these people only think about Muslims in Portugal when specifically asked about them? If we asked two similar questions, one pertaining Muslims in Portugal and another pertaining Muslims in general, would different results be obtained? Which specific characteristics do non-Muslim Portuguese associate with Muslims (Portuguese and others)? How do those characteristics differ from those associated with Muslims as a foreign and distant group? Why is the image associated with Muslims in Portugal not extended to Muslims in general? Which of the two images would be a larger determinant in specific situations of conflict between Muslims and non-Muslims? And, would the societal encounter in Portugal still be almost free of tensions and public demonstrations against Islam if the Muslim presence were to gain more visibility?

Answering these and other questions regarding individual attitudes may not only help us paint a more comprehensive picture of the current situation of the Muslim community in Portugal but also help us understand future events regarding the relationship between Muslims and non-Muslims in Portugal regardless of the positive or negative nature of those events.

The chapter has described certain preferences and attitudes that characterize Muslim leaders and leading Islamic institutions in the country and that have shaped the establishment process of the communities and societal encounters. But in order to understand such choices or strategies, one would need to inquire into the power relations and Muslim experiences under colonial rule, as well as constructions of the "Muslim subject" in Portuguese dominant discourses over time.[30] Given Portugal's medieval and colonial history, the Portuguese variety of Islamophobia certainly leads back to the times of the Empire(s) and beyond. What we can assume by looking at only a part of the history of the current Muslim presence in Portugal is that the preference of the Muslim integration leaders for strategies that exclude what in dominant discourse is called "claims-making" derives from their awareness of Islamophobia. Their social capital and ability to rely on informal networks to negotiate single steps in an ongoing establishment process further contributes to the image of not being "too demanding." Not only the results but already the design of the survey show that the idea that Muslims in Europe should not be "too demanding" is taken as conventional wisdom among the non-Muslim population. The Portuguese Muslim migration intelligence, represented by Muslim leaders who were acculturated both under colonial rule and in Portuguese higher education, is certainly aware of this.

---

30   Abdool K. Vakil, "The Crusader Heritage: Portugal and Islam from Colonial to Postcolonial Identities," in *Rethinking Heritage: Cultures and Politics in Europe,* ed. Robert Peckham (New York: I.B. Tauris, 2003), 29–44.

CHAPTER 9

From the Margins to the Fore: Muslim Immigrants in Contemporary Greece

Panos Hatziprokopiou

On 28 February 2010, a public prayer in Constitution Square, at the heart of Athens, sent a message for peace and love across the world begging God to help Greece overcome its escalating economic crisis. Public religious gatherings in Greece have not been rare in recent decades. One may recall, for instance, the struggles over the Rotonda that took place in Thessaloniki in the mid-1990s, when priests and faithful citizens prayed in public objecting to the conversion of the monument into an archaeological and cultural site.[1] Or the huge nationwide demonstrations in 2000 when church-goers, clerics and Orthodox organizations protested the non-inscription of religious beliefs on the new identity cards issued by the state.[2] That one, however, was unique in that it did not involve people pertaining to the majority Christian Orthodox faith, but to Islam. Even more so, the faithful participating in the prayer were not members of the indigenous Muslim minority described in the previous chapter by Evergeti, but were largely migrants from Arabic and South Asian countries. The occasion was the birthday of the Prophet on February 26, which was publicly celebrated two days later so that it falls on a Sunday. This was the fifth year such an event took place in the Greek capital, and more were to follow in the next few months: the *Eid al Fitr* celebration closing Ramadan on 10 September 2010 in *Kotzia Square*, just across from Athens' Town Hall; and the *Eid ul Adha* of November that year at *Propylaia*, the square overlooked by the historical central University building, the Athens Academy and National Library.

All these events involved peaceful prayers, which the representatives of Muslim communities articulated on the basis of necessity since the Greek capital lacks a central mosque appropriate and large enough to host significant

---

1 Mark Mazower, *Salonica, City of Ghosts: Christians, Muslims and Jews, 1430–1950* (London: HarperCollins, 2004).

2 George Mavrogordatos, "Orthodoxy and Nationalism in the Greek Case," *West European Politics* 26/1 (2003); Victor Roudometof, "The Evolution of Greek Orthodoxy in the Context of World Historical Globalisation," in *Orthodox Christianity in 21st Century Greece: The Role of Religion in Culture, Ethnicity and Politics*, ed. Victor Roudometof and Vassilis N. Makrides (Farnham: Ashgate, 2010).

© KONINKLIJKE BRILL NV, LEIDEN, 2019 | DOI:10.1163/9789004404564_011

numbers of believers during important religious festivities.[3] Considering that they all took place in similarly landmark central locations of Athens, they may be interpreted as public statements and citizenship claims by migrant Muslim communities.[4] As such, open public prayers are indicative of a transformation regarding the position of Islam in Greece, one that involves four interrelated shifts. First, there has been a shift in immigration trends: while the 1990s were characterized largely by immigration from the Balkans, Eastern Europe and the former Soviet Union, recent arrivals involve to a great extent migrants from predominantly Muslim countries of Asia and (to a lesser extent) Africa. In turn, there is a change in relevant perceptions of, and discourses about the migrant "Other": from national/ethnic otherness highlighted primarily through the racialization of the most numerous immigrant group, Albanians, during the 1990s, difference is now constructed in more diversified ways that partly include concerns about the growing Muslim presence in the country. As a result, defining who Greece's Muslims are becomes a complex matter, as the rather "exceptional" case of an (indigenous) Muslim minority, limited geographically to the north-east corner of the country, is being enriched by the growing presence and visibility of people who are of Islamic faith and of a migrant background. However, whilst until recently dominant discourses towards (also immigrant) Muslims reflected mostly the historical association of Islam with Turkey and the Turks, as Greece's essential "Others," they lately increasingly tend to echo uneasy European debates over the acceptance, tolerance and integration of Muslims, and the global frames of Islamophobia constructed around the geopolitics of terrorism.

Significantly under-researched in the context of migration studies in Greece and largely unacknowledged in public discourses until recently, the last two decades or so have witnessed a mushrooming of publications on Greece's "new Islam" and its implications.[5] This chapter offers a descriptive account of

---

3 Anna Triandafyllidou and Hara Kouki, "Muslim immigrants and the Greek nation: The emergence of nationalist intolerance," *Ethnicities* 13/6 (2013).

4 Panos Hatziprokopiou and Venetia Evergeti, "Negotiating Religious Diversity and Muslim Identity in Greek Urban Spaces," *Social and Cultural Geography* 15/6 (2014).

5 Dia Anagnostou and Ruby Gropas, "Domesticating Islam and Muslim Immigrants: Political and Church Responses to Constructing a Central Mosque in Athens," in *Orthodox Christianity in 21st Century Greece: The Role of Religion in Culture, Ethnicity and Politics*, ed. Victor Roudometof and Vassilis N. Makrides (Farnham: Ashgate, 2010). Dimitris Antoniou, "Muslim Immigrants in Greece: Religious Organisation and Local Responses," *Immigrants and Minorities* 22/2–3 (2003); Venetia Evergeti, Panos Hatziprokopiou and Nikolas Prevelakis, "Islam in Greece," in *The Oxford Handbook of European Islam*, ed. Jocelyne Cesari (Oxford: Oxford University Press, 2014) [in press]; KSPM, "In Search of Spaces of Coexistence," project report by the *Centre for Support of Repatriate Migrants and Ethnic Greeks* (2007), accessed May 17,

the complexity and diversity characterizing the "new" Muslim population of Greece, and of the various ways through which it has entered the public sphere in recent years. To this end, the chapter mainly builds on official statistics, empirical studies, relevant material from the daily press and the Internet, and occasionally draws on fieldwork research conducted by Dr Venetia Evergeti and the author during 2010–11.[6] Based on this material, and following from the previous chapter, it tells the story of a transition regarding the "place" of Islam in Greece: from a "peripheral" case in Europe, home to an indigenous Muslim minority, to a "core" one whereby Muslim communities relate to transnational migration.

Even though the chapter was originally written before the events of what came to be called the European/Mediterranean migration/refugee "crisis" of 2015, and latest revisions purposively avoided expanding its scope toward latest developments, the discussion suggests that this transition has been underway over the past decades in ways that have set the ground for current trends and tropes. It is organised into two broad sections: the first traces the statistical representation of the immigrant Muslim population of Greece; the second

---

2012, http://www.kspm.gr; Antonios K. Papantoniou, "Muslim Migrants in Athens," (in Greek) *Ekklisia* 86/5 (2009); Athena Skoulariki, "Old and New Mosques in Greece: A New Debate Haunted by History," in *Mosques in Europe: Why a Solution Has Become a Problem*, ed. Stefano Allievi in collaboration with Ethnobarometer, Network of European Foundations' Initiative on Religion and Democracy in Europe (London: Alliance Publishing Trust, 2010); Anna Triandafyllidou, "Greece: The Challenges of Native and Immigrant Muslim Populations," in *Muslims in 21st Century Europe: Structural and Cultural Perspectives*, ed. Anna Triandafyllidou (London: Routledge, 2010); Anna Triandafyllidou and Ruby Gropas, "Constructing Difference: The Mosque Debates in Greece," *Journal of Ethnic and Migration Studies* 35/6 (2009); Sevasti Troubeta, "'Minorization' and 'Ethnicization' in Greek Society: Comparative Perspectives on Moslem Migrants and the Moslem Minority," in *History and Culture of South Eastern Europe: An Annual Journal / Jahrbücher für Geschichte und Kultur Südosteuropas* 5 (2003); Konstantinos Tsitselikis, "The Religious Freedom of Migrants," in *Greece of Migration: Social Participation, Rights and Citizenship*, ed. Miltos Pavlou and Dimitris Christopoulos (Athens: Kritiki/KEMO, 2004); Tsitselikis, "Greece," in *Yearbook of Muslims in Europe. Volume 1*, ed. Jørgen S. Nielsen et al. (Leiden: Brill, 2009); Tsitselikis, "Greece," in *Yearbook of Muslims in Europe. Volume 2*, ed. Jørgen S. Nielsen et al. (Leiden: Brill, 2010); Tsitselikis, *Old and New Islam in Greece: From Historical Minorities to Immigrant Newcomers* (Leiden: Brill, 2012); Elektra Kostopoulou "From mosque to mosque: past and present images of Islamic space in Greece," *Nationalities Papers* 44/5 (2016).

6 The project "Islam in Greece: Religious identity and practice among indigenous Muslims and Muslim immigrants" was funded by the British Arts and Humanities Research Council. Beginning in March 2010 and lasting for 18 months, it involved key-informant and in-depth interviews with migrant associations, Muslim organizations and lay people, as well ethnographic methods including visits to prayer halls and observations of prayers and religious festivities.

explores its presence and visibility in the public sphere. Critically reflecting on the limits of official data, the former situates Muslim communities among the country's immigrant population, accounts for their relative growth and highlights their diversity. The latter engages more substantially with the book's overarching themes, as set out by the editors' introduction: the politics of institutionalisation, dimensions of transnationalism, and the rise of Islamophobia and racism alongside the making of Muslim subjectivities. These are revisited in the concluding section to question the alleged "exceptionality" of Islam in Greece and to underline its transition from the margins to the fore.

1   Tracing Greece's Immigrant Muslim Population in Official Statistics

Public awareness of, and concern about, Muslims in Greece has been until recently exclusively linked to the indigenous Muslim minority of Thrace, whose history is rooted in the country's Ottoman past and whose fate has been partly shaped by diplomatic relations with Turkey. Immigration, which only became relevant as a major phenomenon since the early 1990s,[7] was not originally associated with the Muslim "Other." The numbers of early newcomers – students, migrants or refugees – from Egypt, Syria, Pakistan and elsewhere since the 1970s remained relatively limited up until about a decade ago and did not trigger much public interest in the rise of new Muslim groups. Nor has the arrival of Albanians in the 1990s, who came to constitute the overwhelming majority of immigrants, stimulated wide discussions about Islam in the Greek context. In general, the discourses concerning immigrants in Greece had focused on their ethnicity and legal status, rather than their religious affiliations.

Even when the public debate on establishing a central Mosque in Athens opened anew with the introduction of a relevant Law in 2000, it focused – partly, at least – on the religious needs of Muslim athletes and visitors during the 2004 Olympic Games, rather than those of Muslim immigrants.[8] Although the history of the debates surrounding the building of a Mosque goes back to the nineteenth century, it was only in the last couple of decades that the lack of formal sites of worship and of Islamic burial sites became associated with the presence and needs of the capital's new residents, and even more recent has been the emergence of "Muslims" as a distinct category related specifically

---

7   E.g., Panos Hatziprokopiou, *Globalisation and Contemporary Immigration to Southern European Cities: Processes of Social Incorporation of Balkan Immigrants in Thessaloniki* (Amsterdam: Amsterdam University Press, 2006).

8   Triandafyllidou and Gropas, "Constructing Difference."

to immigrants. Such a shift is inevitably associated with migratory trends developing since the second half of the 1990s and gaining pace in the 2000s, with new arrivals from Middle Eastern and especially South Asian countries growing considerably, while older Arab and other communities had in the meantime settled down, formed families, acquired legal status, and established businesses and associations. This diverse immigrant Muslim population now outsizes numerically the historical officially-designated minority, comes rarely into contact with its institutions, is excluded from the provisions for religious and cultural rights, which are anyway limited to the territory of Thrace, and, crucially, does not – in its majority – enjoy Greek citizenship.

To define this emergent category of migrant Muslims, however, whether for analytical or political purposes, is far from an easy and straightforward task. Estimating the number of Muslim immigrants in Greece, their share among the total migrant population and their characteristics is a difficult exercise entailing both problems identified elsewhere in Europe[9] and the specifics of the Greek case. Various figures have been given from various sources, and many are deliberately exaggerated – especially those coming from conservative and extreme right political circles that capitalize on fears of a supposed Islamic threat, but also those provided by Muslim migrant associations aiming at raising social awareness.[10] Most scholars engaging in such attempts base their calculations on Census data, or on data on residence permits, and some try to incorporate irregular migrants in their estimations. Since the 1951 Census, however, there is no official data on religious beliefs in Greece, so the only available information comes from nationality statistics. Yet, even well-thought and well-intended estimates are problematic and guesses often appear odd. Skoulariki[11] reviews estimates varying from 200,000 to about 300,000 people. Tsitselikis[12] reports that about one fourth (200,000) of all foreign nationals recorded in the 2001 Census were Muslims (not including Albanians), claiming that "the estimated Muslim population of Greece in 2008 (Greek and non-Greek citizens) was 350,000, making 3.1% of the total population" (including the minority). Anagnostou and Gropas[13] calculate the share of Muslims at 29.5 per cent among the foreign population recorded in the 2001 Census, but give no details of what they base their calculation on.

---

9   Mark Brown, "Quantifying the Muslim Population in Europe: Conceptual and Data Issue," *Social Research Methodology* 3/2 (2000).

10   Tsitselikis, *Old and New Islam in Greece*, 161–162.

11   Skoulariki, "Old and New Mosques in Greece," 305, n. 13.

12   Tsitselikis, "Greece" (2010), 234–235.

13   Anagnostou and Gropas, "Domesticating Islam and Muslim Immigrants," 92.

Considering the relative novelty of mass migration to Greece and the limited access of third country nationals and their descendants to naturalization, data on the nationality of migrants remains the only available point of reference.[14] However, using nationality as a proxy by counting citizens of predominantly Muslim countries may be tricky. This is not only because statistics tell us nothing about who is religious or observing and who is not, but also because clear-cut nationality categories do not strictly coincide with faith groups. Accordingly, we do know that there are segments of Egyptians, Lebanese, or Syrian migrants who are of Christian background, but it is rather impossible to safely estimate their shares among the respective immigrant groups from these countries; in a similar fashion, we cannot be sure about the proportions of Muslims among Nigerians or Indians in Greece – and so on. Additionally, there are particularities specific to Greek history or recent migratory trends. For instance, Turkish nationals residing in Greece may be political refugees of Turkish or Kurdish origin, while a good number of them come from the minority of Thrace, who were deprived of their Greek citizenship upon emigration to Turkey in earlier decades.[15] Similarly, most immigrants from Central Asian former Soviet republics, such as Kazakhstan or Uzbekistan, are expected to be of ethnic Greek origin and thus of Christian Orthodox background.[16] Above all, the vast majority of migrants (52.7 per cent in the 2011 Census, and 68 per cent among migrants holding a valid residence permit at the end of 2017) come from neighbouring Albania – a country with a 70 per cent nominally Muslim population. It would be misleading though to consider that an equivalent proportion of Albanian migrants in Greece are practising Muslims, due

---

14 According to EUROSTAT data on citizenship acquisition, less than 80,000 foreign nationals acquired Greek citizenship between 1991 and 2011, 90 per cent of whom since 2001. It was only in the last few years that legislative changes eased access to citizenship for long term residents and especially for the so-called second generation.

15 Following the 1955 riots against the Greek Orthodox minority of Istanbul, about 50,000 Thracian Muslims who had migrated to Turkey were deprived of their Greek citizenship between 1955 and 1998 on the basis of article 19 of the Greek citizenship code, which was previously applied to communists who fled to Eastern Europe after the Democratic Army's defeat in the Greek civil war. See Dia Anagnostou, "Deepening Democracy or Defending the Nation? The Europeanisation of Minority Rights and Greek Citizenship," *West European Politics* 28/2 (2005).

16 These may be Muslim majority countries, but most migrants from these countries in Greece claimed ethnic Greek origin and were subject to a special legal status that treated them as "repatriates" and eventually granted them citizenship; see, e.g. Panagoula Diamanti-Karanou, "Migration of Ethnic Greeks from the Former Soviet Union to Greece, 1990–2000: Policy Decisions and Implications," *Southeast European and Black Sea Studies* 3/1 (2003).

to historical peculiarities of religion and Islam in Albania as well as to the patterns of Albanian migration and settlement in Greece.

The former relate partly to the historical predicament of Albanian Islam, characterized by a particularly tolerant and flexible approach under the influence of the "pantheist" Bektashi order, which allowed common observation of religious feasts and customs among Muslims and Christians, as well as interfaith relations including marriages, or even conversions.[17] Moreover, the origins of the Albanian nation-state are to be found in a form of nationalism that needed to break ties with Ottoman authority and Turkish identity and at the same time longed for uniting a population with diverse religious affiliations.[18] This unity was achieved by placing emphasis on language, blood and land, the latter two referring to common ancestry and history in a given geographical space, rather than religion, as central elements of Albanian national identity.[19] After World War II, Emver Hoxha's isolationist rule included an absolute banning of religion which picked up in 1967, when Albania was proclaimed the world's first (and only) officially atheist state – and remained so until the collapse of the regime in 1991. Religious activities may have resumed since then, but there were already generations who grew up without any practice of religion at all. Migration to Greece, especially at the early stage, involved mostly people from these younger generations.

On the other hand, a considerable proportion of Albanian migrants in Greece are from Greek roots and thus of Christian Orthodox heritage.[20] Not only did they receive differential treatment by the Greek polity, but they were also thought to be better-welcomed by society at large, which led to peculiar adaptation strategies by non-ethnic Greek migrants that are indicative of a

---

17 It is worth noting that the 15th century Albanian national hero Skanderbeg (Gjerji Kastrioti), known for resistance to Ottoman advancement, was born Christian, converted to Islam and then back to Christianity.

18 Elira Cella, "Albanian Muslims, Human Rights and Relations with the Islamic World," in *Muslim Communities in the New Europe,* ed. Gerd Nonneman, Timothy Niblock and Bogdan Szajkowski (Reading: Ithaca Press, 1996); Miranda Vickers, *The Albanians: A Modern History* (New York: I.B. Tauris, 2006). Intellectuals of the Albanian National Awakening in the late 19th century were also concerned with convincing European powers that Albanians constitute a separate people, against the Ottoman state's official stance that did not acknowledge a distinct Albanian identity, but also against neighbouring nationalisms claiming Albanian Christians as "their own"; see Gazmend Kapllani, "Religion and Albanian National Identity: Myths and Realities," (in Greek) *Synchrona Themata* 81 (2002): 52.

19 Kapllani, "Religion and Albanian National Identity," 52.

20 According to EUROSTAT data on citizenship acquisition, 48,336 Albanian nationals have acquired Greek citizenship between 2007 and 2011; it is assumed that the majority of these are of ethnic Greek origin, and that most remaining Albanian citizens holding ethnic Greek status will have been granted citizenship since then.

FROM THE MARGINS TO THE FORE

flexible, and largely indifferent, approach to religion. Such strategies included practices of name changing, especially adopting Christian Orthodox names when the original ones indicated a Muslim background, as well as official conversions through baptizing, even if these were not necessarily related to faith as such but can rather be seen as adaptation strategies.[21] Undoubtedly, such practices may have been to an extent imposed by the host society's stances, partly reflecting "the continuing ... importance of the Orthodox religion in the Greek collective imagination."[22] Indicative of this is a study conducted in northern Greece in the second half of the 1990s that confirmed sentiments of mistrust towards Albanian migrants partly because of their "Muslim" religion.[23] Considering, however, how widespread "Albanophobia" was throughout the 1990s, direct references to the religion of immigrants have been remarkably scarce. Apart from cases of baptizing, there is little evidence of interest in religion coming from the migrants themselves while public expressions of such an interest have been totally absent. Interestingly, Hatzopoulos and Kambouri[24] report on the reactions they received from Albanian migrants they approached for interviews on the theme of religion and migration: most expressed either their ignorance on the subject or the irrelevance of the research topic in their case. Moreover, among the numerous informal prayer halls operating in Athens, there are none set up by Albanian immigrants, while evidence from our own fieldwork during 2010–2011 suggests that the numbers of Albanians attending prayers in the capital's informal sites of worship are relatively low.

Excluding Albanians, as well as nationals of former Soviet countries, immigrants from Muslim-majority countries exhibit a limited yet growing presence in official statistics. As shown in Table 9.1, from nearly 50,000 recorded in the 2001 Census, about 6.5 per cent among Greece's foreign population, their numbers have almost doubled within a decade with just below 90,000 people recorded in the 2011 Census: one out of ten immigrants in Greece now appears to come from a Muslim country. The number of Pakistanis has tripled: they were the twelfth largest migrant group in 2001, and the fourth in 2011; Bangladeshis

---

21 In the author's study on Albanian migrants in Thessaloniki, one fifth of the sample had declared non-religious, and another ten per cent said they had been baptized in Greece (Hatziprokopiou, *Globalisation and Contemporary Immigration*, 88; see also chapter 8.2.3).

22 Hatziprokopiou, *Globalisation and Contemporary Immigration*, 228.

23 Panagiotis Kafetzis et al., "Empirical Dimensions of Xenophobia," (in Greek) in *Macedonia and the Balkans: Xenophobia and Development*, ed. Aikaterini Michalopoulou et al. (Athens: EKKE & Alexandria, 1998).

24 Pavlos Hatzopoulos and Neli Kambouri, "National Case Study: Thematic Study on Religion," Ge.M.IC. research project, WP 6 – Greece (Athens: Panteion University, 2010), 9–10.

TABLE 9.1   Foreign nationals in Greece originating from Muslim countries, 2001–2011

country of citizenship	2001			2011			2001–2011 % change
	rank	N	%	rank	N	%	
all foreign nationals	–	762,191	6.97	–	911,929	8.43	**19.6**
Albania	1	438036	57.47	1	480,824	52.73	9.8
Muslim countries[a]							
of which:		49,460	6.49		89,325	9.80	80.6
Pakistan	12	11,130	1.46	4	34,177	3.75	207.1
Bangladesh	25	4,854	0.64	12	11,076	1.21	128.2
Egypt	16	7,448	0.98	14	10,455	1.15	40.4
Syria	23	5,552	0.73	18	7,628	0.84	37.4
Turkey	14	7,881	1.03	21	5,157	0.76	-34.6
Iran	37	1,011	0.13	32	1,569	0.57	55.2
Iraq	18	6,936	0.91	25	3,692	0.40	-46.8
Afghanistan	54	371	0.05	19	6,911	0.21	1762.8
Morocco	50	526	0.07	29	1,910	0.17	263.1
Algeria	61	267	0.04	39	1,119	0.12	319.1
Lebanon	33	1,277	0.17	45	876	0.10	-31.4
Somalia	103	27	0.00	46	863	0.09	3096.3
Sudan	55	356	0.05	50	740	0.08	107.9
Senegal	98	37	0.00	54	669	0.07	1708.1
Tunisia	67	231	0.03	56	631	0.07	173.2
Other countries							
e.g. including[b]:		273,887	35.93		335,075	36.74	22.3
India	17	7,216	0.36	11	11,333	0.02	57.1
Nigeria	30	2015	0.22	27	3,285	0.43	63.0
Ethiopia	35	1424	0.16	31	1606	0.21	12.8
Stateless/ Unknown[c]		808	0.01		6,705	0.74	729.8

SOURCE: HELLENIC STATISTICAL AUTHORITY, ACCESSED FEBRUARY 20, 2014, HTTP://WWW
.STATISTICS.GR.

a   Countries with a (nominally) Muslim population of more than 50 per cent (excluding Albania and the former Soviet republics of Central Asia);
b   Examples of migrants from countries with significant Muslim populations;
c   Stateless persons or undeclared nationality

more than doubled, while the numbers of Egyptians, Syrians and Iranians have also grown significantly. Even more spectacular has been the rise of new refugee groups, especially from Afghanistan as well as Somalia, Senegal, and other African countries. Although Census data picture a predominately young, working age and male-dominated population, they also reveal variations reflecting migratory patterns and routes. Among longer-established groups, such as Egyptians or Syrians, women and children formed respectively 23–30 per cent and 16–22 per cent in 2011, and the growth of these shares since 2001 reflect some degree of family formation or reunification. By contrast, women and children were hardly present among South Asians (less than five per cent) and largely remain so; in our interviews with Pakistani migrants we came across men who have been working in Greece for years while their families lived in Pakistan, and this appears to be a common pattern applying to many. What is interesting and common to most groups, however, is that the majority of immigrants from Muslim countries are overwhelmingly concentrated in the Greater Athens area: according to the 2011 Census, nearly 75 per cent of Egyptians, 68.3 per cent of Pakistanis and 78.2 per cent of Bangladeshis lived in the region of Attica (compared to about 45 per cent among the total number of foreign nationals).

Table 9.1 additionally shows that the numbers of stateless persons and of those who have not declared their nationality have also increased substantially, which is indicative of the migration turnaround taking place during the 2000s when Greece came to receive the vast majority of new arrivals entering the EU by crossing the Greek-Turkish border. Clearly then, even if one attempts to go through nationality-based data by acknowledging their limitations and problems, there remains an unknown "hidden" population of immigrants and refugees without documents, many of whom originate from Muslim-majority countries. Official data on undocumented aliens apprehended by the Greek police and coastal guard point to a radical shift around the mid-2000s, with numbers almost doubling in the second half of the decade – as illustrated in Figure 9.1[25]. Among those, the share of Albanians dropped from about 60 per cent in 2006–07 to just over 20 per cent in 2014. By contrast, the shares

---

25   Data are from the Greek Police website, accessed December 4, 2017, http://www.hellenic
      police.gr. Apprehensions spiralled from just over 63,500 in 2005 to 132,524 in 2010, then
      declined with 43,000 in 2013 (possibly due to increased border controls and the economic
      crisis in Greece, but also a broader reshuffling of migratory channels and smuggling
      routes), before rising again since 2014. One should bear in mind that figures are indicative
      of movement but not of actual numbers, reflecting the extent and efficacy of policing and
      counting arrests rather than people (undocumented migrants may have been arrested at
      least twice, e.g., on the border and in Athens).

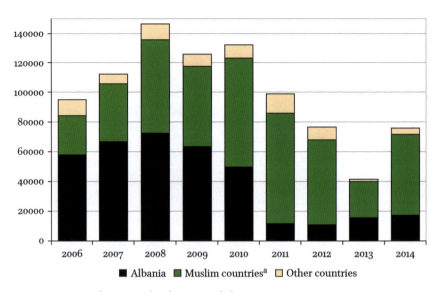

FIGURE 9.1 Apprehensions of undocumented aliens in Greece 2006–2014
SOURCE: GREEK POLICE, ACCESSED DECEMBER 4, 2017, HTTP://WWW.HELLENICPOLICE.GR.
a Counting only nationals of countries with more than 50 per cent Muslim population.

of migrants from Muslim countries, hardly exceeding 10 per cent in 2005, mounted to more than 70 per cent in 2014; the principal nationalities were Afghanistan, Iraq, Pakistan, Palestine and Syria.

Certainly, not all these migrants are "here to stay." For many, Greece is not a chosen destination; a proportion – especially asylum seekers – inevitably transit though Greece on their way to some western European country. Many, however, end up staying for shorter or longer periods due to restrictive EU policies (primarily the Dublin regulation) and long-standing inadequacies of Greek immigration and asylum policy. Thousands are deported on an annual basis, and even more are being detained, while some eventually manage to make it out of the country by irregular means. Even if the refugee crisis may have marked yet another turning point in the contours of Muslim migration to Greece[26], the

---

26 In 2015 alone, more than 860,000 people crossed the Greek-Turkish borders. More than half of them were fleeing war in Syria, and significant shares were from Afghanistan and Iraq; yet the vast majority transited through Greece in search of asylum to other European destinations. Since the EU-Turkey common statement of March 2016 new arrivals are now stranded in Greece, with more than 170,000 having applied for asylum between 2016 and November 2018 (data are from the Greek Asylum Service website, accessed on December 12, 2018, http://asylo.gov.gr/en/).

FROM THE MARGINS TO THE FORE

difficulties arising from ongoing recession has impacted decisively on migratory and settlement patterns, resulting in considerable fluctuations in official statistics.

In the last few years, as a combined result of growing unemployment and of the (until recently) continuing dependence of legal status on formal employment, many migrants shifted back to irregularity as joblessness renders them unable to renew their residence permits, while there is a marked trend of many returning to their countries of origin or re-migrating.[27] Accordingly, the numbers and proportions of legally resident immigrants from Muslim countries since the mid-2000s have grown and then dropped: from less than 46,500 or 10.2 per cent of the total in 2005 to over 55,500 in 2009 and then to about 52,000 or 9 per cent in 2016.[28] Similarly, considering the high incidence of informal employment among migrants in Greece, nationals of the five most represented Muslim countries of origin who were directly insured as paid employees had grown from just over 18,000 in 2004 (8 per cent of the total foreign nationals) to more than 28,000 in 2008 (10.3 per cent of the total), then to just over 19,500 (8,3 per cent) in 2016. On the other hand, migrants of the same nationalities who were insured as self-employed have increased from nearly 1,680 (7.4 per cent of the total) at the fall of 2010 to 2,71 (10.1 per cent) by January 2016.[29]

How are we then to make sense of official data? Beyond any discussion of numbers, the question of Muslim presence in Greece concerns actual religious practice, community organization and collective mobilization, as well as exposure to formal or informal discrimination or Islamophobic prejudice and racism. The material presented in this section suggests that the category of immigrant "Muslims" in the Greek context points to a diverse, mobile and highly fluctuating population whose material circumstances (legal status, employment, social security, etc.) are also shifting. Yet, even if exact numbers remain

---

27   Anna Triandafyllidou, "Migration in Greece: People, Policies and Practices," in *Governing Irregular Migration* (IRMA) project document (Athens: ELIAMEP, 2013), accessed April 15, 2014, http://irma.eliamep.gr/wp-content/uploads/2013/02/IRMA-Background-Report-Greece.pdf.

28   Data on residence permits were provided from the Ministry of the Interior upon request (except for 2016, which were drawn from the Ministry for Migration Policy website, accessed December 4, 2017, www.immigration.gov.gr); they refer to 31 December each year, and mostly concern adults since children are covered by their parents' legal status.

29   Namely Egypt, Syria, Iraq, Bangladesh and Pakistan. Data on immigrants insured as paid employees (referring to August each year) are from IKA, the largest social security fund: IKA website, accessed March 3, 2014 (www.ika.gr); 2016 data (not counting Iraqis) are from the new EFKA website, accessed December 3, 2017 (www.efka.gov.gr). Data on immigrants insured with OAEE as self-employed have been provided to the author upon request.

unknown and the economic crisis currently affects both migratory patterns and living conditions, there has been a trend of growing Muslim presence among Greece's migrant population since the 1990s. The next section explores some qualitative dimensions of this presence and its visibility in the Greek public sphere.

2 The Rise of Immigrant Muslims in the Greek Public Sphere

The key demographics sketched above, but also residential clusters and labour market niches, make the presence of Muslim migrants increasingly visible in Athens, where the majority are concentrated. These, as the population concerned, are characterized by significant diversity. Despite overarching demographic and socio-economic patterns, the brief overview presented above points to the heterogeneity of the immigrant Muslim population, which comprises different national and ethnic origins, diverse migration histories and migratory plans and routes, varying legal statuses and socio-economic conditions. Similarly, there is no single pattern of religious organization and practice among Greece's new Muslim residents since they belong to different Islamic traditions, practice their faith to varying degrees and engage in different modes of collective mobilization in their struggles for rights and recognition. Still, from various forms of mobilization to everyday religious practice, and from State and Church considerations to Islamophobic and racist reactions, the presence of immigrant Muslims has been receiving increasing public attention, and several issues concerning that presence have come to the fore of the Greek public sphere. The following paragraphs offer some examples of how awareness of the presence of the "new" Muslim "Other," here and among "us," has become public in the last two decades.

Religious rights as such, as far as the institutional basis of religious freedom and tolerance is concerned, are certainly safeguarded by the Greek Constitution and a number of international treaties.[30] At the same time, however, there are a number of (political) implications arising from the peculiar relationship between the Orthodox Church and the Greek State,[31] according to which

---

30   The framework for religious freedom in Greece is determined by article 5 (paragraphs 2 and 13) of the Greek Constitution, articles 9 and 14 of the European Convention on Human Rights, articles 18 and 27 of the International Covenant on Civil and Political Rights, articles 14 and 30 of the Convention on the Rights of the Child; see Tsitselikis, "The Religious Freedom of Migrants."

31   Mavrogordatos, "Orthodoxy and Nationalism in the Greek Case"; Roudometof, "The Evolution of Greek Orthodoxy in the Context of World Historical Globalisation."

the Church enjoys a privileged position vis-à-vis other religious groups and maintains the authority to control their activities.[32] For example, the earlier-mentioned 2000 Law on the establishment of a central Mosque in Athens was never implemented, partly due to reactions from the Orthodox Church. The Church's official position was in fact not objecting to the mosque itself, but to its attached Islamic cultural centre; yet the local bishop at Paiania, the district where the Mosque was to be constructed, located near the airport, managed to mobilize religious residents against the construction, arguing that a building of Islamic architecture would create false impressions to visitors who may think Greece is a Muslim country.[33] A new Law, 3512 of 2006, managed to survive conservative objections and currently determines the procedures for finally building the Mosque in Elaionas, a district at the western edge of central Athens. Since then, however, the public debates surrounding the building of a central Mosque in Athens refer to the city's immigrant Muslim residents, and sometimes take into account the opinions of imams, community leaders and representatives.

To be fair, as on other occasions, objections come not only from the Church, but also from ultra-nationalist and extreme right political circles,[34] as well as from conservative politicians within mainstream political parties and their wider considerations of the supposed "political cost."[35] Such objections bear heavy references to Greek national identity, which, because of the strong emphasis on Orthodoxy within it, is thought to be incompatible with Islam.[36] Yet, at the same time, they also entail Orientalist accounts of Islam and the Muslim "other"[37] as backward, incompatible with "western" secular democratic values, oppressive towards women, etc., while at the same time reproduce "imported" prejudices associating Islam with fanaticism and terrorism, following the international current of Islamophobia in the post-9/11 geopolitical order that portrays Muslim populations as a potential threat. To give a rather indicative example, just a few weeks before the public prayer introducing this chapter,

---

32   Tsitselikis, "The Religious Freedom of Migrants"; Tsitselikis, *Old and New Islam in Greece.*

33   Triandafyllidou and Gropas, "Constructing Difference"; Skoulariki, "Old and New Mosques in Greece."

34   Hatzopoulos and Kambouri, "National Case Study."

35   See: Triandafyllidou and Gropas, "Constructing Difference"; Skoulariki, "Old and New Mosques in Greece."

36   Venetia Evergeti and Panos Hatziprokopiou, "On Muslims, Turks and migrants: perceptions of Islam in Greece and the Challenge of Migration," in *Myths of the Other in the Balkans: Representations, Social Practices, Performances*, ed. Fotini Tsibitidou and Nikitas Palantzas (Thessaloniki: www.balkanmyth.com, 2013).

37   Edward Said, *Orientalism* (New York: Vintage Books, 1979).

an organization named "Panhellenic Commission of Patriotic and Christian Associations and Friends of Mount Athos" called for a rally to be held in central Athens on 6 February 2010. As shown in Figure 9.2 below, the poster advertising the event pictured a woman wearing an Afghani-style burka and the stated slogan was "NO: to the Islamization of Greece, to the shrinking of our national borders, to globalization." Although views of this kind may remain marginal and limited to ultra-nationalist and extreme right groups, they have grown in the context of the escalating economic crisis in the country, while anti-immigrant hate-talk and racist attacks increasingly seem to target Muslims.[38] More recent incidents include mobilizations against the building of the central Mosque, which may partly explain why no construction company placed a bid for four consecutive times in the relevant competition, despite the attractive state funding (approximately 900,000 euros), and why procedures still delay even though the project has been finally undertaken by a joint venture involving Greece's four largest construction companies, and building has begun since November 2016. Reports monitor an overall rise of violent racist attacks since 2011, with many of the victims being newcomers from Muslim countries (predominantly Afghanis, Pakistanis, and Egyptians).[39] A crucial development has been the electoral success, in June 2012, of an openly neo-Nazi party, "Chrysi Avgi" (= "Golden Dawn"), members of which are currently facing charges for violent attacks, including at least two murders. Despite ongoing (since autumn 2013) legal action against them, opinion polls reveal a persistent support by a significant segment of the electorate.

Yet, even if extreme racist feelings remain relatively marginal among the wider native population, Islamophobic sentiments are probably gaining pace. Back in 2010–11, Muslim immigrants interviewed during our fieldwork in Athens did not complain about facing prejudice or discrimination on the basis of their religion, but stressed instead the wider difficulties affecting migrants in Greece, underlining problems with the state, the police, the procedures of issuing and renewing their residence permits, as well as problems related to employment and working conditions. Moreover, Islam remains an unknown territory for most native Greeks, even if not inscribed in prejudice. In a 2009 opinion poll, some 77 per cent of respondents said they have limited knowledge of Islam; while about 19–23 per cent responded negatively to concepts such as

---

38   Hatzopoulos and Kambouri, "National Case Study," 3.

39   See, e.g., the Human Rights Watch 2012 report *Hate on the Streets: Xenophobic Violence in Greece*, accessed July 12, 2012, http://www.hrw.org/sites/default/files/reports/greece 0712ForUpload_0.pdf.

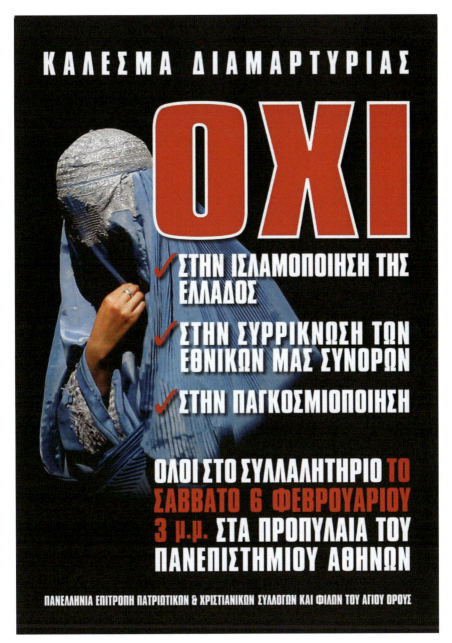

FIGURE 9.2 Extreme right anti-Muslim poster
SOURCE: HTTP://WWW.THERMOPILAI.ORG/CONTENT/SULLALETERIO
-STA-PROPULAIA-OKHI-STEN-ISLAMOPOIESE-TES-ELLADOS

"jihad," "burqa" and the "Islamic veil," similar proportions reacted positively, and very limited shares reacted negatively to "Quran," "Mosques," "Muslims," "Prophet Muhammad" or "Islam."[40] Nevertheless, increasing interaction between immigrants and natives in everyday life brings awareness of the presence and habits of the migrant Muslim "Other," who is often exposed to old stereotypes and newly-formed prejudices surrounding "Muslims" and "Islam." The former sometimes entail persistent historical associations of Islam with Turkey and of Muslims with Turks,[41] which often re-emerge in the encounters of Muslims of immigrant background with native Greeks, including young people born and raised in Greece.[42] The latter increasingly bear similarities to the kind of Islamophobic stereotypes observed elsewhere in Europe. Among Egyptians migrants, for example, those of Christian Coptic background appear to be closer to the host population, whereas Muslims face prejudice associated with their religious habits, such as, e.g., not eating pork or consuming alcohol.[43] Similar differentiations with respect to contacts with the native population have been observed among Christian and Muslim Iraqis.[44] Even if this often remains a *private* matter of interpersonal relations, it partly reflects an increase in contacts between natives and Muslim immigrants, and a rising awareness of the latter's presence.

Similarly, increasing awareness may be related to the immigrants' different religious practice. The key spaces wherein such practice takes place have been informal prayer halls, which mushroomed alongside the settlement of immigrant Muslim communities – from just a few in the 1990s to more than 100

---

40   Public Issue, "Οι Έλληνες και το Ισλάμ: Τι γνωρίζει και τι πιστεύει η κοινή γνώμη" (Greeks and Islam: What Public Opinion Knows and Believes. Public Issue Opinion Surveys), November 17, 2010, accessed February 2, 2013, http://www.publicissue.gr/1395. It is worth noting that recent polls in the context of the migration "crisis" register higher shares of negative views: e.g., despite evidence of widespread compassion and active solidarity in a survey conducted in January 2016, 33 and 51 per cent of respondents reacted negatively to the words "Muslims" and "Islam" respectively. See DiaNEOsis. "Greeks and the refugee problem," February 2016, accessed December 7, 2017, https://www.dianeosis.org/wp-content/uploads/2016/02/immigration_04.pdf.

41   Evergeti and Hatziprokopiou, "On Muslims, Turks and migrants."

42   Papantoniou, "Muslim Migrants in Athens"; Evergeti, Hatziprokopiou and Prevelakis, "Islam in Greece."

43   Nikos Gogonas, "Religion as a Core Value in Language Maintenance: Arabic Speakers in Greece," *International Migration* 50/2 (2010): 113–129.

44   Sophia. I. Wanche, "An Assessment of the Iraqi Community in Greece," report commissioned by the UNHCR Representation in Greece, Evaluation & Policy Analysis Unit, 2004, accessed June 13, 2012, http://www.aina.org/reports/aoticig.pdf.

during 2010–11 – and thus increasingly attract public attention.[45] The studies available testify to some degree of segregation of informal prayer sites along lines of nationality (e.g. between Pakistanis, Bangladeshis and migrants from Arabic countries[46]), but also locality,[47] as well as religious denomination. This diversity by no means undermines the importance of religious practice and of Islamic sites of worship among Athens' Muslim population. For instance, the attachment of Pakistanis to transnational religious networks allows the maintenance of ties with places of origin while providing a source of identity and a space for organizing informal prayer sites in Athens that become central points of reference for locally-based communities in specific districts.[48] The same is observed among Bangladeshis, Egyptians and others.[49] Fieldwork evidence suggests that informal prayer sites re-establish to an extent the function of the mosque at the local level not only as a religious institution, but also as a familiar space within an alien environment, a contact point and base for the community, as well as a hub in transnational space.[50] Although these are in essence *private* venues, usually rented by a religious or immigrant association, they form *public* spaces for the local community of believers and are collectively funded and maintained. Moreover, although they do not, in most cases, publicly denote their character as religious sites, they are still recognized as such by community members and are thus known to neighbours, landlords

---

45   E.g., "Which are the 'Informal Mosques' of Athens," *Kathimerini*, April 13, 2013, accessed March 3, 2014, http://www.kathimerini.gr/33813/article/epikairothta/ellada/poia-einai-ta -atypa-tzamia-ths-a8hnas. However, follow-up visits to informal prayer halls revealed that their number may have been reduced in the meantime, due to financial problems facing mosque communities that have even led to the closure of some venues. On the other hand, legal adjustments seem to have opened the path for some prayer halls to be licenced as sites of worship, with at least four such cases as of January 2017.

46   KPSM, "In Search of Spaces of Coexistence"; Papantoniou, "Muslim Migrants in Athens."

47   Hatziprokopiou and Evergeti, "Negotiating Religious Diversity and Muslim Identity in Greek Urban Spaces."

48   Inam U. Leghari, "Pakistani Immigrants in Greece: From Changing Pattern of Migration to Diaspora Politics and Transnationalism" (paper presented at the *4th LSE PhD Symposium on Contemporary Greece*, LSE-Hellenic Observatory, 25–26 June 2009), accessed October 8, 2010, www.lse.ac.uk/collections/hellenicObservatory/pdf/4th_%20Symposium/PAPERS _PPS/ETHNICITY_IMMIGRATION/LEGHARI.pdf; Antonis Liakos and Emilia Salvanou, "Citizenship, Memory and Governmentality: A Tale of Two Migrant Communities," in *Citizenships and Identities: Inclusion, Exclusion, Participation*, ed. Ann K. Isaacs (Pisa: Plus-Pisa University Press, 2010), accessed October 15, 2014, http://antonisliakos.files .wordpress.com/2011/04/citizenship-and-memory.pdf.

49   KPSM, "In Search of Spaces of Coexistence"; Papantoniou, "Muslim Migrants in Athens."

50   Hatziprokopiou and Evergeti, "Negotiating Religious Diversity and Muslim Identity in Greek Urban Spaces."

and the authorities. Moreover, the very fact that (most) existing prayer halls are *informal*, i.e., not only do they operate in flats, basements, garages and storerooms, but they also lack a formal licence as sites of worship,[51] has resulted in very high fines imposed on migrant Muslim associations in cases where their use of a rented space for religious purposes is brought to court.[52]

The differentiations mentioned above have allowed little space for the various nationality-based and religious organizations to come together in a single formal body of collective representation.[53] Our fieldwork back in 2010–2011 confirmed that, with the exception of the question of Athens' Central Mosque, this still remained the case, also reflecting different politics or approaches to Islam between and within migrant and religious communities. Even so, the diversity of organized collectives and associations is further testimony to the rising migrant Muslim voices in the Greek public sphere. As early as in 1997, a Panhellenic Federation of Supporting Muslims in Greece named "Filotita" was set up in Athens on the initiative of indigenous (minority) Muslims; although it extended membership to migrants of various nationalities,[54] it has been inactive in recent years. In the meantime, the *Muslim Association of Greece* was formed in 2003 by nationals of Arabic countries and has grown to become the largest and perhaps also the most influential organization at present, with a public voice and with ties to a vast network of religious groups and immigrants of diverse ethnic origins.[55] Yet, since 2007, a Greek-Arabic Cultural Centre, partner of the Federation of Islamic Organisations in Europe, functions in south-west Athens attracting migrants of Arabic origin as it hosts the largest operating (informal) mosque with a separate prayer hall for women and also has a library, Quranic education for children and various other activities. Immigrants from South Asian countries, on the other hand, have established their own organizations. Our own fieldwork in Athens located seven Pakistani religious organizations of diverse religious denominations and Islamic

---

51   Such a licence lies under the authority of the Ministry of Education and Religious Affairs and involves consultation with the Orthodox Church; as mentioned, at least four such licences were valid in January 2017.

52   Emilia Salvanou, "Pakistani Migrants at N. Ionia. A Community at the Procedure of Forming: Narratives and Representations through Space and Time," report on the project *Culture, Identity and Movement: A Study in the Social Anthropology of the Everyday Life and Popular Representations of Migrants from Pakistan in Nea Ionia* (Athens: John Latsis Public Benefit Foundation, 2009), accessed April 29, 2012, www.latsis-foundation.org/files/Programmes2008-2009/Dermentzopoulos%20FINAL%20REPORT.pdf.

53   Antoniou, "Muslim immigrants in Greece."

54   Mehmet Imam and Olga Tsakiridi, *Muslims and Social Exclusion* (in Greek) (Athens: Livanis, 2003).

55   Evergeti, Hatziprokopiou and Prevelakis, "Islam in Greece."

traditions, confirming what has been described by other researchers:[56] from neo-Sufi groups including Minhaj-ul-Quran or Dawat-e-Islami, related to the Balrevi movement, to missionary networks such as the Tablighi Jamaat originating from the Deobandi movement; and there are also two Shia associations. These groups are part of transnational networks and maintain ties in countries of origin or diaspora communities in Europe and beyond, while in many cases, relate to one or more informal masjids operating in various parts of Athens; in some cases they are also represented within (non-religious) migrant community organizations. Moreover, at least two virtual organizations – i.e., websites on Islam in the Greek language – offer general information about Islam addressing Muslims in the country.[57]

The open prayers of 2010 that introduced this chapter are perhaps the most indicative example of how Athens' new Muslim residents made their presence – and religious identity – public. Yet, these were among the last such events formally organized by majority Muslim communities to take place in Athens. As with other issues that trigger controversy in the public sphere, the authorities appeared bewildered by Golden Dawn's expanding electoral appeal amidst Greece's escalating financial woes, austerity and the resulting social breakdown and sleepwalked to the adoption of a conservative anti-immigrant discourse and policy measures. In that frame, local authorities in Greater Athens made conscious efforts not to have Islamic festivals celebrated in the open public space, offering instead large stadiums for such purposes, such as the Olympic Stadium in the northern part of the city or the "Peace and Friendship" Stadium in the South. Yet, Muslim organizations chose not to apply for using these venues, for instance, on the occasion of the July 2013 Eid al-Fitr prayers, opting for smaller places, in most cases self-arranged. Notably, the president of the Muslim Association issued a media statement expressing the wish for the 2014 Eid prayer to be hosted in Athens' central mosque, which did not materialize. In the following years, certain groups organised festivities in public space, yet, perhaps in less pronounced locations, without much controversy and despite reactions by the radical right; for example, the regular Ashura commemorations organized annually by a Shi'a Pakistani community at a backstreet outside their premises in Piraeus.[58]

---

56   Leghari, "Pakistani Immigrants in Greece"; George Kassimeris and Antonis Samouris, "Examining Islamic Associations of Pakistani and Bangladeshi Immigrants in Greece," *Religion, State and Society* 40/2 (2012).

57   Islam.gr team, accessed October 13, 2014, http://www.islam.gr; Islam for Greeks website, accessed October 13, 2014, http://islamforgreeks.org.

58   Marios Chatziprokopiou and Panos Hatziprokopiou, "Between the politics of difference and the poetics of similarity: Performing Ashura in Pireaus," *Journal of Muslims in Europe* 6/2 (2017).

Even more importantly, there have recently been several examples of immigrant Muslims' mobilization beyond religious celebrations. On 23 September 2012, the provocative online video entitled "The Innocence of Muslims" caused angry demonstrations by groups of Muslim immigrants in Athens, as it did elsewhere in Europe, as well as in the Muslim world and beyond. Even if religious concerns may lie at the background, such incidents clearly have a more political character, reflecting broader geopolitical imbalances in the relations between "the Muslim world" and "the West" and revealing the marginal position many Muslim migrants have in Greek society in terms of class, status and recognition. The first such incident took place on Friday 22 May 2009, when the centre of Athens was shaken by angry demonstrations involving immigrant Muslims clashing with the police. The reason was a policeman's assault on the Quran during a routine documents inspection a few days earlier. This was the explosive result of a series of cases of discrimination, police harassment and racist violence that affected many migrants and increasingly Muslims. Although the protests went on peacefully on the following days, supported by imams and migrant organizations rejecting violence, this may be seen as the first major migrant "riot" in Greece and concerned specifically Muslims. The case in point is that the presence of Muslim migrants has become public, and so have their demands and claims to the state, not strictly animated by religious needs but also in reaction to domestic troubles or global developments.

3   A Greek or a Muslim Exceptionality? Islam in Greece from National Minorities to Diversified Transnational Communities

This chapter looked at Greece's "new" Muslim residents, their growing presence and visibility in the public sphere and the ways they are portrayed in dominant public discourses. In so doing, it followed from the previous chapter on the indigenous and formally recognised Muslim minority and its historical predicament linked to the country's Ottoman legacy and relations with modern Turkey throughout the 20th century. Although this legacy is still present in perceptions of Islam and Muslims in Greece, it is now challenged in the face of recent migrations and the processes of migrant settlement and public claims put forward by immigrant Muslim communities. Building on the key themes around which all chapters in this book make up a cohesive whole, as outlined in the editors introduction, the chapter argues that Islam in Greece undergoes a shift from a "peripheral" case in Europe, home to an indigenous Muslim minority, to a "core" one whereby Muslim communities relate to transnational migration. Moreover, it showed that even though migrants from Muslim countries remain at a marginal position within Greek society, they have however come centre-stage in the public sphere. Incidents such as the public prayer that opened this chapter or developments regarding the building of Athens' Central Mosque are revealing of the complex politics of *institutionalisation* that are underway: from the migrants' struggles for recognition and claims to space, to the negotiations in established church-state arrangements in order to accommodate, even reluctantly, the new reality of Islamic presence in the country. The establishment of diverse prayer sites and religious networks play a key role in nurturing *transnational experiences* for (some) Muslim migrants in the diaspora, even though the apparent fragmentation according to ethnicity, denomination or Islamic tradition may appear to contradict the *transnationality* of the Ummah. At the same time, *anti-Muslim racism* originally emanating from nationalist hostility to Turkey, in the context of crisis and austerity it alarmingly showed its ugly violent face targeting people of colour and of Muslim faith, while public discourses on new migrations increasingly reflect the *transnationalisation* of global Islamophobia.

The exceptionality reserved for Muslim migration in public discourse over the last few years has been rightly criticized[59], yet is perhaps inevitable in the face of key issues addressed in this chapter, i.e., the growing Muslim presence and visibility, both due to a growth of migratory flows involving increasing numbers of immigrants from Muslim countries, and to a rise of Muslim communities in the public sphere. The exceptionality of Islam and Muslim migrants is rather suggested by an overwhelming focus on religion instead of other, more tangible aspects of migrants' lives in the host country which rather pertain to migrancy as such: legal status, labour market exploitation, racism, families, and transnational ties. In respect to these issues, Muslim immigration is by no means exceptional. The question of a Muslim "exceptionality" may find obvious answers in the kind of claims pursued. The single issue around which Muslims of migrant background mobilized collectively has been the claim for a central mosque. But on the other hand, some degree of collectivity emerges not only as a matter of hetero-identification, but also through organized forms of civic engagement involving public prayers and protests like the ones this chapter began with. As Muslims, they face racism and discrimination and put claims for the practice of their religion and its public recognition; as immigrants, refugees and asylum seekers, they express demands regarding legal status, social rights and citizenship. In that sense, Triandafyllidou may

---

59 Hatzopoulos and Kambouri, "National Case Study."

have been wrong in asserting that "native Muslims mobilize mainly along ethnic lines while Muslim immigrants appear mainly concerned with religious issues."[60] Rather, as Zapata-Barrero noted in the case of Spain, the first concern of immigrants is certainly not religion, but work, home, health and education (or even, in the Greek case, the means to travel to some western European country):[61]

> Religion belongs more to the realm of custom and habit than to the conscious ... realm of belief. When an immigrant publicly affirms her/his faith it may be a real concern, but there are also ingredients of social protest and a process of 'reactive identity', that is an identity that is being constructed as a reaction against an 'other' who has created walls of separation.

The contrast between Greece's "old" (indigenous) and "new" (immigrant) Muslim communities implied above is inevitable, and may suggest another dimension of exceptionality; this time of Greece, as a peculiar case with an indigenous Muslim population. But not even here is the Greek case an exception, as documented by several chapters in this book and as the editors make explicit in their introduction, suggesting that Islam should not be regarded as something "new" or exceptional to Europe, nor is it solely the product of post-war or recent migrations. Nevertheless, in the Greek context, there are certain indispensable 'methodological' differences in discussing comparatively the Muslim minority of Thrace and newly arrived migrants. First, differences in terms of the origins and characteristics of the two groups. The former are a native indigenous population with citizenship rights – however ambivalent these may have been historically in the premises of the Greek nation-state – and at the same time an officially designated entity. The latter are a newly arrived immigrant population, extremely diverse and stratified by nationality, ethnicity, migratory reasons and routes, entry modes and legal status, religious denominations and Islamic traditions. The fact that the minority is by law recognized as a religious community brings religious elements to the fore of the politics over its status while the different nationalities, denominations and Islamic traditions, or the degree of non-practising within the Muslim migrant population

---

60 Triandafyllidou, "Greece," 214.
61 Ricard Zapata-Barrero, "The Muslim Community in the Spanish Tradition: Maurophobia as a Fact, and Impartiality as a Desideratum," in *Multiculturalism, Muslims and Citizenship* ed. Tariq Modood, Anna Triandafyllidou and Ricard Zapata-Barrero (London: Routledge, 2006), 153.

FROM THE MARGINS TO THE FORE

adds to the difficulties in understanding it as a "community." Nevertheless, the dominant view treating them as a homogenous group suggests, as Troubeta has argued, that Muslim migrants are being "ethnicized" like the Muslims of Thrace have been "minoritized."[62] In that sense, the public discourse on Greece's "new" Muslims tends to equate religion to ethnicity, constructing thus the Muslim "other" as an "ethnic" category, as Modood and Ahmad have observed in the post-2005 British context.[63] Yet, this relates to specific hegemonic discourses and historical legacies that are still peculiar to the Greek context:

> Islam, more than any other immigrant religion, became a potential ground for intolerance and racism, as the majority's dominant ideology tend to nationalise social relations and naturalise the predominant position of the majority's religion. Taken into account the historical past of the Greek-Turkish controversy through religion, whereas Islam is traditionally and ideologically associated with the 'enemy other' of the Ottoman past, immigrant Islam is constructed as an alien element to the 'host' society and national ideology.[64]

This narrative is present both in official discourses and policy (e.g., vis-á-vis Athens' central mosque) and in lay encounters between native Greeks and Muslim immigrants in everyday contexts. Its extreme version is manifested in the discourse and politics of the radical right; this, however, even if vested with specifically "Greek clothes" increasingly resembles and repeats extreme right voices everywhere in Europe. This appears to become even more prominent in the aftermath of the migration/refugee "crisis" of 2015–16, when Islamophobia has entered explicitly the public discourse, and islamophobic narratives are not limited to the extreme right or conservative political and church circles, but also to an emerging liberal anti-Muslim rhetoric[65]. After all, what has been labeled as "nationalist intolerance" in the case of Greece, may not be that far from the "liberal intolerance" against (Muslim) immigration that spreads across Europe and beyond.[66]

---

62   Troubeta, "'Minorization' and 'Ethnicization' in Greek Society."
63   Tariq Modood and Fauzia Ahmad, "British Muslim Perspectives on Multiculturalism," *Theory, Culture, Society* 24/2 (2007).
64   Tsitselikis, *Old and New Islam in Greece*, 159.
65   Matilda Chatzipanagiotou and Iason Zarikos, "Workstream 1: Dominant Islamophobic Narratives – Greece," *research project CIK – Countering Islamophobia through the Development of Best Practice in the use of Counter-Narratives in EU Member States*, Working Paper 4 (Centre for Ethnicity and Racism Studies, University of Leeds, 2017).
66   Triandafyllidou and Kouki "Muslim immigrants and the Greek nation."

Nevertheless, increasingly, this narrative comes into conflict with the evolving reality of ethnic and cultural diversity. In this context, any action is no longer without reaction, and the presence of immigrants, Muslim or otherwise, has entered the mainstream in the sense that it became *political*. Whether through organizing in communities, arranging peaceful public prayers in landmark locations, or being involved in confrontational protests in the streets of Athens, immigrants *state* their presence and *place* claims associated with it, addressed to the Greek polity and society at large. The coming into play of migrants in the Greek public sphere increasingly involves a Muslim "component." This may suggest that Greece has shifted from a "peripheral" case, home to an indigenous Muslim minority whose history originates in the Ottoman past, to a situation resembling more the place of, and debates about, Islam in western European countries, whereby Muslim populations have grown as the product of subsequent migratory waves. Yet it would be rather naïve to assume such a linear shift; rather, the rise of an immigrant Muslim presence suggests a radical diversification and transnationalization of the religious and political landscape.

PART 4

Mobilities and Belonging

∴

CHAPTER 10

Iraqi Diaspora and Public Space in a Multicultural Suburb in Finland

Marko Juntunen

What gives the Finnish "Muslim question" its specific character is the fact that a vast majority of Muslims are, on one way or other, linked to questions of asylum; as asylum claimants or their spouses and children. Since the early 1990s nearly three-quarters of the annual asylum claims in Finland are made by Muslims, whose life courses and transnational connections are in multiple ways shaped by the complex and extended conflicts in the Middle East, Central Asia and the Horn of Africa. Migration from these areas towards Finland has continued for nearly three decades and each new cohort adds to the local level diversity in Finland. These conditions shape interactions, tensions and solidarities across the heterogeneous Muslim groups. Therefore, the ethnographic context for studying Muslims in Finland differs in fundamental ways from French, British, German and Dutch urban settings with large and historically rooted Muslim minorities. In this chapter I will address these questions through focusing on the highly diverse Iraqi diaspora in Finland and the ways in which their diverse diasporic experiences shape public suburban Muslim spaces.

In the recent years the ethnography of diasporic Muslim communities in the West has undergone a significant shift from the conventional minority group study to the observation and analysis of complex power relationships, forms of resistance and interaction that emerge as global, transnational and national influence intersects.[1]

On one hand, the ethnography of the Muslim diaspora is about following the transnational everyday life of the diasporans and observing the ways in which religious perceptions emerge as responses to global negotiation concerning

---

1 Pnina Werbner, *Imagined Diasporas among Manchester Muslims: The Public Performance of Pakistani Transnational Identity Politics* (Oxford: James Currey, 2002); Ruba Salih, "The Backward and the New: National, Transnational and Post-National Islam in Europe," *Journal of Ethnic and Migration Studies* 30/5 (2004): 995–1011; Marta Bolognani, "The Myth of Return: Dismissal, Survival or Revival? A Bradford Example of Transnationalism as a Political Instrument," *Journal of Ethnic and Migration Studies* 33/1 (2007), 59–76.

© KONINKLIJKE BRILL NV, LEIDEN, 2019 | DOI:10.1163/9789004404564_012

Muslim belief and practice.[2] On the other hand, it is essential to observe the ways in which diasporic Muslim communities negotiate with Western refugee regimes, multicultural social policies and official and popular discourses on Islam and Muslims.[3] The ethnographer thus must be sensitive to the complex reality in which social categories and contested ideas emerge as global, transnational, national and popular debates meet. Being a diasporic Muslim in the West is something that is constantly negotiated and challenged on a variety of spatial, social and political levels.

Between the years 2005 and 2008, I carried out fieldwork among the Arabic speaking Iraqi diasporans[4] in Finland, and from 2009 to 2013 I followed their transnational networks to Sweden, Holland, Belgium and Iraq.[5] My primary interest was the ways in which the violent fragmentation and sectarianization of Iraqi society since the toppling of Saddam Hussein's Baath party regime in 2003 is shaping the lives of the Iraqi diasporans in Finland. This question became particularly acute around the year 2005 as the heterogeneous diasporans who had escaped from Saddam's Iraq to Finland in the 1990s encountered the

---

2   Ralph Grillo, "Islam and Transnationalism," *Journal of Ethnic and Migration Studies* 30/5 (2004), 861–878; Olivier Roy, *Globalized Islam: The Search For a New Ummah* (London: Hurst & Company, 2004); James Piscatori, "Reinventing the Ummah? The Trans-Locality of Pan-Islam," Lecture to the Tenth Anniversary Conference: Translocality: An Approach to Globalising Phenomena (Berlin: Zentrum Moderner Orient, 26 September 2006); Hisham Hellyer, "Visions & Visualizations: Negotiating Space for European Muslims," *Contemporary Islam* 1/1 (2007), 23–35.

3   Hilary Cunningham and Josiah Heyman, "Introduction: Mobilities and Enclosures at Borders," *Identities: Global Studies in Culture and Power* 11 (2004), 289–302; Andre Gingrich, "Concepts of Race Vanishing, Movements of Racism Rising? Global Issues and Austrian Ethnography," *Ethnos* 69/2 (2004), 156–176; Marianne Gullestad, "Blind Slaves of Our Prejudices: Debating Culture and Race in Norway," *Ethnos* 69/2 (2004), 177–203; Peter Hervik, "The Danish Cultural World of Unbridgeable Differences," *Ethnos* 69/2 (2004), 247–267; Gabriele Marranci, *The Anthropology of Islam* (Oxford: Berg Publishers, 2008), 53–70.

4   Because of the politically and religiously fragmented nature of the Iraqi diaspora in the West, I consciously avoid addressing my interlocutors in ethnicized terms such as Iraqi Arabs. By using the term Arabic-speaking Iraqis I merely wish to point to the fact that my heterogeneous interlocutors are native speakers of Arabic, in contrast to Kurdish-speaking Iraqis who compose roughly fifty percent of the Iraqi diasporans in Finland. All of my interlocutors trace their social roots to central Iraq – mainly to Baghdad, Najaf and Karbala, and to Basra and Samawa in southern Iraq. During the fieldwork periods all interviews, unstructured discussions and participant observation among the Iraqi interlocutors were carried out in Iraqi Arabic and in Modern Standard Arabic.

5   Marko Juntunen, *Prospects for Sustainable Return: Iraqi and Afghan Asylum Seekers in Finland* (Tampere: Tampere Peace Research Institute, 2011); Petri Hautaniemi, Marko Juntunen and Mariko Sato, *Return Migration and Vulnerability: Case Studies from Somaliland and Iraqi Kurdistan* (Helsinki: Development Studies, Department of Political and Economic Studies, Faculty of Social Sciences, University of Helsinki, 2013).

influx of new Iraqi refugees whose histories of persecution differed radically from their experiences of violence. Thirdly, I have observed how the heterogeneous Iraqi refugees adapt their lives vis-à-vis the constantly changing Finnish refugee regime and multicultural policies that contain several discrepancies and contradictions.

This chapter is structured around three specific research questions: How do globally produced religious and political influences shape the public spaces in a multicultural suburban space that hosts Iraqis with contrasting political and religious perceptions and experiences of persecution and violence? What kind of social boundaries emerge when people with very different histories of violence and persecution live side by side in suburban spaces? What happens when the fragmented Iraqi diaspora encounters multicultural social programmes that attempt to build bridges between diasporic communities and the Finnish state?

I begin by describing the primary fieldwork site in Finland, the suburb Varissuo, and introduce the social and political background of the Iraqi diaspora in Finland. After briefly outlining the central contradictions inherent in the Finnish refugee regime, I demonstrate the ways in which the diasporans of the 1990s attempted to come to terms with the increasingly restrictive immigration and refugee policy while attempting to facilitate the migration of relatives fleeing Iraq following the toppling of Saddam's regime in 2003. Finally, by focusing on debates between diasporic Iraqi parents and Finnish specialists on parenting and pre-school education I illustrate the ways in which the sectarian social boundaries emerge as heterogeneous diasporans meet with bureaucratically organized multicultural social programmes.

1   Iraqis in a Multicultural Suburb

The suburb of Varissuo in the town of Turku in southwestern Finland hardly differs from dozens of other Finnish suburbs constructed in the late 1970s and early 1980s for lower- and mid-income groups. Until the middle of the 1990s an overwhelming majority of the inhabitants of the suburb were native Finns. However, the population structure began to change with the influx of UNHCR quota refugees from Vietnam during the late 1980s. Until the early 1990s, Varissuo hosted a reception center for asylum seekers and the number of inhabitants with migrant backgrounds grew gradually.[6] Currently, the suburb hosts

---

6   Jarkko Rasinkangas and Marjukka Laitinen, ed., *Varissuon 30 vuotta – tavoitteista todeksi* (Turku: Kirja-Aurora, 2006).

some 9,000 inhabitants, more than one third of whom have a migrant background, the largest groups being Russians, Iraqis, Iranians, Somali, Kosovars, Bosnians, Albanians and Estonians. The Muslim population in the suburb consists predominantly of individuals and families who fled violence and political crises in Africa, the Middle East and Central Asia. The Muslim diaspora is extremely heterogeneous, as it consists of religiously observant and secular Shi'a Muslims from Iran and Iraq as well as observant and secular Sunnis with a variety of religious orientations and ethnic backgrounds from Iraqi Kurdistan, Somalia, North Africa, and the Middle East.

The approximately 5,000 Iraqis (nearly 50% of whom speak Arabic as a mother tongue) in Finland share their history of refuge with some six million Iraqi diasporans, the majority of whom live in Sweden, Norway, Denmark, Germany, Austria and nearly thirty other countries.[7] The majority of the Iraqis in Varissuo entered Finland between 1996 and 2002 as UNHCR quota refugees from Syria and Jordan and from the refugee camps of Rafha and Artawiya situated in Northern Saudi Arabia. Others found their way to Finland as asylum seekers often after years on the road in Turkey, Greece and Russia. Upon entry, numerous families were placed in small peripheral towns in different parts of the country, but with bleak future options, entire households moved to suburban areas in southern and southwestern Finland.

The Arabic-speaking Iraqi diasporans in Finland, as elsewhere in the refugee communities in Western Europe, display highly diversified political as well as religious affiliations. A considerable number of families are popularly categorized by Iraqis as the "people of the refugee camps" (Arab. *ahl al-mukhayyamāt*) which stereotypically refers to people who spent years in the Rafha and Artawiya camps and who often hold political and religious attitudes favourable to the most influential parliamentary forces of the Shi'a population, namely the Islamic Supreme Council of Iraq (ISCI) and the Iraqi prime minister Nouri al Maliki's Dawa Party. The current leadership of these parties is largely constituted of the exiled activists who spent years in Iran and in Western asylum states. According to my interlocutors who spent several years in these camps, especially ISCI had considerable political and religious influence in Rafha and Artawiya. Today ISCI is largely present in Finland through its International Shahid al Mihrab Organization and runs several Islamic cultural centres in the major cities in Finland.

---

7   "Five Years on Europe is Still Ignoring Its Responsibilities Towards Iraqi Refugees," European Council on Refugees and Exiles, published March 2008, accessed November 12, 2014, http://www.refworld.org/cgi-bin/texis/vtx/rwmain?docid=47e1315c2.

The majority of the quota refugees who were repatriated directly from Syria and Jordan were individuals (and often entire families) persecuted by the Baath party regime because of their more or less direct support for the banned religious and political opposition. Numerous leftist and Shi´a Islamist activists born in the late 1950s and the early 1960s whom I encountered in Varissuo had dramatic personal histories of persecution perpetrated by the Baath regime. More than ten of my interlocutors, all men, suffered years of political imprisonment; six of them had been sentenced to death by Baghdad's notorious revolutionary court. After spending several weeks on death row they were pardoned and transferred to Abu Ghraib prison where they spent up to six years. These men related their prison experiences in a manner that predicted the present-day internal fragmentation in Iraqi society; prison was portrayed routinely as a battlefield between the Baathist regime and opposition forces, but the boundaries between various factions of leftist and religious opposition were also shaped by ethnic, regional and tribal affiliations. To further complicate the profile of the Iraqi diaspora in Finland among the quota refugees accepted by Finland from Syria and Jordan there were also Kurds, Turkomans, Mandaeans and members of various Christian minorities persecuted because of their ethnic and religious backgrounds or their political views. The Iraqi population in general faced severe challenges entering the Finnish labour market. The unemployment rate of the Iraqis reached nearly 80% at the turn of the millennium and the situation improved only slightly (to 67–69%) between 2005 and 2008.

2   The Iraqi Diaspora and Self-applauding Humanitarianism

For the diasporans in Varissuo the administrative discourses and practices of the Finnish refugee regime appeared to contain severe discrepancies, contradictions and forms of indirect institutional marginalization. Over the years of my fieldwork the Finnish state received annually some 750 UNHCR quota refugees,[8] and granted humanitarian protection to 700–900 asylum claimants.[9] However, none of the municipalities in the vicinity of Turku have been willing to house these people in communal housing compounds since the mid-2000s

---

8 "Kiintiöpakolaiset," The Finnish Immigration Service, accessed November 12, 2014, http://www.migri.fi/turvapaikka_suomesta/kiintiopakolaiset.
9 "Turvapaikka- ja pakolaistilastot," The Finnish Immigration Service, accessed November 12, 2014, http://www.migri.fi/tietoa_virastosta/tilastot/turvapaikka-_ja_pakolaistilastot.

largely because the migrant households were already highly concentrated in particular suburban areas in southern and southwestern Finland.

In 2005 there was a highly polarized political debate on immigration and integration that divided even the members of the Finnish Government. "The integration (of migrants) is a completely neglected issue in Finland," Minister of Interior Kari Rajamäki expressed in September 2005. A month later the Prime Minister, Matti Vanhanen, claimed that, "the integration policy has been a success." The same year the forced return of failed asylum claimants to Iran, Iraq and Afghanistan and extended periods of detention of irregular migrants generated extensive critique from the majority church (the Evangelical Lutheran Church of Finland) and numerous NGOs. The administrative discourses were, however, often backed by a rhetoric conveying the exalted and self-applauding humanitarianism of the Finnish state. "Refuge is for those who need it and not for those who exploit it" Minister of Interior Kari Rajamäki stated in 2005.

Humanitarian discourses penetrated even institutions such as the immigration detention centre. The closed and barbwired centre in Helsinki expressed on its Internet home page in 2005 that it aspires "to construct relations of interaction between 'customers' (Finn. *asiakkaat*) and employees." The page further clarified its activities stating that "the 'customers' are guided, supported and advised on issues related to entry and expulsion." The centre maintained that it offers "daily activities" its "customers."

As in many other EU member states, immigration, multiculturalism and Islam began to divide political parties in Finland and these topics were successfully exploited by a number of populist politicians. Echoing developments in Norway, Denmark and Sweden, there was growing public pressure in Finland to reverse a range of policies that could be labeled as multiculturalist.[10] Finland, like its western neighbors, was clearly adopting a more interventionist integration policy including compulsory education in language, initiation programmes for refugees, and increased control over family reunification. Simultaneously, these developments coincided with the re-evaluation of citizenship and formulation of an increasingly rejective asylum policy. Finland introduced several initiatives aimed at reducing the number of unfounded asylum applications, delimiting family reunification and speeding up processing times of asylum claims. In addition, policies of detention and removal of refused asylum claimants were to be revised.[11]

---

10   Tjitske Akkerman and Anniken Hagelund, "Women and Children First! Anti-immigration Parties and Gender in Norway and the Netherlands," *Patterns of Prejudice* 41/2 (2007): 197–214.

11   "Thors: Linjaus irakilaispakolaisten suhteen tarkistettava," YLE *uutiset*, April 27, 2009, accessed November 12, 2014, http://www.yle.fi/uutiset/kotimaa/2009/04/thors_linjaus _irakilaispakolaisten_suhteen_tarkistettava_708459.html.

3 The Influx from Post-occupation Iraq

Surrounded by the contradictory discourses and practices of the refugee regime, nearly all Iraqi households I encountered in Varissuo were urgently trying to facilitate the flight of their relatives from the turmoil of occupied Iraq. I commenced my project 18 months after the dethroning of Saddam Hussein by the international coalition forces when Iraq had fallen into chaos as the collapse of the regime and the dismantling of its military and security institutions created a deadly vacuum. The year 2006 alone witnessed 34,000 civilian casualties; 40% of the families based in Baghdad had lost a member. The occupation produced the largest refugee crisis since the 1947 Palestine Partition with 2 million international refugees and 2.8 million internal refugees.[12]

Financial help was distributed from Finland to relatives who were among the nearly two million Iraqis waiting for their case to be heard by the UNHCR in Syria and Jordan. Many of my interlocutors in Finland were increasingly concerned about the news from EU countries with large Iraqi minorities. In the period of 2006 to 2007, as many parts of Iraq witnessed the bloodiest months of sectarian violence, Germany, Britain, Sweden, and Denmark were particularly determined to deport hundreds of Iraqis whose asylum requests had been rejected by authorities. The migrant regimes in many parts of the EU followed the logic of the German government: with the fall of the Baathist dictatorship, Iraqis were no longer in need of international protection. The Federal Office for Migration and Refugees (BAMF) began its procedures in 2006, and aimed to deprive 4,400 Iraqis of their refugee status, including hundreds of Iraqis already well integrated into the German society. Some 14,000 Iraqis faced deportation from the country, but the lack of air connections and a bilateral agreement with the Government of Iraq prevented Germany from engaging in large-scale deportations.[13] Britain deported 632 people against their will to the Iraqi Kurdistan region between 2005 and 2008. In Sweden, 1,400 Iraqi refugees received letters from the country's Migration Board in which they were informed that measures would be taken to deport them forcibly unless they consented to return voluntarily.[14] As a response, the International Federation of Iraqi Refugees organized demonstrations in several European capitals, including Stockholm

---

12   Al-Mashad al-Iraqi, political discussion program, *al-Jazeera* (Arabic) TV channel, November 16, 2008.

13   "Iraqi Refugee Disaster: Europe Continues to Shirk Its Responsibility," *ProAsyl*, July 21, 2007, http://www.proasyl.de/en/news/newsenglish/news/iraqi_refugee_disaster_dt_vorlage/back/764/.

14   "Iraqi Army Confronted U.K. Deportation Officials on Baghdad Plane," *Guardian*, October 16, 2009, accessed November 12, 2014, http://www.theguardian.com/uk/2009/oct/16/unhcr-uk-baghdad-deportations.

(April 19, 2007) and Helsinki (April 20, 2007). In Denmark, Iraqis represented nearly fifty per cent of the total number of rejected asylum seekers under expulsion order in March 2009.[15] By the year 2009, Britain, Denmark, Sweden, and Norway had ratified bilateral agreements with the Iraqi government to repatriate Iraqi citizens.

According to an estimate by the Finnish Immigration Service in May 2010, the time was ripe for the rejection and removal of asylum seekers coming from autonomous Kurdish regions, southern Iraq, and the capital Baghdad. The reason, it was claimed, was that they no longer needed international protection due to an improved security situation in Iraq. In May 2009, approximately 1,500 Iraqis were waiting in Finland for their asylum decision, and the new guidelines were to be applied to new decisions only. The Immigration Service estimated that the first returns were expected to take place in the spring months of 2010.[16]

The inter-governmental repatriation agreements between the western asylum states and the Government of Iraq received extensive criticism from humanitarian organizations, including the UNHCR and Refugees International. However, for several EU member states, the agreements were interpreted as guarantees that the returns could be implemented without violating the human rights of the displaced Iraqis. As for the Iraqi Government led by a Shi'a coalition, it received the returnees with open arms, since they conveyed an important message to international audiences: the Government of Iraq was on the right path to stabilize the country. However in July 2012 the Iraqi Government suddenly announced that it would refuse to accept any nationals deported from Europe, and threatened to fine airlines carrying rejected asylum seekers.

My interlocutors experienced in very concrete terms the contradictions inherent in the national and international refugee regimes: on one hand, the Finnish state offered asylum to some fortunate ones, distributing social services, housing, education and integration programmes for the ones considered "justified" or "legal," but simultaneously the authorities would deny rights of asylum to their friends and family members fleeing the violence whose claims it held to be unfounded. People certainly knew that the truth did not count – it was critically important to know how to construct one's biography of persecution for the officials of the refugee regime. Numerous of my interlocutors

---

15 "Iraq Reach Deal to Repatriate Iraqi Refugees," *Agence France-Presse* (AFP), May 13, 2009, accessed November 12, 2014, http://www.unhcr.org/cgi-bin/texis/vtx/refdaily?pass=463ef 21123&id=4a0bb8218.

16 "Suomi palauttaa irakilaisia turvapaikanhakijoita," *YLE uutiset*, May 5, 2009, accessed November 12, 2014, http://yle.fi/uutiset/kotimaa/2009/05/suomi_palauttaa_irakilaisia _turvapaikanhakijoita_728142.html.

reported receiving nearly every week telephone calls from friends and family members who were ready to flee from Iraq and inquiring about the ways in which they should construct their narratives for asylum hearings.

The first new arrivals fleeing the post-occupation chaos began to enter Finland from 2005 onwards and in 2007 and 2008 Iraqis were the largest group of asylum claimants in Finland, with some 1,255 cases in 2008. The narratives of the new arrivals constructed an image of the emergence of a conservative religious ethos in the Iraqi public space. Numerous Baghdadis from the secular left-leaning middle class recalled how they had become nearly paralyzed inside their houses without electricity and running water for weeks and months and without exception had experienced cases of murder, rape and kidnappings among friends or relatives. Many women I interviewed in private homes and asylum centres in Turku and Helsinki had experiences of harassment and reported having been threatened by groups of armed young men whom they addressed as sectarian militias. These women reported that they were targeted because of their liberal dress style, professional profile (sport teachers, fashion merchants, doctors, nurses and university lecturers) or reputation as too liberal in terms of their public conduct. Many men and women I interviewed explained that the only option was to leave their homes after having heard that their names were on the "militias" death list.

What was deeply troubling for those Iraqis who had been persecuted by the Baath regime was the fact that among the newcomers there were individuals who had served as civil servants, and public authorities in the Baathist regime of Saddam's era and reported having become targets of the extreme acts of revenge in Iraq. A 62-year-old Sunni Muslim man, a secretary in a local Baathist office in the Dora district in Baghdad I interviewed in a refugee reception centre in Turku showed me pictures of the ruins of his house destroyed by explosives in Baghdad. His wife lost her life in the incident, and the eldest son, a former member of Saddam's National Guard had been kidnapped and killed three days before the incident. Another Sunni Muslim man, a 32-year-old textile merchant from Baghdad, had served two years as an administrative officer at Abu Ghraib prison under the Baath regime and said that he had to flee because of continuous death threats from members of Shi´a militias.

In Varissuo as in Iraq the violence that swept across the country was increasingly often conceptualized in terms of a sectarian crisis between Sunnis and Shi´as. The battle lines were, however, much more blurred and complex. Iraqis were also deeply affected by the religious–secular divide leading to the need for refuge of entire professional groups, such as scientists, university lecturers, doctors, artists, and musicians, as well as members of sexual minorities. The social fabric also fragmented along tribal and ethnic boundary lines and the process found diverse local expressions in different parts of Iraq. In their search for protection people had no other option than to choose their side – which in practice meant identification with a sectarian, religious, ethnic, tribal or political grouping. By 2010 over fifty areas within Baghdad were divided by concrete walls, and there were 1,400 security check points inside the city.[17]

In this chaotic situation, my interlocutors in Varissuo were often unaware of who was targeting their families in Iraq and why. Terms such as sectarian violence and civil war hardly captured the nature of the situation as perceived by my interviewees. What the Iraqis in Varissuo experienced as particularly painful was that violence against civilians was often perpetrated by ordinary people against other ordinary people. Every person I interviewed in Finland could name at least one close relative who had died in turmoil following the military occupation of Iraq in 2003.

4 Suburban Space and the Globalized Sectarian Crisis

Many Iraqis in Varissuo expressed being terrified about the rapid collapse of security in Iraq. It seemed typical, especially for the former members of the educated middle class from Baghdad, to underline how unexpectedly the sectarian boundaries had emerged. In several interview situations, my interlocutors remarked that until the early 1990s people in general were unaware of the sectarian identity of their neighbours.

The use of sectarian political rhetoric, I was told, was part of modern Iraq's political reality. However, sectarianism intensified particularly rapidly after the popular uprising against the regime in 1991 and the resurgence of the popular Shi´a movement, led by the al-Sadr family, during the 13 years of embargo. Subsequently, Saddam Hussein resorted more overtly to religious symbols to legitimize the regime and to present himself as the defender of Sunni hegemony against the West but also against Iran. However, to many diasporic Iraqis such developments were shockingly unexpected.

The sectarian divide also became clearly pronounced on the Arabic satellite channels and Internet news rooms that were frequently followed by my interlocutors. Yusuf al-Qaradawi, one of the most influential Sunni scholars globally and largely respected in several Sunni mosque communities in Finland,[18]

---

17   "1,400 checkpoints inside Iraqi Capital Baghdad," *Azzaman*, March 27, 2010, http://www .azzaman.com/english/index.asp?fname=news\2010-03-27\kurd.htm.

18   In 2005 the largest Sunni Muslim organizations of Helsinki and Turku linked their Internet homepages to *IslamOnline*, one of the largest Islamic web pages, which was

issued a statement in September 2008 that the occupation of Iraq had drawn the entire Muslim world into a growing sectarian rivalry. The rhetoric of al-Qaradawi as well as numerous other Sunni scholars began to render Saddam's person and the military resistance against the occupation of Iraq as defenders of global Sunni-Islam. The attitudes reflecting growing sectarianism were equally heard from numerous Shi'a religious authorities and were echoed as well by the public speeches of Mahmoud Ahmadinejad, President of Iran; Hosni Mubarak, President of Egypt; and King Abdullah II of Jordan to name just a few.

What I encountered in Varissuo was a highly charged social reality where the Iraqis sustained a variety of different positions vis-à-vis the global drama of occupied Iraq. Many individuals acknowledged the presence of sectarian tensions together with tensions resulting from the religious–secular divide but maintained that there was a silent agreement to avoid confrontations by remaining among likeminded people. With rapidly increasing anti-immigration and Islamophobic sentiments in Finland, people did not want to create another basis of negative stereotyping. Many Iraqis explained that globally communicated sectarian tensions together with Islamophobia, a rejective asylum policy and an unwelcoming labor market led to the withdrawal and isolation of Iraqis from Finnish society. My interlocutors thus routinely described their state in Finland with the Iraqi Arabic term "*mutaqawqa*'," meaning "being curled up."

A large majority of my interlocutors expressed strong dislike towards categorizing people – and becoming categorized – along sectarian and secular–religious markers but had to admit that Sunni and Shi'a and religious and secular as social categories were increasingly present. One man, an active member of the Shi'a religious centre associated with the international Shahid al-Mihrab Organization in Turku related in an interview situation in May 2006:

> When the violence commenced in Iraq [after the collapse of the Baath regime in 2003] it clearly had a sectarian basis, because the regime was Sunni and the oppressed were the Shi'a. When justice was done, the sectarian battle started as a sign of change. This same battle travelled abroad. We were against Saddam, but the other Arabs backed him.

---

established in 1997 by the Al-Balagh Cultural Society led by Yusuf al-Qaradawi. See Bettina Gräf, "IslamOnline.net: Independent, Interactive, Popular," *Arab Media & Society* (January 2008), accessed November 12, 2014, http://www.arabmediasociety.com/articles/downloads/20080115032719_AMS4_Bettina_Graf.pdf.

Iraqis in Varissuo were particularly aware of which commercial and social spaces frequented by Iraqis were sites for potential tensions and often seemed alert when talking about political developments in Iraq in public spaces.

Sectarian discourses appeared especially unfortunate for the considerable minority of Iraqis who had no urge to underline any kind of religious component of their public identity. One Iraqi woman, an architectural draughtsman who had fled Iraq in 1994 expressed in an interview in March 2006 that "I just do not want to go to places where others would ask me why I do not wear a headscarf." Her husband, a representative of a secular Iraqi cultural association in Turku, repeatedly told me that he dislikes speaking publicly in situations where large numbers of Iraqis are present such as at parental evenings in schools and kindergartens:

> I notice the disdain on their faces (the more religiously observant parents) as I open my mouth. I don't start my words, as they do by saying: *bismillāh al-rahmān al-rahīm* (In the name of God the Merciful, the Compassionate).

Sectarian social boundaries were underlined in such a variety of ways that I can only provide a few illustrations here. Naming practices for babies, for example, indicated political and religious sentiments of entire families in an unprecedented manner. I was aware of the fact that people had named children in modern Iraq for several generations not only after hegemonic religious persons but persons' names were often adopted from popular public figures and prominent politicians. I soon noted for example that many of my secular male interlocutors, who were born in the late 1950s and early 1960s had first names (or had adopted nicknames) that were associated with popular Arab Nationalists (e.g., Qasim, 'Abd al-Karim – after nationalist president 'Abd al-Karim Qasim) or communist symbolism (*Fawzī* – the Victorious one; *Thā'ir* – Revolutionary etc.). However there was no direct correspondence between the first names of the men from this generation and the religious orientation of their family. Many men who came from families with a tradition as active followers of the Iraqi Communist Party were also named after historically hegemonic Shi'a or Sunni persons.

As the sectarian crisis intensified in occupied Iraq, naming became more clearly a sectarian marker. Naming a child after the hegemonic figures of Shi'a (Ali, Hasan, Husayn, Zaynab) or Sunni Islam (Umar, Uthman, Abu Bakr) was interpreted by Iraqis in Varissuo as a statement about the family's strong sectarian identification.

IRAQI DIASPORA AND PUBLIC SPACE IN A MULTICULTURAL SUBURB

In addition, naming practices drew boundaries between religious and secular families. Rana and Muhsin,[19] a husband and wife serve as an example. They are both non-practising Muslims and they named their child Enkido (born in 2006) after the hero of Gilgamesh. Another secular family with whom I had associated frequently from 2005 onwards had two young daughters, Basra (after the family's home city in Iraq) and Fairuz (after the popular Lebanese singer) marking the family's secular orientation. Muhsin was sharply critical of sectarian naming practices and in May 2006 a few months before the birth of his son Enkido he mentioned ironically that he was thinking about naming his son Kafka: "because our reality [in and out of Iraq] is as chaotic as in the writings of Franz Kafka," he said.

5   Illustrating Multicultural Encounters

Varissuo proved to be a fertile context to illustrate the ways in which the multivocal Iraqi diaspora came to terms with Finnish multicultural policies. In the spring of 2007 the internal violence in Iraq had reached extremely alarming proportions and the Iraqis with whom I spent my time in Varissuo were surfing long hours on the Internet and sitting in front of their television screens to make sense of what was happening. At the same time, a local NGO in Varissuo, Multicultural Home, School and Parenting offered an opportunity for "Arabic-speaking parents" to share their views concerning daycare, school education and roles and responsibilities of parents with Finnish authorities and professionals.

Multicultural social work in suburban contexts in Turku was largely about building bridges with different communities by emphasizing cultural understanding and dialogue. Integration of migrants was a question administered at the community level, involving relevant organizations and representatives. The newly established projects employed increasing numbers of people with a refugee background. These "peer supporters" were then expected to function as cultural interpreters and trust building diplomats between different migrant groups and public authorities. Many of these programmes had clearly realized that so-called community consultation strategies could in practice encourage patriarchal practices, as the voices of the community often meant those of self-defined male leaders. The programmes I followed between 2005

---

19   For the sake of confidentiality and anonymity I use pseudonyms when referring to my interlocutors.

and 2008 were constructed around a repertory of slogans such as "the process of activating migrant families" and "multicultural neighbourhood democracy" that circulated among various NGOs.

Like many other NGOs, Multicultural Home, School and Parenting included two peer supporters; a Palestinian man and an Iraqi Mandaean woman. However, in the context of the highly heterogeneous and politically charged Iraqi diaspora, who could be considered a peer? Anyone with an Iraqi background? Any Muslim? Any Arabic speaker? Over several months, I had observed how projects targeting Iraqis and other refugees in the suburbs of Turku were often only superficially informed about the social realities of the diasporans and, like many Iraqis, I wondered whether lectures on recycling garbage, home fire safety or courses instructing women how to ride bicycles were meeting the most essential needs of the refugees in Varissuo.

Multiculturalism and multicultural work seemed to mean very different things to the administrative personnel, who were predominantly native Finns (women nearly without an exception), and the peer supporters (both men and women) of diasporic background. The administrators often had genuine humanitarian reasons for working in multicultural projects. They, however, shared the frustration that the local and national authorities neglected multicultural work and this fact led to operational discontinuities and financial problems. For these reasons the neighborhood projects "traveled" from quarter to quarter, each time run by a different NGO but with a very similar agenda to the previous one that had run out of funding.

For Iraqi diasporans in Varissuo, multicultural work offered one of the few possibilities of finding a permanent job, but it also created a sphere for wider public participation with the surrounding society. The coordinators were required to construct their position as a community expert who communicates messages between migrants and the local society. Given the heterogeneity of the Iraqi diaspora and the nationally and globally produced tensions surrounding their experience, these positions were contradictory and politically charged. Negotiating the complex political conditions, project coordinators tended to manipulate social boundary lines and filter the information communicated between project administration and the diasporic social fields. This would be necessary if one wanted to maintain affiliations with heterogeneous Iraqis and other Muslim diasporans but also in order to convince the administrative personnel of the project of one's professional skills.

In order to understand the ways in which the sectarian tensions framed the multicultural work in Varissuo I decided to pay specific attention to the parental group discussions organized by the NGO Multicultural Home, School and Parenting. The parental group met five times according to a thematically structured programme. The administration of the NGO had assumed that as Arabic speakers the parents would at least partly share "the same culture" and through dialogue with Finnish specialists invited to the meetings, offer fruitful insights into questions concerning co-operation between educational institutions and Arabic-speaking households. The meetings attracted nine active participants between 22 and 51 years of age, with two to four children. Their backgrounds and subjective understandings on "their" culture differed widely as the Iraqi participants mirrored the heterogeneity of the diaspora. Other participants in the meetings were a Palestinian woman with a refugee background, a Syrian man who worked as an Arabic instructor in a local primary school, and a Moroccan migrant man who was an active participant in the activities of a major Sunni centre in Turku. The discussions were translated by two Arabic–Finnish translators present at the meetings.

I participated in the opening meeting accompanied by my closest interlocutor in Varissuo, Radi, a father of three children and an active member of a left-leaning secular cultural organization. He had been sentenced to death by the Revolutionary Court in Baghdad in 1984, accused of having attempted to flee the country when at war with Iran. He was pardoned from the death sentence after over four weeks on death row, but suffered six years of imprisonment in Abu Ghraib prison and had experienced violent confrontations with the members of Shi'a political activists in the prison. His eldest brother was the only family member remaining in Iraq, as his sister, a sports teacher, had fled the country six months earlier for Syria with her family after experiencing two attempted assassinations and the attempted kidnapping of her son.

Before attending the meeting together with Radi we followed the Iraqi news all afternoon, as a car bomb had exploded in the town of Karbala killing 56 people. A few minutes later the atmosphere changed strikingly as Tiina, a middle-aged local specialist on pre-schooling opened the meeting:

> As parents, you will have to play many different roles. I always say that the small children have small worries, and the big ones have big worries [...] the most important thing that we need from one another is love. You migrants have to think how to transmit your own culture and how to dive into Finnish culture in a way that you do not do it at the cost of your own culture. How do you in your family address human relations? Do you have family members helping you? How do you transmit your culture and take care of it?

Nearly without an exception, the authorities and specialists of education attending the meetings emphasized that they were still in the process of learning how to cope with the social realities of the multicultural suburb. Therefore they believed it was essential for them to gain insights into the cultures, and respect the subjective views on culture upheld by the diasporans.

Marja, a specialist on pre-school education who had worked several years in the eastern suburbs of Turku expressed:

> This multiculturalism is a new thing for us and we hope that you teach us about it. We teach your children about Finnish culture but simultaneously we respect other cultures.

In five sessions, the Finnish specialists never enquired of the participants about their life histories, experiences of violence and persecution, not to mention the transnational social relations through which the diasporic culture was expressed and transmitted.

While expecting people to "share their cultural values" with the authorities, to "preserve them," and to "pass them to their children," the participants clearly also realized that they were expected to enter into discussions concerning deeply politicized, tense and contested (sectarian) issues. Silences, the mutual silencing and conscious avoidance of public discussion about sectarian issues became the parents' means of avoiding potential confrontations.

Abu Thabit expressed this idea in a discussion I carried out with him in May 2007 in a local Shi´a mosque in the following manner:

> The problem is that we have no openness and transparency among the Muslims here (in Turku). This is due to the boundary that exists between us and cannot be transgressed. How, in these conditions could we then cooperate with the Finnish authorities?

The Iraqis and other parents participating in the meetings had another source of deep frustration. The overarching concern of the parents was that the official educational system recognizes and respects their children's cultural difference but constantly produces ambivalent and contradictory practices. Finnish authorities and representatives of NGOs expressed their urge to 'learn about migrants' culture,' and based on the shared information they provided migrant and refugee families institutionalized social and economic support, possibilities for education and vocational training; yet at the same time – and often the very same authorities and professionals – appeared to host exclusive ideas and practices. I wish to illustrate these themes by observing the heated debates the parental group held regarding education and in particular the transmission of Arabic language to their children.

The children's language training was a great concern for the parents. Rana, an Iraqi mother working in a Varissuo daycare centre expressed that many Iraqi children had severe problems of differentiating the geometrical patterns, colours or names of common animals in any language. Many discussions concerning children's training in Arabic language and Islam reflected this deep contradiction; the public schools provided basic training in "home language" and "minority religions" but only for one to two hours a week. In Varissuo's primary school, children from several different age groups and with diverse linguistic qualifications were taught in the same classrooms. From the parents' perspective, teaching had proved to be extremely inefficient and the situation generated many frustrated questions.

> Yusuf, father of two children, asked:
> I would like to know why the Finnish authorities are interested in the fact that our children learn Arabic? How do you see that learning Arabic benefits them?

> Satu, Finnish as a second language teacher, responded:
> So that they learn Finnish better.

> Tuuli, specialist in pre-school education, intervened in the discussion:
> They are Arabic speakers and if they learn Finnish they make their futures in the labor market. Most certainly they will.

> Sini, specialist in pre-school education, added:
> Don't let your children lose their Arabic.

The municipal Department of Education in Turku stated in its programme for the year 2007 that the primary school aimed at assisting the children to "develop their linguistic and cultural foundations" and to make them (migrant children) "more self-assured." For the parents, the situation was not without problems; the home language taught at school was modern standard Arabic, but the real home language of their children was one of many Arabic vernaculars.

An entire session in the parents' group was devoted to discussion on different methods of strengthening the children's vocabulary and finding more effective ways to teach them literary Arabic. Many mothers expressed having tried, for example, reading Arabic children's books available at Varissuo's public library while simultaneously translating them into colloquial Arabic.

Largely as a response to these problems, the major religious organizations in Turku had begun to organize language-training programmes. Two Shi'a

Muslim organizations provided training on weekends but due to sectarian tensions the instruction was only theoretically open to all Arabic-speaking children. The same was true of the language programme provided by the major Sunni mosque in Turku. It was widely shared among my Iraqi interlocutors that language training also necessarily meant in practice the communication of sectarian religious principles.

Yusuf's remark below points out that in Varissuo any debate between the diasporic Muslims and Finnish professionals concerning education approached quite delicate sectarian boundaries. In order to avoid open conflict the Arabic-speaking participants silenced the conversation. Yusuf said:

> There are three categories of us Arabs here in Varissuo; we are Sunni Arabs, Shi´as and Christians. We are three groups. If we talk about Sunnis first, I can only say that all these issues concerning education from daycare to secondary school have been discussed between our Sunni organization (the largest Sunni organization in Turku) and the (Finnish) Ministry of Education. There is no need to waste time in discussions, we have our representatives and we have stated our demands, it's all on paper.

An Iraqi Mandaean woman, Thabita, interrupted in a clearly irritated tone. She commented to the translator in Finnish:

> One moment, you can keep on interpreting, but I just have to comment.

Lost in the hustle and bustle that soon filled the room, the interpreter stopped translating. Then Radi, the president of a left-leaning cultural organization, asked for a word:

> In order not to pull our children into this kind of atmosphere, I think we should stick to the subject and talk about daycare. There should be a seminar for all groups; we all have our opinions on the subject.

The debate was brought to a halt and Annika, another Finnish specialist on preschool education, interrupted and tried to bring the discussion back on track:

> Here in the kindergarten we have only limited resources to teach home languages, yet we try to show respect to the fact that children have different backgrounds. It is wonderful that you seem to know so much about raising children in bilingual contexts. If the parents think that the kindergarten has an important pedagogic role, the children will feel it too. It is important for us to know what kinds of wishes the parents have. So please share your thoughts with us.

6 Multivocal Diaspora

A number of British Muslim writers who were raised in multicultural Western contexts[20] have been particularly active in addressing issues such as the multivocality of Muslim diasporas, the processes of boundary marking between different confessional groups, and the social tensions that emerge in Western Muslim spaces. These themes have received far too little attention among the scholars focusing on Muslim minorities in the West. A number of contemporary trends within the Muslim communities have been interpreted as either sociologically unrepresentative or politically too sensitive issues to tackle. In the Swedish context, Aje Carlbom,[21] for example, claims that social phenomena, such as the moral policing of non-observant Muslims, disputes within and between Muslim communities, and growing social polarization between Muslims and "others," have lacked serious scrutiny. Unfortunately the discussion concerning politically sensitive developments in Western European Muslim communities has been dominated by empirically weakly informed writers with a tendency to essentialize Islam per se as undemocratic and incapable of integrating into Western secular societies.[22]

In this chapter I aimed to introduce one of the possible ways in which ethnographers can engage with the creation of social and symbolic boundaries in a Finnish multicultural suburban setting. My aim was to highlight that the specific character of the Finnish suburban Muslim context can only be understood by focusing on how globally produced sectarian and political discourses intersect with immigrant regimes and multicultural policies. The Iraqi diasporans who hold contrasting religious and political perceptions and different personal histories of persecution must come to terms with the fact that the rapid fragmentation of Iraqi society is in many ways present in the form of social and symbolic boundaries in multicultural suburban contexts in Finland.

The Iraqi diasporans in Finland are caught up in a collision of discourses not only with relation to violence at home; they also stand between the increasingly

---

20   For example, Ziauddin Sardar, *Desperately Seeking Paradise: Journeys of a Sceptical Muslim* (London: Granta Books, 2005); Rageh Omaar, *Only Half of Me: Being Muslim in Britain* (London: Viking, 2006); Ed Husain, *The Islamist: Why I Joined Radical Islam in Britain, What I Saw Inside and Why I Left* (London: Penguin, 2007).

21   Aje Carlbom, "An Empty Signifier: The Blue-and-Yellow Islam of Sweden," *Journal of Muslim Minority Affairs* 26/2 (2006): 245–261.

22   For example, Robert Spencer, *The Myth of Islamic Tolerance: How Islamic Law Treats Non-Muslims* (New York: Prometheus Books, 2005); Bruce Bawer, *While Europe Slept: How Radical Islam is Destroying the West from within* (London: Doubleday, 2006); Oriana Fallaci, *Force of Reason* (New York: Rizzoli, 2006); Melanie Philips, *Londonistan* (New York: Encounter Books, 2006).

contradictory refugee regime and multicultural social policies that essentialize identities in religious or sectarian terms. The widely shared perception on multicultural work in Finland emphasizes on build bridges between diasporic communities and the state. However, the multicultural projects often fail to recognize the internal divisions within the diaspora and thus engenders particular types of responses from the diasporans: silences and forms of silencing that are rooted in cultural and religious differences.

The increased debates on multiculturalism since the 1990s have largely revolved around normative theories with very few empirical studies analysing specific policies and their consequences.[23] This fact is particularly true with regard to the Finnish context. An uncritical respect for cultural difference easily leads to reifying cultural distinctions; it furthermore underlines group boundaries and silences internal debate. This problem has attracted especially gender scholars[24] and thus a detailed and empirically informed ethnographic focus on these themes in different diasporic Muslim contexts, both in the margins and centers of Europe is highly welcome.

---

23 Irene Bloemraad, Anna Korteweg and Yurdakul Gökçe, "Citizenship and Immigration: Multiculturalism, Assimilation, and Challenges to the Nation-State," *Annual Review of Sociology* 34 (2008): 160.

24 Cf. Susan Okin, *Is Multiculturalism Bad for Women?* (Princeton: Princeton University Press, 1999); Sarah Song, "Majority Norms, Multiculturalism, and Gender Equality," *American Political Science Review* 99/4 (2005): 473–489.

CHAPTER 11

Sudanese and Somali Women in Ireland and in Finland: Material Religion and Culture in the Formation of Migrant Women's Identities in the Diaspora

Yafa Shanneik and Marja Tiilikainen

The meaning of 'home' as a space of physical stability and permanence can be lost through migration. The notion of 'home' can instead develop to what David Morley describes as a 'mobile symbolic habitat.'[1] In this chapter, the authors will investigate the meaning and importance of material religion and culture for the formation of migrant women's religious, cultural, ethnic and national identities in the diaspora. The chapter will compare two groups of African women coming from Sudan and Somalia who migrated to two different European countries – Ireland and Finland respectively. The focus of the chapter lies in the investigation of the impact various material objects and symbols have on the women's sense of belonging and self-understanding in a European context. The chapter will examine how Sudanese and Somali women create their private spaces within their houses through particular objects, symbols and artefacts in order to construct a 'home' for themselves in the diaspora.[2] Furthermore, it will examine how these various spaces reflect the women's feelings of belonging and understanding of their identities in the diaspora.[3] Hence, this chapter contributes to the main themes discussed in this edited volume by presenting diasporic experiences of Muslim migrant women in two different European countries. In addition to being situated at the geographical margins of the Europe, the experiences of these and other Muslim women often remain invisible as, compared to men, they are more bound to domestic and private spaces.

Objects and images are visible references of particular religious, cultural, national and/or ethnic identification(s). In other words, they are markers of

---

1 David Morley, *Home Territories: Media, Mobility and Identity* (London: Routledge, 2000), 47.
2 See Manuel A. Vasquez, *More than Belief: A Materialist Theory of Religion* (Oxford: Oxford UP, 2011), 285.
3 See E. Frances King, *Material Religion and Popular Culture* (London: Routledge, 2010), 5.

© KONINKLIJKE BRILL NV, LEIDEN, 2019 | DOI:10.1163/9789004404564_013

difference and belonging. Particular objects become personalized in homes through carrying shared religious, cultural, individual or collective memories.[4] These memories are kinetic and transformed through various objects that are, like the women themselves, deterritorialized and re-territorialized[5] through migration. Some of these memories are preserved through particular objects and gain through displacement new meanings. Some of the women we interviewed insist on maintaining specific memories through holding on to particular objects that fill or mark a space within their private homes. These spaces give these women a sense of stability, a source of belonging, a memory of a past and yearning for a better future. At the same time these memories are associated with loss, pain, instability and uncertainty. Furthermore, in the diaspora the meaning and use of objects may change.

In the following we will demonstrate how two different groups of African Muslim female migrants create a space in their houses through specific objects that carry particular memories, habits, beliefs, rituals and practices and provide the women with various understandings of their identities in the diaspora.[6] These understandings are however not static but in a constant process of shifting meaning according to the personal, educational, financial, legal, political, religious and social situation of the women in the diaspora.

The chapter relies on two sets of data: 11 in-depth interviews conducted by Yafa Shanneik with Northern Sudanese women in Arabic in their homes in Dublin and Cork between September 2009 and February 2012,[7] and ethnographic data collected by Marja Tiilikainen among 22 Somali women in Finland between 1996 and 2002.[8] The Sudanese women studied here represent a well-educated group of migrants whose migration history to Ireland is linked to their academic studies and profession. Within the group, however, two different sub-groups are identified as regards to the length of stay in Ireland, and

---

4 See Danièle Hervieu-Léger, *Religion as a Chain of Memory*, trans. Simon Lee (Cambridge: Polity Press, 2000).

5 See Vasquez, *More than Belief*, 283.

6 See King, *Material Religion and Popular Culture*, 17.

7 This fieldwork is part of the ethnographic research on Muslim migrant women in Ireland which is part of the project 'Islam in Ireland' funded by the Irish Research Council for the Humanities and Social Sciences and the Department of An Taoiseach at the Study of Religions Department at University College Cork. The interviews were conducted in Arabic and are Shanneik's own translations. Some terms used in this chapter are in colloquial Sudanese dialect. The photographs of Figures 11.1–11.6 are taken by Shanneik.

8 The fieldwork was part of Tiilikainen's PhD research in comparative religion at the University of Helsinki, see Marja Tiilikainen, *Arjen islam: Somalinaisten elämää Suomessa* (Tampere: Vastapaino, 2003). The section on Somali women in this chapter includes some Somali language terms. The photographs of Figures 11.7–11.8 are taken by Tiilikainen.

SUDANESE AND SOMALI WOMEN IN IRELAND AND IN FINLAND   247

the degree of their mobility/settlement. The Somali women in this study, in contrast, have entered Finland as asylum seekers or through family reunification processes and they mainly stay at home taking care of their small children. First we will focus on the Sudanese women in Ireland and second on the Somali women in Finland. Finally, some conclusions on the role of material religion and culture in the formation of the studied African migrant women's understanding of their identities will be drawn.

1   Sudanese Women in Ireland

Ireland has a long history of Sudanese migrants coming to Ireland as medical students, trainees or well-established doctors working in hospitals or in their own private practices.[9] The Sudanese women,[10] Shanneik interviewed, emphasized the respected public image of Sudanese migrants in Ireland that is based, in their view, on their professional and educational status. As one of the women says: 'We've been known in Ireland for years. It is "normal" to see Sudanese doctors here.' Shanneik's research focuses on these middle- and upper-class educated and professional women who have lived in Ireland for at least ten years. What interested Shanneik the most in this community is their social communal networks that, to a large extent, have their roots back in Sudan. The transnational connectedness of Sudanese migrant doctors lead to the migration of a large number of Sudanese doctors coming to Ireland to continue their studies and professional careers. In the 1990s a growing number of Sudanese asylum seekers came to Ireland. The status of the majority of this group is, however, still not yet clear even after 20 years in Ireland. A number of Sudanese asylum seekers still live in segregated refugee camps. In contrast to Sudanese asylum seekers, middle- and upper-class educated Sudanese women were able to bring different objects from Sudan to Ireland and are therefore a better group to analyse in terms of the meaning and function of material religion and culture within Sudanese private homes in the diaspora.

The social structure of Sudanese communities is very hierarchal. Gender differences and gender roles are much respected within the Sudanese communities. Although highly educated and having been very active in the public

---

9   This information relies on interview material.

10   From 1992–2010 around 1,300 Sudanese applied for asylum in Ireland. For more information see Oliver Scharbrodt, 'Muslim Migration to Ireland: Past Perspectives and Future Prospects,' *Eire-Ireland: Journal of Irish Studies – Special Edition New Perspectives on Irish Migration* 47/1–2 (2012): 221–243. There are no official numbers of Sudanese migrants in Ireland but it is estimated, according to the interviewees, that their number is about 1,500.

sphere in Sudan the majority of Sudanese women in Ireland whom Shanneik interviewed have given up or have held back their career as medical doctors and devoted their time to bringing up their children. One of the main issues is the Irish system of medical education, which emphasizes the constant move of doctors within Ireland in order to gain further professional knowledge nationwide. The relocation of doctors to different places every few months results in the instability and insecurity of their families. There is a possibility of a family being split up when parents are stationed at different hospitals in different cities. As one of the Sudanese women explains: 'Isn't it enough to be separated from our families in Sudan? There is no need to split our small family life here as well. This is why I stay at home in order to give our children at least familial stability.' In general, priority is given to the men to find an appropriate position. Gender roles among Sudanese migrants shifted after migration, supporting its patriarchal definitions. In Sudan both men and women worked as professionals, while the children were taken care of by extended family members or by someone hired for this purpose. Sudanese women in Ireland feel more restricted in their freedom and mobility than in Sudan where they enjoyed more freedom of movement and self-fulfilment because of stable work conditions and familial support, particularly in regard to childcare.

2 'Sudanese Women on the Move'[11] in Ireland

There are two major groups of Sudanese middle- and upper-class migrants in Ireland. There are those who are still at the beginning of their medical education and constantly relocated from one city to the other. This group continuously disconnect and reconnect with a new environment.[12] As one of the interviewees explains: 'My husband might get a maximum of a one year contract, then he will have to find another place to go.' These people have to keep their baggage as light as possible in order to facilitate their move. When coming to Ireland, however, the women brought a considerable number of objects that reminded them of Sudan and of the people, culture and tradition they had left behind: 'In the past airport regulations weren't as strict as nowadays. We took boxes and boxes full with things like frames, talismans, spices

---

11   The term 'women on the move' was used by the Sudanese women who refer to themselves as *nisa' mutanaqilat* in order to describe their unstable and mobile situation in Ireland. Motasim and Heynen talk in their article about 'people on the move.' See Hanaa Motasim and Hilde Heynen, 'At Home with Displacement? Material Culture as a Site of Resistance in Sudan,' *Home Cultures* 8/1 (2011): 43–70.

12   See Motasim and Heynen, 'At Home with Displacement?.'

and even furniture. We hoped they would give us tranquillity while in the diaspora.' As soon as they had discovered the system of Irish medical education they had to give up some of their objects in order to move with ease: 'I brought my personal valuable belongings such as jewellery and accessories back to Sudan. The more we moved the more the objects I brought with me from Sudan began to disappear. Some I had to give away and some had to be left behind. I was very sad about it but could not change it.'

The only objects these women refused to give or throw away were religious ones. National, cultural and ethnic objects were more likely to be thrown away than religious ones as one of the women explains: 'All my religious frames and talismans travel with me. They give me *baraka* [blessing] and protect my family from evil spirits.' Another interviewee says: 'Yes, I could see my own cultural and ethnic identity shrinking and almost disappearing by each object I had to leave behind or to throw away. But I couldn't allow my religious identity to be taken. Therefore, I kept them travelling with me wherever I went in Ireland.' Maintaining a religious identity seems to be more important than a national or cultural identity in this context. The reason here lies in the women's understanding of objects they associate with religious meaning. They believe that giving a religious object away might have a negative impact on the family; as one of the women explains: 'I would be afraid to throw a frame of Allah's words away. Allah might be angry about that.' Another woman says: 'It is our duty to protect our religious identity in order for Allah to protect us.'

The houses of these women on the move are very barren and ascetic with only a very few religious symbols and frames hanging on the walls or at the entrance. Small mobile objects are now more prioritized than stable ones as they are easier to carry such as the *mebkhara* [pl. *mabakher*], which is any type of vessel made for burning incense [*bukhoor*]. This incense can be from wood or from paste that while burning releases a strong scent usually used to perfume the body, the clothes or the house as an expression of hospitality (Figure 11.1). Some of these *mabakher* have a traditional Sudanese touch with particular outside decorations (colours, designs) expressing their specific geographic location in Sudan. This particularity would be known among Sudanese women and highlighted in each of their social gatherings. *Al-hoq* is another example of 'mobile symbols of permanency.'[13] It is a mortar in which a particular wood with incense is ground to a powder. This powder is used particularly by women to perfume their bodies (Figure 11.2). Women on the move would have a small souvenir version of a larger traditional *hoq* as it is easier to carry. One of the women who however owns a larger traditional *hoq* explained that it is normally

---

13   See Motasim and Heynen, 'At Home with Displacement?,' 58.

FIGURE 11.1
Mebkhara, Dublin, 2010

FIGURE 11.2
Hoq, Cork, 2011

SUDANESE AND SOMALI WOMEN IN IRELAND AND IN FINLAND   251

used by a bride on her wedding night. The *hoq*, as she continues, is traditionally a symbol of transition from the status of a girl to a woman. This transition period is remembered quite often as it symbolizes the purity and innocence of the unmarried girl before entering wedlock; as one of the women explains: 'I took this with me as it reminds me of my feelings on my wedding day: fear of the unknown but also happiness at becoming a mature woman – independent and responsible for my life and my own family.' The *hoq* is usually given to the women by their families before their departure from Sudan as it symbolizes their transition from the local to the global or from the known to the unknown. It also reminds them of where they come from, highlighting the importance of their homeland.

Both objects are part of the material and sensory culture of Sudanese women. The *hoq* is usually placed in a visible space in the living room, functioning as a reminder of their origin that can be seen as well as touched and smelled. The *mebkhara* is carried around the house, filling the rooms with incense. It has a transformative effect on the women, giving them the feeling of being in Sudan: 'Women from back home would feel sometimes a nostalgia remembering the world they have left behind.' Sudanese women believe that this incense gives blessing to the house and protects them from the evil eye, adding to it a religious meaning. The *bukhoor* is a habitual practice that has always been performed back in Sudan and that is insisted on in the diaspora as one of the women explains: 'This practice is, besides the cooking, one of the few things that we perform in Europe that reminds us how Sudan and the people we left behind smell.' In this context, Sally Promey and Shira Brisman introduce the term 'sensory cultures,'[14] which describes the interaction between objects and individuals through their association with different smells, sounds, touches and sights: 'Sensory culture, like material culture, concerns not simply perception and its histories and theories but also things perceived and things produced for sensory apprehension.'[15] Smells are important for Sudanese women as they generate particular memories associated with their homeland and family members.

The *bambar* holds different associations. A *bambar* is a short wooden stool without a backrest. It is light and small. It can be carried around easily and fits in any corner (Figure 11.3). It comes as a souvenir in the form of a medal and is usually hung on a woman's bag. It is a symbol of a temporary sojourn signalling

---

14   See Sally Promey and Shira Brisman, 'Sensory Cultures: Material and Visual Religion Reconsidered,' in *The Blackwell Companion to Religion in America*, ed. Philip Goff (Oxford: Blackwell Publisher, 2010).

15   Promey and Brisman, 'Sensory Cultures,' 198.

FIGURE 11.3
Bambar, Cork, 2011

an imminent departure as one of the women explains: 'It is light, small and has no backrest as if to say, "take a rest but not too long as we will be going soon."' *Al-'angareeb* is also very popular and comes as a souvenir as well. It is a traditional wooden bed woven in the middle. The meaning of this object is twofold: It is used on the wedding night as a symbol of stability and origin. On the other hand, it is used to carry the dead[16] symbolizing both happiness and sadness. Similar to the *hoq* it is a symbol of transition from an unmarried to a married status and from life to death. *Bambar* and *'angareeb* souvenirs are very popular in Sudan as they are given prior to departure to symbolize mobility or transition but also reminding the owner of one's roots and origin.

Mobile symbols are carriers of meaning[17] and very popular among Sudanese women migrants in Ireland. This meaning is central for the women's religious, cultural and national understanding. Women use their private spaces in order to express visibly their belonging and affiliations. Hervieu-Léger describes the function of such objects as symbols of social identification expressing visibly one's attachment to or detachment from a particular community.[18] Religious objects are social identifiers like other cultural, national and ethnic objects that are responsible for the construction of communal and national identities and senses of belonging.[19]

---

16 For more on *al-'angareeb*, see Janice Boddy, *Wombs and Alien Spirits: Women, Men, and the Zār Cult in Northern Sudan* (Madison: University of Wisconsin Press, 1989), 26.
17 See also Motasim and Heynen, 'At Home with Displacement?,' 63.
18 Hervieu-Léger, *Religion as a Chain of Memory*.
19 See also Claire Mitchell, *Religion, Identity, and Politics in Northern Ireland: Boundaries of Belonging and Belief* (Aldershot: Ashgate, 2006), 133 and King, *Material Religion and Popular Culture*.

3 Settled Sudanese Women in Ireland

The other group of Sudanese women migrants in Ireland are those who have lived in Ireland for more than twenty years and who in the meantime have settled into permanent professional positions. They usually own a house and intend to remain in Ireland permanently. Their houses are not as barren and ascetic as the houses of the other group of Sudanese women, but rather exhibit a decorative intensification. The women use their private/domestic spaces to express their feeling of belonging, desire, longing and attachment to an imagined homeland which is highly idealized as a country in which its diverse ethnic and religious groups co-exist peacefully and whose ethnic and religious conflicts are ignored in the diasporic memory of the homeland. Women who have settled in a place sometimes feel more nostalgic and homesick for Sudan than those 'women on the move,' as they know that their stay is permanent. As one of the Sudanese women says: 'The minute you leave home there will never be a return back.' The migrant will never retrieve the feeling of being back home again since space and time have caused loss; as another woman explains: 'When you leave home you will have to consider it lost.' The migrant as well as the people that have been left behind are in constant change – a change that none of the parties, neither the migrant nor the people left behind – are aware of precisely, as one woman describes: 'Whenever I go back home I feel like a stranger and outsider. As if I never lived and shared a life with family and friends there before.' The migrant often experiences loss of roots, attachment and feeling of belonging to family and friends in the homeland. Objects therefore become the tools to hold on to the memories that maintain the links to the homeland and to the people and culture that were left behind, as another woman says: 'After some years you even forget the shared memories with your family and friends back home. I have been here for nearly 20 years now and hardly remember what it means or how it feels to be Sudanese in Sudan.'

This loss of shared memories is compensated for by the construction of a 'little Sudan' in the diaspora.[20] Sudanese women who have settled usually intensify the display of objects in their houses. One of the houses Shanneik visited was filled with different African, Sudanese, Arab and Islamic objects and symbols. One of the main objects that were highlighted is called *gabanat al-qahwa,* which is an Ethiopian-style pot for boiling traditional Arab/Sudanese

---

20   On the construction of a 'New Sudan' in diaspora see Anita Häusermann Fábos, 'Sudanese Identity in Diaspora and the Meaning of Home: The Transformative Role of Sudanese NGOs in Cairo,' in *New Approaches to Migration? Transnationalism and Transformations of Home,* ed. Nadje Al-Ali and Khalid Koser (London: Routledge, 2002), 34–50.

FIGURE 11.4 Gabanat al-qahwa, Cork, 2010

or Ethiopian coffee (Figure 11.4).[21] The woman emphasized the originality of the coffee that is boiled within the *gabanat*. The original coffee (*Al-Qahwa al-Aseela*) reflects the origin (*'asala*) of the people of the house and of the respect they show towards visitors when the coffee is boiled within the *gabanat*. The *gabanat* is also a reminder for the women of their roots, which becomes

---

21 Women on the move would have a traditional Arab pot for boiling coffee called *ghalayet qahwa* or *bakraj qahwa* as it is faster compared to the *gabanat* in which the coffee needs to be boiled for several hours. A *gabanat* is usually of clay and breaks easily.

more important particularly in the diaspora, as one of the women explains: 'You need to know where you come from. A tree without roots is a dead tree.' The ambiguity of identity understandings among Sudanese women can be seen through the example of the *gabanat* where its Ethiopian origin is ignored and instead seen as a symbol of Sudanese culture. Identities can become more porous in the diaspora leading women to see themselves in multiple identities symbolized through different objects. The women at this stage highlight the diversity of African cultures and traditions in Sudan saying: 'In the end we are all Africans, isn't it (*mish kidda*)?'

Among the women interviewed only one has a traditional *bambar* (a wooden stool without a backrest). She used to keep it in her living room in the first years of her stay in Ireland: 'In the past I used to put them in my living room and we used to sit on them.' But now they are stored upstairs underneath the bed. As explained above the *bambar* symbolizes movement and temporality. As this woman's situation became stable and permanent in Ireland she exchanged the *bambar* for a modern armchair (*kanab 'ady*), as they are more comfortable than these wooden stools without backrest on which one sits as if one is 'on the go,' as the woman explains. The exchange of traditional for modern objects is not a symbol of a newly gained prestigious status as these women are already members of the middle- and upper-class. Holding on to traditional objects such as the *bambar* rather symbolizes the woman's preservation of her Sudanese cultural identity. The women gain social capital,[22] to use Bourdieu's term, in making the effort of bringing such traditional objects over to Ireland. In addition, it shows the woman's rejection of dissociating herself from her past. Settled Sudanese women create a small Sudan in their homes in Ireland in order to maintain, at least psychologically, a connection with their home country. Even after bringing the modern armchairs in, the traditional *bambar* is not thrown away but is brought out on special occasions for others to admire. These traditional objects provide the owner with a social capital that shows their loyalty towards their homeland despite their long stay in Europe.

The *mawlid* marks the celebration of the birth of the Prophet Muhammad at which different religious sects and cultural groups in Sudan gather for several days. Colourful *mawlid* dolls and horses decorated with coloured paper are presented to little girls and boys (Figure 11.5). These are traditional presents given to children in Sudan and generally do not have a religious meaning. However, the majority of the Sudanese women, Shanneik interviewed in Ireland, regard these dolls as *baraka* and a symbol of protection – a function

---

22   Pierre Bourdieu, *The Logic of Practice*, trans. Richard Nice (Cambridge: Polity Press, 1990). In addition, see Terry Rey, *Bourdieu on Religion: Imposing Faith and Legitimacy* (London: Equinox, 2007).

FIGURE 11.5
Mawlid doll, Cork, 2010

only associated with Sudanese in the diaspora. One of the Sudanese women keeps the doll in a very central position on an upper shelf in the kitchen. It is a special space in the house as it looks over and through the different rooms. It has a spiritual meaning, as one of the women explains: 'It looks after the house and protects it from the evil eye.' This example reflects Tweed's argument that certain non-religious objects might have religious connotations or, as this case illustrates, religious associations might be assigned to them.[23] The dolls and horses as such do not carry a religious meaning but Sudanese women in the diaspora who do not celebrate the *mawlid* as in Sudan believe they have brought the spirit and the religious atmosphere of the *mawlid* celebration, personified in the dolls and horses, with them to Europe.

The last objects to be introduced in this section are wooden faces of women and men who had undergone particular scarifications (Figure 11.6). Shanneik was told that scarification has long been a tradition in Sudan, performed in order to distinguish the Arabs from the Nubians and other African tribes. It is a sign of beauty for young girls and of bravery and manhood for boys. Different tribes have different ways and designs to scar the faces of young children

---

23   Thomas A. Tweed, 'Space,' *Material Religion* 7/1 (2011): 116–123.

FIGURE 11.6 Scarificated faces, Cork, 2011

(their ages would range between 5 and 12 years). The women however mention in this regard modern transformations within Sudanese society and the disappearance of this tradition particularly among upper-class and educated people: 'We [people of the North of Sudan] stopped doing it but it is still practiced in the South.' Middle- and upper-class Sudanese women reject the praxis of scarification today. However they regard it as an element of Sudanese identity and displace these wooden faces in their homes as folkloristic decorations. One of the Sudanese women has three faces of men and women with different scarifications and ethnic features representing the different ethnicities of Sudan. At the first interview, in February 2011, she idealized her homeland as outlined above and described it as a country 'in which everyone respects the difference of the other but we are in the end all Arabs and Africans.' When Shanneik visited her again at the end of February 2012, she only referred to the particularity of the northern faces ignoring the southern ones. When Shanneik showed particular interest in the faces from the South, she referred to them as *'denka'* highlighting her detachment from them as they are no longer part of Sudan saying: 'As you know they are independent now. We are not united anymore.' A year before the faces were regarded by the woman as a symbol of unity celebrating the diversity of Sudanese culture, whereas they are now ignored and no longer part of the woman's identity.

The women Shanneik interviewed see themselves in multiple identities depending on the context they are in. They express their multiple identifications through objects displayed in their private spaces. Amongst each other, they regard themselves as Sudanese, highlighting however their Khartoum-origin by labelling themselves as *khartoumiyyat*. This identification is emphasized through the display of particular *khartoumy* objects in the house. The hierarchies in Sudanese society are maintained by emphasising the superior educational and social status of Sudanese women from the capital (as the example of the decline of scarification shows). In front of other Arabs and especially in cases where they want to emphasize being different, they label themselves as Africans (*ifriqiyyat*). This is particularly visible by placing African objects in the house such as wooden statues that some Arabs may regard as idols and therefore reject having them in their homes. In front of other African women they turn to identify themselves as Arabs in order to highlight their ethnic and linguistic difference and superiority. The ability to dwell,[24] to use Tweed's term, between various national, ethnic and religious identities helps the women to express visibly their attachment to or detachment from particular groups. It functions as social identifications expressed through the placement of different Arab and African as well as local tribal objects in their homes.

4 Somali Women in Finland

Somalis started to enter Finland as asylum-seekers in 1990 as the central government of Somalia was about to collapse and the country slide into full civil war. Since that time Somalis have remained the largest migrant group in Finland with refugee, Muslim and also African backgrounds. In 2012, the number of native Somali language speakers was almost 15,000, 48% of them being women.[25] According to several studies, Somalis in Finland frequently experience racism and discrimination. For example, according to an EU study 47% of Somalis in Finland reported incidents of discrimination over a period of 12 months.[26] Also, according to a recent study on migrant health and wellbeing,

---

24 Thomas A. Tweed, *Crossing and Dwelling: A Theory of Religion* (Cambridge: Harvard University Press, 2006).

25 Statistics Finland, 'Language According to Age and Gender by Region 1990–2012,' accessed November 12, 2014, http://193.166.171.75/database/StatFin/vrm/vaerak/vaerak_en.asp.

26 *EU-Midis: European Union Minorities and Discrimination Survey. Main Results Report* (European Union Agency for Fundamental Rights, 2009), 36.

36% of the Somali women reported having experienced discrimination and harassment on the street.[27] The unemployment rate among Somalis is high, almost 61% among the women and 46% among the men in 2011.[28] The size of the families has an impact on the employment of Somali women: many mothers prefer to stay at home and take care of their small children. Also, the educational background of women compared to that of men is often lower. Before the war, Somali women in general used to have limited opportunities for education, and women's economic and social position lagged behind that of men.[29] In Finland, it has been reported that Somali women are in a disadvantaged position as almost 12% could not read well or at all, 29% could not understand the official languages of Finland (Finnish or Swedish) sufficiently, and over 28% could not use the Internet.[30]

In Finland, most Somali families live in the metropolitan Helsinki region. They typically live in rental apartments located in neighbourhoods. Somali mothers are busy with taking care of the children and household, and their everyday life is very much home-centred. Daily cooking and cleaning as well as visits to maternity and child health clinics or social offices fill the day. The kitchen is the heart of the female and motherly space at home – cooking is a central part of identity as a woman, mother and wife. A big sack of rice and a several-litre bottle of cooking oil, bought in an ethnic shop, are basic items in a Somali kitchen, where cooking for a big family is an everyday practice.

In Somalia, families usually lived in one- or two-level houses, where they had easy access to a yard that was used by their family only or shared by neighbours. It was easy to let children go out to play as ageing and other family members were easily available to watch them. In Finland, things are much more complicated: particularly in wintertime mothers may avoid going out with children as they find it too difficult and not very inviting to take children to a playground when it is cold, dark and icy. Some mothers may also avoid going out because they feel that their Finnish neighbours do not accept them and complain about things like Somali children using other children's toys in their

---

27 Simo Mannila, Anu E. Castaneda and Inga Jasinskaja-Lahti, 'Syrjintäkokemukset,' in *Maahanmuuttajien terveys ja hyvinvointi*, ed. Anu E. Castaneda et al. (Helsinki: Terveyden ja hyvinvoinnin laitos, 2012), 234.

28 *Somalis in Helsinki* (New York: Open Society Foundations, 2013).

29 Nancy Hawk Merryman, 'Women's Welfare in the Jubba Valley: Somali Socialism and After,' in Catherine Besteman and Lee V. Cassanelli, *The Struggle for Land in Southern Somalia* (Boulder: Westview Press, 1996), 180.

30 Seppo Koskinen, Päivi Sainio and Shadia Rask, 'Sosiaalinen toimintakyky,' in *Maahanmuuttajien terveys ja hyvinvointi*, ed. Anu E. Castaneda et al. (Helsinki: Terveyden ja hyvinvoinnin laitos, 2012), 201–205.

play. Furthermore, Somali mothers in Finland in general seem to prioritize duties inside the home over taking children to play in the yard which is not considered as important as, for instance, cooking. And finally, migrant women often lack social networks through which they can get support and help, and, therefore, they have few people who could share daily tasks and offer them opportunities for rest. In this situation, television, telephone and the Internet are women's channels to reach out from the physical home and stay connected to their extended families, friends and previous home country. In the families that Tiilikainen studied, it was common to follow news from Somalia as well as from Arabic countries through satellite antennas. During Ramadan and Eid festivals, in particular, satellite channels brought Islamic recitations, prayers and celebrations into the living rooms of Somali families in Finland, and strengthened the identities of the women as Muslims as well as created the sense of *umma*, community of all Muslims.

For the Somali women, home is also a central religious space, which is created by sounds, decorations, organization of the space and religious practices.[31] Although many of the women also visited a mosque as they attended Qur'anic schools, lectures or prayers, particularly during the month of Ramadan, women mostly prayed at home. On a wall one could find a prayer schedule – beside a clock and a bus schedule – a picture of Mecca, Qur'anic verses, or a map of the Islamic world where the largest mosques in the world had been marked. A prayer mat was spread at prayer times. Also, religious rituals such as communal recitation of the Qur'an for a sick person might be organized at home.

Tiilikainen once observed a ritual where the Qur'an was recited to a sick Somali woman. A group of men were responsible for the reading, but before the actual ritual took place, female relatives and friends had done a considerable amount of work to prepare the woman's living room as a suitable ritual space: Ordinary furniture had been removed and replaced by mattresses and pillows on which the sheikhs and other men would sit. Female friends had also decorated the room by bringing artificial flowers, framed Qur'anic verses and textiles from their own homes. The women explained that these objects were not mandatory, but created good atmosphere. Moreover, they needed to bring them, because the sick woman 'had become European,' and therefore she did not have many Somali objects in her apartment. Once the men had eaten, prayed and recited the Qur'an to the woman, they left and the women, who had been packed into a small kitchen during the ritual and prepared the

---

31 See also Marja Tiilikainen, 'Illness, Healing, and Everyday Islam: Transnational Lives of Somali Migrant Women,' in *Everyday Lived Islam in Europe*, ed. Nathal M. Dessing et al. (Farnham: Ashgate, 2013), 147–162.

food served to the men, reorganized the place as it used to be. After that was done, the women went to sit and discuss in the living room, and several other female visitors also came and joined them. Interestingly, reorganization of the space had an important ritual significance as it created an 'authentic' cultural and religious context. Furthermore, the women were instrumental in making the ritual space and they possessed the necessary cultural knowledge – and creativity – which enabled them to manage the task in the absence of traditional objects and spaces.

5 Objects and Knowledge of Objects

During fieldwork, an observation that Tiilikainen made in the Somali homes was the lack of objects in general, and Somali cultural objects in particular. Just a few objects reminiscent of home in Somalia could be found: some traditional handicraft, baskets, incense burners, a camel bell or a wooden milk container, personal jewellery and some clothes. In one of the families that Tiilikainen visited, the mother, together with her mother and her daughter had prepared a small model of an *aqal*, a portable nomadic house: they had collected grass in the summer in Finland, and prepared everything by hand, including traditional grass mats. Preparing the small *aqal* was very important for the mother and the grandmother, who could thereby transmit traditional female knowledge to the next generation and pay tribute to the past nomadic culture. In the apartment located in the block of flats in the metropolitan Helsinki, the *aqal* was a constant reminder of the real home in Somalia (Figure 11.7). Another woman explained to Tiilikainen that she had tried not to wear the clothes that she had brought from Somalia, but to keep them well so that they would remain in good condition as long as possible. The same woman had fixed a Somali flag, which

FIGURE 11.7A–B   Traditional aqal, Somaliland, 2006

she had drawn on a piece of paper, beside Qur'anic verses printed on decorative fabric on the wall of her living room. She had done it because 'children know the Finnish flag, but what is the flag of Somalia like?' Sometimes women received gifts from friends who had travelled to Somalia, and those items were treated carefully: Somali coffee, incense, wooden sticks to brush the teeth, or dresses and scarves brought from Somalia were highly appreciated.

Many of the objects that previously had been in daily use in Somalia such as milk vessels, baskets or camel bells had become decorative objects that were kept on a shelf, wall, or in a cupboard and reminded women and their children in the diaspora about their past home and nomadic culture, and through which they could transfer history within the family. Some of the objects, however, still had an important role in rituals. For example, some of the women had a large *xeedho* (or *xeero*), which traditionally plays an important role in the Somali wedding ritual. The *xeedho* is a wedding basket that is beautifully decorated with leather and cowry shells. Inside the *xeedho* there is a bowl in which a special dish called *muqmad* or *oodkac*, made from dates, camel meat (cow meat in Finland) and clarified butter, *subag*, is served during weddings. The *xeedho* has an important symbolic meaning: The container consists of two parts and symbolizes the bride and the groom and their families. Female relatives of the bride dress one of the *xeedho*s to look like a bride, and in addition, close and tie it skilfully with a knotted robe. The groom is expected to solve the task and open the *xeedho* without cutting the long robe and spilling its contents. If he fails, women ridicule and symbolically punish him.[32] As only a few migrant Somali women have *xeedho*s in their homes, they are circulated and borrowed by relatives and friends who need one (Figure 11.8).

The lack of Somali objects can naturally be explained by, first, the refugee background: when Somalis fled from their homes, they had to leave their things behind, or women were forced to sell precious items such as jewellery they might have had while on the move. Moreover, they have not yet had enough time or money to fill their apartments in Finland with decorative or other objects. Second, the lack of objects may be explained by a nomadic culture and the minor value given to objects: Sada Mire argues that in the Somali culture preserving knowledge is more important than preserving objects. The possession of the knowledge of objects is esteemed more highly than the possession of the object itself. This has also been crucial for the survival of nomadic households that have not been able to carry many things with them.[33]

---

32 Also Kathryn McMahon, 'The Hargeisa Provincial Museum,' *African Arts* 21/3 (1988): 68.

33 Sada Mire, 'Preserving Knowledge, Not Objects: A Somali Perspective for Heritage Management and Archaeological Research,' *African Archaeological Review* 24/3–4 (2007): 49–71.

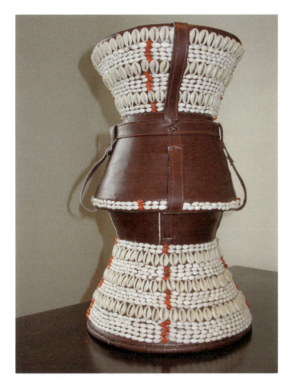

FIGURE 11.8
Xeedho, Finland, 2019

This notion seems particularly fitting in the case of rituals such as the Qur'anic recitation in the diaspora described in the previous section: The knowledge of how to organize the ritual in a culturally new, non-Islamic environment is more important than the possession of individual objects per se.

In the Somali culture, a woman is responsible for the house and its objects. For example, in a nomadic family a woman has the responsibility of erecting the portable house, *aqal*. Therefore, for Somali women important objects are those that have their significance in the domestic, and particularly female, everyday and ritual space. In the diaspora, however, the use and significance of traditionally important objects may be contested by both the Finnish cultural environment and new Islamic interpretations. As an example, we will address some dimensions of fragrance and frankincense in the lives of Somali women.

6 Traditional Objects, Contested Meanings

In the Somali cultural environment, good scent has special meanings: Regardless of gender, a person who wants to dress up is not complete without a drop of perfume or good-smelling oil. Good smell speaks of cleanliness and it is also sexually attractive. *Cadar*, perfume or perfumed oil, is also used for the hands after eating: according to Islamic custom, food is eaten with the right hand, and afterwards when the hands have been washed, they are also perfumed to cover the food smell.

Various types of incense are also used to refresh a person or home. *Uunsi*, a mixture of incense and concentrated perfume is burned to perfume a woman before she goes, for example, to meet her friends or to a wedding party. To perfume herself, a woman may stand above an incense burner, *dabqaad*, and treat herself and her clothes with good-smelling smoke. Moreover, the whole house may be freshened by burning *uunsi*, in particular after cooking, which often entails cooking in oil. Apart from *uunsi*, other types of incense are also used on different occasions.

Frankincense and perfume also have religious and ritual significance. Special types of resin incense and gum such as *foox* are used for religious and healing purposes. For example, at sunset in Somalia, *foox* is commonly burned in homes to prevent mosquitos and also *jinn* spirits from entering the house. For healing purposes, *foox* may be burned together with some herbs or Qur'anic verses written on a piece of paper, prescribed by a religious healer, and a patient fumigated.

Until recently, Somalis have predominantly been Sufi Muslims.[34] Among the women, Sufi *sitaat* rituals have been popular: During the ritual, which is attended and led only by women, distinguished women of early Islam such as the Prophet's daughter Faadumo, his mother Aamina and his wives are being remembered and praised by religious hymns.[35] During the ritual, a religious trance called *muraaqo* may be experienced. Singing of *sitaat*, religious poetry, drumming and rhythmical clapping of the hands is accompanied by burning of frankincense and sprinkling participants with perfume. As a woman explained: 'Whoever mentions the Prophet's name should smell nice.'

---

34 See e.g. I.M. Lewis, *Saints and Somalis: Popular Islam in a Clan-based Society* (London: Haan Associates, 1998).

35 On *sitaat*, see Lidwien Kapteijns with Mariam Omar Ali, 'Sittaat: Somali Women's Songs for the "Mothers of the Believers,"' in *The Marabout and the Muse: New Approaches to Islam in African Literature*, ed. Kenneth W. Harrow (Portsmouth: Heinemann, 1996), 124–141; Lidwien Kapteijns with Maryan Omar, 'Sittaat: Women's Religious Songs in Djibouti,' *Hal-abuur – Journal of Somali Literature and Culture* 2/1–2 (2007): 38–48; Francesca Declich, 'Sufi Experience in Rural Somali: A Focus on Women,' *Social Anthropology* 8/3 (2000): 295–318; Marja Tiilikainen, 'Sitaat as Part of Somali Women's Everyday Religion,' in *Perspectives on Women's Everyday Religion*, ed. Marja-Liisa Keinänen (Stockholm: Stockholm University, 2010), 203–218.

Fragrance and frankincense are also part of spirit possession rituals. *Saar* is a generic term for spirit possession rituals, which are well known in eastern Africa. In Somalia, specific spirits and cults are referred to, for example, as *mingis, sharax, boorane* or *wadaaddo*. Different spirits are fond of different songs, colours, foods and also frankincense. For example, in *mingis* rituals incense called *cuud* and *jaawe* are burned. A patient who suffers from symptoms caused by a spirit is fumigated with incense and often the whole room is dense with smoke. In the *saar* ritual, incense is aimed at inviting the spirits to enter the room where healing takes place, and also the patient.[36]

In Finland, *uunsi* and even other types of frankincense may be found at ethnic shops. In addition, Somali women commonly bring along *uunsi* from the Horn of Africa when they visit home – *uunsi* is a popular gift from female relatives and friends at home in the Horn of Africa. In Finland, however, traditional incense burners are not functional because small pieces of coal are not easily available. Therefore, many women use electric incense burners that they may buy in ethnic shops or, for example, Middle Eastern cities such as Dubai. Alternatively, they may burn incense placed on a piece of folio paper on an electric cooking plate.

Some women have said, however, that in Finland they have decreased the use of *uunsi* because Finnish neighbours have complained about the strong odour that spreads into the corridors of the buildings and neighbouring apartments, or because Finnish people on buses or in offices have frequently reacted to the smell of *uunsi* or strong perfumes around Somalis. Another reason for decreasing the use of frankincense and fragrance among Somali migrants is political-religious change, which has an impact on Somalis both in the diaspora and in the Horn of Africa.

Several studies have documented the increased importance of Islam among Somali migrants following the civil war and exile.[37] Moreover, religious interpretations and practices have gradually been changing. Islamic movements in

---

36 On *zar* (*saar* in Somali) in Eastern Africa, see, e.g., I.M. Lewis, Ahmed Al-Safi and Sayyid Hurreiz, ed., *Women's Medicine: The* Zar-Bori *Cult in Africa and Beyond* (Edinburgh: Edinburgh University Press for the International African Institute, 1991); Janice Boddy, *Wombs and Alien Spirits: Women, Men and the Zār Cult in Northern Sudan* (Madison: The University of Wisconsin Press, 1989); Marja Tiilikainen, 'Somali Saar in the Era of Social and Religious Change,' in *Spirit Possession and Trance*, ed. Bettina E. Schmidt and Lucy Huskinson (London: Continuum, 2010), 117–133.

37 E.g., Rima Berns McGown, *Muslims in the Diaspora: The Somali Communities of London and Toronto* (Toronto: University of Toronto Press, 1999); Celia McMichael, 'Everywhere is Allah's Place: Islam and the Everyday Life of Somali Women in Melbourne, Australia,' *Journal of Refugee Studies* 15/2 (2002): 171–188; Tiilikainen, *Arjen islam.*

Somalia have gained influence since the 1970s, and increasingly since the 1990s, after the collapse of the central government. Among the influential Islamist groups were, for example, the moderate al-Islāh and the politically radical al-Itihād al-Islāmī, which is close to the puritanical Wahhabi and Salafiyya movements of the Arabian Peninsula. At the same time, Sufi Islam in Somalia has become less popular.[38]

In the diaspora, the change can be observed, for example, in how Somali women cover themselves more than before in Somalia where attitudes towards Islamic dress codes used to be very relaxed. Somali women also told Tiilikainen how Somali men even at school or a working place might advise them to wear the hijab. One woman complained that Somali men had remarked that Somali women should not use perfume when they went out so that they would not attract men: 'In Somalia a woman always had perfume when she wanted to dress up, enjoy and go out with her friends. It was like aroma therapy for us. Now a woman should be invisible and unscented!'

Religious change can also be observed in healing practices. The spirit possession of *saar* has been condemned by several contemporary Somali Islamic scholars as non-Islamic, and therefore forbidden. Hence, the practice has been declining or it is not practised openly as it used to be. Sufi *sitaat* rituals also seem to be very rare in the diaspora, although they are still found in Somalia. Some of the women who used to participate in *saar* rituals in Somalia, explained to Tiilikainen how they sometimes secretly organized small spirit possession rituals in Finland with a few trusted friends, or alternatively, tried to treat their spirits alone at home by burning incense and eating special foods. In the two *mingis* rituals that Tiilikainen observed in Finland, *cuud* and *jaawe* were habitually burnt, and indeed, they were central in creating the proper atmosphere and context for the ritual performance.[39]

7   'Home' Expressed through Gendered Spaces among Sudanese and Somali Women in Europe

In this chapter the authors compared two groups of African Muslim women coming from Sudan and Somalia living in Ireland and Finland, investigating

---

38   Andre Le Sage, 'Prospects for Al Itihad & Islamist Radicalism in Somalia,' *Review of African Political Economy* 28/89 (2001): 472–477; Ken Menkhaus, 'Political Islam in Somalia,' *Middle East Policy* IX/1 (2002): 109–123; Marja Tiilikainen, 'Spirits and the Human World in Northern Somalia,' in *Milk and Peace, Drought and War*, ed. Markus Hoehne and Virginia Luling (London: Hurst, 2010), 163–184.

39   Tiilikainen, 'Somali Saar in the Era of Social and Religious Change.'

the meaning and importance of material religion and culture for the formation of the women's religious, cultural, ethnic and national identities in the diaspora. Although different in regard to their migration histories as well as socio-economic and national backgrounds, the two groups show similarities in highlighting the importance of preserving their religious, ethnic, national and cultural identities. This is expressed in the creation of various spaces in their private homes through presenting particular objects and symbols or performing specific religious practices and rituals or transferring gender-specific knowledge from one generation to the next. This attachment and connectivity to their past proves to be important for the interviewed Sudanese and Somali women as it provides them with a sense of belonging and self-understanding in a European context.

The authors also examined how spaces and meaning of spaces are in continuous change as they are re-negotiated and re-formed depending on political, socio-economic or religious changes.[40] This reflects Thomas Tweed's argument that: '[...] political processes, social relations, and economic forces mark religious spaces and, therefore, they are sites where power is negotiated as meaning is made.'[41] Material religion and culture in the form of objects, for example, change in meaning and value in different contexts. As illustrated above, the Sudanese women intensify their display of particular religious, national or ethnic objects in their houses. Particular objects gain in meaning and value through the women's own displacement. Particularly among the settled Sudanese women a feeling of guilt could be observed as they have not returned home after the completion of their medical education in Ireland as originally planned but rather have stayed in Ireland and built a new home in Europe for themselves and for their families. These women try to compensate for this disturbing feeling by showing particularly other Sudanese women in Ireland how much effort they have put into bringing different objects from Sudan to Ireland in order to create a new home with an overstated Sudanese character.

Spaces, as Tweed argues, are, however, also made by perception, imagination and religious practice.[42] Sudanese women on the move in Ireland and Somali refugees in Finland are similar in this regard as both had to travel with light luggage to Europe taking only the necessities and leaving particular objects behind. Both of these groups of women have had to find new alternative ways in which to preserve their religious and ethnic identity in Europe without the possession of particular objects. Sudanese women on the move

---

40   Tweed, 'Space,' 117.
41   Tweed, 'Space,' 121.
42   Tweed, 'Space,' 122f.

would carry a *bambar* or *al-ʿangareeb* souvenir rather than having them as part of their furniture at home. The possession of a smaller version of this furniture in the form of a souvenir hanging on the wall or carried on a handbag would still have a symbolic meaning and remind women of their own roots and origin. This reflects Tiilikainen's observation of Somali women in Finland, who highlight the preservation of their religious, national, ethnic and nomadic identities through the transfer of particular gender-specific knowledge from one generation to the next as the examples of the preparation of the portable nomadic house, *aqal*, or the organization of religious spaces for ritual practices such as the Qurʾanic recitation have shown.

The domestic spaces described in this chapter have been central arenas for the creation of female, cultural and religious identities in the diaspora. Religious and cultural practices and objects provide migrant women continuity and remembrance on one hand, but they also entail tension and contestation, on the other. For example, following the over 20-year-long conflict in Somalia, Somali women's ritual knowledge and the content and practice of Islam itself has been challenged by increasingly rigid interpretations of Islam both in Somalia and in the diaspora, and the space for the expression of sensory culture,[43] such as the use of certain incenses and perfumes, has been reduced.

Both groups of African Muslim women studied here are creative and imaginative in their perception of spaces and objects according to their own socio-economic or political situation and migration context. Sudanese and Somali women in Ireland and Finland create gendered spaces of religious, cultural, national and ethnic memory and practice in order to build a new home in Europe.

---

43   Promey and Brisman, 'Sensory Cultures.'

CHAPTER 12

The Socio-spatial Configuration of Muslims in Lisbon

Jennifer McGarrigle

The religious spatiality of minorities in Europe has attracted attention in recent times. Increasing diversity due to global migration, coupled with recent geopolitics, has raised questions about the visibility of Islam in the city. Perceived threats to social cohesion have included concerns about factious Islamic spaces as a catalyst for further social and spatial fragmentation. Hence, the spatial practices of Muslims in Europe, including patterns of residence, the appropriation of spaces for places of worship, public religious dress and rituals in public space have been subjected to debate.[1] Moreover, such practices have been portrayed as synonymous with the desire to preserve religious identity. Eade[2] writes, "religious identities are intimately bound up with the process of migration, cultural diversity and the relationship between geopolitical events at the global and local levels." In the urban context, the territorialization of religion represents interchanges at the transnational and local levels[3] in the same way that religious practices span both the transnational and the everyday[4]

---

1 For example, Silvio Ferrari and Sabrina Pastorelli, ed., *Religion in Public Spaces – A European Perspective* (Farnham: Ashgate, 2012); Jennifer McGarrigle, *Understanding Processes of Ethnic Concentration and Dispersal: South Asian Residential Preferences in Glasgow* (Amsterdam: University of Amsterdam Press, 2010); John Bowen, *Why the French Don't Like Headscarves: Islam, the State, and Public Space* (Princeton: Princeton University Press, 2007); Jocelyne Cesari, "Mosque Conflicts in European Cities: Introduction," *Journal of Ethnic and Migration Studies* 31/6 (2005): 1015–1024; Armando Salvatore, "Making Public Space: Opportunities and Limits of Collective Action Among Muslims in Europe," *Journal of Ethnic and Migration Studies* 30/5 (2004): 1013–1031.
2 John Eade, "Excluding and Including the 'Other' in the Global City: Religious Mission among Muslim and Catholic Migrants in London," in *The Fundamentalist City? Religiosity and the Remaking of Urban Space*, ed. Nezar AlSayyad and Mejgan Massoumi (London: Routledge, 2011), 284.
3 David Garbin, "The Visibility and Invisibility of Migrant Faith in the City: Diaspora Religion and the Politics of Emplacement of Afro-Christian Churches," *Journal of Ethnic and Migration Studies* 39/5 (2013): 677–696.
4 Olivia Sheringham, "Creating 'Alternative Geographies': Religion, Transnationalism and Everyday Life," *Geography Compass* 4/11 (2010): 1678–1694.

© KONINKLIJKE BRILL NV, LEIDEN, 2019 | DOI:10.1163/9789004404564_014

with places of worship functioning at times as "meso"/ in-between spaces.[5] Levitt[6] contends that places of worship represent "multilayered webs of connection" that function at a global level. Thus, the study of religious spatiality spans various scales from the neighbourhood and city to the global. While the global perspective in religious studies has long been present, implicit in the concept of "world religions,"[7] recent literature has sought to explore the ways in which the local emplacement of migrant faith groups impacts the negotiation of religious identities and reshapes the city[8] through the appropriation of space, the provision of welfare[9] and interactions in the social life of the city. Beyond this, and contrary to the idea that the preservation of religious identities may impede integration, is the evidence that religion generates specific forms of social capital. In the Portuguese case, Fonseca and Esteves[10] found this to be true in varying degrees among the Sunni Muslim, Ismaili and Hindu communities. Similarly, Vilaça[11] found religious communities helped to "open doors [and] establish bridges" for Eastern European migrants in Portugal.

The Portuguese capital is an interesting context to study religiosity and urban space. While increasing religious diversity is a result of recent immigration in a society of traditional religious homogeneity, religious difference remains a somewhat neutral topic. For various reasons postulated in the literature, the same tensions evident in relations between Muslims and non-Muslims

---

5   Manuel Vasquez and Marie Friedmann Marquardt, *Globalizing the Sacred: Religion across the Americas* (New Brunswick: Rutgers University Press, 2003).

6   Peggy Levitt, *God Needs No Passport: Immigrants and the Changing American Religious Landscape* (New York: The New Press, 2007), 15.

7   Kim Knott, "From Locality to Location and Back Again: A Spatial Journey in the Study of Religion," *Religion* 39/2 (2009): 154–160.

8   Kim Knott, "From Locality to Location and Back Again," 154–160; David Garbin, "The Visibility and Invisibility of Migrant Faith in the City," 677–696; Simon Naylor and James Ryan, "The Mosque in the Suburbs: Negotiating Religion and Ethnicity in South London," *Social and Cultural Geography* 3/1 (2002): 39–59; Eade, "Excluding and Including the 'Other' in the Global City."

9   David Conradson, "Expressions of Charity and Action towards Justice: Faith-based Welfare Provision in Urban New Zealand," *Urban Studies* 45/10 (2008): *2117–2141;* Tanja Winkler, "When God and Poverty Collide: Exploring the Myths of Faith-sponsored Community Development," *Urban Studies* 45/10 (2008): 2099–2116.

10   Lucinda Fonseca and Alina Esteves, "Migration and New Religion Townscapes in Lisbon," in *Immigration and Place in Mediterranean Metropolises*, ed. Lucinda Fonseca et al. (Lisbon: Luso-American Foundation, 2002): 255–291.

11   Helena Vilaça, *Imigração, Etnicidade e Religião: O Papel das Comunidades Religiosas na Integração dos Imigrantes da Europa de Leste*. Estudos OI: 30 (Lisbon: ACIDI, 2008), 84.

in other socio-political realities across Europe are less evident.[12] The Muslim community, while small in number, is internally heterogeneous in terms of doctrine, origin and class.[13] Moreover, while much has been written on the ethnic geography of Lisbon, the nexus between religion and space has been given less attention.

This chapter explores various elements of the religious spatiality of Muslims in Lisbon and is structured as follows. The first section contextualizes the increasing religious diversity in Lisbon as a post-colonial and post-immigration phenomenon. Next, a spatial analysis of religious landscapes, conceived as residence and collective spatial appropriation for worship, is conducted for the Lisbon Metropolitan Area (LMA). Census data[14] on religion from 2001 and 2011 are mapped and processes underlying patterns of local emplacement are then explored using qualitative data from interviews conducted in 2012 with, primarily, Sunni religious leaders.[15] In the following section, to complement the spatial analysis of Muslims in the city, Islamic places of worship, associations and educational establishments are mapped at two different points in time (2001 and 2014). The dichotomy of invisibility and visibility in relation to

---

12 Nina Clara Tiesler, "No Bad News from the European Margin: The New Islamic Presence in Portugal," *Islam and Christian-Muslim Relations* 12 (2001): 71–91.

13 José Mapril and Nina Clara Tiesler, "Portugal," in *Yearbook of Muslims in Europe. Volume 5*, ed. Jørgen S. Nielsen et al. (Leiden: Brill, 2013), 517–530; Abdool Karim Vakil, "Do Outro ao Diverso: Islão e Muçulmanos em Portugal: História, Discursos, Identidades," *Revista Lusófona de Ciência das Religiões* III/5–6 (2004): 296; Nina Clara Tiesler, "No Bad News from the European Margin," 71–91; Nina Clara Tiesler, "Novidades do Terreno. Muçulmanos na Europa e o Caso Português," *Análise Social* XXXIX/173 (2005): 827–849; Nina Clara Tiesler and David Cairns, "Across Difference: Portuguese Muslim Youth as Portuguese Youth?," in *Youth on the Move: European Youth and Geographical Mobility*, ed. David Cairns (Morlenbach: VS Verlag, Springer, 2010), 107–115.

14 To overcome limitations with census data, mainly due to the fact that the "religion" question in the census is facultative resulting in a substantial percentage of non-response, it is supplemented by a mapping of places of worship and interviews with religious leaders. Thus, we rely largely on the cross-reading of the data and not on a single source. Given the fact that the presence of Muslims is related strongly to immigration, one may imagine that data by nationality would provide a good picture of spatial patterning. However, with high levels of naturalization and in some cases citizenship rights linked with the ex-Portuguese colonies it is hard to trace the extent of the groups over migration waves and generations. Hence, in methodological terms it is difficult to quantify and map the Muslim population based solely on census data.

15 Semi-structured interviews were conducted with 21 religious leaders/community presidents of both formal and informal places of worship. All interviewees are male of migrant background and between 30 and 60 years of age. Interviews were recorded, transcribed and analysed using qualitative software.

peripheralization and centrality in the city and particular forms of spatial appropriation is discussed. The remaining sections of the chapter focus on two interconnected themes: first, the local emplacement and formation of communities in line with diversities within the Islamic community that produce different affiliations and appropriations of space; and second, the social role of religious bodies and associated institutions in transforming local dynamics and in generating social capital.

1 Increasing Religious Diversity in a Post-colonial and Post-immigration Setting

Despite the historic links with Islam in Portugal, dating back to Al-Andalus, the modern Muslim minority is a very recent result of the process of decolonization and labour migration in the context of globalization. With the exception of a small group of Indo-Mozambican students studying in Lisbon during the 1950s, it was not until after the transition to democracy in 1974 and the subsequent independence of the colonies that Muslim migrants began to arrive from Portuguese-speaking African countries. Initially, the largest group arrived from Mozambique and included both Sunni and Isma'ili Muslims. While a smaller number of this group was black African, the majority were of Indian origin and of higher socio-economic status. Beginning in the 1980s, with particular expression in the 1990s and beyond, a second group of Sunni Muslim migrants arrived from Guinea-Bissau with a different socio-economic profile from the Indo-Mozambicans. Several particularities render Islam in Portugal distinct; Tiesler[16] highlights the relatively notable presence of Isma'ilis,[17] the constitution of the Sunni community and the role of the elite and middle class. From the beginning, the Muslim minority was heterogeneous in terms of class, socio-cultural characteristics and doctrine. Intra-group diversity has increased further with the more recent wave of immigration from South Asia, namely India, Pakistan and Bangladesh, and other African countries including Guinea, Senegal and Morocco. Subsequently, while Sunni Muslims comprise the vast majority, new Islamic denominations have been introduced into Portugal, including African-cultured Sufism and the Barelwi (*ahl-i sunna wa'l-jamā'at*), Deobandi and Tablighi Jama'at movements.

As in other Western societies, the ongoing debate on secularization prevalent since the 1960s has been challenged in Portugal both by the cultural

---

16   Nina Clara Tiesler, "No Bad News from the European Margin," 71–91.

17   It is estimated that there are around 8,000 Ismailis in Portugal.

THE SOCIO-SPATIAL CONFIGURATION OF MUSLIMS IN LISBON 273

TABLE 12.1. Religious affiliation in Portugal and the Lisbon Metropolitan Area, population aged 15 and over, 1981–2011

	1981		1991		2001		2011	
	PT	LMA	PT	LMA	PT	LMA	PT	LMA
Non-response	14.2	19.7	17.6	24.1	9.04	13.8	8.3	12.1
% of valid responses								
Catholic	94.5	87.4	94.6	88.1	92.9	85.6	88,30	78.4
Orthodox	0.04	0.06	0.16	0.16	0.22	0.32	0,69	1,06
Protestant	0.58	1.17	0.54	1.04	0.61	1.16	0,92	1,65
Other Christian	0.89	1.69	1.15	2.18	1.55	2.55	1,98	3,22
Jewish	0.08	0.13	0.05	0.08	0.02	0.04	0,04	0,05
Muslim	0.06	0.21	0.13	0.33	0.15	0.49	0,25	0,68
Other non-Christian	0.06	0.14	0.14	0.31	0.18	0.41	0,35	0,69
No religion	3.78	9.19	3.27	7.86	4.33	9.48	7,46	14,20

SOURCE: INE, 1981, 1991, 2001 AND 2011 CENSUSES

embeddedness of Christian, mainly Catholic, traditions and values[18] and an increasing religious diversity from the emergence of new religious beliefs and practices.[19] Over the past 30 years, Portuguese society has remained predominantly Catholic (Table 12.1). At the national level, according to census data, the religious make-up of the population is changing slowly, with small decreases in the number of Catholics and increases in non-profession. However, in the capital city one can observe a consistent decrease in the number of self-proclaimed Catholics as well as a subsequent increase in non-profession and a higher percentage of non-response. Moreover, the proportion of followers of other religions in the LMA, albeit small, has been consistently higher than the national average given the concentration of immigrants in the city. As such, the weight of Muslims in the population is roughly three times the national average and other non-Christians – including Hindus – around twice. The number of followers of other non-Catholic Christian religions is also higher in the LMA, resulting in large part from migration from Africa, Brazil and Eastern Europe.

---

18   Daniele Hervieu-Leger, *Religion as a Chain of Memory* (Cambridge: Polity Press, 2000).
19   Sheringham, "Creating 'Alternative Geographies,'" 1678–1694; John Eade, "Excluding and Including the 'Other' in the Global City."

TABLE 12.2   Muslim population aged 15 or over in Lisbon Metropolitan
Area, by main nationalities and country of birth, 2011

Country	Nationality	Country of birth
Portugal	5944	2033
Guinea-Bissau	3165	5357
Pakistan	862	1087
Bangladesh	424	553
Senegal	349	430
Guinea	333	404
Mozambique	263	2474
Morocco	214	327
India	114	307
Bulgaria	85	89

SOURCE: INE 2011 CENSUS

It is important to stress that while the Muslim population is certainly small in comparison with other European countries, it is not particularly easy to quantify. Values differ substantially when official data is compared to community estimates. According to 2011 census data, the Muslim population aged over 15 numbers slightly over 20,000 nationwide and around 14,000 in the LMA. On the other hand, estimates in the literature of the total Muslim population are between 48,000 and 55,000[20] and those of religious leaders interviewed in 2012 range from 40,000 to 60,000. Moreover, recent onward migration from Portugal, in the context of the current economic crisis, has had an impact on the Muslim community.

While census data can only be considered indicative, they point to a considerably heterogeneous group in terms of origin and verify the correlation between Muslim presence and recent immigration. The main nationality of Muslims living in the LMA is Portuguese, followed by nationals from Guinea-Bissau (Table 12.2). When country of birth is considered, Mozambique follows Guinea-Bissau as the second most important country of origin, confirming the Muslim presence as being in large part a post-colonial phenomenon. In addition, more recent flows from Asia and other African countries are also visible

---

20   José Mapril and Nina Clara Tiesler, "Portugal" in *Yearbook of Muslims in Europe. Volume 5*, ed. Jørgen S. Nielsen et al. (Leiden: Brill, 2013), 517–530.

THE SOCIO-SPATIAL CONFIGURATION OF MUSLIMS IN LISBON   275

in the data, with the largest group from Pakistan followed by Bangladesh, Senegal, Morocco and a smaller number from India.

2   Religious Cartographies and New Religious Landscapes

Recent immigration, besides contributing to the religious and cultural heterogeneity of Lisbon, has played a role in recent processes of urban fragmentation and in the transformation of the socio-spatial structure of the metropolis.[21] Over half of the immigrants present in Portugal are concentrated in the LMA. Lisbon, like other Southern European cities, has quite a diverse ethnic population, which, coupled with other socio-economic characteristics, has an effect on spatial distribution and economic integration. In general, the Portuguese literature has tended to focus on the ethnic geography of Lisbon and little has been written on the spatiality of religion.[22] The settlement patterns of minority and migrant groups tend to be more peripheralized in Southern European cities and levels of segregation lower than in Northern European cities.[23] The spatial distribution of migrants in Lisbon and their position in the housing market is complex and related to the specific processes of urban development, housing policy and market trends that coincided with their time of arrival. From the 1980s into the early 2000s, housing construction increased substantially in Portugal leading to urban sprawl into suburban and peri-urban areas and population loss in the city centre. Public and private support for home ownership led to an increase in owner occupancy from which some earlier migrants from Portuguese-speaking African countries benefited. Newer migrants, however, lacking the conditions to purchase property, are overwhelmingly represented in the private rented market.[24] On the one hand, while over-supply, resulting in cheap rents and labour incorporation, drew migrants arriving from Guinea, Eastern Europe and Brazil in the 1990s to peripheral and even peri-urban areas, the informal private rental market attracted mainly Asian migrants to the city

---

21   Jorge Malheiros, "Immigrants, Residential Mobility, Socio-ethnic Desegregation trends and the Metropolises Fragmentation Thesis: The Lisbon Example," in *Minority Internal Migration in Europe*, ed. Nissa Finney and Gemma Catney (London: Ashgate, 2012): 65–88.
22   With the exception of Lucinda Fonseca and Alina Esteves, "Migration and New Religion Townscapes in Lisbon," 255–291.
23   Jorge Macaísta Malheiros and Francisco Vala, "Immigration and City Change: The Lisbon Metropolis at the Turn of the Twentieth Century," *Journal of Ethnic and Migration Studies* 30/6 (2004): 1065–1086.
24   Jorge Malheiros, "Immigrants, Residential Mobility, Socio-ethnic Desegregation trends and the Metropolises Fragmentation Thesis," 65–88.

centre. These complex settlement patterns result not only in lower levels of segregation, but in a centre/suburban-periphery dichotomy.[25] Still, evidence suggests that forms of marginalization exist given the poor housing conditions often experienced by migrants[26] and their propensity to pay higher rents.[27] This challenges the traditional assumption that migrant dispersal, lower levels of concentration and presence in the owner occupied market are indicative of spatial integration or social inclusion.[28]

The bifurcated ethnic structure of Lisbon, a specific local condition, is replicated in the spatial distribution of Muslims in the city (Maps 12.1 and 12.2). One can observe simultaneous patterns of centralization and suburbanization. The Muslim population has remained highly centralized over the two census periods, with over one fifth represented in the City of Lisbon (Map 12.2). The number of Muslim followers has grown, particularly in the most central parishes around Mouraria in the historic part of the city centre, which continues to be an area of reception for new migrants (Map 12.1 and 12.2), and also close by in Anjos. The private rental market in the area attracts migrants, many of whom have informal rental arrangements or sublet housing in poor condition. While this part of the city has a high population turnover, there is also evidence of place-making strategies among the Asian and, in particular, the Bangladeshi community.[29]

Parallel to patterns of centralization among the Muslim population, there are processes of suburbanization extending into the first and second suburban rings on the periphery of the metropolitan area. In the 1980s and 1990s, the

---

25 Sonia Arbaci, "Patterns of Ethnic and Socio-Spatial Segregation in European Cities: Are Welfare Regimes Making a Difference?," in *Immigration and Place in Mediterranean Metropolises*, ed. Lucinda Fonseca et al. (Lisbon: Luso-American Foundation, 2002), 83–116; Vassilis P. Arapoglou, "Immigration, Segregation and Urban Development in Athens: The Relevance of the LA Debate for Southern European Metropolises," *The Greek Review of Social Research* 121 (2006): 11–38.

26 Sonia Arbaci, "(Re)Viewing Ethnic Residential Segregation in Southern European Cities: Housing and Urban Regimes as Mechanisms of Marginalisation," *Housing Studies* 23/4 (2008): 589–613; Sonia Arbaci and Jorge Malheiros, "De-segregation, Peripheralisation and the Social Exclusion of Immigrants: Southern European Cities in the 1990s," *Journal of Ethnic and Migration Studies* 36/2 (2010): 227–255; Jorge Malheiros, "Immigrants, Residential Mobility, Socio-ethnic Desegregation Trends and the Metropolises Fragmentation Thesis."

27 Jorge Malheiros and Lucinda Fonseca, *Acesso à Habitação e Problemas Residenciais dos Imigrantes em Portugal* (Lisbon: ACIDI, 2011).

28 Sonia Arbaci and Jorge Malheiros, "De-segregation, Peripheralisation and the Social Exclusion of Immigrants: Southern European Cities in the 1990s," 227–255.

29 José Mapril, "Bangla Masdjid: Islão e Bengalidade Entre os Bangladeshianos em Lisboa," *Análise Social* XXXIX/173 (2005): 851–873.

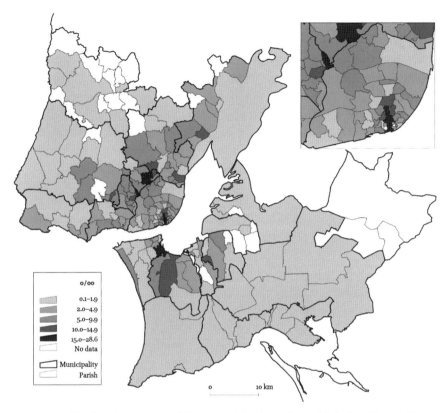

MAP 12.1   Muslims (over 15 years old) per 1000 inhabitants, by parish, Lisbon Metropolitan Area, 2001
SOURCE: INE 2001 CENSUS

largest group of Muslims resided in Lisbon and the municipality of Loures, which included Odivelas at the time. Other settled communities also consolidated in other peripheral municipalities.[30] Since 2001, while the Muslim population has continued to grow in the suburban municipalities to the north of Lisbon, especially in Amadora and Odivelas, the most notable expansion has been in Sintra in the second suburban ring (Map 12.2). The municipality of Sintra now hosts almost the same share of the total Muslim population as the City of Lisbon. This is, in part, indicative of the internal residential mobility of settled migrants but is also due to housing supply as a result of the continuing urban sprawl at the time of arrival of later migrants.

Patterns of clustering can be observed across the metropolitan area on a micro scale. The largest cluster of Muslims at the smaller scale of parish is in

30   Namely Seixal, Cascais, Almada (mostly in the parish of Laranjeiro), Sintra and Amadora.

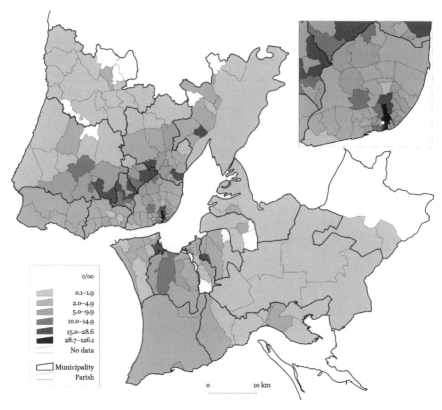

MAP 12.2 Muslims (over 15 years old) per 1000 inhabitants, by parish, Lisbon Metropolitan Area, 2011
SOURCE: INE, 2011 CENSUS

the suburban parish of Odivelas, which has progressively increased over each census period. Other larger clusters are in the historic city centre as mentioned previously. Along the suburban railway line from Lisbon to Sintra, there is a line of neighbouring areas running through Amadora – Mina, Brandoa, Damaia and Venteira – to the commuter suburbs of Sintra – most notably, Tapada das Mercês and Cacém where small clusters of Muslim followers mainly from Guinea-Bissau and Guinea Conakry reside. Consequently, the number of informal places of worship has grown to facilitate this population, creating different local religious groups (Map 12.4 and 12.5).

In contrast, with the exception of the traditional Muslim area of settlement of Laranjeiro, the municipalities on the south bank of the River Tagus have lost relative shares and growth rates have been low and in some places negative over the last census period. It is unclear if this is due to international migration

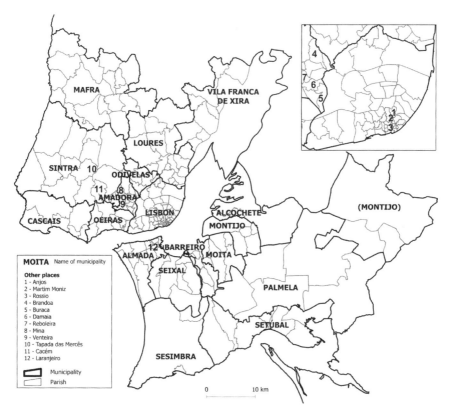

MAP 12.3   Municipalities and other places, Lisbon Metropolitan Area

after 2008 related to the economic crisis or to internal residential mobility. In general terms, patterns of settlement are differentiated by nationality, with Asians, notably Bangladeshis, more concentrated in the city and in Odivelas and Africans or Indo-Mozambicans represented to a greater degree in the first and second suburban rings.

Processes underlying the spatial distribution of Muslims in Lisbon were explored during in-depth interviews with central and local community leaders.[31] The mental mapping conducted by the interviewees of their perception of the distribution of Muslims in Lisbon confirmed the spatial analysis of census data in terms of location. However, their estimates of the dimensions of the community were higher than the official data. The interviewees stressed

---

31   For a study from the perspective of residents see Jennifer McGarrigle "Islam in urban spaces: The residential incorporation and choices of Muslims in Lisbon" *Journal of Ethnic and Migration Studies* 42/3 (2016): 437–457.

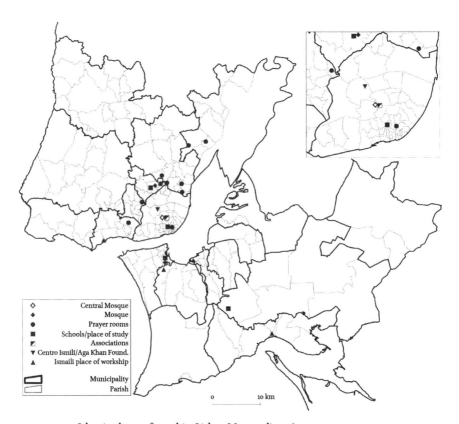

MAP 12.4   Islamic places of worship, Lisbon Metropolitan Area, 2001

the uniqueness of Lisbon in comparison with other European cities due to the spatial dispersion of Muslims. One leader of Indo-Mozambican origin relates this to social integration more generally.

> It turns out that we have no 'ghetto neighbourhood' as is the case in some European countries that is to say that the Muslim population eventually integrates itself into society.

Or in the words of one religious leader, from Guinea-Bissau, responsible for a suburban mosque, "there are countries that when immigrants arrive, they move to areas where other Muslims live. Here all main areas in the city have mosques. There is always a mosque nearby." Some leaders referred to a gradual habitation of apartments around places of worship.

Initial neighbourhood settlement was a function of the specific phase of urban development of the city at the time of migration, housing market

MAP 12.5   Islamic places of worship, Lisbon Metropolitan Area, 2014

mechanisms and access to the formal and informal sectors. As such, there was little distinction between migrants according to religion. Indeed, the account given by the following leader, of Indo-Mozambican origin, is proximate to the process of migrant insertion more generally in the city:

> When Muslims arrived [in Portugal] at the beginning, houses were cheaper in the surrounding areas [of Lisbon] … We are talking about the 70s, when there was no metro, only bus. People came to Lisbon to do their work and then returned to these residential areas, to Odivelas, Póvoa de Santo Adrião. So we are talking about from Odivelas to Santo António dos Cavaleiros, and later when we are talking about Sintra, Amadora, Cacém, Tapada das Mercês….

Or again, one leader from Guinea-Bissau explains the process of settlement in the suburban municipality of Amadora:

> People choose this area because it was an area that had many shanties, as we say, it had lots of space for very cheap houses ... it was easier to arrange a much cheaper house, to the contrary of [other areas]...

While structural factors resulted in pioneers settling in the first suburban ring and beyond, continuing settlement was a result of networking among family and friends. One community leader sums this up, "settling here in the area depended on family members that came first, because when we came here [from Guinea-Bissau] we already had friends or family members that helped us."

As mentioned previously, processes of settlement of Muslims in the metropolitan area beginning in the 1970s are not easy to distinguish from the insertion of immigrants in general into urban neighbourhoods. Nonetheless, this initial process of settlement is important for understanding the specific dynamics of the local emplacement of Muslims and the subsequent formation of local religious and diasporic communities, spaces and organizations.

3   (In)Visible Places of Worship and Appropriation of Space

The Islamic Community of Lisbon (*Comunidade Islamica de Lisboa – CIL*) was established in 1968 by a small group of students from Mozambique who had arrived in the 1950s. The evolution of the CIL and its attempt to assert Muslim presence has been well documented in the literature[32] and is in essence synonymous with the institutionalization of Islam in Portugal.[33] Rather than asserting otherness, CIL has tried to integrate into the social and political milieu, first in the framework of colonialism and then in the post-colonial period.[34] Still, it was only in the latter period marked by the simultaneous transition from authoritarianism to democracy and from state Catholicism to religious freedom that CIL managed to build the Central Mosque in Lisbon. Before the inauguration of the Central Mosque, built on land donated by the City Council,[35] two mosques were opened in converted buildings in local neighbourhoods in

---

32   Jared Larson, *Demographic and Migration Transition in Spain and Portugal: Catholic Contexts and Secular Responses,* MIGRARE Working Paper 5 (Lisbon: CEG, 2010).

33   Abdool Karim Vakil, "Do Outro ao Diverso."

34   Mário Artur Machaqueiro, "Portuguese Colonialism and the Islamic Community of Lisbon," in *Colonial and Post-Colonial Governance of Islam: Continuities and Ruptures,* ed. Marcel Maussen, Veit Bader and Annelies Moors (Amsterdam: University of Amsterdam Press, 2012).

35   Donations from oil-rich Middle Eastern countries were invested in the Islamic infrastructure in Lisbon, principally in the building of the Central Mosque.

THE SOCIO-SPATIAL CONFIGURATION OF MUSLIMS IN LISBON 283

Laranjeiro (1982) and Odivelas (1983), with the latter finished in Islamic architectural style.

Conflicts related to the establishment of Islamic places of worship in other European cities have been well documented in the academic literature.[36] Portugal is distinct in this sense as the politics of the built environment have been relatively neutral, except for one protest over the opening of the mosque in Odivelas that was resolved peacefully and some instances of vandalism.[37] The spatial distribution of prayer rooms and mosques reflects quite clearly the increased Islamic presence in the city and the expansion of the Muslim community beyond the traditional areas of settlement of Odivelas and Laranjeiro. Throughout the 1990s, various places of worship, mainly prayer rooms, were established to serve growing populations of Muslims in local neighbourhoods. This has territorialized parts of the urban landscape through the conversion of non-religious spaces, comparable to the strategies adopted by immigrant churches of other denominations in Lisbon and other cities.[38] By 2000, as can be observed in Map 12.4, besides the three mosques and Isma'ili places of worship, there were approximately ten of these prayer rooms frequented mainly by Sunni Muslims in Lisbon.[39] Over the period between 2000 and 2014, there has been a clear proliferation of places of worship in line with the changes in the distribution of Muslims (Map 12.5). The increase in new mosques and prayer rooms reflects the diversification of migrant-sending countries and associated differences in religious tendencies and language. Four new prayer rooms were established along the Linha de Sintra[40] in the north-western suburbs of Amadora and Sintra[41] where mainly African communities have settled. In addition,

---

36   For example, Seán McLoughlin, "Mosques and the Public Space: Conflict and Cooperation in Bradford," *Journal of Ethnic and Migration Studies* 31/6 (2005): 1045–1066; Simon Naylor and James Ryan, "The Mosque in the Suburbs: Negotiating Religion and Ethnicity in South London," *Social and Cultural Geography* 3/1 (2002): 39–59.

37   Since the writing of this chapter there has been some polemic surrounding the City Council's plan to construct a new mosque in Mouraria.

38   Afe Adogame, "Raising Champions, Taking Territories: African Churches and the Mapping of New Religious Landscapes in Diaspora," in *The African Diaspora and the Study of Religion, ed.* Theodore Louis Trost (New York: Palgrave Macmillan, 2007), 21–46; Afe Adogame, "From House Cells to Warehouse Churches? Christian Church Outreach Mission International in Translocal Contexts," in *Traveling Spirits: Migrants, Markets and Mobilities*, ed. Gertrud Hüwelmeier and Kristine Krause (London: Routledge, 2010), 165–185.

39   The prayer rooms were located in Póvoa de Santo Adrião in Odivelas, Portela, Quinta do Mocho, Santo António dos Cavaleiros and Feitas in Loures, Colina do Sol in Amadora, Forte da Casa and Vilalongo in Vila Franca de Xira, Caraxide in Oeiras and Martim Moniz in the historic centre of the city.

40   A main commuter suburban railway line.

41   These are located in Mina, Damaia, Reboleira, Buraca and Cacém.

in 2007, a mosque was established by migrants from Guinea-Conakry in Tapada das Mercês, a suburb on the urban margins of the LMA close to the town of Sintra. New places of worship have also been established to the south of the river, in particular a prayer room in Barreiro, and one in Setúbal frequented by mostly francophone Africans. Finally, as the historic city centre continues to be a dynamic area of new reception for Muslims from diverse origins, new places of worship have been established to cater for them. The Bangladeshi place of worship was formalized under the name of Mesquita Baitul Mukarram and a new Bengali Muslim prayer room, occupying a disused shop, opened one street away.[42] Furthermore, African communities established two places of worship in basements in Anjos and Rossio in the city centre.

In large part, the prayer rooms are located in suburban areas in converted apartments and garages, often in back streets or in basements or shops in the city. Signing is usually discreet or in some cases completely absent, especially when private spaces are used in residential buildings. Thus, they tend to blend in with the wider urban environment. Effectively, makeshift spaces have become sacred places challenging, in the words of Garbin, "the idea of an essential and radical dichotomy between sacred and profane, between religious and secular."[43] The transformation of these inconspicuous places in peripheral areas into places of worship has served to create invisibility and attenuate Muslim presence in the city. In contrast, the Central Mosque that presides over an important square – Praça de Espanha – in the heart of the city, the Aisha Siddika Mosque in Odivelas and the impressive Isma'ili mosque in Laranjeiras on the north-western edge of the City of Lisbon have transformed parts of the urban landscape. The use of traditional architectural styles, custom-building and prime locations creates symbolic visibility in the urban landscape and reflects, at least in part, socio-economic and class differences within the Islamic community. Such differences are evident in the higher incidence of informal and makeshift places of worship among the West African and new Asian communities that often lack facilities for women. The provision for women in the three original mosques built by Indo-Mozambicans render them important for Muslim women living in the city. In the historic city centre, while places of worship are undistinguishable by architectural style, faith is visible due to public religious practices. For instance, Muslims gather in the central square in Martim Moniz to celebrate *Eid-ul-fiṭr* at the end of Ramadan. Moreover, the religious spaces in the city centre represent a juncture of various geographical scales and different forms of mobility at both the city level and internationally.

---

42 As mentioned previously, since the writing of this chapter the City Council of Lisbon plans to construct a mosque in Mouraria to serve this community.

43 David Garbin, "The Visibility and Invisibility of Migrant Faith in the City," 682.

They serve as convenient places of worship for the local downtown population, non-residents who are frequenting particular spaces in the city centre for leisure or work, and new international migrants. The dichotomy of centralization and peripheralization in terms of patterns of settlement and the local emplacement of Muslim communities, including the appropriation of local spaces for worship, clearly influences the visibility or otherwise of Muslims at the scale of the metropolitan area. This is not to say that local communities in peripheral areas are invisible. To the contrary, as oftentimes at the finer scale of the neighbourhood, they are contributing through the provision of services for the community.

4   Local Emplacement and Intra-group Differentiation

Studying the local emplacement of Muslim communities in Lisbon leads inevitably to the reconnection of religion with social, ethnic and cultural characteristics. It is true that the interplay between Islam and diversity has been discussed widely, to the extent that the usefulness of "Muslim" as a term has been subject to debate.[44] Vakil[45] problematizing to some extent the notion of one Portuguese Islamic community, writes that the various theological strands and the different associations that have been established in Portugal, whether institutionalized or not, and regardless of the links between them, need to be studied in terms of "their own community dynamic in each local context." In a similar vein, Werbner[46] argues that in the British case Islam is divided into both ethnic and national terms as other affiliations produce what Grillo[47] refers to as "nationally-bounded transethnic Muslim collectivities." Likewise, in Lisbon, diasporic settings have been developed by religious communities at the local level. One interviewee of Indo-Mozambican origin, while stressing the importance of the Islamic community and notions of brotherhood in general, observed the following:

> Even though we have approximately 40 mosques and places of worship scattered throughout the country, there are mosques in which there are more Muslims from a certain origin attending that particular mosque.

---

44   Tariq Modood, "Muslims and the Politics of Difference," *The Political Quarterly* 74 (2003): 100–115.

45   Abdool Karim Vakil, "Do Outro ao Diverso," 296.

46   Pnina *Werbner,* "Theorising Complex Diasporas: Purity and Hybridity in the South Asian Public Sphere in Britain," Journal of Ethnic and Migration Studies 30/5 (2004): 895–911.

47   Ralph Grillo, "Islam and Transnationalism," *Journal of Ethnic and Migration Studies* 30/5 (2004): 861–878.

Ethnicity, language and country of origin are important aspects in group formation that influence the specific mosques that Muslims attend and to some extent the particular neighbourhoods in which they live. One Guinean leader of a small suburban mosque explains this well:

> In Lisbon you have the mosque of the Guineans, that of the Pakistanis, that of the Bangladeshis, do you see? The reason is pure and simple they are all Muslims, but they speak different languages.

In this sense, local community formation has served to strengthen ethnic and cultural bonds and create internal differentiation within the wider Islamic community in Lisbon. Still, several of the interviewees were quick to dissociate residential settlement patterns and the accumulation of social capital based on origin ties from the "Muslim-ness" of the migrants. This was expressed most poignantly by the community leaders of Indo-Mozambican origin as illustrated by the following quote:

> The cultural factor is very important ... when we talk about the Muslims who came from India, Pakistan or Bangladesh, immigrants alone with friends, it is normal to a certain extent that they live together ... it is not a religious factor but one of support, or because they have a brother who knows a cousin who has a friend who is here [in Portugal].

Nonetheless, granting the role that ethnic and cultural ties play in assisting new migrants in the immigration and settlement process, places of worship play an integral role in ethno-cultural preservation. As such, there is a reinforcing interchange between religion and ethnic background. One leader in Amadora, originally from Guinea-Bissau, explained to the Irish interviewer why there were two mosques within a 15-minute walking distance of one another:

> Here, [in this mosque] the majority, around 80 per cent, are from Guinea-Bissau. There in [that mosque, another mosque within walking distance] 70 per cent are from Guinea-Conakry because that prayer room has a particular geographical origin. When you're here [in Lisbon], you may meet with Europeans but when you meet the Irish, you know the culture and have goals in common ... The attitude is the same, even the food, everything...

Even in local diasporic settings, intra-group differences influenced the composition of particular congregations. For example, as the following quote from

THE SOCIO-SPATIAL CONFIGURATION OF MUSLIMS IN LISBON   287

a central religious figure illustrates, political party loyalties among the highly centralized Bangladeshi community led to two different places of worship in the same neighbourhood, albeit the Bangladeshi leader contends it is a question of space.

> How am I going to explain this? For, example a Portuguese is affiliated to a [football] club, Sporting, Benfica or Porto. Well, a Bangladeshi is affiliated to a [political] party. They try to transport these party divisions outside of their country. So, probably the first mosque was frequented by members of party A and the second is frequented more by members of party B.

Generally speaking, within spaces of worship plurality is accommodated, particularly in terms of specific ethnic and cultural differences; however, certain tensions can also occur. At times, different cultural interpretations resulted in altered religious practices that strained relations between those of Indo-Mozambican origin and West Africans. One Guinea-Bissauan leader of a prayer room and association in the suburbs of the city describes this:

> In [that] Mosque, the leaders are of Indian or Pakistani origin. They do not accept it if a woman does not cover her head.... The fact that I didn't have a beard was seen as a problem. As the mosque is being managed by them, they make the rules there ... We Africans do not have much beard. In Africa it rains for 6 months. People have to work in agriculture. Can a person with burka work in high temperatures or rain? ... It is a matter of culture, not religion ... Islam respects each person in their natural state. Islam teaches "we dignify the sons of Adam" it does not say we dignify Muslims. We are all worthy, it respects each as they are ...

Beyond the role of culture, such tensions are embedded in wider social hierarchies as economic disparities often result in differentiated capacities to adhere to specific practices. One example is the affordability of and access to halal meat. Some leaders who worked mainly with the Guinea-Bissauan community described how consuming only halal meat was a burden for families due to the current financial crisis. In contrast, other conservative Sunnis perceived this as moderation related to more lenient cultural interpretations.

Different branches of Islam and various religious tendencies have been gradually transposed to Portugal over successive migration waves, from African-cultured Sufism to Deobandi, Barelwi and Tablighi groups introduced by more recent waves of Asian migrants. One religious leader related how differences between traditional Sunni Muslims and Barelwi followers, mostly from Pakistan and Indian, in Odivelas, had resulted in two separate mosques a stone's throw away from one another.

While local urban settings and local community dynamics are crucial to our understanding of the spatiality of Islam in Lisbon and processes of belonging to local neighbourhoods, there are links between places of worship and associations that play into a wider sense of community. One interviewee refers to the Central Mosque as being the "mother" mosque, saying that, "even though we are separated from the community we are connected to it." Various connections related to different needs and mobilities create opportunities for congregating with others.[48] On a practical note, makeshift places of worship often lack necessary facilities for ceremonies that bring people to the larger mosques for weddings and other special events. Women also gather, in particular, in the Central Mosque, albeit one leader contends that despite the shared space of worship, "they are organized according to their country of origin." Everyday mobility takes people out of their neighbourhoods and into other spaces in the city. One interviewee describes how the place of worship he frequents depends on the place he is at a given time:

> When we are in Lisbon, if we are working and the call to prayer is approaching, we normally go to the Central Mosque. There are many places of worship ... they are small communities. For instance, I know people who try to visit a different place of worship every month.

5   The Social Role of Local Religious Communities

Cultural sameness and common understandings coupled with shared migration and integration experiences created the foundation for mutual assistance and a supportive environment. In many local communities in Lisbon, informal support had evolved into organized services. To this end, not unlike the process Ley[49] described in Canadian immigrant churches, bonding capital eventually extended to bridging capital as local communities gained recognition due to their role in service provision. Tiesler[50] also notes the fact that local Muslim

---

48   The Tablighi Jamaʻat move between the mosques in the city, in the words of one interviewee from Mozambique, "to strengthen our faith."

49   David Ley, "The Immigrant Church as an Urban Service Hub," *Urban Studies* 45/10 (2008): 2057–2074.

50   Nina Clara Tiesler, "No Bad News from the European Margin," 71–91.

religious communities adapted to European models of community organization and a significant proportion formed associations, which have a strong socio-cultural component. Several of the local African associations interface between the local community and the local authorities acting as access points to public and third-sector resources. Accounts from Islamic associations, as well as municipal councils in the LMA, point to the acceptance of some local African-Muslim leaders as agents of local power.

The policy relevance of local social support initiatives has generated important social capital that has attracted the attention of local authorities. The role of these associations is reminiscent of the way that civil society institutions and the Catholic Church have traditionally compensated for the weak welfare state. Increasing poverty after the recent economic crisis in Portugal has accentuated the importance of local social support, albeit itself under increasing financial strain. While the associations born out of local religious communities represent a specific ethnic and cultural group, at times services are extended to include other local residents. Like other immigrant associations in Lisbon, even if certified by the High Commission for Immigration and Intercultural Dialogue,[51] their initiatives are almost always area-based and confined to a local area. Pires[52] contends that their "scope of action at the local level is a characteristic of less-educated, poor communities."

One religious leader from Guinea-Conakry in the suburbs stated, "in the case of the council, they don't work with the religious side of things, just with the community side. The religious part depends on us, on what each one can give." Nonetheless, the contact with local authorities provided a platform for local religious communities to negotiate particular forms of funding, land for burials and planning permission for more permanent religious facilities anticipated in the future.

A main concern and objective of the associations, emphasized throughout the interviews, relates to cultural preservation and the transmission of religious and cultural values to the second generation. One leader of a suburban association from Guinea-Conakry describes his experience:

> I got together with some other colleagues and had a meeting and we thought about where we could eventually leave our children on the

---

51   The "Alto Comissariado para a Imigração e Diálogo Intercultural" is a public institution responsible for public policy on the integration of immigrants and ethnic minorities in Portugal.

52   Sonia Pires, "Guinea-Bissau Immigrant Transnationalism in Portugal: A Substitute for a Failed State?," *African and Black Diaspora: An International Journal* 6/2 (2013): 17.

weekend so that they could learn the culture of their parents, their fathers' culture.

The mosques have socio-moral roles in the community through the provision of religious education, in particular for children, on one hand, and, on the other, informal education to improve language skills, educational performance or job training. The president of an association in the suburbs describes the initiatives undertaken by his particular local community notably with support from the Isma'ili community and the local council:

> At the cultural level our plan of activities includes a football team for children, support with school work and Portuguese, English and Arabic classes. We work across all aspects. K'Cidade[53] provides us with a computer room that we use for training.

Transnational practices to preserve religious and cultural identities, including recruiting imams from the country of origin, are played out alongside clear efforts to improve the social insertion of the members of the local community into the host society. In other words, the bifurcated objectives of local community organizations include the complex interplay between working toward integration and prosperity in Portugal and simultaneously maintaining and transmitting ethno-religious values and practices. Both, however, as the following quote illustrates, are considered essential as social and economic integration is considered crucial for the construction of positive representations of Islam in Portuguese society:

> When I was second Imam in [that] mosque, I began to realize that there were many Muslims outside of Lisbon, from Damaia, Amadora to Sintra. The government's integration programme has strategic intentions, but this aspect was not developed. The main central mosque and those in Odivelas and Laranjeiro are too far away, people can't afford to travel there. It is not only that, there is a need to help parents with the integration of their children. Many of them don't know what's written on the work contract that they have signed. We need to have an integrated European education for Muslims; we are in Portugal so we teach Portuguese. We have fewer problems in Portugal than the rest of Europe, but we have to fight for this every day by teaching our children, to ensure that Islam is well represented.

---

53   K'Cidade is an urban community development programme promoted by the Aga Khan Foundation.

THE SOCIO-SPATIAL CONFIGURATION OF MUSLIMS IN LISBON

Conversely, the Indo-Mozambican leaders interviewed distanced themselves from integration discourse, rather stressing their strong Portuguese identity and role in promoting social solidarity:

> The Muslims who came from Mozambique in the 70s and 80s arranged houses, began to work without any problem, without difficulty to integrate; we speak Portuguese, our culture is Portuguese, our habits and customs are more or less identical. We can't say that we are more integrated or better integrated as this is our country. The Portuguese Muslim community is one of the oldest communities in the country; it is exemplary, different in comparison with other Islamic communities in Europe. The cultural factor is very important when we are talking about integration in whatever society.

The distinction of the "Portuguese Muslim community", in leaders' narratives, from other European Muslims relates strongly to the fact that many of the community leaders from Mozambique were Portuguese citizens before they arrived in Portugal. Subsequently, the immigrant integration agenda pertains, from the informants' perspectives, to other members of the Muslim community who arrived in different socio-legal contexts. In fact, a strong social solidarity agenda is central to the communities' social work. From another perspective, the notion of a Portuguese Muslim Community reflects the CIL's dialogue and self-representation in the public sphere, which has been built upon a discourse of cultural identification and belonging on the basis of citizenship. Close links with the political elites of the country, higher socio-economic status and educational performance[54] exemplify this.

6   Diverse Islam in the City

We see here, then, that the "Portuguese Muslim Community" can only be understood in the context of the national and ethnic sub-collective Muslim groups that are represented in different spaces across the city. In a city with a relatively small Muslim population, there are numerous places of worship reflecting diversity within Islam and the spatial organization of Muslims in the metropolitan area. In general terms, broader trends in the ethnic geography of the city are replicated with a clear central/peripheral pattern that creates both visibility in the city centre and invisibility on the urban margins. Initial

---

54   The Islamic College, established by this community in Palmela, is one of the top-ranking secondary schools in the metropolitan area, and ranked in first place in 2009.

settlement was largely driven by structural factors and the time of migration and later consolidated by networking among family, nationality and ethno-cultural groups resulting in differentiated settlement patterns. To this end, there has been a proliferation of religious spaces that reproduce differences in denomination, nationality, ethnicity, language and even transnational political participation. Subsequently, the structuring of the Muslims in Lisbon by cultural and national origin results in local community development that reaches beyond religion to include cultural and, at times, social provision. The adaption of the organizational structures of associations at the local level has carved out an important role for several of the religious communities, particularly those from Western Africa. They mediate between public institutions and the local community and oftentimes represent an access point to public and third-sector resources.

In the case of Lisbon, overt controversies or tensions related to Muslim and non-Muslim relations and the visibility of Islam in territorial terms have largely been avoided. One may ask why this is so. Obvious answers lie in history, the smaller number of Muslims relative to other traditional immigration countries and lower levels of segregation. Indeed, this fragmentation distinguishes the spatiality of Muslims in Lisbon from other contexts. Moreover, as argued here, the dynamic renegotiation of religious identities and practices in local neighbourhoods by migrant communities has led to insertion from the grassroots. The heterogeneous Islamic community is configured in multiple places of worship and micro-clusters that help preserve and transmit ethno-cultural practices, yet, simultaneously, reduce visibility at the city level. In some local areas, however, in spite of challenges, community dynamics are recasting encounters between local residents and modes of civic participation. On a final note, while a multiplicity of affiliations forms a plural Islam, there are ties that link the diverse local communities and the central community to varying degrees, creating a web of relations that spans space and differences across the metropolitan area.

Acknowledgements

The research presented here was funded by the Portuguese Foundation for Science and Technology (FCT) in the ambit of the project PTDC/CS-GEO/113680/2009 "Socio-spatial integration of Lisbon's religious minorities: residential patterns, choice and neighbourhood dynamics."

References

Adogame, Afe. "Raising Champions, Taking Territories: African Churches and the Mapping of New Religious Landscapes in Diaspora." In *The African Diaspora and the Study of Religion*, edited by Theodore Louis Trost, 21–46. New York: Palgrave Macmillan, 2007.

Adogame, Afe. "From House Cells to Warehouse Churches? Christian Church Outreach Mission International in Translocal Contexts." In *Travelling Spirits: Migrants, Markets and Mobilities*, edited by Gertrud Hüwelmeier and Kristine Krause, 165–185. London: Routledge, 2010.

Ahmad, Feroz. *The Making of Modern Turkey*. London: Routledge, 1993.

Akkerman, Tjitske and Anniken Hagelund. "Women and Children First! Anti-immigration Parties and Gender in Norway and the Netherlands." *Patterns of Prejudice* 41/2 (2007), 197–214.

Alasuutari, Pertti. "Suunnittelutaloudesta kilpailutalouteen: Miten muutos oli ideologisesti mahdollinen?" In *Uusi jako: Miten Suomesta tuli kilpailukyky-yhteiskunta*, edited by Risto Heiskala and Eeva Luhtakallio, 43–64. Helsinki: Gaudeamus, 2006.

Alexandris, Alexis. *The Greek Minority of Istanbul and the Greek-Turkish Relations 1918–1974*. Athens: Centre for Asia Minor Studies, 1978.

Allen, Chris. "Justifying Islamophobia: A Post-9/11 Consideration of the European Union and British Contexts." *American Journal of Islamic Social Sciences* 21/3 (2004): 1–25. Accessed November 11, 2014. http://i-epistemology.net/attachments/847_Ajiss21-3%20-%20Allen%20-%20Justifying%20Islamophobia.pdf.

Allen, Chris. *Islamophobia*. Farnham: Ashgate, 2010.

Allievi, Stefano. "Islam in the Public Space: Social Networks, Media, and Neo-communities." In *Muslim Networks and Transnational Communities in and across Europe*, edited by Stefano Allievi and Jørgen S. Nielsen, 1–27. Leiden: Brill, 2003.

Allievi, Stefano. "How the Immigrant Has Become Muslim: Public Debates on Islam in Europe." *Revue Européenne des Migrations Internationals* 21/2 (2005): 135–163.

Anagnostou, Dia. "Breaking the Cycle of Nationalism: The EU, Regional Policy and the Minority of Western Thrace, Greece." *South European Society and Politics* 6/1 (2001): 99–124.

Anagnostou, Dia. "Deepening Democracy or Defending the Nation? The Europeanisation of Minority Rights and Greek Citizenship." *West European Politics* 28/2 (2005): 335–357.

Anagnostou, Dia and Ruby Gropas. "Domesticating Islam and Muslim Immigrants: Political and Church Responses to Constructing a Central Mosque in Athens." In *Orthodox Christianity in 21st Century Greece: The Role of Religion in Culture, Ethnicity and Politics*, edited by Victor Roudometof and Vassilis N. Makrides, 89–109. Farnham: Ashgate, 2010.

294 REFERENCES

Anderson, Joel. "Situating Axel Honneth in the Frankfurt School Tradition." In *Axel Honneth: Critical Essays: With a Reply by Axel Honneth*, edited by Danielle Petherbridge. Leiden: Brill, 2011.

Andreades, Kostas G. *The Moslem Minority in Western Thrace*. Amsterdam: Adolf Hakkert, 1980.

An-Na'im, Abdullahi Ahmed. "Global Citizenship and Human Rights: From Muslims in Europe to European Muslims." In *Religious Pluralism and Human Rights in Europe: Where to Draw the Line?*, edited by M.L.P. Loenen and Jenny E. Goldschmidt, 13–55. Antwerp-Oxford: Intersentia, 2007.

Anoniou, Dimitris. "Muslim Immigrants in Greece: Religious Organisation and Local Responses." *Immigrants and Minorities* 22/2–3 (2003): 155–174.

Arapoglou, Vassilis. "Immigration, Segregation and Urban Development in Athens: The Relevance of the LA Debate for Southern European Metropolises." *The Greek Review of Social Research* 121 (2006): 11–38.

Ararse, Abdi-Hakim Yasin. "Suomalaiset muslimit ja syyskuun 11. päivä." In *Mitä muslimit tarkoittavat? Keskustelua islamilaisista virtauksista Suomessa ja Europaassa*, edited by Tuomas Martikainen and Tuula Sakaranaho, 139–155. Turku: Savukeidas, 2011.

Arbaci, Sonia. "Patterns of Ethnic and Socio-Spatial Segregation in European Cities: Are Welfare Regimes Making a Difference?" In *Immigration and Place in Mediterranean Metropolises*, edited by Lucinda Fonseca, Jorge Malheiros, Natália Ribas-Mateos, Paul White and Alina Esteves, 83–116. Lisbon: Luso-American Foundation, 2002.

Arbaci, Sonia. "(Re)Viewing Ethnic Residential Segregation in Southern European Cities: Housing and Urban Regimes as Mechanisms of Marginalisation." *Housing Studies* 23/4 (2008): 589–613.

Arbaci, Sonia and Jorge Malheiros. "De-segregation, Peripheralisation and the Social Exclusion of Immigrants: Southern European Cities in the 1990s." *Journal of Ethnic and Migration Studies* 36/2 (2010): 227–255.

Armando, Salvatore. "Making Public Space: Opportunities and Limits of Collective Action Among Muslims in Europe." *Journal of Ethnic and Migration Studies* 30/5 (2004): 1013–1031.

Asad, Talal. *Genealogies of Religion*. Baltimore: The John Hopkins University Press, 2003.

Bader, Veit. "The Governance of Islam in Europe: The Perils of Modelling." *Journal of Ethnic and Migration Studies* 33 (2007): 871–886.

Baldwin-Edwards, Martin. "Immigrants in Greece: Characteristics and Issues of Regional Distribution." *Mediterranean Migration Observatory Working Paper 10*. Athens: Panteion University, 2008. Accessed 17 October, 2014. http://www.mmo.gr/pdf/publications/mmo_working_papers/MMO_WP10.pdf.

REFERENCES

Barker, Martin. *The New Racism: Conservatives and the Ideology of the Tribe.* London: Junction Books, 1981.

Bastos, Susana, Bastos, José. *Portugal Multicultural.* Lisboa: Edições Fim de Século, 1999.

Basu, Amrita. "Introduction." In *The Challenge of Local Feminisms,* edited by Amrita Basu. Boulder: Westview Press, 1995.

Baughn, Lisa. "Islamic Education in Europe." *Euro-Islam.info.* Accessed March 19, 2012. http://www.euro-islam.info/key-issues/education.

Bawer, Bruce. *While Europe Slept: How Radical Islam is Destroying the West from Within.* London: Doubleday, 2006.

Bäckström, Anders and Grace Davie, ed. *Welfare and Religion in 21st Century Europe: Volume 1. Configuring the Connections.* Farnham: Ashgate, 2010.

Becker, Lawrence C. "Crimes against Autonomy: Gerald Dworkin on the Enforcement of Morality." *William and Mary Law Review* 40/2 (1999): 959–973.

Beckman, Ludvig. *The Frontiers of Democracy: The Right to Vote and its Limits.* Basingstoke: Palgrave MacMillan, 2009.

Bernardo, Luís. "The Accommodation of Islam in Portugal and the Republic of Ireland: A Comparative Case Study." Unpublished MA Thesis, Lisbon: ICS – UL, 2010.

Berns McGown, Rima. *Muslims in the Diaspora: The Somali Communities of London and Toronto.* Toronto: University of Toronto Press, 1999.

Bloemraad, Irene, Anna Korteweg and Yurdakul Gökce. "Citizenship and Immigration: Multiculturalism, Assimilation, and Challenges." *Annual Review of Sociology* 34 (2008), 153–179.

Boddy, Janice. *Wombs and Alien Spirits. Women, Men and the Zār Cult in Northern Sudan.* Madison: The University of Wisconsin Press, 1989.

Bolognani, Marta. "The Myth of Return: Dismissal, Survival or Revival? A Bradford Example of Transnationalism as a Political Instrument." *Journal of Ethnic and Migration Studies* 33/1 (2007), 59–76.

Bonte, Pierre, Anne-Marie Brisebarre and Altan Gokalp, eds. *Sacrifices en Islam: Espaces et Temps d'un Rituel.* Paris: CNRS Editions, 2002.

Borou, Christina. "The Muslim Minority of Western Thrace in Greece: An Internal Positive or an Internal Negative Other?" *Journal of Muslim Minority Affairs* 29/1 (2009): 5–26.

Bourdieu, Pierre. "Genèse et structure du champ religieux." *Revue Française de Sociologie* 12/3 (1971): 295–334.

Bourdieu, Pierre. *The Logic of Practice.* Translated by Richard Nice. Cambridge: Polity Press, 1990.

Bowen, John. "Beyond Migration: Islam as a Transnational Public Space," *Journal of Ethnic and Migration Studies,* 30/5 (2004): 879–894.

Bowen, John. *Why the French Don't Like Headscarves: Islam, the State, and Public Space.* Princeton: Princeton University Press, 2007.

Brenner, Neil, Jamie Peck and Nik Theodore. "Variegated Neoliberalization: Geographies, Modalities, Pathways." *Global Networks* 10/2 (2010): 182–222.

Brown, Mark. "Quantifying the Muslim Population in Europe: Conceptual and Data Issue." *Social Research Methodology* 3/2 (2000): 87–101.

Brown, Wendy. *Regulating Aversions: Tolerance in the Age of Identity and Empire.* Princeton: Princeton University Press, 2008.

Bruinessen, Martin van and Stefano Allievi, eds. *Producing Islamic Knowledge: Transmission and Dissemination in Western Europe.* London: Routledge, 2011.

Brunnbauer, Ulf. "The Perception of Muslims in Bulgaria and Greece: Between the 'Self' and the 'Other.'" *Journal of Muslim Minority Affairs* 21/1 (2001): 39–61.

Bujis, Frank J. and Jan Rath. "Muslims in Europe: The State of Research." IMISCOE Working Paper No 7. Amsterdam: IMES, 2006. Accessed June 11, 2012. http://library. imiscoe.org/en/record/314221.

Buzan, Barry, Ole Wæver and Jaap de Wilde. *Security: A New Framework for Analysis.* London: Lynne Rienner Publishers, 1998.

Byrnes, Timothy A. and Peter J. Katzenstein, eds. *Religion in an Expanding Europe.* Cambridge: Cambridge University Press, 2006.

Cadge, Wendy. "De Facto Congregationalism and the Religious Organizations of Post-1965 Immigrants to the United States: A Revised Approach." *Journal of the American Academy of Religion* 76/2 (2008): 344–374.

Cardeira da Silva, Maria, "O sentido dos árabes no nosso sentido," *Análise Social* 173 (2005): 781–806

Carlbom, Aje. "An Empty Signifier: The Blue-and-Yellow Islam of Sweden." *Journal of Muslim Minority Affairs* 26/2 (2006), 245–261.

Casanova, José. *Public Religions in the Modern World.* Chicago: University of Chicago Press, 1994.

Casanova, José. "Immigrants and the New Religious Pluralism: A European Union/ United States Comparison." In *Democracy and the New Religious Pluralism*, edited by Thomas Banchoff, 59–83. Oxford: Oxford University Press, 2007.

Casanova, José. "The Secular, Secularizations, Secularisms." In *Rethinking Secularism*, edited by Craig Calhoun, Mark Juergensmeyer and Jonathan VanAntwerpen, 54–75. New York: Oxford University Press, 2011.

Castles, Francis, Peter Starke and Herbert Obinger. "Convergence towards Where: In What Ways, If Any, Are Welfare States Becoming More Similar?" *Journal of European Public Policy* 15/7 (2008): 975–1000.

Castles, Stephen and Mark J. Miller. *The Age of Migration: International Population Movements in the Modern World.* Fourth Edition. New York: The Guilford Press, 2009.

REFERENCES

Cella, Elira. "Albanian Muslims, Human Rights and Relations with the Islamic World." In *Muslim Communities in the New Europe*, edited by Gerd Nonneman, Timothy Niblock and Bogdan Szajkowski, 139–152. Reading: Ithaca Press, 1996.

Central Statistics Office. *Census 1991: Volume 5 – Religion*. Dublin: Government of Ireland, Stationery Office, 1995.

Central Statistics Office. *Census 2011 Profile 7 – Religion, Ethnicity and Irish Travellers*. Dublin: Government of Ireland, Stationery Office, 2012. Accessed October 9, 2014. http://www.cso.ie/en/media/csoie/census/documents/census2011profile7/Profile,7 ,Education,Ethnicity,and,Irish,Traveller,entire,doc.pdf.

Central Statistics Office. "Statistical Tables." In *Census 2011 Profile 7 – Religion, Ethnicity and Irish Travellers*. Dublin: Government of Ireland, Stationery Office, 2012.

Central Statistics Office. "Population 1901–2011." Accessed November 1, 2013. http://www .cso.ie/Quicktables/GetQuickTables.aspx?FileName=CNA13.asp&TableName =Population+1901+-+2011&StatisticalProduct=DB_CN.

Centre for Support of Repatriate Migrants and Ethnic Greeks. "In Search of Spaces of Coexistence." Project report KSPM, 2007. Accessed May 17, 2012. http://www.kspm .gr. (In Greek.)

Cesari, Jocelyne. *When Islam and Democracy Meet: Muslims in Europe and in the United States*. New York: Palgrave Macmillan, 2004.

Cesari, Jocelyne. "Mosque Conflicts in European Cities: An Introduction." *Journal of Ethnic and Migration Studies* 31/6 (2005): 1015–1024.

Cesari, Jocelyne. "Mosques in French Cities: Towards the End of a Conflict?" *Journal of Ethnic and Migration Studies* 31/6 (2005): 1025–1043.

Cesari, Jocelyne. "Muslim Identities in Europe: The Snare of Exceptionalism." In *Islam in Europe: Diversity, Identity and Influence*, edited by Effie Fokas and Aziz Al-Azmeh. Cambridge: Cambridge University Press, 2007.

Cesari, Jocelyn. "The Securitisation of Islam in Europe." Research Paper No. 14. CEPS Challenge, 2009. Accessed November 26, 2013. http://aei.pitt.edu/10763/1/1826.pdf.

Chatziprokopiou, Marios and Panos Hatziprokopiou. "Between the Politics of Difference and the Poetics of Similarity: Performing Ashura in Pireaus." *Journal of Muslims in Europe* 6/2 (2017): 198–215.

Chebel d'Appollonia, Ariane and Simon Reich, eds. *Immigration, Integration, and Security: America and Europe in Comparative Perspective*. Pittsburgh: University of Pittsburgh Press, 2008.

Chubb, Basil. *The Government and Politics of Ireland*. Stanford: Stanford University Press, 1982.

Ciciora, Alice C. "Integrating Ireland's Muslims: Attitudes of Muslim and Irish Elites towards Value Compatibility and the Mainstreaming of Islam." *Journal of Muslim Minority Affairs* 30/2 (2010): 199–216.

Clogg, Richard. *A Concise History of Greece.* Cambridge: Cambridge University Press, 1995.

Clogg, Richard, ed. *Minorities in Greece: Aspects of a Plural Society.* London: Hurst and Company, 2002.

Coakley, John. "Society and Political Culture." In *Politics in the Republic of Ireland,* edited by John Coakley and Michael Gallagher, 25–49. London: Routledge, 2004.

Conradson, David. "Expressions of Charity and Action towards Justice: Faith-based Welfare Provision in Urban New Zealand." *Urban Studies* 45/10 (2008): 2117–2141.

Constitution of Ireland (1937). http://www.taoiseach.gov.ie/eng/Historical_Information/The_Constitution/.

Cosgrove, Olivia, Laurence Cox, Carmen Kuhling and Peter Mulholland. *Ireland's New Religious Movements.* Cambridge: Cambridge Scholars Publishing, 2011.

Crouch, Colin. *Social Change in Western Europe.* Oxford: Oxford University Press, 1999.

Crouch, Colin and Wolfgang Streeck. *The Diversity of Democracy: Corporatism, Social Order and Political Conflict.* Cheltenham: Edward Elgar, 2006.

Cruz, Manuel Braga da and Natália Correia Guedes. *A Igreja e a Cultura Contemporânea em Portugal 1950–2000.* Lisbon: Universidade Católica, 2001.

Csergö, Zsuzsa and James M. Goldgeier. "Nationalist Strategies and European Integration." In *The Hungarian Status Law: Nation Building and/or Minority Protection,* edited by Zoltán Kantor, Balázs Majtényi, Osamu Ieda, Balázs Vizi and Ivan Halász, 270–302. Sapporo: Slavic Research Centre, Hokkaido University, 2004.

Cunningham, Hilary and Josiah McC. Heyman. "Introduction: Mobilities and Enclosures at Borders." *Identities: Global Studies in Culture and Power* 11/3 (2004): 289–302.

d'Appolonia, Ariane Chebel and Reich, Simon, ed., *Immigration, Integration, and Security: America and Europe in Comparative Perspective.* Pittsburgh: University of Pittsburgh Press, 2008.

Davie, Grace. *The Sociology of Religion.* Los Angeles: Sage Publications, 2007.

Dean, Mitchell. *Governmentality: Power and Rule in Modern Society.* London: Sage Publications, 1999.

Dechlich, Francesca. "Sufi Experience in Rural Somali: A Focus on Women." *Social Anthropology* 8/3 (2000): 295–318.

Demetriou, Olga. "Prioritizing Ethnicities: The Uncertainty of Pomak-ness in the Urban Greek Rhodope." *Ethnic and Racial Studies* 27/1 (2004): 95–119.

Diamanti-Karanou, Panagoula. "Migration of Ethnic Greeks from the Former Soviet Union to Greece, 1990–2000: Policy Decisions and Implications." *Southeast European and Black Sea Studies* 3/1 (2003): 25–45.

DiaNEOsis. "Greeks and the refugee problem," February 2016. (In Greek.) Accessed December 7, 2017, https://www.dianeosis.org/wp-content/uploads/2016/02/immigration_04.pdf.

REFERENCES

DiMaggio, Paul J. and Walter W. Powell. "The Iron Cage Revisited: Institutional Isomorphism and Collective Rationality in Organizational Fields." *American Sociological Review* 48/2 (1983): 147–160.

Divani, Lena. *Greece and Minorities*. Athens: Nefeli, 1995. (In Greek.)

Dobbelaere, Karel. *Secularization: A Multi-Dimensional Concept*. London: Sage Publications, 1981.

Dovidio, John F., John C. Brigham, Blair T. Johnson and Samuel L. Gaertner. "Stereotyping, Prejudice and Discrimination: Another look." In *Stereotypes and Stereotyping*, edited by C. Neil Macrae, Charles Stangor and Miles Hewstone, 165–208. New York: Guilford, 1996.

Dragonas, Thalia and Anna Fragoudaki. "Educating the Muslim Minority of Western Thrace." *Islam and Christian Relations* 17/1 (2006): 21–41.

Dragonas, Thalia, and Anna Fragoudaki, ed. *Addition, not Subtraction/Multiplication, Not Division*. Athens: Metehmio, 2008. (In Greek.)

Eade, John. "Excluding and Including the 'Other' in the Global City: Religious Mission among Muslim and Catholic Migrants in London." In *The Fundamentalist City? Religiosity and the Remaking of Urban Space*, edited by Nezar AlSayyad and Mejgan Massoumi. London: Routledge, 2011.

Esping-Andersen, Gøsta. *The Three Worlds of Welfare Capitalism*. Princeton: Princeton University Press, 1990.

Esping-Andersen, Gøsta. *The Social Foundations of Post-Industrial Economies*. Oxford: Oxford University Press, 2003.

EU-Midis. *European Union Minorities and Discrimination Survey. Main Results Report*. European Union Agency for Fundamental Rights, 2009. Accessed November 13, 2014. http://fra.europa.eu/fraWebsite/attachments/eumidis_mainreport_conference -edition_en_.pdf.

Eurostat. "Population on 1 January." Accessed November 5, 2013. http://epp.eurostat .ec.europa.eu/tgm/table.do?tab=table&language=en&pcode=tps00001&table Selection=1&footnotes=yes&labeling=labels&plugin=1.

Evans, Peter and Dieter Rueschemeyer, ed. *Bringing the State Back In*. Cambridge: Cambridge University Press, 1985.

Evergeti, Venetia. "Boundary Formation and Identity Expression in Everyday Interactions: Muslim Minorities in Greece." In *Crossing European Boundaries: Beyond Conventional Geographical Boundaries*, edited by Jaro Stacul, Christina Moutsou, and Helena Kopnina, 176–196. Oxford: Berghahn Books, 2006.

Evergeti, Venetia and Panos Hatziprokopiou, ed. *Islam in Greece: Religious Identity and Practice among Indigenous and Migrant Muslims*. Athens: Okto Publishers, forthcoming 2015. (In Greek.)

Evergeti, Venetia, Panos Hatziprokopiou and Nikolas Prevelakis. "Islam in Greece." In *The Oxford Handbook of European Islam*, edited by Jocelyne Cesari, 350–390. Oxford: Oxford University Press, 2014.

Fallaci, Oriana. *Force of Reason*. New York: Rizzoli, 2006.

Fanning, Bryan. *Immigration and Social Change in the Republic of Ireland*. Manchester: Manchester University Press, 2007.

Fanning, Bryan and Fidele Mutwarasibo. "Nationals/Non-Nationals: Immigration, Citizenship and Politics in the Republic of Ireland." *Ethnic and Racial Studies* 30/3 (2007): 439–460.

Faria, Rita Gomes. "Marroquinos em Portugal: Imigração, religião e comunidade," *Lusotopie* 14/1 (2007): 205–221.

Favell, Adrian. *Philosophies of Integration: Immigration and the Idea of Citizenship in France and Britain*. Basingstoke: Palgrave Macmillan, 2001.

Fábos, Anita Häusermann. "Sudanese Identity in Diaspora and the Meaning of Home: The Transformative Role of Sudanese NGOs in Cairo." In *New Approaches to Migration? Transnationalism and Transformations of Home*, edited by Nadje Al-Ali, and Khalid Koser, 34–50. London and New York: Routledge, 2002.

Featherstone, Kevin, Dimitris Papadimitriou, Argyris Mamarelis and Georgios Niarchos. *The Last Ottomans: The Muslim Minority of Greece, 1940–1949*. Basingstoke: Palgrave Macmillan, 2011.

Ferrari, Silvio. "The Secularity of the State and the Shaping of Muslim Representative Organizations in Western Europe." In *European Muslims and the Secular State*, edited by Jocelyne Cesari, and Seán McLoughlin, 11–23. Aldershot: Ashgate, 2005.

Ferrari, Silvio and Sabrina Pastorelli, ed. *Religion in Public Spaces – A European Perspective*. Farnham: Ashgate, 2012.

Ferriter, Diarmaid. *The Transformation of Ireland*. Woodstock: Overlook Press, 2005.

Fetzer, Joel S. and J. Christopher Soper. *Muslims and the State in Britain, France, and Germany*. Cambridge: Cambridge University Press, 2005.

Finnish National Board of Education. *Perusopetuslain muutosten vaikutukset uskonnon ja elämänkatsomustiedon opetukseen sekä koulun toimintaan* [The Implications of the Changes in the Basic Education Act for the Education of Religion and Ethics as well as other practices of schools]. Helsinki: Finnish National Board of Education, 2003.

Finnish National Board of Education. *National Core Curriculum for Basic Education Intended for Pupils in Compulsory Education*. Helsinki: Finnish National Board of Education, 2004.

Finnish National Board of Education. *Perusopetuksen opetussuunnitelman perusteet* [National Core Curriculum for Basic Education]. Helsinki: Finnish National Board of Education, 2004.

Finnish National Board of Education. *Perusopetuksen muiden uskontojen opetussuunnitelman perusteet* [National Core Curriculum of Other Religions for Basic Education]. Helsinki: Finnish National Board of Education, 2006.

Fiske, Susan T., Amy J.C. Cuddy, Peter Glick and Jun Xu. "A Model of (Often Mixed) Stereotype Content: Competence and Warmth Respectively Follow From Perceived Status and Competition." *Journal of Personality and Social Psychology* 82/6 (2002): 878–902.

Flynn, Kieran. "Understanding Islam in Ireland." *Islam and Christian-Muslim Relations* 17/2 (2006): 223–238.

Fonseca, Lucinda and Alina Esteves. "Migration and New Religion Townscapes in Lisbon." In *Immigration and Place in Mediterranean Metropolises*, edited by Lucinda Fonseca, Jorge Malheiros, Natália Ribas-Mateos, Paul White and Alina Esteves, 255–291. Lisbon: Luso-American Foundation, 2002.

Fragopoulos, Ioannis. "Mosque, Square, Coffee-Shop: Social Mobility and Spatial Organization in a Mountainous Minority Community of Thrace." *Ethnologia* 13/5 (2007): 5–48. (In Greek.)

Galeotti, Anna Elisabetta. "Citizenship and Equality: The Place for Toleration." *Political Theory* 21/4 (1993): 585–605.

Gang, Ira N., Francisco L. Rivera-Batiz and Myeong-Su Yun. "Economic Strain, Ethnic Concentration and Attitudes towards Foreigners in the European Union." Discussion paper No. 578. Institute for the Study of Labor, September 2002.

Garbin, David. "The Visibility and Invisibility of Migrant Faith in the City: Diaspora Religion and the Politics of Emplacement of Afro-Christian Churches." *Journal of Ethnic and Migration Studies* 39/5 (2013): 677–696.

Garner, Steve. "Babies, Bodies and Entitlement: Gendered Aspects of Access to Citizenship in the Republic of Ireland." *Parliamentary Affairs* 60/3 (2007): 437–451.

George, Alexander and Andrew Bennett. *Case Studies and Theory Development in the Social Sciences.* Cambridge: MIT Press, 2005.

Gerholm, Tomas and Yngve Lithman, eds. *The New Islamic Presence in Western Europe.* London: Mansell's, 1988.

Gill, Anthony James. *The Political Origins of Religious Liberty.* Cambridge: Cambridge University Press, 2008.

Ging, Debbie and Jackie Malcolm. "Interculturalism and Multiculturalism in Ireland: Textual Strategies at Work in the Media Landscape." In *Resituating Culture*, edited by Gavan Titley. Strasbourg: Council of Europe Publishing, 2004.

Gingrich, Andre. "Concepts of Race Vanishing, Movements of Racism Rising? Global Issues and Austrian Ethnography." *Ethnos* 69/2 (2004): 156–176.

Gogonas, Nikos. "Religion as a Core Value in Language Maintenance: Arabic Speakers in Greece." *International Migration* 50/2 (2010): 113–129.

Gräf, Bettina. "IslamOnline.net: Independent, Interactive, Popular." *Arab Media & Society* January (2008). Accessed November 13, 2014. http://www.arabmediasociety .com/articles/downloads/20080115032719_AMS4_Bettina_Graf.pdf.

Greek Police. "Statistical data." Accessed February 25, 2014. http://www.hellenicpolice.gr.

Gresch, Nora, Leila Hadj-Abdou, Sieglinde Rosenberger and Birgit Sauer. "Tu felix Austria? The Headscarf and the Politics of 'Non-Issues.'" *Social Politics: International Studies in Gender, State & Society* 15:4 (2008): 411–432.

Grillo, Ralph. "Islam and Transnationalism." *Journal of Ethnic and Migration Studies* 30/5 (2004): 861–878.

Grillo, Ralph and Katy Gardner. "Transnational Households and Ritual: an Overview." *Global Networks* 2/3 (2002): 179–191.

Grillo, Ralph and Benjamin Soares. "Transnational Islam in Western Europe." *ISIM Review* 15:11 (2005).

Group-Focused Enmity in Europe. Accessed October, 2013. http://www.uni-bielefeld.de/ikg/zick/gfe_project.htm.

Gullestad, Marianne. "Blind Slaves of Our Prejudices: Debating Culture and Race in Norway." *Ethnos* 69/2 (2004): 177–203.

Habermas, Jürgen. *The Theory of Communicative Action. Volume 1: Reason and Rationalisation of Society.* Boston: Beacon Press, 1984.

Habermas, Jürgen. *The Theory of Communicative Action. Volume 2: Lifeworld and System: A Critique of Functionalist Reason.* Boston: Beacon Press, 1987.

Haddad, Yvonne Yazbeck. *Muslims in the West: From Sojourners to Citizens.* Oxford: Oxford University Press, 2002.

Hammer, Thomas. *Democracy and the Nation State. Aliens, Denizens and Citizens in a World of International Migration.* Aldershot: Ashgate, 1990.

Haralambidis, Michael. *National Issues.* Athens: Gordios, 1994. (In Greek.).

Hatziprokopiou, Panos. *Globalisation and Contemporary Immigration to Southern European Cities: Processes of Social Incorporation of Balkan Immigrants in Thessaloniki.* Amsterdam: Amsterdam University Press, 2006.

Hatziprokopiou, Panos. "Migrants, Islam and Greek National Identity." In *Indigenous Muslims in Greece: Case Studies of Europe's Autochthonous Muslims*, edited by Venetia Evergeti. London: Springer, forthcoming.

Hatziprokopiou, Panos and Venetia Evergeti. "Negotiating Religious Diversity and Muslim Identity in Greek Urban Spaces." *Social and Cultural Geography* 15/6 (2014): 603–626.

Hatzopoulos, Pavlos and Neli Kambouri. "National Case Study: Thematic Study on Religion." Ge.M.IC. research project (Gender, Migration and Intercultural Communication in South-East Europe), WP 6 – Greece. Athens: Panteion University, 2010.

Hautaniemi, Petri, Marko Juntunen and Mariko Sato. *Return Migration and Vulnerability: Case Studies from Somaliland and Iraqi Kurdistan.* Helsinki: Development

REFERENCES 303

Studies, Department of Political and Economic Studies, Faculty of Social Sciences University of Helsinki, 2013.

Hefner, Robert and Muhammad Zamman, eds. *Schooling Islam: The Culture and Politics of Modern Muslim Education.* Princeton: Princeton University Press, 2001.

Heikkilä, Markku, Jyrki Knuutila and Martin Scheinin. "State and Church in Finland." In *State and Church in the European Union*, edited by Gerhard Robbers, 519–536. Second Edition. Baden-Baden: Nomos, 2005.

Heiskala, Risto. "Kansainvälisen toimintaympäristön muutos ja Suomen yhteiskunnallinen murros." In *Uusi jako: Miten Suomesta tuli kilpailukyky-yhteiskunta?*, edited by Risto Heiskala and Eeva Luhtakallio, 14–42. Helsinki: Gaudeamus, 2006.

Heiskala, Risto and Eeva Luhtakallio, eds. *Uusi jako: Miten Suomesta tuli kilpailukyky-yhteiskunta?* Helsinki: Gaudeamus, 2006.

Helleiner, Jane. *Irish Travellers: Racism and the Politics of Culture.* Toronto: University of Toronto Press, 2000.

Hellenic Statistical Authority. "Population statistics": *2001 Census* detailed results; *2011 Census* preliminary results." Accessed February 20, 2014. http://www.statistics.gr.

Hellyer, Hisham. "Visions & Visualizations: Negotiating Space for European Muslims." *Contemporary Islam* 1/1 (2007): 23–35.

Hendriks, Aart. "Dealing with Different Religious Convictions and Practices." In *Religious Pluralism and Human Rights in Europe: Where to Draw the Line?*, edited by M.L.P. Loenen and Jenny E. Goldschmidt, 147–154. Antwerp-Oxford: Intersentia, 2007.

Herbert, David and Max Fras. "European Enlargement, Secularisation and Religious Re-publicisation in Central and Eastern Europe." *Religion, State and Society* 37/1–2 (2009): 81–97.

Hermansen, Marcia. "Hybrid Identity Formations in Muslim America: The Case of American Sufi Movements." *The Muslim World* 90/1–2 (2000): 158–197.

Hervieu-Léger, Danièle. *Religion as a Chain of Memory.* Translated by Simon Lee. Cambridge: Polity Press, 2000.

Hervik, Peter. "The Danish Cultural World of Unbridgeable Differences." *Ethnos* 69/2 (2004): 247–267.

Herzfeld, Michael. *Ours Once More: Folklore, Ideology, and the Making of Modern Greece.* Austin: University of Texas Press, 1987.

Hickman, Mary J., Lyn Thomas, Sara Silvestri and Henri Nickels. *"Suspect Communities"? Counter-Terrorism Policy, the Press, and the Impact on Irish and Muslim Communities in Britain.* London: London Metropolitan University, 2011. Accessed October 9, 2014. http://www.city.ac.uk/__data/assets/pdf_file/0005/96287/suspect-communities -report-july2011.pdf.

Hirschkind, Charles, "Granadan Reflections," *Material Religion* 12:2 (2016): 209–232.

Hirschon, Rene. "The Consequences of the Lausanne Conventions: An Overview." In *Crossing the Aegean: An Appraisal of the 1923 Compulsory Population Exchange between Greece and Turkey,* edited by Rene Hirschon, 13–20. Oxford: Berghahn Books, 2003.

Holma, Markku. "Finland." In *Religious Education in Europe. A Collection of Basic Information about RE in European Countries,* edited by Peter Schreiner, 37–41. Münster: ICCS / Comenius-Institute, 2000.

Holmer-Nadesan, Majia. "Organizational Identity and Space for Action." *Organization Studies* 17/1 (1996): 50.

Holtz, Peter, Janine Dahinden and Wolfgang Wagner. "German Muslims and the 'Integration Debate': Negotiating Identities in the Face of Discrimination." *Integrative Psychological and Behavioral Science* 47/2 (2013): 231–248.

Honneth, Axel. *The Struggle for Recognition: The Moral Grammar of Social Conflicts.* Cambridge: Polity Press, 1995.

Honneth, Axel. *The Pathologies of Individual Freedom.* Princeton: Princeton University Press, 2001.

Honneth, Axel. "Invisibility: On the Epistemology of Recognition." *Aristotelian Society* 75/1 (2006): 111–126.

Human Rights Watch. "Hate on the Streets: Xenophobic Violence in Greece." Report 2012, accessed July 12, 2012. http://www.hrw.org/sites/default/files/reports/greece 0712ForUpload_0.pdf.

Hunter, Shireen. *Islam, Europe's Second Religion: The New Social, Cultural and Political Landscape.* Westport: Praeger, 2002.

Husain, Ed. *The Islamist: Why I Joined Radical Islam in Britain, What I Saw Inside and Why I Left.* London: Penguin, 2007.

IKA. "Research and Statistics Department." Accessed March 3, 2014. http://www.ika.gr.

Ikäheimo, Heikki and Arto Laitinen, ed. *Recognition and Social Ontology.* Leiden: Brill, 2011.

Imam, Mehmet and Olga Tsakiridi. *Muslims and Social Exclusion.* Athens: Livanis, 2003. (In Greek.)

Inglis, Tom. *Moral Monopoly: The Rise and Fall of the Catholic Church in Modern Ireland.* Dublin: University College Dublin Press, 1998.

Inglis, Tom. "Catholic Identity in Contemporary Ireland: Belief and Belonging to Tradition." *Journal of Contemporary Religion* 22/2 (2007): 205–220.

Inglis, Tom. "Individualisation and Secularisation in Catholic Ireland." In *Contemporary Ireland: A Sociological Map,* edited by Sara O'Sullivan, 67–82. Dublin: University College Dublin Press, 2007.

Islamin uskonnon opetussuunnitelman perusteet peruskouluun ja lukioon [The Overall Curriculum of Islam for Comprehensive and Upper-secondary Schools]. Opetushallituksen päätös 3/430. Helsinki: Finnish National Board of Education, 1995.

Jaakkola, Magdalena. *Maahanmuuttajat suomalaisten näkökulmasta: Asennemuutokset 1987–2007*. Helsinki: City of Helsinki Urban Facts, 2009.

Jalovaara, Ville and Tuomas Martikainen. "Suomi maallistumisen jälkeen: valtiokirkollisuudesta uskontojen markkinoihin." In *Religions återkomst: brytningspunkter i kyrkan, religionen och kulturen*, edited by Tuomas Martikainen and Ville Jalovaara, 27–39. Helsingfors: Magma, 2010.

Jamisto, Annukka. "Opetussuunnitelman valmisteluprosessi ja monikulttuurinen koulu." In *Monikulttuurisuus ja uudistuva katsomusaineiden opetus*, edited by Tuula Sakaranaho and Annukka Jamisto, 117–125. Helsinki: University of Helsinki, 2007.

Jensen, Sune Qvotrup. "Othering, Identity Formation and Agency." *Qualitative Studies* 2/2 (2011): 63–78. Accessed October 9, 2014. http://ojs.statsbiblioteket.dk/index.php/qual/article/view/5510/4825.

Jessop, Bob. *State Theory: Putting the Capitalist State in its Place*. University Park: Pennsylvania State University Press, 1990.

Jessop, Bob. *State Power: A Strategic-Relational Approach*. Cambridge: Polity, 2007.

Johnson, Michele. *Being Mandinga, Being Muslim: Transnational Debates on Personhood and Religious Identity in Guinea-Bissau and Portugal*. Urbana-Champaign: University of Illinois, 2002.

Joppke, Christian. "The Retreat of Multiculturalism in the Liberal State: Theory and Policy." *The British Journal of Sociology* 55/2 (2004): 237–257.

Juntunen, Marko. *Prospects for Sustainable Return: Iraqi and Afghan Asylum Seekers in Finland*. Tampere: Tampere Peace Research Institute, University of Tampere 2011.

Jusdanis, Gregory. "East is East – West is West: It's a Matter of Greek Literary History." *Journal of Modern Greek Studies* 5 (1987): 1–14.

Kafetzis, Panagiotis, Aikaterini Michalopoulou, Eudokia Manologlou and Paris Tsartas. "Empirical Dimensions of Xenophobia." In *Macedonia and the Balkans: Xenophobia and Development*, edited by Aikaterini Michalopoulou, Paris Tsartas, Maria Giannisopoulou, Panagiotis Kafetzis and Eudokia Manologlou, 171–222. Athens: ΕΚΚΕ & Alexandria, 1998. (In Greek.)

Kapllani, Gazmend. "Religion and Albanian National Identity: Myths and Realities." *Synchrona Themata* 81 (2002): 50–58. (In Greek.)

Kapteijns, Lidwien with Mariam Omar Ali. "Sittaat: Somali Women's Songs for the 'Mothers of the Believers.'" In *The Marabout and the Muse. New Approaches to Islam in African Literature*, edited by Kenneth W. Harrow, 124–141. Portsmouth: Heinemann, 1996.

Kapteijns, Lidwien with Maryan Omar. "Sittaat: Women's Religious Songs in Djibouti." *Hal-abuur, Journal of Somali Literature and Culture* 2/1–2 (2007): 38–48.

Karakasidou, Anastasia. "Vestiges of the Ottoman Past: Muslims Under Siege in Contemporary Greek Thrace." *Cultural Survival* 19/2 (1995). Accessed November 13, 2014.

https://www.culturalsurvival.org/ourpublications/csq/article/vestiges-ottoman
-past-muslims-under-siege-contemporary-greek-thrace.

Karolewski, Ireneusz Pawel and Andrzej Marcin Suszycki, ed. *Nationalism and European Integration: The Need for New Theoretical and Empirical Insights.* London: Continuum, 2007.

Karvonen, Hanna. "Salaam Aleikum. Islamin opettajien käsityksiä omasta työstään ja uskonnonopetuksesta Helsingin kouluissa." Minor thesis, University of Helsinki, Department of Teacher Education, 1998.

Kassimeris, George and Antonis Samouris. "Examining Islamic Associations of Pakistani and Bangladeshi Immigrants in Greece." *Religion, State and Society* 40/2 (2012): 174–191.

Katsikas, Stefanos. "Millets in Nation-States: The Case of Greek and Bulgarian Muslims, 1912–1923." *Nationalities Papers* 37/2 (2009): 177–202.

Katzenstein, Peter. "Small States and Small States Revisited." *New Political Economy* 8/1 (2003): 9–30.

Kemnitz, Eva-Maria von. "Muslims as Seen by the Portuguese Press 1974–1999: Changes in the Perception of Islam." In *Intercultural Relations and Religious Authorities: Muslims in the European Union*, edited by W.A.R. Shadid and P.S. van Koningsveld, 7–26. Leuven: Peeters, 2002.

Ketola, Kimmo. "Uskontotilanteen muutos ja suomalaisten suhtautuminen eri uskontoihin." In *Uskonnon ylösnousemus: Kirkon, uskonnon ja kulttuurin murros*, edited by Tuomas Martikainen and Ville Jalovaara, 44–51. Helsingfors: Magma, 2010.

Ketola, Kimmo. "Uskonto suomalaisessa yhteiskunnassa 1600-luvulta nykypäivään." In *Moderni kirkkokansa: Suomalaisten uskonnollisuus uudella vuosituhannella*, Kimmo Kääriäinen, Kati Niemelä and Kimmo Ketola, 17–52. Tampere: Kirkon tutkimuskeskus, 2003.

Kettani, Houssain. "World Muslim Population: 1950–2020." *International Journal of Environmental Science and Development* 1/2 (2010).

Khan, Adil H. "Transnational Influences on Irish Muslim Networks: From Local to Global Perspectives." *Journal of Muslim Minority Affairs* 31/4 (2011): 486–502.

Khan, Adil H. "Creating the Image of European Islam: The European Council for Fatwa and Research and Ireland," in *Muslim Political Participation in Europe*, ed. Jørgen S. Nielsen Edinburgh: Edinburgh University Press, 2013, 224.

Khan, Adil H. "Narratives of Muslim Migration to Ireland." *The Muslim World* 107/3 (2017): 401–431.

Khiabany, Gholam and Milly Williamson. "Veiled Bodies – Naked Racism: Culture, Politics and Race in the Sun." *Race & Class* 50/2 (2008): 69–88.

Kiliç, Sevgi. "The British Veil Wars." *Social Politics: International Studies in Gender, State and Society* 15/4 (2008): 433–454.

REFERENCES

Kimanen, Anuleena. "Voimaa tiedosta. Islamin kouluopetuksen merkitys eräille espoolaisille musliminuorille." Minor thesis, University of Helsinki, Department of Teacher Education, 2011.

King, E. Frances. *Material Religion and Popular Culture*. London: Routledge, 2010.

Kissane, Bill. "The Illusion of State Neutrality in a Secularising Ireland." In *Church and State in Contemporary Europe: The Chimera of Neutrality*, edited by John Madeley and Zsolt Enyedi, 73–94. London: Frank Cass, 2007.

Kjær, Anne Mette. *Governance*. Cambridge: Policy Press, 2004.

Knott, Kim. *The Location of Religion: A Spatial Analysis*. London: Equinox, 2008.

Knott, Kim. "From Locality to Location and Back Again: A Spatial Journey in the Study of Religion." *Religion* 39/2 (2009): 154–160.

Knott, Kim, Elizabeth Poole and Teemu Taira. *Media Portrayals of Religion and the Secular Sacred*. Farnham: Ashgate, 2013.

Koikkalainen, Anu. *Uskonnonopetus ja ihmisoikeudet*. Helsinki: Ihmisoikeusliitto, 2010. Accessed June 13, 2012. http://ihmisoikeusliitto.fi/images/pdf_files/uskonnonopetus .pdf.

Koliopoulos, John S. and Thanos Veremis. *Greece: The Modern Sequel. From 1821 to the Present*. London: Hurst and Company, 2002.

Koopmans, Ruud, Marco Giugni and Florence Passy. *Contested Citizenship: Immigration and Cultural Diversity in Europe*. Minneapolis: University of Minnesota Press, 2005.

Koskinen, Seppo, Päivi Sainio and Shadia Rask. "Sosiaalinen toimintakyky." In *Maahanmuuttajien terveys ja hyvinvointi: Tutkimus venäläis-, suomalais- ja kurditaustaisista Suomessa*, edited by Anu E. Castaneda, Shadia Rask, Päivikki Koponen, Mulki Mölsä and Seppo Koskinen, 199–207. Helsinki: National Institute for Health and Welfare, 2012.

Kozlowski, Gregory C. "Imperial Authority, Benefactions and Endowments (Awqāf) in Mughal India." *Journal of the Economic and Social History of the Orient* 38/3 (1995): 355–370.

Kristeva, Julia. "Word, Dialogue, and Novel." In *The Kristeva Reader*, edited by Toril Moi. Oxford: Basil Blackwell, 1986.

Kuru, Ahmet. *Secularism and State Policies towards Religion: The United States, France and Turkey*. Cambridge: Cambridge University Press, 2009.

Laitinen, Arto. "On the Scope of 'Recognition': The Role of Adequate Regard and Mutuality." In *Philosophy of Recognition: Historical and Contemporary Perspectives*, edited by Hans Cristoph Schmidt am Busch and Christopher Zurn. Plymouth: Lexington Books, 2010.

Lambton, Ann. "Awqāf in Persia: 6th–8th/12th–14th Centuries." *Islamic Law and Society* 4/3 (1997): 298–318.

Landman, Nico. "Imams in the Netherlands: Homemade Better than Import." *ISIM Newsletter* 2:5 (1999).

Larson, Jared. *Demographic and Migration Transition in Spain and Portugal: Catholic Contexts and Secular Responses*. MIGRARE Working Paper 5. Lisbon: CEG, 2010.

Larsson, Göran and Egdūnas Račius. "A Different Approach to the History of Islam and Muslims in Europe: A North-Eastern Angle, or the Need to Reconsider the Research Field." *Journal of Religion in Europe* 3/3 (2010): 350–373.

Latvala, Piia. *Valoa itään? Kansanlähetys ja Neuvostoliitto 1967–1973*. Helsinki: Suomen Kirkkohistoriallinen Seura, 2008.

Laurence, Jonathan. "Managing Transnational Islam: Muslims and the State in Western Europe." In *Immigration and the Transformation of Europe*, edited by Craig Parsons and T.M. Smeeding, 251–273. New York: Cambridge University Press, 2006.

Laurence, Jonathan. "The Corporatist Antecedent of Contemporary State Islam Relations." *European Political Science* 8/3 (2009): 301–315.

Laurence, Jonathan. *The Emancipation of Europe's Muslims: The State's Role in Minority Integration*. Princeton: Princeton University Press, 2012.

Le Sage, Andre. "Prospects for Al Itihad and Islamist Radicalism in Somalia." *Review of African Political Economy* 28/89 (2001): 472–477.

Leghari, Inam U. "Pakistani Immigrants in Greece: From Changing Pattern of Migration to Diaspora Politics and Transnationalism." Paper presented at the 4th LSE PhD Symposium on Contemporary Greece, LSE–Hellenic Observatory, June 25–26, 2009. Accessed October 8, 2010. http://www.lse.ac.uk/collections/hellenic Observatory/pdf/4th_%20Symposium/PAPERS_PPS/ETHNICITY_IMMIGRATION/ LEGHARI.pdf.

Lempinen, Hennariikka. "'Pitäisi olla taikuri.' Islamin opettajien käsitykset islamin uskonnon opetuksesta peruskoulussa." Master's thesis, University of Helsinki, Faculty of Theology, 2002.

Lentin, Ronit. "Ireland: Racial State and Crisis Racism." *Ethnic and Racial Studies* 30/4 (2007): 610–627.

Levitt, Peggy. *God Needs No Passport: Immigrants and the Changing American Religious Landscape*. New York: The New Press, 2007.

Lewis, Bernard. *The Emergence of Modern Turkey: Studies in Middle Eastern History*. Oxford: Oxford University Press, 2001.

Lewis, I.M. *Saints and Somalis: Popular Islam in a Clan-based Society*. London: Haan Associates, 1998.

Lewis, I.M., Ahmed Al-Safi and Sayyid Hurreiz, eds. *Women's Medicine: The Zar-Bori Cult in Africa and Beyond*. Edinburgh: Edinburgh University Press for the International African Institute, 1991.

REFERENCES 309

Ley, David. "The Immigrant Church as an Urban Service Hub." *Urban Studies* 45/10 (2008): 2057–2074.

Liakos, Antonis and Emilia Salvanou. "Citizenship, Memory and Governmentality: A Tale of Two Migrant Communities." In *Citizenships and Identities: Inclusion, Exclusion, Participation*, edited by Ann K. Isaacs. Pisa: Plus-Pisa University Press, 2010. Accessed October 15, 2014. http://antonisliakos.files.wordpress.com/2011/04/citizenship-and-memory.pdf.

Lister, Ruth. "Citizenship: Towards a Feminist Synthesis." *Feminist Review* 57 (Autumn 1997): 28–48.

Loenen, M.L.P. and J.E. Goldschmidt, eds. *Religious Pluralism and Human Rights in Europe: Where to Draw the Line?* Antwerp–Oxford: Intersentia, 2007.

Loja, Fernando Soares. "Islam in Portugal." In *Islam, Europe's Second Religion*, edited by Shireen Hunter, 191–203. London: Praeger, 2002.

Lowi, Theodore J. "Four Systems of Policy, Politics, and Choice." *Public Administration Review* 32/4 (1972): 298–310.

Lukiolaki [Upper-Secondary Education Act] 6.6.2003 / 455, 9§. Finlex – Valtion säädöstietopankki. Accessed July 7, 2013. http://www.finlex.fi/.

Mac Éinrí, Piaras. *Immigration into Ireland: Trends, Policy Responses, Outlook*. Cork: Irish Centre for Migration Studies, 2001.

Mac Éinrí, Piaras. "Immigration: Labour Migrants, Asylum Seekers and Refugees." In *Understanding Contemporary Ireland*, edited by B. Bartley and R. Kitchin, 236–248. London: Pluto Press, 2007.

Machaqueiro, Mário Artur. "Portuguese Colonialism and the Islamic Community of Lisbon." In *Colonial and Post-Colonial Governance of Islam: Continuities and Ruptures*, edited by Marcel Maussen, Veit Bader and Annelies Moors, 211–232. Amsterdam: University of Amsterdam Press, 2012.

Madeley, John. "A Framework for the Comparative Analysis of Church–State Relations in Western Europe." In *Church and State in Contemporary Europe: the Chimera of Neutrality*, edited by John Madeley, and Zsolt Enyedi, 23–50. London: Frank Cass, 2003.

Madeley, John. "Unequally Yoked: The Antinomies of Church–State Separation in Europe and the USA." *European Political Science* 8/3 (2009): 273–288.

Mahmood, Saleha S. "A Word about Ourselves." *Journal of Muslim Minority Affairs* 31/4 (2011): 467–468. Accessed October 9, 2014. http://dx.doi.org/10.1080/13602004.2011.636255.

Maijala, Leena. "Islamin opetus kouluissa – oppilaiden puheenvuoro." Accessed January 13, 2009. http://www.teologia.fi/opinnaytteet/pro-gradut/414-islamin-opetus-kouluissa-oppilaiden-puheenvuoro.

Mair, Peter and Liam Weeks. "The Party System." In *Politics in the Republic of Ireland*, edited by John Coakley and Michael Gallagher. London: Routledge, 2004.

Malheiros, Jorge Macaista. *Imigrantes na Região de Lisboa: Os Anos da Mudança, Imigração e Processo de Integração das Comunidades de Origem Indiana.* Lisbon: Colibri, 1996.

Malheiros, Jorge. "Immigrants, Residential Mobility, Socio-Ethnic Desegregation Trends and the Metropolises Fragmentation Thesis: The Lisbon Example." In *Minority Internal Migration in Europe*, edited by Nissa Finney and Gemma Catney, 85–88. London: Ashgate, 2012.

Malheiros, Jorge and Lucinda Fonseca. *Acesso à Habitação e Problemas Residencais dos Imigrantes em Portugal.* Lisbon: ACIDI, 2011.

Malheiros, Jorge and Francisco Vala. "Immigration and City Change: The Lisbon Metropolis at the Turn of the Twentieth Century." *Journal of Ethnic and Migration Studies* 30/6 (2004): 1065–1086.

Mamdani, Mahmood, *Good Muslim, Bad Muslim: America, The Cold War and the Roots of Terror*, London, Penguin Random House, 2005.

Mandaville, Peter. *Transnational Muslim Politics: Reimagining the Umma.* New York: Routledge, 2001.

Mandel, Ruth. *Cosmopolitan Anxieties: Turkish Challenges to Citizenship and Belonging in Germany.* Durham: Duke University Press, 2008.

Mannila, Simo, Anu E. Castaneda and Inga Jasinskaja-Lahti. "Syrjintäkokemukset." In *Maahanmuuttajien terveys ja hyvinvointi: Tutkimus venäläis-, suomalais- ja kurditaustaisista Suomessa*, edited by Anu E. Castaneda, Shadia Rask, Päivikki Koponen, Mulki Mölsä and Seppo Koskinen, 229–239. Helsinki: National Institute for Health and Welfare, 2012.

Mantouvalou, Katerina. "Equal Recognition, Consolidation or Familiarisation? The Language Rights Debate in the Context of the Minority of Western Thrace in Greece." *Ethnicities* 9/4 (2009): 477–506.

Mapril, José. "Bangla Masdjid: Islão e Bengalidade Entre os Bangladeshianos em Lisboa." *Análise Social* XXXIX/173 (2005): 851–873.

Mapril, José. "The New South Asians: The Political Economy of Migrations between Bangladesh and Portugal." *Revista Oriente* 17 (2007): 81–99.

Mapril, José. "'Bons' Muçulmanos: Educação Islâmica e Cidadania na Área Metropolitana de Lisboa." In *Religião em Movimento: Imigrantes e Diversidade Religiosa em Portugal e Itália*, edited by Helena Vilaça and Enzo Pace, 37–54. Porto: Estratégias Criativas, 2010.

Mapril, José. "'Aren't You Looking for Citizenship in the Wrong Place?' Islamic Education, Secular Subjectivities and the Portuguese Muslim." *Religion and Society: Advances in Research* 5 (2014): 65–82.

Mapril, José and Nina Clara Tiesler. "Portugal." In *Yearbook of Muslims in Europe. Volume 5*, edited by Jørgen S. Nielsen, Samim Akgönül, Ahmet Alibašić and Egdūnas Račius, 517–530. Leiden: Brill, 2013.

Maréchal, Brigitte. "Institutionalisation of Islam and Representative Organisations for Dealing with European States." In *Muslims in the Enlarged Europe: Religion and Society*, edited by Brigitte Maréchal, Stefano Allievi, Felice Dassetto and Jørgen S. Nielsen, 151–182. Leiden: Brill, 2003.

Maréchal, Brigitte. *The Muslim Brothers in Europe: Roots and Discourse*. Leiden: Brill, 2008.

Maréchal, Brigitte, Stefano Allievi, Felice Dassetto and Jørgen S. Nielsen, ed. *Muslims in the Enlarged Europe: Religion and Society*. Leiden: Brill, 2003.

Maroukis, Thanos. "Country Report: Greece." Report for the project CLANDESTINO Undocumented Migration: counting the uncountable – data and trends across Europe, EU 6th Framework Programme, 2008. Accessed June 26, 2012. http://irregular -migration.net/typo3_upload/groups/31/4.Background_Information/4.4.Country _Reports/Greece_CountryReport_Clandestino_Nov09_2.pdf.

Marranci, Gabriele. *The Anthropology of Islam*. Oxford: Berg Publishers, 2008.

Martikainen, Tuomas. *Immigrant Religions in Local Society: Historical and Contemporary Perspectives in the City of Turku*. Åbo: Åbo Akademi University Press, 2004.

Martikainen, Tuomas. "The Governance of Islam in Finland." *Temenos* 43/2 (2007): 243–265.

Martikainen, Tuomas. "Muslimit suomalaisessa yhteiskunnassa." In *Islam Suomessa: Muslimit arjessa, mediassa ja yhteiskunnassa*, edited by Tuomas Martikainen, Tuula Sakaranaho and Marko Juntunen, 62–84. Helsinki: Suomalaisen Kirjallisuuden Seura, 2008.

Martikainen, Tuomas. "Finland." In *Yearbook of Muslims in Europe. Volume 3*, edited by Jørgen S. Nielsen, Samim Akgönül, Ahmet Alibašić, Brigitte Maréchal and Christian Moe, 187–196. Leiden: Brill, 2011.

Martikainen, Tuomas. "The Global Political Economy, Welfare State Reforms, and the Governance of Religion." In *Post-Secular Society*, edited by Peter Nynäs, Mika Lassander and Terhi Utriainen, 71–93. New Brunswick: Transaction Publishers, 2012.

Martikainen, Tuomas. "Finland." In *Yearbook of Muslims in Europe. Volume 5*, edited by Jørgen S. Nielsen, Samim Akgönül, Ahmet Alibašić and Egdūnas Račius, 237–246. Leiden: Brill, 2013.

Martikainen, Tuomas. "Multilevel and Pluricentric Network Governance of Religion." In *Religion in the Neoliberal Age: Political Economy and Modes of Governance*, edited by Tuomas Martikainen and François Gauthier, 129–142. Ashgate: Farnham, 2013.

Martikainen, Tuomas. "Reframing Islam and Muslim Identities: Neoliberalism, Minority Governance and the Welfare State in Finland." In *Living Islam in Europe. Muslim Traditions in European Contexts*, edited by Dietrich Reetz. Forthcoming..

Maussen, Marcel. *Making Muslim Presence Meaningful*. Amsterdam, Amsterdam School for Social Science Research working paper 2005.

Maussen, Marcel. *The Governance of Islam in Western Europe: A State of the Art Report.* IMISCOE Working Paper No. 16. Amsterdam: IMISCOE, 2007. Accessed November 26, 2013. http://www.iom.lt/documents/GovernanceofIslam.pdf.

Maussen, Marcel. *Constructing Mosques: The Governance of Islam in France and the Netherlands.* Amsterdam: Amsterdam School for Social Science Research, 2009.

Mavrogordatos, George. "Orthodoxy and Nationalism in the Greek Case." *West European Politics* 26/1 (2003): 117–136.

Mavromatis, Georgios. *The Children of Kalkantza: Education, Poverty and Social Exclusion in a Muslim Community of Thrace.* Athens: Metehmio, 2005. (In Greek.)

Mazower, Mark. *Salonica, City of Ghosts: Christians, Muslims and Jews, 1430–1950.* London: HarperCollins, 2004.

McGarrigle, Jennifer. *Understanding Processes of Ethnic Concentration and Dispersal: South Asian Residential Preferences in Glasgow.* Amsterdam: University of Amsterdam Press, 2010.

McLoughlin, Seán. "Mosques and the Public Space: Conflict and Cooperation in Bradford." *Journal of Ethnic and Migration Studies* 31/6 (2005): 1045–1066.

McMahon, Kathryn. "The Hargeisa Provincial Museum." *African Arts* 21/3 (1988): 64–68, 87–88.

McMichael, Celia. "'Everywhere is Allah's Place': Islam and the Everyday Life of Somali Women in Melbourne, Australia." *Journal of Refugee Studies* 15/2 (2002): 171–188.

McVeigh, Robert. "'Ethnicity Denial' and Racism: The Case of the Government of Ireland against Irish Travellers." *Translocations* 2/1 (2007): 90–133. Accessed October 9, 2014. http://www.translocations.ie/docs/v02i01/translocations-v02i01-06.pdf.

Meaney, Geraldine. *Sex and Nation: Women in Irish Culture and Politics.* Cork: Attic Press, 1991.

Mekos, Zafirios. *The Responsibilities of the Mufti and Greek Legislation.* Athens: Sakkoulas, 1991. (In Greek.)

Menkhaus, Ken. "Political Islam in Somalia." *Middle East Policy* IX/1 (2002): 109–123.

Merryman, Nancy Hawk. "Women's Welfare in the Jubba Valley: Somali Socialism and After." In *The Struggle for Land in Southern Somalia. The War Behind the War*, edited by Catherine Bestemand and Lee V. Cassanelli, 179–198. Oxford: Westview Press, 1996.

Messina, Anthony. "The Politics of Migration to Western Europe: Ireland in Comparative Perspective." *West European Politics* 32/1 (2009): 1–25.

Metcalf, Barbara. *Making Muslim Space in North America and Europe.* Berkeley: University of California Press, 1996.

Metcalf, Barbara. *"Traditionalist" Islamic Activism: Deoband, Tablighis, and Talibs.* Leiden: I.S.I.M., 2002.

Michail, Domna. "From 'Locality' to 'European Identity': Shifting Identities among the Pomak Minority in Greece." *Ethnologia Balkanika* 7 (2003): 140–157.

REFERENCES 313

Migdal, Joel. *State in Society*. Cambridge: Cambridge University Press, 2001.

Ministry of the Interior. *Safety First: Internal Security Programme. Government Plenary Session 8 May 2008*. Publications of the Ministry of the Interior 25/2008. Helsinki: Ministry of the Interior, 2008.

Ministry of the Interior. *Turvallinen elämä jokaiselle. Sisäisen turvallisuuden ohjelma*. Ministry of the Interior, 2008.

Ministry of the Interior. *Sisäisen turvallisuuden toimeenpanon ohjelma. Väliraportti 1/2010*. Helsinki: Ministry of the Interior, 2010.

Ministry of the Interior. *A Safer Tomorrow – Internal Security Programme*. Helsinki: Ministry of the Interior, 2012.

Minkenberg, Michael. "The Policy Impact of Church–State Relations: Family Policy and Abortion in Britain, France, and Germany." *West European Politics* 26/1 (2003): 195–217.

Minkenberg, Michael. "Democracy and Religion: Theoretical and Empirical Observations on the Relationship between Christianity, Islam and Liberal Democracy." *Journal of Ethnic and Migration Studies* 33/6 (2007): 887–909.

Minkenberg, Michael. "Religious Legacies, Churches, and the Shaping of Immigration Policies in the Age of Religious Diversity." *Politics and Religion* 1/3 (2008): 349–383.

Mire, Sada. "Preserving Knowledge, not Objects: A Somali Perspective for Heritage Management and Archaeological Research." *African Archaeological Review* 24/3–4 (2007): 49–71.

Mitchell, Claire. *Religion, Identity, and Politics in Northern Ireland: Boundaries of Belonging and Belief*. Aldershot: Ashgate Publishing, 2006.

Modood, Tariq. "Anti-Essentialism, Multiculturalism and the 'Recognition' of Religious Groups." *The Journal of Political Philosophy* 6/4 (1998): 378–399. Accessed October 9, 2014. http://dx.doi.org/10.1111/1467-9760.00060.

Modood, Tariq. "Muslims and the Politics of Difference." *The Political Quarterly* 74 (2003): 100–115.

Modood, Tariq and Fauzia Ahmad. "British Muslim Perspectives on Multiculturalism." *Theory, Culture, Society* 24/2 (2007): 187–213.

Modood, Tariq, Anna Triandafyllidou and Ricard Zapata-Barrero, eds. *Multiculturalism, Muslims, and Citizenship: A European Approach*. London: Routledge, 2006.

Modood Tariq, *Still Not Easy Being British: Struggles for a Multicultural Citizenship*. London. Thretham Books, 2010.

Mohr, Irka. "Islamic Instruction in Germany and Austria: A Comparison of Principles Derived from Religious Thought." *Cahiers d'études sur la Méditerranée orientale et le monde turco-iranien* 33 (2002): 149–166.

Monsma, Stephen V. and J. Christopher Soper. *The Challenge of Pluralism: Church and State in Five Democracies. Religious Forces in the Modern Political World*. Lanham: Rowman and Littlefield, 1997.

Montgomery, Victoria. "Ireland." In *Yearbook of Muslims in Europe. Volume 5*, edited by Jørgen S. Nielsen, Samim Akgönül, Ahmet Alibašić and Egdūnas Račius, 333–349. Leiden: Brill, 2013.

Moors, Annelies and Ruba Salih. "'Muslim Women' in Europe: Secular Normativities, Bodily Performances and Multiple Publics." *Social Anthropology* 17/4 (2009): 375–378.

Morley, David. *Home Territories: Media, Mobility and Identity*. London: Routledge, 2000.

Motasim, Hanaa and Hilde Heynen. "At Home with Displacement? Material Culture as a Site of Resistance in Sudan." *Home Cultures* 8/1 (2011): 43–70.

Mouffe, Chantal. *The Return of the Political*. London: Verso, 1993.

National Consultative Committee on Racism and Interculturalism. *The Muslim Community in Ireland: Challenge some of Myths and Misinformation*. Dublin: National Consultative Committee on Racism and Interculturalism, 2008.

Naylor, Simon and James Ryan. "The Mosque in the Suburbs: Negotiating Religion and Ethnicity in South London." *Social and Cultural Geography* 3/1 (2002): 39–59.

Nielsen, Jørgen S. *Muslims in Western Europe*. Second Edition. Edinburgh: Edinburgh University Press, 1995.

Nielsen, Jørgen S. *Muslims in Western Europe*. Third Edition. Edinburgh: Edinburgh University Press, 2004.

Nielsen, Jørgen S., ed. *Muslim Political Participation in Europe*. Edinburgh: Edinburgh University Press, 2013.

Nielsen, Jørgen S., Samim Akgönül, Ahmet Alibašić, Brigitte Maréchal and Christian Moe, eds. *Yearbook of Muslims in Europe. Volume 1*. Leiden: Brill, 2009.

Nielsen, Jørgen S., Samim Akgönül, Ahmet Alibašić and Egdūnas Račius, eds. *Yearbook of Muslims in Europe. Volume 5*. Leiden: Brill, 2013.

Nokelainen, Mika. *Vähemmistövaltiokirkon synty: Ortodoksisen kirkkokunnan ja valtion suhteiden muotoutuminen Suomessa 1917–1922*. Helsinki: Suomen Kirkkohistoriallinen Seura, 2010.

O'Malley, Eoin. *Contemporary Ireland*. Dublin: Palgrave Macmillan, 2011.

O'Regan, Mary. "Explaining Media Frames of Contested Foreign Conflicts: Irish National 'Opinion Leader' Newspapers' Frames of the Israeli- Palestinian Conflict (July 2000 to July 2004)." *Networking Knowledge: Journal of the MeCCSA Postgraduate Network* 1/2 (2007): 1–25.

Okin, Susan. *Is Multiculturalism Bad for Women?* Princeton: Princeton University Press, 1999.

Omaar, Rageh. *Only Half of Me: Being Muslim in Britain*. London: Viking, 2006.

Omi, Michael. "'Slipping into Darkness': The (Re)Biologization of Race." *Journal of Asian American Studies* 13/3 (2010): 343–358.

Onniselkä, Suaad. "Islamin opetus koulussa." In *Mitä muslimit tarkoittavat? Keskustelua islamilaisista virtauksista Suomessa ja Euroopassa*, edited by Tuomas Martikainen and Tuula Sakaranaho, 122–138. Turku: Savukeidas, 2011.

REFERENCES   315

Østergaard-Nielsen, Eva. *Transnational Politics: Turks and Kurds in Germany*. London: Routledge, 2003.

Papantoniou, Antonios K. "Muslim Migrants in Athens." *Ekklisia* 86/5 (2009): 348–360. (In Greek.)

Parekh, Bhikhu. "British Citizenship and Cultural Difference." In *Citizenship*, edited by G. Andrews, G. London: Lawrence & Wishart, 1991.

Parekh, Bhikhu. "Religion and Public Life." In *Church, State and Religious Minorities*, edited by Tariq Modood, 16–22. London: Policy Studies Institute, 2007.

Peach, Ceri. "Britain's Muslim Population: An Overview." in *Muslim Britain: Muslim Communities under Pressure*, edited by Tahir Abbas, 29. London: Zed Books, 2005.

Pędziwiatr, Konrad. *The New Muslim Elites in European Cities: Religion and Active Social Citizenship amongst Young Organized Muslims in Brussels and London*. Saarbrücken: VDM Verlag Dr Müller, 2010.

Peek, Lori. "Becoming Muslim: The Development of a Religious Identity." *Sociology of Religion*, 66:3 (2005).

Perusopetuslaki 6.6.2003 / 454 [The Basic Education Act]. Finlex – Valtion säädöstieto-pankki. Accessed July 7, 2013. http://www.finlex.fi/.

Pew Templeton Global Religious Futures Project. *The Future of the Global Muslim Population: Projections for 2010–2030*. Washington: Pew Research Center, Forum on Religion & Public Life, 2011.

Phalet, Karen, Fenella Fleischmann and Snezana Stojcic. "Ways of 'Being Muslim.'" In *The European Second Generation Compared: Does the Integration Context Matter?*, edited by Maurice Crul, Jens Schneider and Frans Lelie. Amsterdam: Amsterdam University Press, 2012. Accessed October 9, 2014. http://www.oapen.org/search?identifier=426534;keyword=crul.

Philips, Melanie. *Londonistan*. New York: Encounter Books, 2006.

Pierson, Paul. "Increasing Returns, Path Dependence, and the Study of Politics." *American Political Science Review* 94/2 (2000): 251–268.

Pires, Sonia. "Guinea-Bissau Immigrant Transnationalism in Portugal: A Substitute for a Failed State?" *African and Black Diaspora: An International Journal* 6/2 (2013): 145–173.

Piscatori, James. "Reinventing the Ummah? The Trans-Locality of Pan-Islam." Lecture to the 10th Anniversary Conference: Translocality: An Approach to Globalising Phenomena, Zentrum Modern Orient, Berlin, September 26, 2006.

Polis, Adamantia. "Notes on Nationalism and Human Rights in Greece" *Journal of Modern Hellenism* 4 (1987): 147–160.

Polis, Adamantia. "Greek National Identity: Religious Minorities, Rights and European Norms." *Journal of Modern Greek Studies* 10 (1992): 171–195.

Poole, Elizabeth and John E. Richardson, ed. *Muslims and the News Media*. London: I.B Tauris, 2006.

Popkewitz, Thomas S. "The Production of Reason and Power: Curriculum History and Intellectual Traditions." *Journal of Curriculum Studies* 29/2 (1997): 131–164.

Poulton, Hugh. *The Balkans: Minorities and States in Conflict.* London: Minority Rights Publication, 1995.

Promey, Sally and Shira Brisman. "Sensory Cultures: Material and Visual Religion Reconsidered." In *The Blackwell Companion to Religion in America*, edited by Philip Goff, 177–205. Oxford: Blackwell Publisher, 2010.

Psomiades, J. Harry. *The Eastern Question: The Last Phase.* Thessaloniki: Institute for Balkan Studies, 1968.

Public Issue. "Οι Έλληνες και το Ισλάμ: Τι γνωρίζει και τι πιστεύει η κοινή γνώμη" [Greeks and Islam; what public opinion knows and believes. Public Issue Opinion Surveys]. November 17, 2010. Accessed February 2, 2013. http://www.publicissue.gr/1395. (In Greek.)

Pyykkönen, Miikka. "Integrating Governmentality: Administrative Expectations for Immigrant Associations in Finland." *Alternatives* 32/2 (2007): 197–224.

Pyykkönen, Miikka. *Järjestäytyvät diasporat: Etnisyys, kansalaisuus, integraatio ja hallinta maahanmuuttajien yhdistystoiminnassa.* Jyväskylä: University of Jyväskylä, 2007.

Pyysiäinen, Markku. *Tunnustuksellinen, tunnustukseton ja objektiivinen uskonnonopetus. Opetussuunnitelma-analyysi Suomen ja Ruotsin peruskoulun uskonnonopetuksen tavoitteista ja sisällöstä.* Helsinki: Kirjapaja, 1982.

Raittila, Pentti and Mari Maasilta. "Silmäyksiä islamin esittämiseen suomalaisessa journalismissa." In *Islam Suomessa: Muslimit arjessa, mediassa ja yhteiskunnassa*, edited by Tuomas Martikainen, Tuula Sakaranaho and Marko Juntunen, 225–243. Helsinki: Suomalaisen Kirjallisuuden Seura, 2008.

Ramadan, Tariq. *To Be a European Muslim.* Leicester: Islamic Foundation, 1999.

Rana, Junaid. *Terrifying Muslims: Race and Labour in the South Asian Diaspora.* Durham: Duke University Press, 2011.

Rantala, Kati and Pekka Sulkunen, ed. *Projektiyhteiskunnan kääntöpuolia.* Helsinki: Gaudeamus, 2006.

Rasinkangas, Jarkko and Marjukka Laitinen, ed. *Varissuon 30 vuotta – tavoitteista todeksi.* Turku: Kirja-Aurora, 2006.

Rentola, Kimmo. "Suojelupoliisi kylmässä sodassa 1949–1991." In *Ratakatu 12: Suojelupoliisi 1949–2009*, edited by Matti Simola, 9–120. Helsinki: WSOY, 2009.

Rey, Terry. "Marketing the Goods of Salvation: Bourdieu on religion." *Religion* 34/4 (2004): 331–343.

Rey, Terry. *Bourdieu on Religion: Imposing Faith and Legitimacy.* London: Equinox, 2007.

Riccio, Bruno. "Transnational Mouridism and the Afro-Muslim Critique of Italy." *Journal of Ethnic and Migration Studies* 30/5 (2004): 929–944.

Ricoeur, Paul. *The Course of Recognition.* Translated by David Pellauer. Cambridge: Harvard University Press, 2005.

Rissanen, Inkeri. "Teaching Islamic Education in Finnish Schools: A Field of Negotiations." *Teaching and Teacher Education* 28/5 (2012): 740–749.

Rose, Nikolas. *Powers of Freedom: Reframing Political Thought.* Cambridge: Cambridge University Press, 1999.

Rottman, Susan B. and Myra M. Ferree. "Citizenship and Intersectionality: German Feminist Debates about Headscarf and Antidiscrimination Laws." *Social Politics* 15/4 (2008): 498.

Roudometof, Victor. "The Evolution of Greek Orthodoxy in the Context of World Historical Globalisation." In *Orthodox Christianity in 21st Century Greece: The Role of Religion in Culture, Ethnicity and Politics,* edited by Victor Roudometof and Vassilis N. Makrides, 23–38. Farnham: Ashgate, 2010.

Roy, Olivier. *Globalized Islam: The Search For a New Ummah.* London: Hurst & Company, 2004.

Said, Edward. *Orientalism.* New York: Vintage Books, 1979.

Sakaranaho, Tuula. *Religious Freedom, Multiculturalism, Islam: Cross-reading Finland and Ireland.* Leiden: Brill, 2006.

Sakaranaho, Tuula. "Pienryhmäisten uskontojen opetus ja monikulttuurisuuden haasteet." In *Katsomusaineiden kehittämishaasteita. Opettajankoulutuksen tutkinnnonuudistuksen virittämää keskustelua,* edited by Arto Kallioniemi and Eero Salmenkivi, 3–16. University of Helsinki: Department of Teacher Education, 2007.

Sakaranaho, Tuula. "Islam ja muuttuva katsomusaineiden opetus koulussa." In *Islam Suomessa: Muslimit arjessa, mediassa ja yhteiskunnassa,* edited by Tuomas Martikainen, Tuula Sakaranaho and Marko Juntunen, 157–181. Helsinki: Suomalaisen Kirjallisuuden Seura, 2008.

Sakaranaho, Tuula. "Religious Education in Finland." *Temenos* 49/2 (2013): 225–254.

Sakaranaho, Tuula, Anne Alitolppa-Niitamo, Tuomas Martikainen and Marja Tiilikainen. "Religion in Migration: Studies on Muslims in Finland." In *New Challenges for the Welfare Society,* edited by Vesa Puuronen, Antti Häkkinen, Anu Pylkkänen, Tom Sandlund and Reetta Toivanen, 124–39. Joensuu: Publications of the Karelian Institute, University of Joensuu, 2004.

Sakaranaho, Tuula and Eero Salmenkivi. "Tasavertaisen katsomusopetuksen haasteet: pienryhmäisten uskontojen ja elämänkatsomustiedon opetus Suomessa." *Teologinen Aikakauskirja* 114/5 (2009): 450–470.

Saktanber, Ayse and Gül Çorbacıoğlu. "Veiling and Headscarf Skepticism in Turkey." *Social Politics* 15/4 (2008): 519.

Salih, Ruba. "Reformulating Tradition and Modernity: Moroccan Migrant Women and the Transnational Division of Ritual Space," *Global Networks* 2/3 (2002): 219–231.

Salih, Ruba. "The Backward and the New: National, Transnational and Post-National Islam in Europe." *Journal of Ethnic and Migration Studies* 30/5 (2004): 995–1011.

Salvanou, Emilia. "Pakistani Migrants at N. Ionia. A Community at the Procedure of Forming: Narratives and Representations through Space and Time." Report on the project Culture, Identity and Movement: A study in the social anthropology of the everyday life and popular representations of migrants from Pakistan in Nea Ionia, 12–87. Athens: John Latsis Public Benefit Foundation, 2009. Accessed April 29, 2012. www.latsis-foundation.org/files/Programmes2008-2009/Dermentzopoulos%20FINAL%20REPORT.pdf.

Santos, Paula Borges. *Igreja Católica, estado e sociedade, 1968–1975: O caso Rádio Renascença.* Lisbon: Imprensa de Ciências Sociais, 2005.

Saraiva, Clara and José Mapril. "Scenarios of Death in Contexts of Mobility: Guineans and Bangladeshis in Lisbon." In *The Power of Death*, edited by Ricarda Vidal, and Maria José Blanco. Oxford: Berghahn Publishers, 2014.

Sardar, Ziauddin. *Desperately Seeking Paradise: Journeys of a Sceptical Muslim.* London: Granta Books, 2005.

Sayyd Salmon. "BrAsians: Postcolonial People, Ironic Citizens" in *A Postcolonial People: South Asians in Britain*, eds. Ali, N. et al. London, Hurst & Co. 2006, 1–10

Scharbrodt, Oliver "Islam in Ireland: Organising a Migrant Religion." In *Ireland's New Religious Movements*, edited by Olivia Cosgrove, Laurence Cox, Carmen Kuhling and Peter Mulholland, 318–336. Newcastle: Cambridge Scholars Publishing, 2011.

Scharbrodt, Oliver. "Muslim Migration to Ireland: Past Perspectives and Future Prospects." *Eire-Ireland: Journal of Irish Studies – Special Edition New Perspectives on Irish Migration* 47/1–2 (2012): 221–243.

Scharbrodt, Oliver and Tuula Sakaranaho, eds. "Islam in the Republic of Ireland." Special Issue of *Journal of Muslim Minority Affairs* 31/4 (2011).

Schattschneider, Elmer. *The Semi-Sovereign People.* New York: Holt, Rinehart and Winston, 1960.

Scheinin, Martin. "Koulujen uskonnonopetus ihmisoikeuksien näkökulmasta." *Teologinen Aikakauskirja* 106/6 (2001): 515–517.

Schiller, Nina Glick, Linda Basch and Cristina Blanc-Szanton. "Transnationalism: A New Analytic Framework for Understanding Migration." *Annals of the New York Academy of Sciences* 645 (1992): 1–24.

Schmitter, Philippe and Gerhard Lehmbruch. *Trends toward Corporatist Intermediation.* London: Sage Publications, 1979.

Schneider, Jens and Maurice Crul. "New Insights into Assimilation and Integration Theory." *Journal Ethnic and Racial studies* 34/4 (2010): 1144.

Schreiner, Peter. "Introduction." In *Religious Education in Europe: A Collection of Basic Information about RE in European Countries*, edited by Peter Schreiner, 7–11. Münster: ICCS / Comenius-Institute, 2002.

Scott, James C. *Domination and the Arts of Resistance: Hidden Transcripts*. New Haven: Yale University Press, 1992.

Seppo, Juha. *Uskonnonvapaus 2000-luvun Suomessa*. Helsinki: Edita, 2003.

Seyppel, Tatjana. "Pomaks in Northeastern Greece: An Endangered Balkan Population." *Journal of Muslim Minority Affairs* 10/1 (1989): 41–49.

Shaheen, Jack G. *Reel Bad Arabs: How Hollywood Vilifies a People*. Northampton: Olive Brach Press, 2009.

Sheringham, Olivia. "Creating 'Alternative Geographies': Religion, Transnationalism and Everyday Life." *Geography Compass* 4/11 (2010): 1678–1694.

Silvestri, Sara. "Public Policies towards Muslims and the Institutionalisation of 'Moderate' Islam in Europe: Some Critical Reflections." In *Muslims in 21st Century Europe*, edited by Anna Triandafyllidou, 45–58. London: Routledge, 2010.

Simola, Matti. "Suojelupoliisin organisaatio 1992–2009." In *Ratakatu 12: Suojelupoliisi 1949–2009*, edited by Matti Simola, 255–270. Helsinki: WSOY, 2009.

Simola, Matti, ed. *Ratakatu 12: Suojelupoliisi 1949–2009*. Helsinki: WSOY, 2009.

Sinno, Abdulkader H., ed. *Muslims in Western Politics*. Bloomington: Indiana University Press, 2009.

Skjeie, Hege. "Headscarves in Schools: European Comparisons." in *Religious Pluralism and Human Rights in Europe: Where to Draw the Line?*, edited by M.L.P. Loenen, and J.E. Goldschmidt. Antwerp-Oxford: Intersentia, 2007.

Skocpol, Theda. *States and Social Revolutions*. Cambridge: Cambridge University Press, 1979.

Skoulariki, Athena. "Old and New Mosques in Greece: A New Debate Haunted by History." In *Mosques in Europe: Why a Solution Has Become a Problem*, edited by Stefano Allievi in collaboration with Ethnobarometer, 300–317. Network of European Foundations' Initiative on Religion and Democracy in Europe. London: Alliance Publishing Trust, 2010.

Skovgaard, Jakob and Bettina Gräf, eds. *Global Mufti: The Phenomenon of Yusuf al-Qaradawi*. London: C. Hurst & Co, 2009.

Smith, Anthony D. *Nations and Nationalism in a Global Era*. Cambridge: Polity Press, 1998.

Somalis in Helsinki. New York: Open Society Foundations, 2013. Accessed November 13, 2014. http://www.opensocietyfoundations.org/reports/somalis-helsinki.

Song, Sarah. "Majority Norms, Multiculturalism, and Gender Equality." *American Political Science Review* 99/4 (2005): 473–489.

Soper, J. Christopher and Joel S. Fetzer. "Religious Institutions, Church-State History and Muslim Mobilisation in Britain, France and Germany." *Journal of Ethnic and Migration Studies* 33/6 (2007): 933–944.

Spencer, Robert. *The Myth of Islamic Tolerance: How Islamic Law Treats Non-Muslims*. New York: Prometheus Books, 2005.

320 REFERENCES

Statistics Finland. "Language According to Age and Gender by Region 1990 – 2012." Accessed November 13, 2014. http://193.166.171.75/database/StatFin/vrm/vaerak/vaerak_en.asp.

Statistics Finland. "Population by Sex and Area 31.12.2012 and Increase of Population." Accessed November 1, 2013. http://pxweb2.stat.fi/database/StatFin/vrm/vaerak/vaerak_en.asp.

Statistics Portugal. *Censos 2011: Resultados Definitivos*. Accessed November 1, 2013. http://www.ine.pt/scripts/flex_definitivos/Main.html.

Stevens, Lorna, Stephen Brown and Pauline Maclaran. "Gender, Nationality and Cultural Representations of Ireland: An Irish Woman's Place?" *European Journal of Women's Studies* 7/4 (2000): 405–421.

Sulkunen, Pekka. "Projektiyhteiskunta ja uusi yhteiskuntasopimus." In *Projektiyhteiskunnan kääntöpuolia*, edited by Kati Rantala and Pekka Sulkunen, 17–38. Helsinki: Gaudeamus, 2006.

Taira, Teemu. "Islamin muuttuva julkisuuskuva: Tapaustutkimus Helsingin Sanomista 1946–1994." In *Islam Suomessa: Muslimit arjessa, mediassa ja yhteiskunnassa*, edited by Tuomas Martikainen, Tuula Sakaranaho and Marko Juntunen, 200–224. Helsinki: Suomalaisen Kirjallisuuden Seura, 2008.

Tarrow, Sidney. "The Strategy of Paired Comparison: Toward a Theory of Practice." *Comparative Political Studies* 43/2 (2010): 230–259.

Tatari, Eren. "Theories of the State Accommodation of Islamic Religious Practices in Western Europe." *Journal of Ethnic and Migration Studies* 35/2 (2009): 271–288.

Taylor, Charles. *A Secular Age*. Cambridge: Harvard University Press, 2007.

Tiesler, Nina Clara. "Muçulmanos na Margem: A Nova Presença Islâmica em Portugal." *Sociologia, Problemas e Práticas* 34 (2000): 117–144.

Tiesler, Nina Clara. "No Bad News from the European Margin: The New Islamic Presence in Portugal." *Islam and Christian-Muslim Relations* 12/1 (2001): 71–91.

Tiesler, Nina Clara. "Novidades do Terreno: Muçulmanos na Europa e o Caso Português." *Análise Social* XXXIX/173 (2005): 827–849.

Tiesler, Nina Clara. "Islam in Portuguese–Speaking Areas: Historical Accounts, (Post) Colonial Conditions and Current Debates." *Lusotopie* 14/1 (2007): 91–101.

Tiesler, Nina Clara. "Muslim Transnationalism and Diaspora in Europe: Migrant Experience and Theoretical Reflection." In *Transnationalism: Diasporas and the Advent of a New (Dis)Order*, edited by Eliezer Ben-Rafael and Yitzhak Sternberg, 417–440. Leiden: Brill, 2009.

Tiesler, Nina Clara. "Portugal." In *Yearbook of Muslims in Europe. Volume 3*, edited by Jørgen S. Nielsen, Samim Akgönül, Ahmet Alibašić, Hugh Goddard and Brigitte Maréchal, 447–458. Leiden: Brill, 2011.

Tiesler, Nina Clara, and David Cairns. "Representing Islam and Lisbon Youth: Portuguese Muslims of Indian-Mozambican Origin." *Lusotopie* 14/1 (2007): 223–238.

REFERENCES

Tiesler, Nina Clara and David Cairns. "Across Difference: Portuguese Muslim Youth as Portuguese Youth?" In *Youth on the Move: European Youth and Geographical Mobility*, edited by David Cairns, 107–115. Frankfurt: VS Verlag, 2010.

Tiesler, Nina Clara and José Mapril. "Portugal." In *Yearbook of Muslims in Europe. Volume 4*, edited by Jørgen S. Nielsen, Samim Akgönül, Ahmet Alibašić and Egdūnas Račius, 469–480. Leiden: Brill, 2012.

Tiilikainen, Marja. *Arjen islam. Somalinaisten elämää Suomessa*. Tampere: Vastapaino, 2003.

Tiilikainen, Marja. "Sitaat as Part of Somali Women's Everyday Religion." In *Perspectives on Women's Everyday Religion*, edited by Marja-Liisa Keinänen, 203–218. Stockholm: Stockholm University, 2010.

Tiilikainen, Marja. "Somali Saar in the Era of Social and Religious Change." In *Spirit Possession and Trance*, edited by Bettina E. Schmidt and Lucy Huskinson, 117–133. London: Continuum, 2010.

Tiilikainen, Marja. "Spirits and the Human World in Northern Somalia." In *Milk and Peace, Drought and War*, edited by Markus Hoehne and Virginia Luling, 163–184. London: Hurst, 2010.

Tiilikainen, Marja. "Illness, Healing, and Everyday Islam: Transnational Lives of Somali Migrant Women." In *Everyday Lived Islam in Europe*, edited by Nathal M. Dessing, Nadia Jeldtoft, Jørgen S. Nielsen and Linda Woodhead, 147–162. Farnham: Ashgate, 2013.

Tohidi, Nayereh and Jane H. Bayes. "Women Redefining Modernity and Religion in the Globalized Context." In *Globalization, Gender, and Religion: The Politics of Women's Rights in Catholic and Muslim Contexts*, edited by Jane Bayes and Nayereh Tohidi. New York: Palgrave Macmillan, 2001.

Toprak, Binnaz. *Islam and Political Development in Turkey*. Leiden: Brill, 1981.

Triantafyllidou, Anna. "National Identity and the Other." *Ethnic and Racial Studies* 21/4 (1998): 593–612.

Triandafyllidou, Anna. "Greece: The Challenges of Native and Immigrant Muslim Populations." In *Muslims in 21st Century Europe: Structural and Cultural Perspectives*, edited by Anna Triandafyllidou, 199–217. Oxon: Routledge, 2010.

Triandafyllidou, Anna, "Migration in Greece: People, Policies and Practices." Governing Irregular Migration (IRMA), project document. Athens: ELIAMEP, 2013. Accessed April 15, 2014. http://irma.eliamep.gr/wp-content/uploads/2013/02/IRMA-Background-Report-Greece.pdf.

Triandafyllidou, Anna and Ruby Gropas, "Constructing Difference: The Mosque Debates in Greece." *Journal of Ethnic and Migration Studies* 35/6 (2009): 957–975.

Troubeta, Sevasti, "'Minorization' and 'Ethnicization' in Greek Society: Comparative Perspectives on Moslem Migrants and the Moslem Minority." *History and Culture of South Eastern Europe: An Annual Journal / Jahrbücher für Geschichte und Kultur Südosteuropas* 5 (2003): 95–112.

Troubeta, Sevasti. *Constructing Identities for the Muslims of Thrace: The Example of Pomaks and Gypsies*. Athens: Kritiki, 2001. (In Greek.)

Tsitselikis, Konstantinos. "The Legal Status of Islam in Greece." *Die Welt des Islams* 44/3 (2004): 402–431.

Tsitselikis, Konstantinos. "The Religious Freedom of Migrants." In *Greece of Migration: Social Participation, Rights and Citizenship*, edited by Miltos Pavlou and Dimitris Christopoulos, 267–302. Athens: Kritiki/KEMO, 2004.

Tsitselikis, Konstantinos. "The Pending Modernisation of Islam in Greece: From Millet to Minority Status." *Südosteuropa* 55/4 (2007): 354–372.

Tsitselikis, Konstantinos. "Greece." In *Yearbook of Muslims in Europe. Volume 1.*, edited by Jørgen S. Nielsen, Samim Akgönül, Ahmet Alibašić, Brigitte Maréchal and Christian Moe, 151–161. Leiden: Brill, 2009.

Tsitselikis, Konstantinos. "Greece." In *Yearbook of Muslims in Europe. Volume 2.*, edited by Jørgen S. Nielsen, Samim Akgönül, Ahmet Alibašić, Brigitte Maréchal and Christian Moe, 233–244. Leiden: Brill, 2010.

Tsitselikis, Konstantinos. *Old and New Islam in Greece: From Historical Minorities to Immigrant Newcomers*. Leiden: Brill, 2012.

Tsitselikis, Konstantinos. "Greece." In *Yearbook of Muslims in Europe. Volume 5.*, edited by Jørgen S. Nielsen, Samim Akgönül, Ahmet Alibašić and Egdūnas Račius, 308–318. Leiden: Brill, 2013.

Turner, Bryan S. *Religion and Modern Society: Citizenship, Secularization and the State*. Cambridge: Cambridge University Press, 2011.

Tweed, Thomas A. *Crossing and Dwelling: A Theory of Religion*. Cambridge: Harvard University Press, 2006.

Tweed, Thomas A. "Space." *Material Religion* 7:/1 (2011): 116–123.

Uittamo, Marita. *Uskontojen ja elämänkatsomusaineiden opetuksesta Espoossa*. Espoo: Espoon kaupunki, 2001.

Uskonnonvapauslaki 6.6.2003/ 453 [Freedom of Religion Act]. Finlex – Valtion säädöstietopankki. Accessed July 7, 2013. http://www.finlex.fi/.

Vakil, AbdoolKarim. "Questões Inacabadas: Colonialismo, Islão e Portugalidade." In *Fantasmas e Fantasias Imperiais no Imaginário Português Contemporâneo*, edited by Ana Paula Ferreira and Margarida Calafate Ribeiro, 257–297. Porto: Campo das Letras, 2003.

Vakil, AbdoolKarim. "The Crusader Heritage: Portugal and Islam from Colonial to Postcolonial Identities." in *Rethinking Heritage: Cultures and Politics in Europe*, edited by Robert Shannan Peckham, 29–44. London and New York: I.B. Tauris, 2003.

Vakil, AbdoolKarim. "Do Outro ao Diverso: Islão e Muçulmanos em Portugal: História, Discursos, Identidades." *Revista Lusófona de Ciência das Religiões* 3/5–6 (2004): 283–312.

REFERENCES

Vakil, AbdoolKarim. "Comunidade Islâmica em Portugal." In *Dicionário Temático da Lusofonia*, edited by Fernando Alves Cristóvão, 186–189. Lisbon: Associação de Cultura Lusófona-Instituto Camões, 2005.

Vakil, AbdoolKarim, Fernando Monteiro and Mário Machaqueiro. *Moçambique: Memória Falado do Islão e da Guerra*. Coimbra: Almedina, 2011.

Vakil, Abdoolkarim and Sayid, Salman, ed., *Thinking Through Islamophobia*. London: Hurst, 2011.

Valiulis, Maryann. "Gender, Power and Identity in the Irish Free State." *Journal of Women's History* 6/4 (1995): 117–136.

Van der Veer, Peter "Transnational Religion: Hindu and Muslim Movements," *Global Networks* 2/2 (2002): 95–111

Vasquez, Manuel and Marie Friedmann Marquardt. *Globalizing the Sacred: Religion across the Americas*. New Brunswick: Rutgers University Press, 2003.

Vasquez, Manuel A. *More than Belief: A Materialist Theory of Religion*. Oxford: Oxford University Press, 2011.

Vasta, Ellie. "From Ethnic Minorities to Ethnic Majority Policy: Multiculturalism and the Shift to Assimilationism in the Netherlands." *Ethnic and Racial Studies*, 30/5 (2007).

Vickers, Miranda. *The Albanians: A Modern History*. New York: I.B. Tauris, 2006.

Vilaça, Helena. *Da Torre de Babel às Terras Prometidas: Pluralismo Religioso em Portugal*. Porto: Edições Afrontamento, 2006.

Vilaça, Helena. *Imigração, Etnicidade e Religião: O Papel das Comunidades Religiosas na Integração dos Imigrantes da Europa de Leste*. Estudos OI: 30. Lisbon: ACIDI, 2008.

Wanche, Sophia I. "An Assessment of the Iraqi Community in Greece." Report commissioned by the UNHCR Representation in Greece, Evaluation and Policy Analysis Unit, 2004. Accessed June 13, 2012. http://www.aina.org/reports/aoticig.pdf.

Warner, Carolyn M. *Confessions of an Interest Group: The Catholic Church and Political Parties in Europe*. Princeton: Princeton University Press, 2000.

Warner, R. Stephen. "Immigration and Religious Communities in the United States." In *Gatherings in Diaspora: Religious Communities and the New Immigration*, edited by R. Stephen Warner and Judith Wittner, 3–34. Philadelphia: Temple University Press, 1998.

Werbner, Pnina. *Imagined Diasporas among Manchester Muslims: The Public Performance of Pakistani Transnational Identity Politics*. Oxford: James Currey, 2002.

Werbner, Pnina. *Pilgrims of Love: An Ethnography of a Global Sufi Cult*. London: Hurst & Company, 2003.

Werbner, Pnina. "Theorising Complex Diasporas: Purity and Hybridity in the South Asian Public Sphere in Britain." *Journal of Ethnic and Migration Studies* 30/5 (2004): 895–911.

Werdmölder, Hans. "Headscarves at Public Schools: The Issue of Open Neutrality Reconsidered." In *Religious Pluralism and Human Rights in Europe: Where to Draw the Line?*, edited by M.L.P. Loenen, and J.E. Goldschmidt, 155–165. Antwerp-Oxford: Intersentia, 2007.

Whyte, John Henry. *Church and State in Modern Ireland, 1923–1970*. Dublin: Gill and Macmillan, 1971.

Williams, Kevin. "Faith and the Nation: Education and Religious Identity in the Republic of Ireland." *British Journal of Educational Studies* 47/4 (1999): 317–331.

Wimmer, Andreas and Nina Glick Schiller. "Methodological Nationalism and Beyond: Nation-state Building, Migration and the Social Sciences." *Global Networks* 2/4 (2002): 301–334.

Winkler, Tanja. "When God and Poverty Collide: Exploring the Myths of Faith-sponsored Community Development." *Urban Studies* 45/10 (2008): 2099–2116.

Yar, Majid. "Honneth and the Communitarians: Toward a Recognitive Critical Theory of Community." *Res Publica* 9/2 (2003): 101–125. Accessed October 9, 2014. http://dx.doi.org/10.1023/A:1024191816597.

Yilmaz, Ferruh. "Right Wing Hegemony through the Immigration Debate in Europe." *Current Sociology* 60/3 (2012): 368–381.

Yuval-Davis, Nira. *Gender and Nation*. London: Sage Publications, 1997.

Zapata-Barrero, Ricard. "The Muslim Community in the Spanish Tradition: Maurophobia as a Fact, and Impartiality as a Desideratum." In *Multiculturalism, Muslims and Citizenship,* edited by Tariq Moddood, Anna Triandafyllidou and Ricard Zapata-Barrero, 143–161. London and New York: Routledge, 2006.

Zeghal, Malika. "The 'Recentering' of Religious Knowledge and Discourse: The Case of al-Azhar in Twentieth-Century Egypt." In *Schooling Islam*, edited by Robert W. Hefner and Muhammad Qasim Zaman, 107–130. Princeton: Princeton University Press, 2007.

Zenginis, Efstrations. *Bektatism in Western Thrace: Contribution to the History of the Distribution of Islamism in the Greek Space*. Thessaloniki: IMXA, 1988. (In Greek.)

Ziaka, Angeliki. "Muslims and Muslim Education in Greece." In *Islamische Erziehung in Europa/Islamic Education in Europe,* edited by Ednan Aslan, 141–178. Vienna: Bohlau, 2009.

Index

9/11 13, 32, 35, 60, 69, 117, 161, 162, 180, 182,
    187, 188, 211

Afghanistan 5, 207, 208, 230
Africa 24, 72, 96, 100, 112, 199, 226, 228, 265,
    273, 287
Africanization 10
Aga Khan Foundation 60, 280, 290
Ahmad 221
Ahmadinejad, Mahmoud 235
al Islah 266
Al Itihad al Islaami 266
Al-Andalus 272
    see also Al Andaluz 12, 13
Albania 203, 204, 206, 208
Albanophobia 205
al-Qaradawi, Yusuf 94, 98, 104, 234, 235
Anagnostou, Dia 202
Antoniou, Dimitris 134
Arab 41, 72, 107–109, 202, 226, 235, 236,
    253–258, 260
    see also Arabic 147, 199, 215, 216, 226, 228,
    234–239, 240–246, 260, 290
Asad, Talal 91, 111
Association 1, 5, 11, 34, 35, 37, 38, 43, 94, 105,
    129, 178, 199, 215, 216, 217, 236, 287, 289,
    290
asylum seekers 5, 208, 219, 227, 228, 232,
    247, 258
Atatürk, Mustafa Kemal 121
attitudes 161–179, 180–197, 228, 235, 266
Austria 83, 88, 172, 178, 228
authenticity 21, 110, 111
authority 21, 39, 54, 91, 92–111, 168, 169, 204,
    211

Bahrain 95
Baldwin-Edwards, Martin 116
Balkans 7, 112, 116–119, 124, 199
Bangladesh 10, 11, 206, 209, 272, 274, 275, 286
Barelwi 12, 272, 287, 288
Basu, Amrita 166
Bayes, Jane H. 173
Bektashi 134, 204
Belgium 2, 49, 178, 236

Bosnia 5, 8
Brisman, Shira 251
British Empire 121, 122
Buddhism 78
Bulgaria 118, 119, 132, 274
burials 35, 289

Carlbom, Aje 243
Casanova, José 28, 51
Catholic Church 54–65, 175, 184, 187, 289
centralization 276, 285
centre/periphery 276
charity 98, 120
church–state 4, 24, 29, 45, 49, 219
    see also state–religion 17, 18, 20, 45–48,
    53, 54, 56, 61, 62, 64
children 63, 75, 81, 85, 130, 135, 152, 153, 176,
    207, 216, 226, 236, 239–242, 247, 248,
    255, 256, 259, 260, 262, 289, 290
citizenship 1, 5, 8, 12, 17, 19, 22, 45, 65, 112,
    113, 116, 125, 128–130, 142, 150, 152, 153,
    163–169, 171–174, 179, 183, 186, 199, 202,
    203, 219, 220, 230, 291
civil society 16, 28, 33, 43, 60, 91, 102, 107, 289
Clogg, Richard 120, 122
coercive isomorphism 38–43
colonial legacies 16, 19, 24
colonialism 137, 157, 282
Concordat 17, 57, 58, 60, 61
Constantinople 114, 115, 119, 120
constitution 149, 151, 162, 198, 210, 272
convert 143, 148, 163
    see also converts 6, 9, 73, 137, 143, 146, 149
corporatism 45, 47, 48, 54, 57, 58, 60
Council of Europe 49
Crul, Maurice 171
cultural racism 16
culture 23, 46, 60, 71, 74, 85, 106, 114, 115, 128,
    133, 135, 155, 168, 169, 171, 172, 173, 176,
    193, 194, 239, 240, 245, 247, 248, 251, 253,
    255, 258, 261–263, 267, 268, 286, 287,
    290, 291
curriculum 12, 20, 42, 70, 71, 75, 79–86, 115,
    186
Cyprus 118, 128

INDEX

Democracy 128, 170, 238, 272, 282
Denizenship 144, 149, 150
Denmark 228, 230, 231, 232
Deobandi 12, 101, 217, 272, 287
Diaspora 217, 219, 225–229, 237–239, 243–249, 251, 253, 255, 256, 262, 263, 265–268
diasporic community 23, 225, 226, 227, 282
DiMaggio, Paul 39
Discrimination 58, 71, 116, 128, 135, 153, 154, 156, 157, 174, 180, 187, 188, 209, 218, 219, 258, 259
Divani, Lena 122
Diversification 20, 222, 283
Diversity 20, 27, 30, 38, 47, 48, 54, 58, 61–63, 73, 78, 85, 96, 102, 170, 173, 182, 183, 200, 201, 210, 215, 216, 222, 225, 255, 258, 269–273, 285, 291
Dublin 8, 9, 21, 55–66, 92–111, 137–160

Egan, Shekinah 163, 172
Egypt 201, 203, 207, 212, 214, 215, 235
Espoo 72, 73, 77, 81
Essentialism 139
Esteves, Alina 270
Estonia 228
Ethics 61, 75, 76, 77
ethnic hierarchy 6
ethnicity 7, 54, 113, 116, 117, 132, 134, 137, 152, 162, 165, 172, 182, 201, 219, 220, 286, 292
ethno-nationalism 22, 161
European Council for Fatwa and Research 55, 94, 95, 98, 104, 109
European Union 2, 4, 27, 43, 57, 162, 180
Evangelical Lutheran Church of Finland 75, 230
Evergeti, Venetia 21, 198, 199

Family 21, 24, 49, 77, 93, 94, 101, 108, 138, 139, 140, 142, 143, 145, 146, 147, 150, 151, 154, 156, 157, 188, 207, 230, 232, 233, 234, 236, 237, 239, 247, 248, 249, 251, 253, 259, 262, 263, 282, 292
Federation of Islamic Organisations in Europe 216
Ferrari, Silvio 27
Ferree, Myra M. 167
Fetzer, Joel S. 40

Financial crisis 287
Finnish Security Intelligence Service 31, 41, 67
Fonseca, Lucinda 270
former Yugoslavia 5
Fras, Max 177
freedom of religion 5, 29, 30, 75, 81, 86
functional differentiation 48
funding 21, 27, 37, 38, 40, 43, 44, 93, 97, 99, 105, 212, 238, 289

Garbin, David 284
Gastarbeiter 15
Geertz, Clifford 91
Gender 153, 155, 161, 164, 165, 168, 169, 174, 175, 177, 179, 244, 247, 248, 263, 267, 268
Gerholm, Thomas 14
Globalization 3, 10, 137, 212, 272
Governance 19, 28, 29, 32, 33, 35, 42, 56, 67, 68, 70, 71, 74, 77, 78, 79, 83, 85, 86, 87, 282
Governmentality 16, 17
Greek Orthodoxy 115, 119
Grillo, Ralph 15, 282
Gropas, Ruby 202
Guinea-Bissau 10, 11, 182, 183, 272, 274, 278, 280, 281, 282, 286, 287
Gülen movement 98

Habermas, Jürgen 139
Halal 8, 12, 287
Halawa, Hussein 55, 100, 104
Hatzopoulos, Pavlos 205
Hayes, Brian 170, 171, 176
Heiskala, Risto 28
Herbert, David 177
Hierarchy 6, 71, 92, 95, 102, 103, 133
Hijab 144, 154, 163, 166, 167, 168, 169, 175, 266
Hindu 58, 61, 162, 195, 270, 273
Honneth, Axel 21, 138, 139, 140, 141, 152, 158

Iivonen, Pekka 82
Imams 94, 95, 97, 98, 99, 100, 101, 102, 103, 104, 105, 106, 107, 108, 109, 110, 148, 211, 218, 290
Immigration 7, 9, 10, 19, 30, 31, 41, 69, 107, 108, 136, 137, 138, 157, 163, 164, 171, 172, 178, 188, 195, 199, 201, 208, 219, 221, 227,

INDEX

230, 232, 235, 270, 271, 272, 275, 286, 289, 292

Inglis, Tom 62

inter-religious relations 17

Islamic Community of Lisbon 1, 11, 17, 59, 60, 183, 184, 282

Islamic Council of Finland 19, 20, 27, 29, 33, 34, 38, 42, 70

Islamic Cultural Centre of Ireland 55, 93, 94, 95

Islamic education 14, 16, 67, 68, 70, 72, 73, 81, 82, 85, 86, 99, 100

Islamic Supreme Council of Iraq 228

Islamization 13, 212

Islamophobia 13, 16, 19, 46, 63, 137, 181, 185, 197, 199, 201, 211, 219, 221, 235

Isma'ili 10, 63

see also Islamili 270, 280

Jew 118

see also Jewish 52, 53, 61, 63, 273

Jordan 228, 229, 231, 235

Kambouri, Neli 205

Karakasidou, Anastasia 113

Kazakhstan 203

Kemalism 125

Khan, Adil Hussain 91–110

Khiabany, Gholam 170

Kiliç, Sevgi 178

Kindergarten 236, 242

King Abdullah II 235

Kingdom of the Serbs, Croats and Slovenes 122

Korais, Adamantions 115

Kosovo 5, 6

Kristeva, Julia 165

Kurdistan 228

Kurds 6, 127, 229

Kuru, Ahmet 53, 65

Kuwait 95

labor market 235, 241

Larsson, Göran 2

Laurence, Jonathan 47, 50, 57, 61, 65

Law 5, 8, 11, 17, 21, 31, 40, 55, 57, 58, 59, 60, 71, 74, 78, 100, 104, 108, 118, 123, 125, 127, 129, 149, 151, 152, 185, 201, 211, 220

Leadership 21, 96, 97, 99, 102, 126, 146, 147, 157, 185, 228

legal opportunity structure 74, 86

legal regulation 4

Ley, David 288

Libya 95

Lisbon 1, 11, 17, 23, 24, 58, 59, 60, 65, 183, 184, 185, 187, 195, 269, 271, 272, 273, 274, 275, 276, 277, 278, 279, 280, 281, 282, 283, 284, 285, 286, 288, 289, 290, 292

Lithman, Yngve 14

local community 24, 99, 104, 105, 106, 153, 154, 156, 157, 215, 279, 286, 288, 289, 290, 292

local emplacement 270, 271, 272, 282, 285

Lutheran 4, 5, 30, 72, 73, 75, 76, 77, 78, 80, 81, 82, 87, 230

Maktoum Foundation 55, 93, 94, 95, 110

Mamede, Suleiman Valy 60

Maréchal, Brigitte 14

Marginalization 32, 134, 181, 229, 276

material religion 245, 246, 247, 267

Maussen, Marcel 70

Media 1, 3, 12, 13, 14, 22, 24, 29, 34, 47, 48, 66, 68, 78, 108, 112, 118, 148, 153, 155–157, 164, 180, 181, 186, 187, 195, 217

Memories 143, 144, 246, 251, 253

Men 1, 133, 167, 207, 229, 233, 236, 238, 245, 248, 256, 257, 259, 260, 261, 266

Metcalf, Barbara 14

methodological nationalism 3

Michail, Domna 134

Middle East 5, 7, 72, 96, 103, 112, 117, 225, 228

Migration 3, 5, 8, 9, 10, 15, 24, 30, 34, 49, 50, 55, 62, 117, 126, 127, 132, 180, 183, 189, 197, 199, 200, 203, 204, 205, 207, 208, 210, 218, 219, 220, 221, 225, 227, 231, 245–248, 267–278, 280, 287, 292

Minaret 16

Minkenberg, Michael 49

Minority 5, 7, 8, 11, 17, 18, 20, 29–31, 35, 40, 42–44, 54, 69, 71, 74, 76, 81–83, 86, 112, 113, 116–121, 123–136, 157, 162, 166–170, 177, 182, 183, 195, 198, 199, 200, 201, 202, 216, 218, 220, 222, 225, 236, 241, 272, 275

Misrecognition 22, 139, 141, 142, 143, 144, 146–157

328   INDEX

Modood, Tariq 221
Morley, David 245
Morocco 10, 15, 206, 272, 275
Mosque 1, 6, 8, 11, 12, 14, 16, 21, 34, 35, 37, 41,
    59, 60, 79, 91, 93–110, 123, 129, 147, 148,
    149, 155, 181, 184, 198, 201, 211, 212, 215,
    216, 217, 219, 221, 234, 240, 242, 260,
    280–290
Mouride 15
Mozambique 10, 17, 182, 183, 184, 185, 195,
    272, 274, 282, 291
Mubarak, Hosni 235
Muhammad cartoons controversy 32, 37
multicultural work 238, 244
multiculturalism 71, 85, 130, 165, 170, 183,
    230, 238, 240, 244
Muslim Brotherhood 97, 98, 108
Muslimness 13, 19, 181, 186

national identity 7, 9, 13, 17–18, 21, 112,
    113–115, 119–120, 161, 164–166, 169, 173,
    178, 204, 211
national security 31–33, 41, 68, 151
nationalism 3, 7, 15, 22, 43, 61, 65, 113–114,
    116, 130, 161, 166–167, 180, 198, 204
nationality 6, 24, 107, 113–114, 116, 129, 164,
    183, 185, 202–203, 206–207, 215–216, 219,
    220, 271, 274, 279, 292
neighbourhood 102, 238, 259, 270, 280,
    282–283, 285–288, 292
neoliberalism 24, 78
Netherlands 2, 14, 45, 49–50, 63, 69, 170,
    190–192, 194, 230
    Holland 101, 236
New Public Management 20, 28, 32, 43, 78
New Religious Movements 58–59, 63–64,
    182
news media 164
NGO 230, 237–240, 253
Nigeria 100, 203, 206
North Africa 7, 72, 107, 238
    see also Africa
Norway 63, 228, 230, 232

Ombudsman for Minorities 35–37, 39–40,
    43
Onniselkä, Suaad 84
opportunity structure 29, 38, 40, 71, 74,
    86–87

organisation 29, 116, 216
    civil society organizations 43, 60
    grassroots organizations 108–109
    Islamic organizations 4, 5, 10, 31, 34–35,
        40–41
    mosque organizations 93–95, 97, 99–100,
        107, 109–110, 147
    Muslims organizations 6, 9, 29, 40, 42,
        69, 91–93, 97–98, 109, 111, 185, 200, 217,
        234, 242
    religious organizations 5, 21, 28, 35, 37,
        113, 135, 210, 216, 241
    representative organizations 20, 27, 39
    student organizations 107
    umbrella organizations 34, 57, 95, 184,
        186
Orthodox 4, 7, 18, 30–31, 42–43, 52–53,
    73, 75–76, 80–81, 113–115, 119, 122,
    124, 162, 170, 198, 203–205, 210–211,
    216, 273
Ottoman Empire 3, 7, 17–18, 112–116, 118–121,
    125, 135, 201, 204, 218, 221–222
outsiders 9, 91, 95, 97, 106, 108, 171, 253

Pakistan 10–11, 15, 40, 59, 100–101, 104, 196,
    201, 205–209, 212, 215–217, 272, 274–275,
    286–288
Palestine 208, 231, 238–239
path dependence 33, 42–43
persecution 23, 132, 227, 229, 232–233, 240,
    243
Pires, Sonia 289
plurality 48, 56, 58, 68, 71, 77–78, 80, 135, 137,
    178, 287, 292
Poland 51, 190–191, 194
Policarpo, José 187
Polis, Adamantia 114
political Islam 50, 99
political party 7, 12, 14–16, 149, 211, 230, 287
political participation 15, 149, 292
politics 4, 19, 21, 46–48, 50, 65, 96, 103, 110,
    117, 131, 182, 199, 201, 216, 219–221, 269,
    283
Pomaks 7, 127, 131–132, 133–135
Popkewitz, Thomas 79
Portugal 1–2, 4–5, 10–12, 17–18, 20, 22–24,
    45–55, 57–65, 113, 180–197, 270–276,
    281–283, 285–287, 289–291
Portuguese Empire 3, 10, 182–183, 188, 271

INDEX

Portuguese Islam   10, 13, 18, 23, 49, 54, 60,
63–64, 181–192, 195–197, 272–275, 285,
290–291
post-Cold War   3, 5, 29, 34
Powell, Walter   39
power   21, 34, 61–62, 64–65, 79, 91–92, 95–96,
167, 179, 267, 289
  relations   66, 95, 165, 169, 185, 197, 225
  structures   21, 91, 111
prayer room   6, 12, 280–281, 283–284,
286–287
prejudice   84, 135, 180, 182, 188, 190, 209,
211–212, 214, 226
Promey, Sally   251
public authorities   20, 27, 35–36, 38–43, 233,
237
public religion   22, 161
public schools   6, 31, 70, 162, 166, 170–171, 176,
178, 241
  see also school
public sphere   13, 16–18, 21, 23, 92, 153, 165,
172, 175, 177–179, 186, 200–201, 210,
216–219, 222, 291
Pyykkönen, Miikka   33, 38

Qatar   95
Quinn, Ruairi   170–171
quota refugees   5, 227–229
  see also refugee

race   117, 135, 137, 155
racialization   16, 199
racism   2, 4, 6, 12, 13, 16, 24, 71, 135, 155, 162,
171, 175, 201, 209, 219, 221, 226, 258
Račius, Egdūnas   2
radicalisation   17, 27, 32, 42
radio   11, 187
Rajamäki, Kari   230
recognition   1, 11, 19, 21–22, 30–31, 55, 62,
77–78, 91, 96–99, 110–111, 112, 120, 127,
136, 137–154, 156–158, 162, 177, 181, 210,
218–219, 288
refugee   5–6, 8, 23, 55, 72, 108, 122, 124, 182,
185, 195, 200–201, 203, 207, 208, 219, 221,
226–233, 237–240, 244, 247, 258, 262,
267
  see also quota refugee
regulation   4, 29, 30, 56, 58, 65, 70–71, 77, 79,
85, 123, 163, 165, 170, 172, 208, 248

religion   1–7, 9, 23, 28–33, 39, 41, 46, 54,
56–57, 78, 85–87, 91–92, 103, 110, 112,
114–117, 120–123, 125–126, 128–129, 132,
134–135, 137, 146–147, 151, 153–156,
161–162, 164–165, 168, 172, 174–179, 181,
204–205, 212, 219–221, 245, 247, 267,
269–271, 275, 281, 285–287, 292
  Islamic religion   3, 7, 14, 136, 144, 148–149,
153–154, 156
  minority religion   20, 29–31, 42–44, 69,
71, 74–76, 81–83, 241
  other religions   1, 30, 75, 80, 82–83, 176, 273
  see also public religion
  religion of intolerance   190, 192–193
  see also state-religion relations
religionization   78
religious dialogue   1, 15, 49, 54, 102, 186, 188,
237, 239, 289, 291
religious diversity   30, 47–48, 58, 61–63, 173,
182–183, 270–273
religious education   6, 20–21, 31, 35, 42,
67–83, 86–88, 92, 99–100, 102–104, 186,
290
representative council   36–37
resource mobilization   29, 38, 40–41
re-territorialization   269
Ricoeur, Paul   146
rights   17, 22, 30, 53, 57, 74, 79, 113, 121,
123–124, 126, 128, 130–131, 140–141,
165–166, 172, 210
  broadcasting   59
  civil   6–7, 144, 169, 219–220, 271
  human   149, 151, 168, 210, 232
  religious   75
  women's   92, 164, 179
Rissanen, Inkeri   85
Roma   7, 131–135
Romania   122
Rottman   168
Royal College of Surgeons in Ireland
  (RCSI)   8, 55, 100
Ruba, Salih   15
Russian Empire   3–5, 29, 30, 118

Said, Edward   6
Salafiyya   98, 100, 106, 266
Saudi Arabia   95, 100–101, 108, 228, 266
Schattschneider, Elmer   47
Schneider, Jens   171

scholars (religious) 97–99, 102–103, 106, 108–109, 234–235, 266

school 8, 20, 35, 42, 56–57, 67–68, 70–88, 115, 120, 123, 125–128, 130, 163, 167–169, 175–177, 227, 236–242, 260, 266, 280–281, 290–291
  see also public schools

sectarianism 23, 104, 108–109, 226–227, 231, 233–238, 240, 242–244

sectarianization 226

secularization 4, 12, 15, 19, 24, 30, 51, 53, 56–57, 64, 77, 86–87, 131, 134, 161, 170, 175–178, 181, 211, 228, 233, 235–237, 239, 243, 272, 284

securitization 17, 19, 29, 31–33, 38, 41–43, 67–69, 117, 150–152, 182, 234

Senegal 10, 15, 206–207, 272, 274–275
  see also Africa

sensory culture 251, 268

service provision 288

Shahid al Mihrab Organization 228, 235

Shi'a 11, 79, 84, 100, 109, 217

silence 22–23, 181, 192, 196, 242
  silencing 23, 240, 244

Skoulariki, Athena 202

social capital 28, 60, 181, 195, 197, 255, 270, 272, 286, 289

social fragmentation 23

Somalia 5, 6, 23, 72, 77, 206–207, 228, 245–247, 258–268

Soper, J. Christopher 40

South Africa 8, 55, 100
  see also Africa

South Asia 5, 7, 9, 55, 59, 96, 98, 100–101, 103–104, 107, 182, 198, 202, 207, 216, 272

Soviet Union 5, 31, 41, 199

space 8, 14–15, 17, 23–24, 46, 101, 105, 107, 117, 157–158, 188, 204, 214–219, 225, 227, 234, 243, 245, 256, 259–261, 263, 266–268, 270–272, 282–283, 285, 287–288, 291–292
  public space 11, 19, 215, 217, 225, 227, 233, 236
  private space 245–246, 251–253, 258, 269, 284

Spain 12, 45, 49–50, 63, 220

spatiality 23, 269, 270–271, 275, 288, 292

state autonomy 48

state–religion relations 17–18, 20, 45–48, 53–56, 61–65

statistics 5, 59, 117, 190, 200–209

stereotypes 135, 155, 188, 214

Stevens, Lorna 166

stigmatization 108, 133

student 8, 10–11, 17, 55, 74–76, 80, 100, 107, 128, 154, 177, 201, 247, 272, 282

subjectivity 13, 161

Sub-Saharan Africa 5
  see also Africa

suburb 11, 23, 225, 227–230, 234, 237–238, 240, 243, 275–290

suburbanisation 276

Sudan 23, 206, 246–258, 266–268

Sufism 104, 106, 264, 266, 272, 287
  neo-Sufi 217

Sunni 5–6, 10–11, 18, 21, 58, 60, 84, 100, 109, 134, 137–138, 148, 157, 182, 184, 228, 233–236, 239, 242, 270–272, 283, 287–288

Sweden 4, 30, 226, 228, 230–232

Switzerland 45, 49, 63, 125

symbol 23, 64, 91, 110, 161, 167–168, 172–177, 186, 234, 236, 243, 245, 249–257, 262, 267–268, 284

Syria 201, 203, 206–209, 228–229, 231, 239

Tablighi Jamaat 16, 98, 217, 272, 287–288

Tampere 5, 67–68, 80, 86–87

Tariqa 12

Tatar 4–6, 30, 69, 72, 75, 80, 118

television 11, 102, 187, 234, 237, 260

terrorism 4, 17, 27, 32, 35, 41–42, 95, 117, 151, 171, 191–196, 199, 211
  counterterrorism 67
  war on terror 4, 187

Thrace 7–8, 17, 21, 112–114, 116, 118–136, 201–203, 220–221

Tiesler, Nina Clara 22, 180, 272, 288

Tohidi, Nayereh 173

translocal 15

transnational religious movements 15

transnationalism 15–19, 49–50, 55, 94, 97, 103, 200–201, 215, 217–219, 222, 225–226, 240, 247, 269, 290, 292

Treaty of Lausanne 7, 119–131, 136

Triandafyllidou, Anna 219

Troubeta, Sevasti 221

INDEX 331

Tsitselikis, Kosntantinos 5, 202
Turkey 5–7, 15, 18, 21, 72, 113–136, 175,
185–186, 199, 201, 203–208, 211, 214,
218–219, 221, 228
Turkoman 229
Turku 227, 229, 233–242
Tweed, Thomas A. 23, 256, 258, 267

'ulama 97, 100, 102–103, 106
see also scholars (religious)
umma 16, 96, 219, 260
UNHCR 5, 227–229, 231–232
United Kingdom 2, 14, 45, 63, 69, 161, 170,
178–179, 190
urbanization 30, 125, 133, 225, 269–270, 275,
280, 282–284, 288, 290–291
Uzbekistan 203

Vakil, AbdoolKarim 59, 60, 285
Vanhanen, Matti 230
veil 16, 22, 161–179, 214
see also hijab

Vietnam 227
violence 23, 188, 190, 218, 227–228, 231–235,
237, 240, 243

Wahhabi 100, 266
war on terror 4, 187
see also terrorism
Watt, Philip 175
Werbner, Pnina 285
Werdmolder, Hans 174
Williamson, Milly 170
women 1, 12, 23, 92, 107, 109, 133, 143–144,
146–147, 154, 162–179, 187–188, 207, 211,
216, 233, 238, 245–268, 284, 288
World War I 119, 135
World War II 3, 41, 126, 204
worship 23, 98, 201, 205, 215–216, 269–271,
278, 280–288, 291–292

Yuval-Davis, Nira 165, 174

Zapata-Barrero, Ricard 220